WHERE ONCE THEY STOOD

WHERE ONCE THEY STOOD

NEWFOUNDLAND'S ROCKY ROAD TOWARDS CONFEDERATION

RAYMOND B. BLAKE & MELVIN BAKER

© 2019 University of Regina Press

All rights reserved. No part of this work covered by the copyrights hereon may be reproduced or used in any form or by any means—graphic, electronic, or mechanical—without the prior written permission of the publisher. Any request for photocopying, recording, taping or placement in information storage and retrieval systems of any sort shall be directed in writing to Access Copyright.

COVER AND TEXT DESIGN: Duncan Noel Campbell, University of Regina Press
COPY EDITOR: Nadine Coderre
PROOFREADER: Dallas Harrison
INDEXER: Patricia Furdek
COVER ART: An angry St. John's crowd marching on the Colonial Building, the Newfoundland seat of power, during the Great Depression, 1932. Reproduced with permission of The Rooms Provincial Archives, A19-20, St. John's, NL.

Library and Archives Canada Cataloguing in Publication

Title: Where once they stood : Newfoundland's rocky road towards Confederation / Raymond B. Blake & Melvin Baker.
Names: Blake, Raymond Benjamin, author. | Baker, Melvin, author.
Description: Includes bibliographical references and index.
Identifiers: Canadiana (print) 20189068000 | Canadiana (ebook) 20189068019 | ISBN 9780889776197 (hardcover) | ISBN 9780889776074 (softcover) | ISBN 9780889776081 (PDF) | ISBN 9780889776098 (HTML)
Subjects: CSH: Newfoundland and Labrador—Politics and government—1855-1934. | Newfoundland and Labrador—Politics and government—1934-1949. | Newfoundland and Labrador—History—1855-1934. | Newfoundland and Labrador—History—1934-1949.
Classification: LCC FC2173.2 .B53 2019 | DDC 971.8/02—dc23

University of Regina Press, University of Regina
Regina, Saskatchewan, Canada, S4S 0A2
TEL: (306) 585-4758 FAX: (306) 585-4699
WEB: www.uofrpress.ca

We acknowledge the support of the Canada Council for the Arts for our publishing program. We acknowledge the financial support of the Government of Canada. / Nous reconnaissons l'appui financier du gouvernement du Canada. This publication was made possible with support from Creative Saskatchewan's Creative Industries Production Grant Program and with the help of a grant from the Federation for the Humanities and Social Sciences, through the Awards to Scholarly Publications Program, using funds provided by the Social Sciences and Humanities Research Council of Canada.

For Ben and Robert, who joked the story we
tell here was a case of *No B'y, Yes B'y*
— RAYMOND BLAKE

For Emily Baker Nash (1951–2016)
— MELVIN BAKER

CONTENTS

PREFACE —ix

INTRODUCTION   Newfoundland: A Place in Search of Security—1

CHAPTER 1   Rejecting Canada and Embracing the Newfoundland Nation, 1864–1869—21

CHAPTER 2   The Nation Turns Inward, 1870–1901—65

CHAPTER 3   Prosperity, Confederation, and the Dominion of Newfoundland before and after the Great War, 1902–1927—105

CHAPTER 4   Despair, Government by Commission, and a Slow Rebuild, 1928–1941—157

CHAPTER 5   The National Convention, Social Citizenship, and Newfoundland's Future, 1941–1946—197

CHAPTER 6   Constitutional Options Explored: Delegations to London and Ottawa, 1946–1948—231

CHAPTER 7   Referendum, Social Citizenship, and Canada: Newfoundland Becomes a Province, 1948–1949—263

CONCLUSION —303

ENDNOTES —311
BIBLIOGRAPHY —361
PHOTO CREDITS —381
INDEX —383

PREFACE

When scholars, students, and citizens turn their attention to the making of Canada and Confederation, they focus almost exclusively on the period from the early 1860s to 1867. That year, 1867, after all, was when several British colonies came together and created Canada as a nation-state. Canadians have marked the anniversary of that important moment on a number of occasions with considerable pomp and ceremony, notably and most recently in 2017 with the sesquicentennial—that is, the 150th anniversary—of Canadian Confederation. To many Canadians, however, their provinces did not become a part of Canada until the years after 1867, and for First Nations and other Indigenous Peoples the origins of Canada extend far earlier than that date. While Manitoba, British Columbia, and Prince Edward Island joined in the years immediately following 1867, Saskatchewan and Alberta became provinces nearly four decades later. Confederation took a very long time in Newfoundland. It remained outside of Canada until 1949, more than eight decades after 1867.

This book considers the issue of Confederation in Newfoundland politics from the early 1860s, when—like the other British North American colonies—it seriously turned its focus to union, until 1949, when it finally became a province of Canada. We are particularly interested in those periods when the union of Newfoundland with Canada was a clear issue in Newfoundland politics, such as in 1869 and 1948, as well as when it was considered tangential or even a distraction by political leaders and their parties. The issue of Confederation was used frequently by a variety of politicians to smear their opponents and to score favour with the electorate. We begin that journey with Frederic Bowker Terrington Carter and Ambrose Shea's dispatch by the Newfoundland government to monitor the constitutional talks in Quebec City in 1864, through Newfoundland's 1869 election on whether or not to join the other British North Americans in union, to the attempts at economic development and diversification in the late nineteenth and early twentieth centuries as ways to stave off Confederation. Throughout those decades, cleavages began to develop between St. John's and the rest of the colony, tension that would ultimately factor prominently in the decision of Newfoundlanders to become part of Canada in 1949. We also consider the rise of the Fishermen's Protective Union, which provided the first inklings of organized discontent among Newfoundland's fishermen and their families and their demands for a greater share of the country's wealth through what we term *social citizenship*, which also became pivotal in the debate about Confederation in the late 1940s. Throughout those periods, we keep our focus on Newfoundland's growing relations with Canada and Newfoundland's flirting with the possibility of union, as well as Canada's interest in Newfoundland. We continue the focus into the First World War and the collapse of the Newfoundland economy in the 1930s when Canada's influence grew in Newfoundland and the consideration of union with Canada was never far from the public agenda. Finally, we turn to the Second World War when Canadian and American troops "occupied" much of Newfoundland, then to the National Convention that considered constitutional options for Newfoundland in the postwar period, and finally to the 1948 referendum campaigns when, after decades of saying "no" to Confederation, Newfoundlanders resisted the international trend favouring smaller and smaller independent nations. At last, they said "yes" to union with Canada.

We believe that in the pages that follow we offer an important reinterpretation of Newfoundland's journey to Canada and Confederation, which does not in any way diminish the work of past and current historians and other academics and scholars who, each in his and her own way have contributed, collectively and immensely, to the understanding of Newfoundland's path to union with Canada. In fact, we acknowledge gratefully their tremendous efforts and have benefitted from their prodigious and important work. In particular, the scholarship of fellow historians and, in many cases, great friends, Peter Neary, Malcolm MacLeod, James Hiller, Andrew Smith, Jeff Webb, Sean Cadigan, Ged Martin, Frederick Jones, Sid Noel, Richard Gwyn, Kurt Korneski, John FitzGerald, Corey Slumkoski, Karen Stanbridge, Patrick O'Flaherty, David MacKenzie, Phil Buckner, and others, has provided immense insight into what follows below.

Despite the efforts of earlier academics and historians, many Canadians, particularly those in Newfoundland and Labrador, want to believe that Newfoundland's decision to join Canada in 1948 was simply a great conspiracy orchestrated by the British and Canadian governments and that the Newfoundlanders themselves were never told about the horrible deeds being perpetrated against them. Conspiracy theories might make for good entertainment, but they unfortunately contribute to the propagation of mistruths and myths, and they certainly make for poor history. It is good history that we are interested in promoting here, and to do that we turn our focus on Newfoundland voters, especially those who participated in pivotal campaigns and elections, particularly in 1869 and 1948—but at other times too—when they had to make a decision on whether or not they would support union with Canada. For a long time, the losers—if we can use that word loosely to identify (1) those who did not prevail in bringing Newfoundland into Canada on the 1869 vote on Confederation and (2) those who failed to keep Newfoundland out of Canada in 1949—have blamed the ignorance and stupidity of voters for why the result in 1869 went against Confederation, and why in 1948 the vote went against those who favoured a return to responsible government and had campaigned against Confederation. We show here that in those two contests over Confederation, Newfoundland voters themselves made informed decisions. We demonstrate that Newfoundland voters should not be explained away as ill-informed, illiterate, and easily swayed by prejudice and hysteria or by the emotional appeal of demagogues, not in 1869 and not in 1948. We challenge the long-standing idea that Confederation was rejected in 1869 and accepted in 1948 because of the stupidity and ignorance of the voter or because the electorate was uneducated and poor and, hence, did not really understand the issues. We argue that Newfoundlanders, in fact, made informed and rational choices for rejecting Confederation in 1869 and for choosing Canada in 1948. By 1948, we also contend, a new relationship had emerged between state and citizen—a social citizenship whereby the state would provide all Newfoundlanders a basic level of social and economic stability and well-being to which many were unaccustomed but naturally aspired. This shift in the notion of citizenship from political and constitutional imperatives to social and economic ones was a decisive factor in the narrow vote for Confederation because it promised voters full participation in the state's economic, social, and political life. In 1869, political citizenship was an important factor in the decision to reject union with Canada, but by 1949, social citizenship, combined with political citizenship, gave the advantage to the Confederate side. Moreover, unlike in 1869 when women could not vote, by 1948 they could, and we believe the votes of women made an important difference to the outcome.

For us, the question of social citizenship is at the heart of the movement for union with Canada in 1948. Appeals to nationalism and patriotism had worked well in the past for those who wished to chart an independent course for Newfoundland within the British Empire; by the 1940s much had changed, especially with the impact of the Great Depression of the 1930s and the coming of the Second World War, which ended in 1945. The shift in conceptions of citizenship from the political to the social, from the 1860s to the 1940s, was critical to Newfoundland's acceptance of Confederation in 1948. The debate over Confederation in the 1940s was between the old regime that had largely controlled Newfoundland since it was first settled by Europeans and a new group that advocated for a new relationship between state and citizen, one that championed an interventionist government promising to promote the social and economic well-being of the average citizen. That established elite—reactionary, conservative, and out of touch with many of the people, especially those in the outports and throughout rural Newfoundland and in Labrador—had nothing new to offer voters or any alternative to the attraction of Canadian social programs. Confederation meant the entitlement to certain rights and benefits from the state and the hope of a better life through improved education, health care, basic services, and social security programs. The Confederates tapped into the yearning among Newfoundlanders for improved economic circumstances, the desire for economic and social security, and an all-around better way of life.

Newfoundlanders were not tricked into political union with Canada in 1948. They knew what they were doing. Confederation was not primarily about constitutions or sectarianism. It was about the self-interest of voters, not about being duped or cheated or misled or being ignorant of what was happening. Newfoundlanders acted in their own self-interest when they chose union with Canada just as they had acted in their own self-interest when they had earlier rejected it. Like other citizens elsewhere around the world, they confronted their leaders and were motivated by their own plight. In the 1940s, they were part of an emerging voice throughout the developed world that wanted a more activist government. They were part of a movement that wanted their state and their government not merely to control aspects of the economy to ensure great economic security but also to ensure a better standard of living for all citizens.

This book has been a collaborative effort, and we are grateful for the help we have received along the way. The archivist is always the historians' best friend, and we wish to acknowledge those archivists who have been so generous with their time and assistance, particularly Linda White and Paulette Noseworthy at the Archives and Special Collections and the library staff at the Centre for Newfoundland Studies, both at Memorial University Libraries. Melanie Tucker at the Rooms Provincial Archives of Newfoundland and Labrador and the staff at the Maritime History Archives, Memorial University, have been helpful, as were archivists at Library and Archives Canada and the National Archives of Ireland. We would also like to acknowledge the research assistance of University of Regina history students Stewart Kerr and Jessica Lohner, as well as the Social Sciences and Humanities Research Council for its Insight Grant to Raymond Blake. Thanks as well to Don Walsh, a digitization services technician at the Digital Archives Initiative at Memorial University, and Judy Rudofsky, Executive Officer of the Johnson Family Foundation, who helped with securing appropriate images included here. We wish to thank, too, Kate Baltais for reading the entire manuscript and offering invaluable and sage advice and saving us from our own pens, and Daniel Whittle, an aspiring historian, for his careful read of several of the early chapters of the book. Karen Clark, acquisitions editor at the University of Regina Press, and Kelly Laycock, managing editor, have been an absolute joy to work with, as have their colleagues. Nadine Coderre brought a wonderfully sharp eye to our prose and offered excellent advice as copy editor. We also wish to acknowledge the support of the University of Regina through the President's Publishing Fund and the Faculty of Arts Publication Fund.

We wish to acknowledge, too, with thanks and generosity not only the excellent comments and suggestions of the two anonymous readers of our manuscript but also the efficient and timely manner in which they read the manuscript. Their comments and useful suggestions helped to greatly improve our work. That the readers were both able to review the manuscript in what must have been less than four weeks from when they received it is extraordinary. In the academic publishing world, where authors sometimes wait months for readers' reports, we were delighted with the speed and enthusiasm with which those readers undertook the task of reviewing our manuscript.

Finally, on a personal note, Raymond Blake wishes to acknowledge once again his appreciation to his colleagues at the University of Regina, friends, and extended family for their continued interest in his work. I am so lucky and happy to be a university professor and to have a wonderful and loving family that continues to take an interest in the history that I try to write. Ben, Robert, and Wanda make all of this worthwhile and nothing would be possible or even worthwhile without them. Similarly, Melvin Baker wishes to acknowledge the support of his brother Leslie and family and friends, especially good friend Betty Archibald, and those who form the membership of an informal monthly history group collectively known as the "Hollywood History Group."

INTRODUCTION

NEWFOUNDLAND: A PLACE IN SEARCH OF SECURITY

CONFEDERATION WAS DEBATED MORE INTENSELY, AND for a longer period, in Newfoundland than in any other province. Although in 1864 it participated in a series of conferences with other British North American colonies to consider union, it was not until 1949 that it became a part of Canada. Even then, Newfoundlanders voted only narrowly in a national referendum for this change in their status. In the intervening decades, however, the issue of Confederation with Canada was never far from their minds, and for the most part they were not in favour. Even so, leading politicians in Canada and Great Britain, as well as some in Newfoundland, continued to promote the idea of the original makers of Canada that Newfoundland should be included. Before the two 1948 referenda that finally settled the matter in favour of Confederation, only once, in 1869, did Newfoundlanders themselves cast their ballots directly on the question of joining Canada. Nevertheless, in many of the general election campaigns between 1869 and 1932—the last time Newfoundlanders went to the polls before surrendering responsible government in 1934 in the midst of an imminent financial collapse— union with Canada was an underlying issue. In various campaigns, both the incumbent parties and opposing hopefuls openly and explicitly declared their opposition to joining Confederation. But frequently, too, politicians of all stripes considered Confederation as one effective way out of a variety of economic, social, and financial problems confronting Newfoundland and its people.

This book is the story of Newfoundland's eighty-five-year ambiguous and troubled relationship with the Canadian Confederation. The relationship had three partners. Although often a suitor, Canada was, at critical moments, disinterested and prickly, perhaps believing that union was inevitable and that Newfoundland would eventually fall into its lap. Britain was never a suitor but always the concerned and worried parent; its goal from the 1860s was to have Newfoundland and Canada united. After 1869, Newfoundland had sought independence as it pursued a separate destiny from Canada. Like Canada, from the mid-nineteenth century it was a self-governing colony, and from 1907 a dominion, making it equal in status to Canada, but it never adopted the designation of a dominion until the end of the Great War in 1918 when there was a heightened sense of nationalism spawned by its gallant, though costly, war effort. It continued to use the British civil service to conduct much of its external affairs, however. The 1931 *Statute of Westminster* again recognized Newfoundland as a dominion, but the new constitutional powers, including several dealing with extraterritoriality, were never adopted. Neither were the judicial powers of the UK Parliament curtailed, nor marine and admiralty courts enacted (as they had been in Canada and several other dominions), largely because Newfoundland's legislators were distracted by a looming debt crisis. In fact, a riot in 1932 discouraged the government from bringing forward legislation to adopt various sections of the *Statute of Westminster*.[1] Nonetheless, in 1931 Newfoundland made the prime minister responsible for external affairs, and it adopted a national flag. By 1934, it was neither a dominion nor a colony as it had suspended responsible government—government responsible for and accountable to the people, not to the Crown or its representatives—and accepted a British-appointed Commission of Government to rule the country. Its pre-1934 constitutional status was restored before it became a part of Canada in 1949. During this period, some Newfoundlanders saw union with such a prosperous and promising partner as Canada as being perhaps both wise and sensible, while others vehemently opposed such a proposition. However, consummating the union in 1949 allowed Newfoundlanders

INTRODUCTION

the satisfaction of knowing that they alone, through a majority vote, had made their own decision to become a province of Canada.

Newfoundland was often an outlier in the world of geopolitics. In the mid-nineteenth century, nationalism had emerged as a powerful impulse spurring increasing momentum among smaller political units towards ever-greater political integration through the unification of kindred peoples. This resulted in the creation of new nation-states, such as Italy, Germany, and Argentina, to name just three of many. Newfoundland, however, turned its back on the wider nation-building project in British North America. Having won responsible government in 1855, the Crown colony of Newfoundland was self-governing in local matters and fully responsible for its own finances. In 1869, it ignored pressure from many in the St. John's mercantile and professional elite and from the Imperial government in London, opting against joining the Canadian Confederation and voting in favour of forging its own path to nation building. Periodically, as Canada extended its boundaries and dominance over the northern half of North America and forged a new sense of national identity from the Atlantic to the Pacific, Newfoundlanders would toy with the idea of Confederation, while also clinging tenaciously to their own identity. Later, in the middle of the twentieth century, Newfoundlanders, once again, went against the international trend. That was another period promoting national self-determination, a key element of the Atlantic Charter in 1941. Groups of people around the world who shared a common past and ethnicity and had forged some sort of national community together sought, through either the gun or the ballot box, to break from an Imperial overlord in search of independence, political autonomy, and self-determination. In 1948, Newfoundlanders rejected at the ballot box independent statehood in favour of membership, as a province, in Canada. This was an unusual choice for a liberal democracy, especially given that Newfoundland had previously enjoyed its status as a dominion in its own right and could have joined the post–Second World War community of nations with a seat in the Commonwealth, in the United Nations, and in defence alliances such as the North Atlantic Treaty Organization. Instead, it chose provincial status within the Canadian Confederation. Editorial content in Ireland, which long had a close association with Newfoundland, noted, for instance, the peculiarity of its choice: "Just when Eire is about to make what is considered a forward move in its constitutional evolution, Newfoundland came into the news because it is seriously contemplating what many will describe as a retrograde step—that of joining the Canadian Confederation as the tenth province or state." Yet the *Irish Examiner* acknowledged the Newfoundlanders' strong spirit of local patriotism, adding that economics was a stronger imperative: "Left to itself, Newfoundland can have little hope of becoming a strong, modernized state within the lifetime of the present generation."[2]

For those Newfoundlanders who favoured self-determination, the 1948 decision was—and has remained to this day for many—a source of great rancour, embarrassment, and shame. Some of those who consider union with Canada to have been a horrible and misguided decision believe that Newfoundlanders were misled and duped into Confederation or that union was imposed by outsiders without the people in Newfoundland being told what was going on. Those who had opposed union cried within days of Canada accepting the results of a second referendum on July 22, 1948, that Newfoundland was the victim of a terrible conspiracy. Peter Cashin, a long-time Newfoundland politician, had complained to Governor Sir Gordon Macdonald forthwith that the British had orchestrated an illegal and unconstitutional process forcing Newfoundland into Canada. Others followed over the years with similar contentions. A 1992 film, *Secret Nation*, written by Edward Riche and directed by Mike Jones, tells the story of a graduate student in history who stumbles across evidence that the British and Canadians had been working together to rig the referendum and pass Newfoundland off to Canada.[3] The most recent example is Greg Malone, activist and television personality, who is convinced that the British and the Canadian governments conspired to railroad Newfoundland into Confederation and that Britain fixed the vote, or at least fudged the result, to get the outcome it desired. In *Don't Tell the Newfoundlanders*, Malone argues that Newfoundlanders were the victims of a terrible conspiracy to bring about union without them knowing what terrible acts were being perpetrated secretly to force their country into Canada. Like many others before him, Malone points his finger in disdain at the outport voters, who gave overwhelming support to the Confederate cause.[4] In his narrative of Confederation, Malone argues

INTRODUCTION

that it was dastardly and undemocratic for the British government not to heed the advice of the Law Society of Newfoundland—"the cream of the country's legal community," as he puts it—when it submitted a petition bearing thirty-two signatures demanding that the 1948 referendum include only the recommendations of the National Convention and leave Confederation with Canada off the ballot. Yet he neglects to mention a rival petition with more than fifty thousand signatures from other Newfoundlanders—mostly outport loggers and fishers and their wives, as well as other women throughout the country—asking that Confederation be placed on the referendum ballot. Although many of those fifty thousand might have been poorly educated compared with the thirty-two lawyers, they were leaders in their communities and the *sine qua non* of Newfoundland society. In Malone's view, however, they were among the Judas Iscariots who had betrayed Newfoundland.[5]

It was not only in 1948 that those who lost the Confederation battle blamed the largely illiterate fishermen and outport people for the outcome of a critical vote on union with Canada. After the election rejecting Confederation in 1869, Newfoundland Governor Sir Stephen Hill had also attributed the failure of Confederation to the stupidity and ignorance of Newfoundlanders. Writing to his superiors in London, he had chastised voters, claiming that intelligent and wise men simply could not possibly reason with such a class of degenerates "who live in a primitive state of existence." He suggested that Britain forge ahead with union, nonetheless, as he believed that the people of Newfoundland would eventually be thankful that a better class of people had made the right decision for them.[6] Similar sentiments were expressed again in 1948. P.E. Outerbridge, St. John's businessman and determined anti-Confederate, saw union with Canada resulting from a bribe and blamed "the ignorant and avaricious outporters [for] hand[ing] over [Newfoundland] to Canada as a free gift on July 22."[7] John G. Higgins, a Rhodes Scholar and later a prominent St. John's lawyer who joined the anti-Confederate movement, was similarly dismissive of what he considered the ignorant and uneducated outport voter:

> The story of the Union of Newfoundland with Canada is a sordid one, a contemptible act of political chicanery perpetrated on a simple people by men holding high positions who have

forgotten the primary tenets of public morality and natural justice. The people should never have been asked to vote on a matter which was so complicated and so abstruse as confederation. This is a matter for experts.[8]

The Monitor, the official publication of the Roman Catholic Church in Newfoundland, did not mince words in its condemnation of those who voted for Confederation. It blamed both "cunning propagandists," notably Confederate leader Joseph R. Smallwood, and the British government for deceiving Newfoundlanders. Both understood fully, it maintained, that "it was possible to bamboozle an uninformed and inexperienced electorate once . . . they [Newfoundlanders] had come to believe in the silly notion of a benevolent Ottawa distributing free monthly checks [in the form of family allowances and old age pensions] to them and their families."[9] In both 1869 and 1948, then, those on the losing side contended that if the process had been fair, and if the voters had been as wise as they themselves were, the outcome would have been different. What those people forget is that persuasion is the art and essence of democracy.

Many commentators have already weighed in on Newfoundland's journey to Canada, but 2019, which is the 150th anniversary of its rejection of Confederation in 1869 and the 70th anniversary of union with Canada, provides an appropriate time to consider once again the long history of the Confederation issue in Newfoundland.[10] While being indebted to those historians who have come before us, we believe that new historiographies and new ways of looking at the past allow for a re-examination of some of the myths surrounding the successes and failures of Newfoundland's long history with Confederation. Recent scholars have questioned some of the earlier notions about Confederation. They have, for instance, challenged the argument that the larger political union of British North America in 1867 was the result of pragmatism. In the case of Newfoundlanders, in particular, we believe that earlier claims that they remained outside of the union because propagandists were able to successfully peddle their lies and prejudices among a gullible and illiterate fisher folk also need reconsideration.[11] We agree with scholars such as Janet Ajzenstat, Peter J. Smith, Andrew Smith, Kurt Korneski, and others that the acceptance or rejection of

INTRODUCTION

Confederation cannot be explained simply by pragmatism, prejudice, and the appeal of propagandists, or more recent writers who contend that voters in the case of Newfoundland in 1869 and 1948 were duped.[12] The reasons for the success or failure of those embracing or rejecting Confederation are far more complex than that; above all, we must see voters, especially in 1869 and 1948, when the ballot question was quite clear, to be making decisions based on their own assessment of the situation. Andrew Smith, for instance, argues in a recent essay that the politics of taxation was central to the struggle over Confederation throughout British North America, including in Newfoundland in the 1860s. Such opposition to taxation was linked to the distrust of a distant and perhaps uncaring state, sentiments that were rampant in the mid-nineteenth century. Smith contends that Canadian Confederation was an ideological struggle about classical liberal ideas on taxation as well as a debate on state powers.[13] Newfoundlanders, as we suggest below, were animated in the 1869 election campaign about the two most onerous aspects of Canadian citizenship: the prospect of higher taxes and the power of the state to force them into military service, which had been common for those in the Newfoundland fishery until after the War of 1812. In 1869, Newfoundlanders decisively cast their ballots on how those policies might impact them, and they voted against Confederation with Canada as a result.

Of course citizens are capable of irrationality in their ballot choices and are, indeed, more than capable of making seemingly strange decisions when voting. The impulse for historians to assert that voters make choices based on irrationality or hysteria is greatest when literacy rates and education levels of citizens are low, as they were in Newfoundland and Labrador from the 1860s and even into the late 1940s. In those instances, scholars and pundits are quick to assume that decisions with which they disagree or find appalling resulted from the stupidity and ignorance of voters. Such an explanation is especially easy when large numbers of citizens from certain geographical areas with similar literacy and education levels vote in a similar way. Explanations that attack the voter as incompetent are not particularly useful, valid, or enlightening, and certainly they do not allow for an understanding of the fears, hopes, dreams, and anxieties that citizens may have when they vote. There indeed may be instances when voters might be without formal

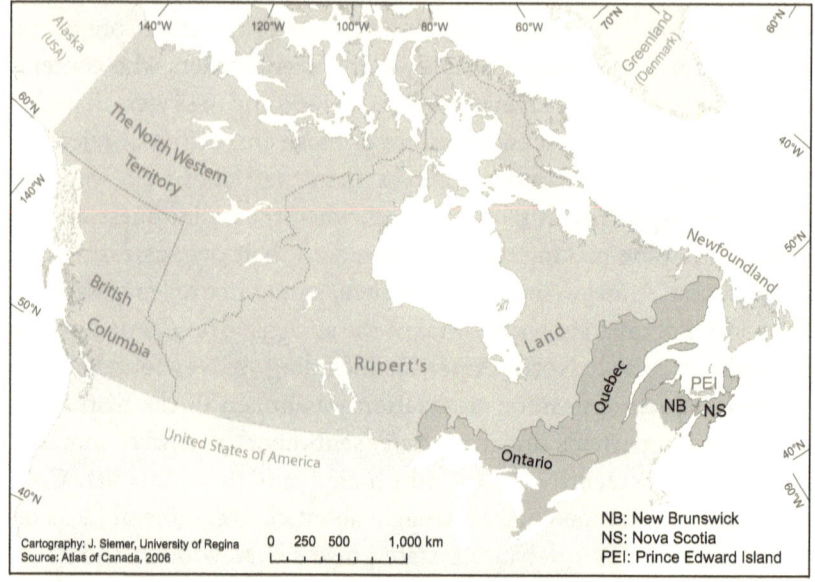

Canada, 1867. Of the Atlantic colonies, Newfoundland and Prince Edward Island did not join in 1867.

education, but that does not mean they are necessarily unintelligent and uninformed as they wrestle with important political, economic, and social matters, including the constitutional future of their state or whether or not they might be pressed into military service against their will or taxed too heavily. We believe one must move beyond the idea of misinformed and obtuse voters and notions of hysteria, prejudice, and irrationality as explanatory factors in understanding the collective reasoning why voters in Newfoundland from the mid-1860s through to 1948 voted as they did on union with Canada.

Despite the literacy rates and the levels of education in Newfoundland being among the lowest in all of British North America in the 1860s, voters in 1869 still likely made informed, rational choices when voting. Newfoundland voters should not be dismissed as failing to understand the issues at stake. James Murray was an unsuccessful candidate in the 1882 general election for the constituency of Burgeo-LaPoile, in one of the most isolated regions of the country, and his account is instructive, especially when considered along with some of the other historical accounts of the excitement generated during

INTRODUCTION

elections in Newfoundland at the time.[14] Murray later noted that the "people in the Outports know little and care less about the general politics of the country or about the general management of public affairs" but that they do care about their own situation. He had found during his campaign that political rallies and other election events were well attended and that the citizenry demonstrated "the existence of a wonderful quickness of apprehension, and of capacity and eagerness to understand more important matters."[15] Moreover, campaigns in Newfoundland were loud, highly visible public events. The processions, arches, torches, rallies and meetings, and gunfire from muskets to welcome candidates were, like the act of voting itself, instruments of state building in the new democracy that had been established after the achievement of responsible government in 1855, or perhaps even earlier with the coming of representative government in 1832. They were also all manifestations of political participation, and Murray wrote that he learned quickly "how important a part 'flags,' 'guns,' and 'processions' play in Outport election campaigns" and how "cheeringly large audiences" came to public halls and other venues to hear candidates during the campaigns.[16] These instruments created for citizens the reality of the Newfoundland state as a distinct entity, even if the country was often divided by regional and local interests. For many voters, too, the campaigns were confirmation that they were, indeed, part of the British world, and in that world participation in the election process was important. They embraced the notions of political citizenship that were widely prevalent throughout the British world at that time, demonstrated perhaps by the huge attendance at political meetings. James Murray also noticed, for instance, when he visited in late fall, just weeks before polling day, that voters had posted in their homes a circular that he had distributed by mail in April.[17] For many Newfoundlanders voting was not only an honour but also a performative duty and a means of protecting themselves, their families, and their communities from potential harms. In those early, post-1855 years after Newfoundland earned responsible government, conceptions of citizenship were largely based on political citizenship, which was then loosely defined as the connection between a male electorate and the Newfoundland state. The simple act of voting and having a say in the democratic process helped reify the presence of the state and the voters' ties to it in the minds of Newfoundland voters. Canada and Canadians were seen as outsiders in that mentality.

Regularly held elections and the process of voting, along with the various campaign trappings, helped to create the institutional framework necessary for the legitimization of the new Newfoundland state. Citizens participated in these events to express their disapproval or approval of candidates, the policies they promised, and the narratives they created. Through their demands and participation in the political process, citizens believed—and hoped—that they were able to shape legislation and general public policy. Newfoundland voters thus had a voice, sometimes a gentle murmur but at other times a loud roar, in the election campaigns, and through their voting they became keenly aware of their status as citizens. Voting was perhaps the most ritualistic symbol of Newfoundland's political culture, and the simple act of casting a vote was an essential way to participate in the political process and make a public gesture as a citizen.[18] For a brief moment in the democratic process, they were the centre of attention with their voting, and elections were an important form of citizenship (along with roadwork as a means of poor able-bodied relief). Thus, through the electoral process, the voter was enrolled as a citizen and became "an autonomous individual as a political subject."[19] Voting bestowed power, although only men were voters at this time. Elections and voting were instruments not of an imagined nation but of a real one, and citizens likely voted in a manner that best reflected their goals and aspirations as well as their fears. In the 1869 election in Newfoundland, 78 percent of eligible voters turned out to cast their ballots, an indication surely that they valued their political and constitutional rights.[20]

Voting in the 1869 election, then, was a performance of citizenship rights for men, a self-conscious realization that as Newfoundlanders they had indeed triumphed in the achievement of self-government and were the equals of others in the British new world. They were distinct, even unique, because of that achievement of political citizenship. Politicians throughout the 1869 campaign nurtured and kindled Newfoundlanders' objection, for instance, to the presence of France on their northern shores and their fears of new policies, including the possibility of increased taxation or military service, if they threw in their lot with Canada. What some have termed the "exaggerations" and "lies"

INTRODUCTION

about Canada perpetrated by the anti-Confederate leadership should be seen, instead, as part of electoral "performances," where a narrative is created, both real and imagined, that voters then evaluate and either accept or reject. Campaign strategies brought voters within the arch of patriotic citizenship. The anti-Confederate leadership implored voters to accept their state as an instrument of the people; fishermen and others were reminded they were not separate from the state but very much a part of it and that it was their duty to protect their state from outsiders such as the Canadians. Citizens were admonished that voting for union with Canada made them "traitors" of Newfoundland. It was patriotism with a considerable swagger.

That was a very powerful message. In 1869, voters cast their ballots on the basis of their perceived reality and the perceived reality often differed depending on where voters resided and worked. They considered the issues presented to them—and they rejected Canada. To dismiss these voters as emotional, irrational, and incompetent participants in the political process for voting as they did is to misunderstand Newfoundlanders and how democracy worked. These issues that animated the 1869 campaign remained at the core of the debates about joining Confederation until a new narrative was created in the 1930s and 1940s that citizens found better suited to their circumstances, a new narrative both more believable and more attractive. In both 1869 and 1948, a majority of voters accepted a narrative that resonated with their view of the world and one they could connect with their own experiences, identities, and knowledge. In each case, the stories told and the narratives constructed were compatible with how citizens understood and perceived their world.[21]

Issues of state and nation were also important in the debates over union with Canada in the late 1940s. The debates on Newfoundland's constitutional future had elements of prejudice, emotion, and misinformation, as these things invariably do in hotly contested electoral campaigns. Nevertheless, Newfoundland's major Roman Catholic publication, *The Monitor*, was wrong to declare shortly after the Confederate victory in 1948 that "it is indeed pitiable that there are still adult people whose minds are so susceptible to propaganda that they can be persuaded to behave with utter stupidity."[22] Wrong, too, are scholars who have attributed such power and causal explanation to those sentiments.[23] Although some Newfoundlanders still nostalgically long for the world they believe they lost after 1949, that world is mostly an illusion because, in fact, independent Newfoundland was rarely economically robust and healthy. Most Newfoundlanders knew full well what they were voting on in 1948, as they had in 1869. The long-term struggle that Newfoundland had in providing its citizens with a decent standard of living, with acceptable public amenities, was understood by most voters—particularly those in rural parts of the country—and it played a critical role in the outcome of the 1948 referenda. Those promoting Confederation in the 1940s were also well aware of that stark reality and promised in union with Canada a new relationship between state and citizen. They offered a social citizenship that would provide to all Newfoundlanders a basic level of social, economic, and cultural well-being to which many were unaccustomed and full participation in the state's economic, social, and political life.[24]

For much of the long, recorded history of humankind, the status of citizenship held little meaning. Communities were commonly bound together through ties of kinship, through personal bonds established between tribespeople and chief, between feudal vassal and lord, between subject and monarch, and, in Newfoundland, between fisher and merchant. Loyalty and fear were the glue that kept communities together. In Newfoundland, governing was largely a preserve of the colonial and professional elite in St. John's who had established directly or through their surrogate agents a client-patron relationship with citizens. From the Age of Enlightenment through the period of the French and American Revolutions and, indeed, throughout most of the nineteenth century, citizenship everywhere had long been associated with civil, legal, and political rights. It was political citizenship. In the Newfoundland Confederation debates of the 1860s, for instance, the anti-Confederate campaign often resorted to such notions of political citizenship to suggest that by throwing their lot in with Canada, Newfoundlanders would be surrendering those cherished notions of democratic rights they had won as British subjects in 1855 with the granting of responsible government.

In the late nineteenth and early twentieth centuries, the concept of citizenship became more abstract and sophisticated, to be interpreted more broadly and not merely as something narrowly juridical

INTRODUCTION

and political. Especially with a rise in literacy rates, a citizen came to understand that being a member of a state should bring status and the enjoyment of rights not bestowed by a tribal chief, an overlord, a sovereign, or even a St. John's fish merchant. By the mid-1940s, citizens in Newfoundland and elsewhere came to believe that citizenship did not simply define membership in a particular national community but also came to mean that they were entitled to certain social and material rights and benefits by virtue of their common status as citizens of a nation-state. These rights and benefits had become a recognized need during the Progressive Era in the early twentieth century—best reflected in Newfoundland by the success of William Coaker and the Fishermen's Protective Union, which he founded in 1908. The movement for social citizenship gathered impetus during the Great Depression and was embraced by Allied leaders during the Second World War, especially after the signing of the Atlantic Charter in Placentia Bay on August 14, 1941, and the publication of the British report, *Social Insurance and Allied Services*, by Sir William Beveridge in 1942. Many of the principles of the Atlantic Charter and the Beveridge Report were haphazardly put into social welfare legislation in many countries in the postwar period.

British sociologist T.H. Marshall was critical in bringing scholarly attention to the new conception of citizenship. He developed around the concept of citizenship a sociological theory of the political development of rights and obligations that recognizes social movements and group conflicts. An inherent tension arose between civil and political citizenship, on the one hand, and social citizenship, on the other, a process that became evident in Newfoundland's National Convention of 1946–48 and in the referendum campaigns that followed, which pitted union with Canada against a return to responsible government. Marshall considered the expansion of social citizenship to be a direct challenge to the hierarchical class structure: "It is clear that in the twentieth century citizenship and the capitalist system have been at war." Social citizenship was associated with social rights that came largely with the emergence of the welfare state, but it also came to include the provision of public services such as electrification, health care, public education, and a host of others. It included "the whole range from the right to a modicum of economic welfare and security to the right to share to the full in social heritage and to live the life of a civilised being according to the standards prevailing in society."25

Not only had social citizenship replaced political citizenship as the major change in the conception of citizenship in Newfoundland by the time of the 1940s debate on Confederation, but also citizenship had, by then, been expanded to include women. Women had been barred from voting in the 1869 election on Confederation and in other campaigns where the Confederation question was present, and there is no way of determining whether or not the outcomes in those instances would have been different if women had had the right to vote. By the time of the 1948 referenda, however, voting rights for women were well established. In fact, the granting of the franchise to women represents an important milestone and achievement in the evolving conceptions of citizenship in Newfoundland. After 1925, when women aged twenty-five and older were eligible to vote, gender certainly emerged as a major factor in the outcomes of all electoral contests. After the franchise was extended to women, political parties attempted to appeal to that group of voters, and in the first general election after winning the vote more than 90 percent of eligible women cast a ballot and undoubtedly played an important role in the outcome of the 1928 election and probably contributed significantly to the victory of Sir Richard Squires, who ironically in the early 1920s had opposed female suffrage.

The expanded electorate with the addition of female voters and changed notions of citizenship represent two key differences between the Confederation campaign of 1948 and earlier incarnations of the Confederation question. Historically, gender and race have been central to contestations about dimensions and meanings of citizenship, but in Newfoundland, where the vast majority of residents traced their lineage to the British Isles, race at that time does not appear to have been a dominant factor, although Newfoundland's Indigenous Peoples were clearly ignored, as we discuss below. The inclusion of women in the electoral process after 1925, however, was important and clearly linked to the rise in social citizenship. It is difficult to make a precise case regarding the importance of female voters, given the lack of exit polling and other types of measurement of voter intentions, to provide a gendered breakdown of voting patterns; however, given that 88 percent and 84 percent of Newfoundlanders, respectively, cast ballots in the

INTRODUCTION

two referenda, it is highly probable that the promise of a welfare state and the promotion of social citizenship in the campaigns would have appealed to female voters, especially to mothers. Winning the female vote was important, and the Confederates better capitalized on this than did those who campaigned for a return to responsible government.

A majority of the Newfoundlanders, including female voters, who marked their ballots in the second referendum on July 22, 1948, did so with hopes for a particular and better way of life as a Canadian province. In the first referendum, on June 3, the Commission of Government had placed third and was subsequently dropped on the run-off ballot. In the second vote, many of those who had wanted the Commission to continue very likely voted for Confederation, an indication, certainly, that they saw in union with Canada—as they had in the Commission—a measure of economic security as well as an unwillingness to place the affairs of the country again in the hands of local politicians who had led the country in the days of responsible government. Had the anti-Confederate forces offered responsible government *and* some social welfare programs, they might have won the referendum. But precisely by explicitly disparaging such programs and state supports for citizens, their chances for victory were made less likely. Victory in the final referendum wasn't actually as simple as selling one's soul and birthright for a "mess of pottage"—however, if citizens elsewhere were benefitting from social welfare programs at this point in history, why shouldn't Newfoundlanders? Accusations from those associated with the country's elite, particularly those in St. John's that considered outport voters crass, greedy, and selfish materialists because of their excitement over Canada's social programs, did little to help the anti-Confederate cause. Outport people firmly believed that the Water Street merchants and other members of the elite had benefitted enormously from an economic and political system that had existed for several generations but had often left them with barely enough to survive. They welcomed a new approach to statecraft and new leaders who promised a new and different way of managing the affairs of state.

Above all, those who voted for union with Canada hoped for a decent, prosperous future with a more secure standard of living than the one to which they had been accustomed as an independent country with its own responsible government. As historian Jeff Webb has pointed out, many of the neo-nationalists in Newfoundland are the right-wing heirs of the Responsible Government League. They denigrated the arrival of social programs, such as family allowances and unemployment insurance, which came with Confederation, for creating a dependency among Newfoundlanders, and their paternalistic ideology was out of touch with the lives of most Newfoundlanders in the pre-union period.[26] Joseph R. Smallwood, however, in the 1940s, one of the leaders of the Confederate movement, was never shy in saying then and later that "Newfoundland joined Canada mostly for Newfoundland's sake. Newfoundland was the smaller of the two, the poorer of the two, the weaker of the two; and it was because we believed that Newfoundland would get the better of the bargain that Newfoundlanders agreed to unite their country with Canada."[27] Smallwood promoted a fear of the uncertainties associated with an independent path for Newfoundland, yet he believed that within Canada's federal system, Newfoundlanders could flourish and thrive, thus ensuring Newfoundland's survival as a distinct self-governing entity or "nation." Canada's benevolence and its institutionalization of financial transfers—to individuals and to subnational governments—would maximize citizens' well-being and allow Newfoundland to modernize and remake itself economically and socially. Although the phrase was not yet in use in 1949, Smallwood believed that Canada was a "multinational state," a political community that made space for and accepted the legitimacy of the various communities making up the federation. Because of the economic and social challenges that had beset Newfoundlanders for generations, Smallwood denigrated the notion of an independent self-governing Newfoundland "nation" in the National Convention and created a new narrative that he hoped would resonate with the voters' own experiences. Within Canada, he said, Newfoundland could become precisely that—a "nation" with its own unique and special past, but also a province of Canada that would have, or at least have access to, the fiscal resources of a larger state necessary to enable its people to live in prosperity and with hope.[28] In one telling exchange in the National Convention on the proposed terms of union with Canada, Smallwood promoted his vision of Newfoundland as a cultural nation. He insisted in one instance during debate on referring to Maggoty Cove in St. John's (where public health and biological research had been

INTRODUCTION

recently undertaken), even though St. John's delegate Gordon Higgins asked Smallwood to "please not say Maggoty Cove," perhaps because of the stigma associated with the parasite. Smallwood retorted, "We may change Newfoundland into a province, but it will always be Newfoundland, and we will keep our Maggoty Cove."[29]

Newfoundlanders were the only Canadians to vote in a referendum to enter Confederation, but even then Indigenous Peoples remained largely excluded from the process.[30] Such instruments of direct democracy as the referendum invite citizens to consider difficult political questions and predict the outcomes of the choices available—sometimes without all of the necessary information—by selecting a "yes" or "no" answer. A referendum is a blunt instrument with which to measure public sentiment. When given such an opportunity, citizens frequently vent their frustrations with the powerful elites that have long run their governments and managed the affairs of their state often, they believe, without much regard for citizens' well-being. Referenda always allow one side to play the anti-establishment card and present itself as the outsiders standing up for the people against entrenched elites. Frequently, voters rely on either the messaging of charismatic politicians or the leanings of trusted authority figures, and they accept from the available narratives the one they find most compelling. In various European countries, particularly in the United Kingdom and Spain in 2016 and 2017, respectively, politicians used the referendum campaigns to remind citizens who felt they had been left behind or had not received their fair share of the nation's wealth, that their social and economic conditions could be different if they repudiated and replaced the existing constitutional or economic arrangements with which they were familiar and which they were convinced had not worked for them. Referendum campaigns are usually binary and polarizing in nature, but the winning side in most referenda has a political leader who has convinced enough citizens that they have a real voice in the outcome.[31] Many of these elements were present in the two Newfoundland referenda, which brought finality to a long-standing and simmering issue, but Newfoundlanders also had ample opportunities to fully understand the options on which they were voting in 1948. The debate on union with Canada began, not in the weeks before the actual vote, but in 1946 with elections to a National Convention. Longer campaigns do not necessarily make for a better-informed citizenry, but intense and passionate campaigns—as the campaigns of the late 1940s in Newfoundland were—do tend to create a more knowledgeable electorate better able to understand the issues involved and make more informed choices.[32] The second referendum in 1948 settled Newfoundland's constitutional relationship with Canada, an issue that had first emerged in the mid-1860s.

Social citizenship, nationalism, conflicting conceptions of state, and voter behaviour are central themes through which Newfoundland's evolving relationship with Canada over the issue of union can be explained. These themes are pivotal to understanding the decisions of the various Newfoundland governments and political parties and the citizens themselves at various times from the 1860s to the 1940s. The Newfoundlanders who negotiated the draft terms of union in 1947 and then the final terms in 1948, and those who campaigned for Confederation, were acutely aware of the economic and social disparities existing between Newfoundland and much of Canada at the time. They believed, however, that Newfoundland would have a secure and prosperous future within Confederation. To them, the promise of Confederation and the Canadian federal system provided economic and social security for all provinces and citizens, regardless of place. Smallwood, who in 1949 was to become the first premier of Newfoundland, believed that the Canadian state was benevolent and that it would be an active and autonomous agent distributing the virtues and benefits of Canadian citizenship to the people of the new province. After 1949, Newfoundlanders had a new national anthem. Although they joined in the singing of "O Canada," for many the "Ode to Newfoundland" with its resounding finale "God guard thee, Newfoundland" remains strong in their hearts, even to this day. Having relinquished their dreams for political sovereignty in an independent and separate country, the memory of their independence and notions of what might have been would, nonetheless, remain prevalent. Provincial politicians are still able to tug on those emotions when necessary in their disputes with Ottawa. Doing so today means that they are both Newfoundlanders and Canadians.

In the pages that follow, we consider the long period of history from Newfoundland's rejection of Canada in 1869 to its joining it finally in

INTRODUCTION

1949. We consider the political culture of Newfoundland, the fluidity of its political parties, and how its regional differences impacted politics. We consider, too, how union with Canada figured into the political debates. Like Canada, Newfoundland attempted to develop its interior through the building of railways that brought Canadian entrepreneurs, particularly Robert Reid, and Canadian banking and financial institutions to the colony when its development strategies saddled it with almost insurmountable debt. Newfoundland quarrelled with Canada when the Canadians interfered with its attempts to forge trade relationships with the United States, but it also sought efficient ferry connections with Nova Scotia and lobbied hard for Canada to contribute to the cost of such connections. It fought Canada for control over Labrador, yet once it secured the territory it frequently attempted to barter it away to Canada, often at an exorbitant price. The issue of union seemed to be a constant in the Canada-Newfoundland relationship, but Newfoundland was generally most keen to consider union when it encountered financial difficulties, and then, of course, Canada was not particularly interested; when the economic conditions were favourable, Newfoundland was much less interested in discussing union with Canada. During and after the Second World War, there were enough Canadians and Newfoundlanders interested in union to make it possible, and, at that time, both countries believed that union was beneficial for both. For Newfoundlanders, Confederation brought a measure of financial security and economic stability that might help them avoid another national debt crisis, but the dreams of 1867 were fulfilled only when a majority of voters embraced the promise of social citizenship that Canada—and not independence and a return to responsible government—could provide in 1949.

CHAPTER 1

REJECTING CANADA AND EMBRACING THE NEWFOUNDLAND NATION, 1864–1869

NEWFOUNDLAND'S JOURNEY TO THE CANADIAN CONfederation was long and complex. The idea for a union of the British territory in North America, which Newfoundland had been a part of since 1497, has a similarly long and complicated history. Among the first to promote such a union was inventor and printer Benjamin Franklin, one of the American Founding Fathers who drafted the Declaration of Independence and the Constitution of the United States. In 1754, worried about persistent and deadly attacks from French military in New France and their Indigenous allies, the famed statesman and diplomat invited leading gentlemen to Albany, New York, to discuss the creation of a union that could organize a common defence network and promote greater commerce among British peoples in North America. It is not clear if he envisioned Newfoundland being part of such a confederacy, but like so many other attempts throughout the early nineteenth century, his efforts came to naught. Newfoundland was obviously interested in the well-being of the rest of British North America, nonetheless. Soldiers and sailors of the Royal Newfoundland Regiment of Fencible Infantry, formed in 1795, rushed to the defence of Canada during the War of 1812 and fought gallantly at Fort George, Fort York, and throughout the Niagara Peninsula and at Fort Mackinac, where they helped repel an American attack. Yet Newfoundland showed little enthusiasm several decades later when James William Johnston of the Nova Scotia legislature attempted to reignite interest in a union of the British colonies.[1] His impassioned pleas that forging such a confederation would realize a "dream as old as the English presence in America" fell on deaf ears. When, however, Alexander Tilloch Galt, the united Province of Canada's minister of finance, raised the possibility of hosting a conference to explore a federal union in 1858, Newfoundland expressed considerable interest.[2] But those plans, too, were soon abandoned as the British government did not share Galt's enthusiasm at that time. When the idea resurfaced a few years later, the state of affairs in North America had changed considerably. There was then significant interest for the project in both the Maritime colonies and the Canadas. The Maritime legislators had arranged a conference for the first week of September 1864 in Charlottetown to discuss legislative union of the Maritime colonies. Newfoundland was not invited, however, and only learned about it through a fortunate stroke of serendipity.

Newfoundland premier and attorney general Hugh W. Hoyles (1861–65) happened to be in Halifax visiting his wife's family when plans were being made for the Charlottetown Conference. It might be possible that he had timed his holiday to learn about the plans then being contemplated for a union of the British North American colonies as the St. John's press were reporting on the plans for Maritime union. Educated at Pictou Academy, Hoyles had received his legal training under Nova Scotia's attorney general Samuel George Archibald, making him, at the time, one of the few Newfoundland politicians born and educated in British North America. Canada was not an unknown land to Newfoundlanders. Canadian magazines and news stories were available throughout the colony, including reports by early August 1864 of the impending meeting at Charlottetown. Travel and trade between the colonies were commonplace. Like many of his contemporaries on the mainland and, indeed, throughout much of Europe and elsewhere, Hoyles saw little hope for economic, cultural, and social expansion in small political units. He believed that a union of the British colonies might offer the best solution to some of Newfoundland's persistent economic problems.

Hoyles personally reached out to the leading members of the Nova Scotia government, including Dr. Charles Tupper, premier and provincial secretary, and asked if Newfoundland might be included in the upcoming conference. The premier of Newfoundland made it clear, however, that his interest was "solely on his own responsibility, [and] without authority either from the Government or the Legislature." Hoyles reminded Tupper that the "determination of this question, so far as Newfoundland was concerned, would altogether rest" with its voters—a position that would be expressed explicitly by Newfoundland leaders time and again in the years to come.[3] Although he was clearly interested in union, Hoyles distinguished himself in Halifax with a timidity and caution that would characterize his approach to the issue of Confederation throughout his tenure.

Tupper, meanwhile, was apologetic. He and his colleagues had given no thought whatsoever to Newfoundland joining their proposed union. Somewhat awkwardly, he confessed to Hoyles that they felt "Newfoundland had no wish to become a party to it." If, however, that proved not to be the case, "the other Colonies would not object to Newfoundland entering the proposed Union." Tupper then invited Hoyles to Charlottetown as Newfoundland's unofficial representative so that Hoyles might see first-hand what was being contemplated. But Hoyles politely refused. He had to return to St. John's to greet the new governor, Sir Anthony Musgrave (1864–69), who was set to arrive early that September and would prove to be a determined supporter of Confederation. Hoyles had no reason to fear that Newfoundland would again be forgotten, however. Tupper assured him that "at the Convention the question of the introduction of Newfoundland should be considered, with a view of providing for her admission," should its legislature wish to join "a Legislative Union with the other Maritime Provinces, upon such terms as might be equitable." If cautious, Hoyles was also persistent and enthusiastic about the Charlottetown Conference. Before departing Halifax, he asked Tupper one more time that he ensure "the Government of Newfoundland . . . be furnished with the fullest and earliest information of the proceedings" at Charlottetown.[4]

NEWFOUNDLAND AND THE QUEBEC CONFERENCE

The plans at Charlottetown did not unfold as Tupper and his fellow Maritimers had anticipated.[5] Like the Newfoundlanders, the Canadians had learned of the conference, but unlike Hoyles they had no intention of passing on it. They requested an invitation and arrived in Prince Edward Island with a renewed interest in the federal union that Galt had recommended a few years earlier. The Maritime politicians embraced the Canadian proposal for a larger federation of all of British North America and agreed to a second conference, in Quebec City, that October. The extent of Canadian leadership and dominance at Charlottetown was evident in the invitation to Newfoundland to join the conference at Quebec. It came not from Tupper but from John A. Macdonald, attorney general from Canada West, who would play a leading role in making the Dominion of Canada and, indeed, become its first prime minister in 1867. Macdonald telegraphed Hoyles from Halifax, on September 12, that an official invitation would arrive shortly from Charles Stanley Monck(the fourth Viscount Monck)—governor general of the Province of Canada (1861–67) and first governor general of Canada (to November 1868)—but he hoped that Hoyles would immediately confirm his participation.[6] Then Macdonald and the other politicians set off on a tour of Maritime towns to make themselves better acquainted with the region; they did not, however, venture across the Cabot Strait to Newfoundland.

The Newfoundland government acted quickly, if cautiously, on Macdonald's invitation and decided to go to Quebec City. Premier Hoyles believed that Confederation could provide more effective management for Newfoundland's important fisheries and much-needed capital to fuel economic diversification and development. Nevertheless, Hoyles was not to be Confederation's major advocate, nor would he venture up the St. Lawrence to Quebec City. The Executive Council in St. John's decided, after "mature deliberation," that the Newfoundland delegates would not be given authority to bind the government or legislature "to any ulterior proceeding." It was resolute in its decision, insisting that the legislature—not the delegates at Quebec—reserve "the fullest right and power of assenting to, dissenting from or, if advisable, of proposing modifications of any terms that may be proposed" at the Quebec

CHAPTER 1

Premier Hugh William Hoyles chose Frederic Bowker Terrington Carter (left), an Anglican and a Conservative, and Ambrose Shea (right), a Catholic and a Liberal, to attend the Quebec Conference in October 1864. Both were convinced that Newfoundland should join Canada.

Conference.[7] The Newfoundland government also decided, as had the colonial governments from throughout British North America, that the issue of union would not be a "party question." Like Tupper and other colonial leaders, Hoyles sought a bipartisan approach to deciding union. He invited Ambrose Shea, leader of the Opposition and a member of Newfoundland's Roman Catholic community, to join Hoyles's chief lieutenant, Frederic Bowker Terrington Carter, Speaker of the House and a member of Newfoundland's Protestant community, in Quebec City. The Newfoundland delegation was the smallest and the only one not led by its premier or a minister of the Crown.[8]

Shea and Carter realized immediately the possibilities that union offered. In this, they were really soulmates with Tupper and Samuel Leonard Tilley, premier of New Brunswick, who believed their colonies could be part of something better and more grandiose—a "British America, stretching from the Atlantic to the Pacific, [that] would in a few years exhibit to the world a great and powerful organization, with British Institutions, British sympathies, and British feelings, bound indissolubly to the throne of England."[9] Shea's father had emigrated from County Tipperary to St. John's in the early 1780s, and Shea saw himself as a native Newfoundlander, not a Briton who happened to be living in St. John's. He came from the older Irish tradition that had favoured cooperation with the British; however, by the time Newfoundland won a measure of self-government in 1832, notions of working with Britain had largely fallen out of favour with many Irish Catholics in Newfoundland, as well as with those in Ireland. Shea had welcomed the founding in 1840 of the Natives' Society of Newfoundland, which was committed to promoting the interests of the colony's native-born (rather than newcomers and British merchants who spent several months each year in the colony) regardless of religion or ethnicity. He became its president in 1846, even though he endured fierce attacks from many fellow Catholics and from priests for promoting his non-sectarian views. Shea supported responsible government, which was achieved in 1855, and free trade—or reciprocity—with the United States. He was among the first to stress the importance of diversifying the colony's economy and to embrace the notion of a trans-island railway as a means of achieving greater national self-sufficiency. Like other members of his family, Shea resisted clerical interference in public life, and as editor of his newspaper, the *Newfoundlander*, he promoted the interests of Newfoundland without much regard to religion. He even became leader of the Liberal Party, although this was an unlikely home for him given that it was long favoured by the Roman Catholic establishment and dominated by recent immigrants from Ireland, who harboured a tremendous dislike for all things British in their fervent Irish nationalism and their struggle for Home Rule.[10] Despite his support for Confederation, Shea could never be its champion, as the Catholic hierarchy was aligned against him, and he was never able to bring the Catholic voter to his side.

It would eventually fall to Carter to lead the Confederation movement in Newfoundland, but it had been in law and business rather than politics that his family had come to prominence. His family had arrived in Newfoundland from Devon in the southwest of England in the mid-1700s and had established operations at Ferryland and then in St. John's. His grandfather, William Carter, was appointed a judge of the vice-admiralty court, and his father and uncle were magistrates. Frederic studied law in England, and on his return to St. John's in 1842,

CHAPTER 1

Shea and Carter at the Quebec Conference, 1864, standing fourth and fifth from the left, respectively.

he was admitted to the Newfoundland Bar. He soon became part of the St. John's elite and was active in the Natives' Society. Like many of his Anglican and Conservative contemporaries, he was opposed to the granting of responsible government, but he soon came to terms with it and won election (by acclamation) to the Newfoundland House of Assembly in 1855. He was later a Conservative member of a delegation sent by the Newfoundland Assembly to London to protest a draft agreement concluded between Britain and France that would have given France an exclusive fishery along parts of the French Shore. Carter had strongly protested the draft agreement as it was negotiated without Newfoundland's consent, and he believed it would be detrimental to Newfoundland's interests. When his close friend, Premier Hoyles, formed a ministry in 1861, Carter was chosen as Speaker of the House of Assembly and was an integral part of the Conservative government as it struggled to find solutions to the colony's social and economic problems, notably the expenditure on poor relief and economic uncertainty.[11]

Carter and Shea departed St. John's for Quebec City on September 23, 1864.[12] En route, they passed a vessel bringing a letter from Charles Tupper asking Premier Hoyles to send five delegates to

Quebec instead of the two who were then making their way up the St. Lawrence River. Tupper had invited them to join the Nova Scotia delegation departing from Pictou on October 16, which would have given the Newfoundlanders a great opportunity to learn what had transpired at Charlottetown—but this was not to be.[13] Although the smallest delegation at Quebec City, arriving without any knowledge of the discussions at Charlottetown, Shea and Carter would earn, nevertheless, a revered place in Canadian history as two of the original Fathers of Canadian Confederation. They appeared in Jules I. Livernois's now famous photograph of the delegates in Quebec, taken on October 27, 1864, and in Robert Harris's 1884 painting, *Conference at Québec in 1864*. For many in St. John's, however, there was no such veneration for the pair. "Generations yet unborn," an anti-Confederate was later to write,

> Will curse the day
> Carter and Shea
> Crossed the Sea
> To barter away
> The rights of Terra Nova![14]

Such doggerel was a sign of the difficulties that lay ahead for Shea, Carter, and other Newfoundlanders favouring union with Canada.

At Quebec City, Shea and Carter were instant and enthusiastic supporters of union, although there was no disguising the fact that both were mere observers of the proceedings. Shea was elected one of the secretaries to the conference, perhaps an indication of the others' eagerness to have Newfoundland join their ranks. When delegates toured Canada East and Canada West following the Quebec Conference, Carter spoke glowingly of Confederation to the Quebec Board of Trade and again in Toronto. "I hope sincerely," he said, "if this confederation is formed, that it will tend effectually to destroy that party spirit and those prejudices, and that acerbity of feeling which have lamentably prevailed; for we generally find the intensity of the acerbity is proportioned to the narrowness of limits."[15] In Carter's view, the smaller and more isolated the pit, the fiercer the rats; Carter had witnessed sectarian upheaval in Newfoundland politics and knew

CHAPTER 1

first-hand the perils of an isolated and fragile economy such as Newfoundland's. Union, he believed, would diminish the religious strife, stabilize Newfoundland's political climate, and spur economic growth and development.[16] In Montreal, Shea spoke to a receptive audience of the mutual benefits of union, and with Carter he signed a formal report warning that union could not be rejected "without aggravating the injurious consequences of our present isolation."[17] A Montreal newspaper praised the Newfoundland pair for their "tact and sagacity and [their] large and enlightened views . . . [which] seemed moved by one will and purpose—to guard the interests of Newfoundland and, at the same time, to promote the grand design."[18]

Shea and Carter reported to the House of Assembly in early January 1865 on the 72 Resolutions agreed to at Quebec. Plans for the new country were ambitious, they said. Macdonald had launched the conference by providing "an exposition of the whole question" of union for their benefit, as they had missed the discussions in Charlottetown. He had opened with an elaborate statement showing the benefits of union and the great opportunities it would bring to all of them collectively and that they could never hope to attain as individual and isolated provinces. Provision was being made for the admission as provinces into the union, on equitable terms, of Newfoundland, British Columbia, and Prince Edward Island.[19] Confederation was to be a federal union under the British Crown that would "protect the diversified interests of the several Provinces, and secure efficiency, harmony and permanency in the working of the Union," while avoiding the mistakes of the American system. Shea and Carter said they embraced—like others gathered at Quebec—a constitution that shared responsibility between competing provincial and national interests, and found balance between unity and diversity, while still forging a national economy. There was recognition in Quebec in 1864 of the linguistic, religious, cultural, and geographical diversity of Canada. Canadians might never have a common sense of national identity, they reported, but it was hoped they would share a common sense of purpose and of citizenship. Shea and Carter believed that plans for the new country could provide a design for social cohesion while recognizing distinctions of diversity. Newfoundland's cultural uniqueness and identity would be secure in such an arrangement. Shea and Carter believed all could prosper and flourish in the new nation, although it is now evident that, like others at Quebec, they ignored the Indigenous Peoples in Newfoundland and Labrador and, indeed, those throughout British North America.[20]

In addition to the General Legislature or Parliament, which included a Legislative Council or Senate with regional equality, each province would have its own government to deal with local matters. The colonies would surrender control over customs duties, the major source of income for all provinces, including Newfoundland. In return, the federal government would provide each province with an annual subsidy of 80 cents per capita of its population so that they would not have to impose abhorrent direct taxation to make up for the lost revenue. Although the grant was substantial, and large enough to meet the needs of the other provinces, it would be insufficient for Newfoundland because of its limited population. To mitigate that situation, Newfoundland could transfer to the federal government all ungranted or unoccupied lands, mines, minerals, and royalties in exchange for an annual subsidy of $150,000 (roughly $2.6 million in 2018 dollars). Newfoundland would, however, retain the right to build roads and bridges on the surrendered lands. The delegates also appreciated that Newfoundland's per capita debt was much *lower* than that of any of the other provinces, except Prince Edward Island. At a time when government debt generally, and the possibility of higher taxes to finance an ever-expanding expenditure, generated considerable concern and fear among citizens, the delegates gathered at Quebec City recognized that they could not expect Newfoundlanders to shoulder the cost of the debt already accumulated by the other colonies without some compensation in return. Because the federal government would absorb the huge debt of the mainland colonies, it offered to Newfoundland as compensation the interest at 5 percent on the difference between Newfoundland's debt at the time of union and the average amount of indebtedness per head of the population of the Province of Canada, Nova Scotia, and New Brunswick. The payments to offset Newfoundland's lower public debt were to be made twice annually and were intended to keep taxes low in Newfoundland.[21] In sum, the aggregate grant from Ottawa, the new union's capital, to Newfoundland was to be approximately $370,000 annually, though that amount would rise with the population. With locally generated revenues of about $5,000, and with the federal government assuming the cost of government services (approximately $150,000) then borne by the Newfoundland government, as a province Newfoundland would have surplus revenue of $124,000 to use annually for a variety of purposes.[22] Shea and Carter believed that the Quebec arrangement placed "the question of our means on a satisfactory footing."[23]

Confederation, Shea and Carter maintained, would also improve and diversify the Newfoundland economy by creating free trade with the rest of Canada and improving the Island's communications with the rest of the world. The Confederation arrangement would also stabilize the financial situation through substantial and predictable revenues. In fact Newfoundland would enjoy, Carter believed, "such progress as no person at present contemplated." He predicted that the tone and quality of political life and discussion would also improve. Only through Confederation, he insisted, could Newfoundland be "relieved from that isolation which has so long retarded our progress."[24] It was also Carter's hope that with union the British merchants who had gained so much financially from their trade in Newfoundland would invest their gains in the new province rather than retire to England, as so many of them did, to spend the fortunes amassed in Newfoundland.[25]

Carter and Shea concluded their report to the Newfoundland House of Assembly by noting that "men of all parties were present at the Conference, from the various British North American Provinces, but the influence of local differences found no place in the deliberations." They also praised the high-minded and philosophical approach of the politicians at Quebec: "We feel warranted in asserting our belief that no inquiry was ever conducted under a higher sense of the responsibility of the occasion, or with a more single desire to arrive at the best results for the great interests at stake." While acknowledging that their report did not cover every "individual view" of every delegate, the 72 Resolutions were "unreservedly adopted" at Quebec, they pointed out. They noted, too, that while their instructions were not to bind Newfoundland to anything at the conference, they fully supported the proposed union: "We have but to state that we affixed our signatures as individuals to that report with the full conviction that the welfare of the colony will be promoted by entering the Union it proposes, and that we cannot reject it without aggravating the injurious consequences of our present isolation."[26] Confederation, they believed, was Newfoundland's best hope for economic progress and financial stability.

Shea and Carter's report and their enthusiastic recommendation for Confederation to the House of Assembly marked Newfoundland's unofficial but measured launch of the campaign for union with Canada. Nevertheless, this first attempt at union was so decisively defeated in 1869 that most political parties largely steered clear of any serious embrace of Canada for more than eighty years; the issue of union did, however, remain part of the political debate and discourse throughout those eight decades. There is no single reason for Newfoundland's rejection of Confederation in the 1860s, but several explanations have been offered to explain why Newfoundland remained outside of the Canadian nation-building project until 1949. Writing at the end of the nineteenth century, the magistrate, politician, and historian Daniel W. Prowse wrote, "I very much doubt if any terms would have been accepted" in 1869. Those opposed to union were many, he added, and the anti-Confederate forces were "powerful in organization" and had in the leading opponent to union, Charles Fox Bennett, a "most able and indefatigable political campaigner." A member of the House of Assembly in 1865,[27] Prowse had supported Confederation, and he lamented "the awful tales that were told about taxation, about ramming new-born babes down Canadian cannon, 'bleaching their bones on the desert sands of Canada.' " They had a "tremendous effect upon the simple out-harbor people." Moreover, he asserted, for Newfoundlanders the sufferings of their forefathers at the hand of the French navies from Quebec and their Indigenous allies during the seventeenth- and eighteenth-century military conflicts for control of the colony still reverberated in their memories, and they had little desire to forge a new nation with their former adversaries. Further, Prowse lamented, the appeal to Irish descendants in Newfoundland, many of whom hated the union of their homeland with Britain, by the anti-Confederates— who compared the union of their new country with British Canada— was very effective. All those factors combined, he believed, proved effective, with the predictable result being "an overwhelming defeat for

CHAPTER 1

Charles Fox Bennett (1793–1883) led a vigorous campaign against Confederation in 1869.

the Confederate party." The union of all of the British North American colonies is "a consummation devoutly to be wished," Prowse concluded, but in 1869, such a dream was "simply annihilated."[28]

Much has been written on the events of 1869 in the years since Prowse offered his explanation for Newfoundland's rejection of Confederation, but the outline of the narrative remains largely unchanged even if the details of that narrative are now better known. As historian Allan MacPherson Fraser noted in the mid-1940s, at a time that Newfoundland was again considering Confederation, many of the conditions in the 1860s, such as the fear of declining markets with the termination of the free-trade agreement with the United States, a political stalemate in the Canadas, fear of an American invasion, and a growing debt crisis that had facilitated union in the other British North American colonies, were absent in Newfoundland. Even so, Fraser casts Charles Fox Bennett, the anti-Confederate leader, as "a born master of the art of propaganda," who played on the "fears and passions of the ignorant sector of the electorate."[29] Like Prowse, Fraser and others have suggested that if the illiterate, uneducated fishermen were only wiser, the outcome would have been different. In the euphoria surrounding the 100th anniversary of the Charlottetown Conference in 1964, W.L. Morton, a passionate Canadian nationalist historian, took up this theme and lamented the fact that in Newfoundland "the incipient 'Liberal' and 'Conservative' parties were neither coherent nor principled" but merely agglomerations of "sentiment and interest" that took advantage of a poverty-stricken and illiterate people. It was unfortunate, intoned Morton, that the decision on the entrance of Newfoundland into Confederation would be left to such folks.[30]

When he examined Newfoundland's rejection of Confederation in Canada's centennial year, St. John Chadwick, a former British civil servant who assisted the National Convention in 1946, was nothing short of contemptuous of Newfoundland society in its rejection of Canada. "The great bulk of the population," he wrote, "bred to adversity, drawn from the poorest quarters of the British Isles, consistently undernourished and largely illiterate, proved fertile breeding ground for rumour and sectarian passions" that the "Establishment" and "the merchant oligarchy" were quick to exploit for "their own varying reasons." The "body politic was far from healthy," he concluded, as if this was sufficient explanation for Newfoundland's rejection of Canada.[31] More recently, James K. Hiller, who has written extensively and with great insight and passion on Newfoundland's history, shows that reason and truth are often the first casualties of political campaigns, as they are in war, and he argues, too, that the anti-Confederates "worked on the ignorance, credulity, and conservatism of rural Newfoundland and without difficulty created a deep fear of Canada" that was impossible for the Confederate side to overcome. In an obvious show of sympathy for the Confederates, Hiller notes that in southeastern constituencies, for instance, "reason has so obviously failed to work on the minds of these voters that only four confederate candidates could be found."[32]

CHAPTER 1

Can the defeat of Confederation be explained by the appeal of emotion and propaganda? This is too simplistic an explanation. The period was complicated, complex, and messy. One cannot, above all, ignore the world view that Newfoundland voters had at the time, even if the elites lamented the incompetence of the average voter who, they believed, was too ill-informed to vote intelligently and, in their view, make the correct choice. Voters may have lacked intimate details of the debates in the House of Assembly in St. John's and of the negotiations over terms of union in Ottawa; it does not follow, however, that they were in any real sense incompetent to judge the direction of their government and what it should do on the major policy issues of the campaign. The contempt that has been demonstrated in the literature for the people—*the demos*—in 1869 is lamentable.[33]

BUILDING A NEW APPROACH TO THE CONFEDERATION DEBATES

The 150th anniversary of Newfoundland's embrace, at the polls, of its own independence is an appropriate moment to consider new ways of thinking about the 1869 election.[34] To do so, it is useful to recall that others have already raised questions about previous interpretations of those Confederation debates. Frederick Jones notes that historians have for too long regarded the 1869 campaign as a "triumph of emotion," adding that although ordinary voters "were certainly not sophisticated . . . they were not fools." He also asks whether the case against union really was as "unreasonable" as some have suggested, a question that Patrick O'Flaherty, too, has recently pondered.[35] Andrew Smith brings a sophisticated and thoughtful analysis to the debate by examining the opposition to taxes that came from wealthy merchants and poor fishermen alike and that marked the campaigns in 1869 as an ideological struggle between interventionist Toryism and classical liberalism.[36]

To look afresh at the events surrounding the issue of Confederation in Newfoundland, it is important to acknowledge that in the 1860s Newfoundland was, indeed, great neither in population nor in wealth. Many of its 162,000 residents were dispersed along the coastline, dependent on the cod and seal fisheries, which together accounted for 95 percent of exports and employed approximately 90 percent of the working population. Any decline in catches, such as occurred throughout much of the 1860s, created social and economic paralysis. The early years of that decade witnessed an economic depression, precipitated largely by local conditions, notably a succession of poor catches in the cod and seal fisheries, by market difficulties in Europe and South America, and by a potato blight; combined, these circumstances contributed to extraordinary economic and social hardship. In the four years prior to 1865, Newfoundland's debt doubled from £18,000 to £36,000 as the Crown colony endured its worst economic depression in a generation.[37] The government ran a current account deficit, and relief payments accounted for nearly a quarter of it as demand for poor relief became rampant, but such borrowing did not bring Newfoundland's accumulated debt anywhere close to that of its neighbouring colonies.[38] The other British North American colonies had borrowed much larger amounts but mostly to invest in canals, railways, and other infrastructure.

Newfoundland was also marked by sectarian and racial divisions, a problem that plagued it for much of the nineteenth century and would continue to do so periodically into the twentieth. Immigrants tended to come from either the Protestant west of England or the Roman Catholic south of Ireland. Most arrived between 1760 and 1830, with the Irish settling mostly on the Avalon Peninsula, and the English farther north and west, into Conception Bay and along the south coast. St. John's became home to both groups, which brought with them the prejudices and hostilities of their homelands, and these soon found their way into the colony's political life. The sectarian lines became further entrenched with the establishment of denominational schools in 1843, a system that continued until 1998. The dominant religious groups forged an unwritten agreement in the 1860s that they would share, proportionately, representation in the legislature and in the Executive Council and in the dispensation of government patronage.[39] It was hoped that by informally institutionalizing such sectarian practices the colony would be somewhat free of religious animosity.[40] Sometimes it worked.

One of the greatest challenges in the mid-nineteenth century for Newfoundland was its struggle with the quality of human capital as defined by literacy and education, "an increasingly essential tool in the modern world for fashioning a better personal and national life." Historian David Alexander, who had turned his attention to those matters before his untimely death, suggested that "literacy and education are essential to a lively intellectual life wherein the goals of a country are effectively debated, defined, and efficiently implemented."[41] Others have noted that the link between illiteracy and labour productivity may be tenuous at best, but Alexander suggested that the "implications in terms of class social relations and the quality of public life and public decision making" are far more important. Education and literacy must have a mass presence in a society for social transformation and liberation to begin. Alan Macpherson's analysis of records for the Parish of Hermitage on the south coast has estimated a literacy rate among the young married population of only 18 percent in the late 1860s compared with 90 percent of bridegrooms who were able to sign the marriage register in the Thirteen Colonies at the time of the American Revolution.[42] Wide differences in educational skills and information between a governing elite and the mass of the population, Alexander noted, "can breed an unwarranted deference on the one hand and a selfish noblesse oblige on the other. It also breeds a sluggish intellectual life and an unimaginative and inefficient debate about the goals of society and how they might be realized." Low levels of educational attainment and low literacy rates contribute to a political culture that gives durability to populist politics. They also foster a political culture that fails to produce a vibrant and effective democracy. Civil and social engagement, including political knowledge, political engagement, and voter turnout, are impacted by education and literacy levels.[43] This is all true, but voters nonetheless understood their own world no matter how limited it might have seemed to the governing and economic elites.[44]

A stable democracy and a functioning society require both education and diversified economic development, and Newfoundland had neither in the 1860s despite earlier attempts by the House of Assembly to encourage alternative industries to the fishery.[45] Most of the country's wealth was in the hands of a small group of merchants, primarily concentrated in St. John's and Conception Bay. The fishery operated on a credit system, whereby fishermen were advanced in the spring supplies for the fishing season as well as molasses, pork, tea, and a few other staples to sustain their families, with the hope that at the end of the season the catch would be enough to settle their accounts. Merchants charged as much as possible for the items advanced on credit and paid as little as possible for the fish delivered in the autumn. Even in a good year, most fishermen barely made enough to cover their debts. Governor Sir Alexander Bannerman (1857–64), writing in 1863, described it as "a most vicious system which had long prevailed in Newfoundland," and a succession of poor catches resulted in making fishermen "disheartened, indifferent, and indolent."[46] As a result, most fishermen existed in poverty or on its boundaries, and the fish merchants and the colony's elite, known as the Water Street merchants, exerted a powerful hold over Newfoundland, controlling all aspects of its economy, including local banking and the meagre manufacturing sector. They also controlled the Legislative Council (upper house in the Newfoundland legislature) and their proxies, the House of Assembly. Moreover, their considerable influence was further exerted through the powerful Chamber of Commerce. They saw the economy, especially the fishery, as their own and ensured that the state would not intervene in their domain. As a result, unlike the fisheries of other countries, there was no strict and sustained government regulatory involvement in this sector in Newfoundland until the 1930s—perhaps providing a clear indication of how the merchant class or "fishocracy" had come to control the Newfoundland state for its own gains. Nor was there any control exerted over how merchants decided to dispense credit to the fishermen and their families. It was a system of servitude that existed in most fishing communities and an arrangement that had created a class system between merchants and fishermen.[47]

By the early 1860s, many people in Newfoundland had recognized that the fishery alone would not be able to support the Island's growing population. Although much political thought and discussion on the increased use of technology, reforms to education, and the importance of economic diversification had animated the rest of North America, and were prevalent throughout the other British colonies, such debate was only beginning in Newfoundland in the 1860s. The Island had won a measure of self-rule with the institution of responsible government in 1855, largely because of the reform efforts of the Catholic politicians and priests.[48] In his 1863 pastoral message, for instance, the Roman

CHAPTER 1

Catholic bishop of St. John's, John Thomas Mullock, had stressed the urgency of finding alternative sources of employment, and in his 1864 Speech from the Throne, Governor Bannerman warned that widespread poverty would be the end result if the economy did not expand beyond the fisheries. In Newfoundland there had been no great clamour, such as had reached a feverous pitch in the rest of North America, for railway development and expansion into the interior.

Hoyles was among the first politicians to recognize the systemic and structural problems plaguing the economy. He attempted to stimulate activity in fisheries other than cod, notably in the trade of herring, salmon, and mackerel, and to expand the cod sector to the Grand Banks. His young protégé, William Whiteway, who in 1865 became Speaker of the Assembly and a keen supporter of Confederation, believed that Canada would help develop the bank fishery that he believed crucial for economic diversification and prosperity.[49] He believed only the Canadian government had the capacity to support the construction of larger vessels to allow Newfoundlanders to search out new fishing grounds, although the powerful Chamber of Commerce initially opposed Confederation because it believed Canada would have little interest in promoting the Newfoundland fishery.[50] Hoyles also encouraged efforts to diversify from the fishery, especially with a geological survey in 1864 to examine the mineral potential of the Island.

In 1866, Hoyles's successor as premier, Frederic Carter (1865–69), followed with a scheme of bounty payments for the clearing and cultivation of new land in the hope that people would mix farming and lumbering with their fishing activities. There was also growing government interest in the French Shore—that part of the Newfoundland coast that Britain had given to France in 1713 to maintain its fishery. Just a few years earlier, in 1857, the British government had outraged Newfoundlanders when it signed a convention giving France a more secure hold on the northern coasts than had been provided in the ambiguous eighteenth-century treaties. London's goal was to maintain good relations between England and France, but Newfoundlanders saw the convention as a betrayal of their interests. Citizens were indignant, lowering the British flag to half-mast and raising the American one in protest. The legislature passed a resolution condemning the convention and criticizing the British government for ignoring the local Assembly. So unanimous and vociferous was the opposition that the British colonial secretary, Henry Labouchere, withdrew the convention and conceded the principle that "the consent of the community of Newfoundland is regarded by Her Majesty's government as the essential preliminary to any modification of their territorial and maritime rights."[51] The government also sponsored the Geological Survey of Newfoundland that was inaugurated in 1864 under the directorship of Alexander Murray, an assistant to William Logan, who had begun a geological survey of the Province of Canada in the 1840s. Murray found that parts of the Newfoundland coastline, including along the French Shore, had tremendous potential for farming and mining, and in 1867 he published an article, "Mineral Resources of Newfoundland," wherein he noted that if those two were simultaneously undertaken "I see no reason to doubt the capability of the island to raise all the necessities of life for its inhabitants." It was hoped that many of those struggling in the Newfoundland fishery could find economic security in those parts of the Island away from the sea, and if developed properly these areas could attract more British settlement.[52]

The Hoyles and Carter governments had both come to realize that the traditional shore fishery had reached its capacity and that it would not be able to sustain a growing population. As historian Kurt Korneski points out, by the 1860s two general philosophies of development had emerged in Newfoundland. One was a state-centred approach modelled essentially on what was happening in the Province of Canada. In that model, development was driven by heavy borrowing, often by the state, large-scale exploration for resources and new lands, and government-supported infrastructure development. The other approach, more classically liberal and laissez-faire, emphasized low taxes, free trade, and private investment; development was best left to individual entrepreneurs and to markets. These two approaches to development were played out in the Confederation debates of the 1860s, with Confederates like Hoyles and Carter promoting a "British" and transcontinental future for Newfoundland that would see it joining, through union, the other British North American colonies and looking to the Canadian state for its economic salvation. The anti-Confederates, however, saw Newfoundland pursuing its own development and independence within the British Empire and exploiting its resource-rich hinterland for the benefit of Newfoundlanders, not Canadians.[53]

Given the economic and social situation in the 1860s, it was relatively easy for earlier historians to draw a connection between Newfoundland's political culture and economy, its level of illiteracy, rates of poverty and income insecurity, and the rejection of union with Canada. If only voters, they surmised, had been better educated and better informed, less stricken with religiosity and sectarianism, wealthier and less reliant on the Water Street merchants, then surely they would have opted for joining Confederation. In political entities such as Newfoundland's, where there was no secret ballot, and individuals had to declare their vote in public at a polling station, voting intimidation was common. Fish merchants, priests, and others were also known to use their power and authority to influence—perhaps even determine—the outcomes of elections. Moreover, in the 1869 election, polling stations were few in number and separated by considerable distances that could not be easily traversed. The voting regulations allowed for the use of "proxy" votes. A male voter, more than fifteen miles from a polling booth, could authorize another to cast his vote (only men could vote at this time) by issuing a written notice and completing the appropriate form. Such practices led to fierce competition among candidates and some considerable pressure being exerted on voters. The proxy often went to the candidate who had the power to impact the voter's well-being.[54] Merchants were especially powerful in this regard, and in a highly polarized election—such as that in 1869—they exerted considerable pressure to win votes, particularly in outport communities. Yet even a better educated electorate might have still voted against union, believing that Newfoundland and its people would be better off on their own and that they could better undertake economic expansion and diversification on their own. The arguments of the anti-Confederates were not so far-fetched that they would not potentially have swayed an educated population.

Another factor to consider in understanding the 1869 debate is the conundrum of Newfoundland identity and nationalism vis-à-vis Confederation and the new Canadian state. One could argue that Newfoundland lacked a powerful figure such as a George-Étienne Cartier or a Thomas D'Arcy McGee. Those two Canadian Confederates had argued successfully in predominantly French-speaking and Catholic Quebec that Confederation was in no way an attempt to unite Canadians around a single national loyalty, but only to unite an array of diverse religious and linguistic communities, which might possibly develop into a single united people under a national government without destroying local identities. Newfoundland had long been a fragmented society, and by the 1860s there had developed some accommodation on important sectarian differences in the hopes of creating a good and just state. Perhaps citizens needed reassurances that all ethnicities and religious groups would be protected in the new union, but there was no such rhetoric coming from the Newfoundland Confederates in 1869. Rather, the anti-Confederates warned repeatedly—and successfully—that those gains, for instance in denominational education, especially for Catholics, would be threatened in a largely Protestant Canada, even if Catholics were the majority in certain sections of the new country. The prominent anti-Confederate leaders were able to cultivate the fears and animosities of a people who worried about losing their identity. Moreover, voters had to make a choice within the social context in which they lived. As James Murray, a merchant and politician who represented the constituency of Burgeo-LaPoile as an independent (1889–94), found in his first (and unsuccessful) campaign shortly after the rejection of Confederation, the demand for political, social, and economic equality predominated in outport Newfoundland. The solution to these challenges often revolved around issues such as taxation, access to poor relief, concerns about military service, and high prices—matters of immediate interest in the everyday lives of most citizens.[55]

With the achievement of responsible government in Newfoundland in 1855, these notions of creating a fairer society took on a national dimension for the first time, as citizens came to believe that the solution to their problems rested with their own state. Voters weighed the options presented to them in 1869, and retaining their self-governing status and rejecting Confederation with Canada seemed the best protection against unwanted intrusion from a distant state (particularly in the form of military service and increased taxes). Newfoundlanders had known only too well how their fishery was a nursery for the British naval forces and how their fellow fishermen had been pressed into service for decades. As Keith Mercer has shown, press gangs were neither

CHAPTER 1

illegal nor unusual in Newfoundland and operated almost with impunity until 1815, the end of the Napoleonic Wars and the War of 1812. Still, fishermen resented such tactics and often fought back against them as they had in 1794, when Lieutenant Richard Lawry of the HMS *Boston* led a press gang ashore in St. John's. He was attacked and killed by a crowd there when he attempted to press some of their own into naval service.[56] It is not surprising then that some fifty years later fishermen in the late 1860s were worried when Bennett and others warned that union with Canada would lead to unwanted military service for them in distant lands. Moreover, their conception of place and their national identity centred on and served the Newfoundland state, where their ethnic and religious identities were relatively secure. The rejection of Confederation was an important step in the creation of a distinct Newfoundland identity. Let us turn now to those debates in 1869 to see how the campaign on Confederation actually unfolded.

THE CAMPAIGN FOR CONFEDERATION

The 1865 Speech from the Throne had called for a "calm examination" of union. When debate began in the House of Assembly, there was no great enthusiasm for union, and members were almost evenly divided on the matter. Eighteen members spoke against it, and twenty-one expressed moderate support for it, although some supporters identified problems with the 72 Resolutions agreed to at Quebec. Premier Hoyles remained interested and warned prophetically that within "half a century the united colonies of British North America would be one of the world's strongest nations and that Newfoundland, if it remained outside and continued in isolation, would become bankrupt."[57] Yet he quickly understood that important factions in his party and others, more generally throughout the colony, were opposed to union. Merchants, fearing increased taxation and a reorientation of their traditional patterns of trade from Britain and the United States to Canada, were worried. Newfoundland's trade and traffic were indeed directed towards Europe, the Caribbean, and the United States rather than westward to Canada. Many of the merchants, too, regarded England as their home, and they returned there "after acquiring sufficient competence," in the words of

Governor Bannerman in 1859; they had no desire to break the British connection.⁵⁸

The Catholic bishops and many of the clergy had come from Ireland, and they feared that a union with the largely Protestant and British colonies would create for Newfoundland all of the evils that had come with the union of Ireland and England; thus, they were equally opposed.⁵⁹ This fear would prove to be immense as the debate over Confederation intensified. Carter and Shea's prediction of broad public support for the Confederation agreement never materialized, but Edward Cardwell, secretary of state for the colonies, advised Governor Anthony Musgrave, Bannerman's successor in 1864, to encourage the Newfoundland legislature to decide on Confederation as quickly as possible. He was extremely disappointed that Newfoundland delegates had not joined other British North Americans when they met in London in June 1865 to finalize plans for union and to write the *British North America Act* (in 1982 incorporated into Canada's Constitution).⁶⁰

Given the divided opinion, Hoyles, who had earlier insisted that the people should decide on union, became ever more convinced that a decision on the matter would have to depend on the results of a general election, but it would be Carter who would have to build a winning team. In 1865, he succeeded Hoyles as premier and proceeded to build a coalition that included Liberal stalwarts Ambrose Shea, former premier John Kent (1858–61), and Ambrose's brother, E.D. Shea. He hoped they might carry Newfoundland into union with Canada and bridge some of the sectarian differences that had long marked politics in Newfoundland and which Carter saw as a scourge on the body politic. James Hiller points out that the coalition of 1865 set an important precedent in Newfoundland politics, as leading politicians came to believe that the government "should represent all religious denominations, which should receive a fair proportion of seats in the legislature and positions in the civil service ... [and at the same time] open the way for party divisions based on factors other than religious affiliation."⁶¹ Still, Carter's Conservative-led coalition remained predominantly Protestant, with only a smattering of Liberals, Catholics, and Methodists. Even his promise to share patronage on a proportional basis among Catholics, Anglicans, and Methodists failed to break the opposition that remained a strong force against Confederation. Carter's coalition

CHAPTER 1

won the 1865 election—but union with Canada had not been a major issue in that campaign.

Little active public discussion on union took place in Newfoundland in either 1866 or 1867, but Shea reported to John A. Macdonald, on May 14, 1867, that he hoped union could be arranged before the end of that year.[62] When the Dominion of Canada came into being on July 1, 1867, the Newfoundland government had to make a decision if it would join. Nothing had really changed since 1864, and Newfoundland still had little reason to be enthusiastic about continental integration. The major incentives that had created sufficient interest in the Maritimes and the Canadas to make union possible in the mid-1860s held little appeal in Newfoundland. Its trade and traffic were still towards Europe and the Eastern Seaboard, not towards the interior of North America. There was no American threat of invasion, as was the case in the Canadas, and the Fenians who posed a threat to the mainland provinces mattered little to Newfoundlanders. The Royal Navy provided all the defence Newfoundland needed. Westward continental expansion held no appeal, and Canada's plans to acquire Rupert's Land and construct the Intercolonial Railway from Halifax to Quebec stirred no excitement on the Island. Political squabbling and deadlock in the Canadas were not Newfoundland's concern, and Newfoundland's debt, compared with that of the other colonies, remained minimal: in 1865 it was one-quarter that of either Nova Scotia or New Brunswick—and a fraction of that of the Province of Canada.[63] In 1867, the net debt of the Government of Canada was $75.7 million.[64]

Moreover, Confederation held little promise for resolving the issue of the French Shore, whereby France enjoyed considerable rights in the northern and western regions of Newfoundland. And the fears of competition from Canada—in the fisheries and in manufacturing—remained. Furthermore, the Canadian tariff would have hit Newfoundland hard in the immediate aftermath of union in 1867, raising taxes by as much as 44 percent if the tariff rate in 1864 had been applied.[65] Even so, Governor Musgrave contacted Macdonald in December 1867 about terms, and Macdonald replied his government was prepared to make the same concessions to Newfoundland as it had to New Brunswick and Nova Scotia. On the subject of the militia, which was to become an issue later, Macdonald acknowledged that all "inhabitants of the Dominion should be bound to share in the defence of their common country," and it would be "improper to stipulate" that Newfoundlanders would not be required to serve beyond the boundaries of their province. Still, Macdonald thought that given their seafaring traditions Newfoundlanders would be most suitable for marine or naval defence.[66]

Carter's government had lost little optimism for union when the matter took centre stage. In 1869, prompted by Governor Musgrave, Premier Carter finally seized the initiative, sensing that the persistent economic difficulties in the fishery might convince people to see joining Confederation favourably. Supporters of Confederation continued to argue that only Canada had the wherewithal to inject new capital into the fishery and get inshore fishermen out of their "miserable cockleshells of punts which can only creep close along the shore when all is calm, and must fly in and abandon perhaps the best fishing at the first ripple of a breeze" and into large boats to increase their range and productivity.[67] With another poor fishing season and revenues continuing to decline, the government had increased taxes on such staples as flour, pork, butter, and tea, and after 1865 it levied a 20 percent increase on most other imported items. Alarmed at those tax increases, many merchants began to change their outlook and saw union and increased government intervention as means of not only lowering taxation but also spurring economic diversification and ushering in a new era of economic security. Many of the colony's political and economic elite agreed that the economy had to be diversified away from the sea, and increasingly they saw joining Confederation as possibly stimulating economic growth, improving social and economic conditions for most citizens, and reducing out-migration from the Island. Economic growth and increased productive capacity, many felt, lay in the interior with new investment in the Island's mineral and timber resources and in further industrialization. Confederation might offer a solution to the lingering economic crisis. Confederates became more vocal in advocating their cause. Moreover, union now had the support of all newspapers in St. John's except the *Patriot*. Union also had the strong backing of Governor Musgrave and the British Colonial Office. Anti-Confederate feeling among the St. John's Irish ran high, however, and one petition in 1868 against political union with Canada garnered

CHAPTER 1

No Confederation !
Reduced (not Increased) Taxation !!

Let us keep our Fisheries to Ourselves ! —— Let us keep our Lands, Mines and Minerals to Ourselves ! ! —— Let us keep our Revenue to Ourselves ! ! !

Newfoundland for the Newfoundlanders.
NO REWARDS FOR TRAITORS.
No Militia Laws for Our Young Men
NO DRAFTING FOR OUR SAILORS.

Let us Stick to our Old Mother Country, Great Britain, the TRUE Land of the Brave and Home of the Free!!

LET US NEVER CHANGE THE UNION JACK FOR THE CANADIAN BEAVER!!

NEVER GIVE TO CANADA THE RIGHT OF TAXING US.

Anti-Confederate propaganda, 1869. The anti-Confederates campaigned on higher taxes and capitalized on the fear of Canadian conscription of young men.

more than two thousand signatures and the endorsement of ten leading mercantile firms.[68]

In early 1869, Premier Carter introduced the draft terms for union from the Quebec Conference into the Newfoundland legislature. "It would be well . . . to travel a little and visit that magnificent province [Canada], as well as Nova Scotia and New Brunswick, which were advancing so rapidly in material prosperity, and in all that tended to make a people great and respected," he said. "These countries were all more prosperous than we are." Many of Carter's arguments for union would be similar to those that would prove successful in 1948: for instance, Carter told the House of Assembly that voters "should support this confederation on account of their children." Confederation would provide cheaper imports, thus immediately providing a net benefit to citizens.[69] By a vote of seventeen to seven, the legislature agreed to send a delegation, consisting of Carter, Methodist Nicholas

Stabb and Roman Catholic John Kent from the House of Assembly, and Peter G. Tessier, a member of the Legislative Council and a representative of the St. John's Chamber of Commerce, to Ottawa to negotiate terms for Newfoundland's entry into Confederation.

Canada was generous in the 1869 negotiations, offering nearly everything Newfoundland demanded, including a promise that there would be no export levy placed on Newfoundland fish and even pledging modifications to the federal *Militia Act* that would exempt Newfoundlanders from serving in mainland Canada.[70] The federal government agreed to assume Newfoundland's debts and liabilities and to provide an annual payment of $106,000 to make up for the difference in the per capita debts of Canada and Newfoundland. Newfoundland was to receive a grant of 80 cents per capita or $104,000 annually on an upward-escalating scale as the population increased. It would receive $150,000 annually from the transfer of Crown lands and mineral rights to the federal government rather than the $175,000 that it had sought, but it had the option of retaining the lands and forfeiting the subsidy before union occurred. Further, a special subsidy of $35,000 was provided, bringing the total annual financial payments to Newfoundland to $408,922, an increase of $40,000 from the amounts negotiated at the Quebec Conference. Ottawa would also be responsible for a variety of services, including the pay and upkeep of judges, the governor, post offices, customs houses, steamer service, fishery patrols, lighthouses, and the geological survey. Those services cost Newfoundland $260,000 annually. It was believed that as a province Newfoundland would have sufficient revenues to meet its needs; however, the revenues were largely fixed, while expenditures would surely have increased. Union also promised to deal with Newfoundland's isolation—a pivotal issue for the Confederates—through the provision of efficient steamer connections to Canada and Great Britain that included as well a mail-boat service between Halifax and St. John's and a passenger service in the summer season between Montreal and St. John's. Canada promised an efficient coastal steamboat service connecting the outport communities on the Island and in Labrador with St. John's, the colonial capital. The Canadian government agreed to encourage the development of the fisheries through a subsidy to promote diversification in the herring and salmon species. Confederation would not interfere with the denominational education system that divided an annual grant for schooling between Protestants and Catholics in proportion to population.[71]

On June 10, 1869, the Parliament of Canada approved the entry of Newfoundland into the Dominion of Canada under section 146 of the *British North America Act*. Governor General Lord Lisgar (1869–72) wrote to Colonial Secretary Earl Granville that the terms had been "agreed upon with the delegates specially sent for the purpose of discussing them by the Government and Parliament of Newfoundland," adding that he expected the terms to be "acceptable to and be sanctioned by the constituencies of that Island at the general election which is to take place in the course of the ensuing autumn."[72] Granville wrote to Colonel Sir Stephen Hill (1869–76), who had succeeded Musgrave as governor, that he hoped "nothing will occur in Newfoundland to delay a measure from which I confidently anticipate advantage both to the Dominion of Canada and to the Colony."[73] The terms were adopted by the Newfoundland House of Assembly on March 5, 1869, by a vote of seventeen to seven, the same divide that had agreed to send the delegation to Ottawa.

The ensuing election, however, would prove to be the undoing of the arrangement worked out with Macdonald's government. Unlike Charles Tupper, who pushed the Confederation package through the Nova Scotia legislature without an election, and John A. Macdonald, who saw a one-issue election on a subject such as union with Canada as possibly playing into the hands of tyrants and demagogues, Frederic Carter was a democrat who rejected the Burkean notion of elected representatives making decisions for the people who elected them. Carter believed that voters should, indeed, have the final say on Newfoundland's constitutional future. He had refused to go to the people immediately after the Assembly approved the terms to capitalize upon the disarray within the Liberal Party and possibly secure victory. Instead, he followed the well-established tradition of holding the vote at the end of the fishing season, although possibly, so it was rumoured, he had promised Confederation's most vocal opponent, Charles Fox Bennett, that he would not hold an early vote as it was important to provide sufficient time for all voters to become familiar with the issue.[74] The delay proved costly as it afforded the opposition time to mobilize. The delay also provided time for economic conditions to improve, thereby diminishing a powerful incentive for voters to accept joining Confederation. Carter and Shea had been promoting union since the Quebec Conference in 1864 as the only way to stabilize and improve the Newfoundland economy, but they were not willing to sacrifice the proper democratic process to political opportunism to achieve their objective. It was an opportunity lost, however, as the economy improved markedly throughout 1869, and fishermen enjoyed one of the best fishing seasons in a decade. With the return of prosperity, one of the powerful arguments in favour of union had vanished.

Political parties had accepted the denominational compromise that Carter had forged before the 1865 election for sharing the political spoils between the major religious groups. Nevertheless, sectarianism and ethnic identity had become firmly entrenched in the political culture of Newfoundland and, as the debates on Confederation demonstrate, almost impossible to overcome. The Irish Catholic minority viewed Confederation as a British plot akin to that of the *Act of Union* of 1801 that had brought their beloved Ireland under English domination. Spurred on by the Limerick-born Bishop John Thomas Mullock, the Irish were largely aligned against Confederation. It was a British plan, Mullock had earlier reminded his faithful: union with Canada would undermine Newfoundland's local culture, threaten Irish influence, and end denominational education. As Sean Cadigan points out, Mullock had attempted to restrain the Irish nationalist elements within the Newfoundland Catholic Church over Newfoundland's economic development,[75] but he never advocated the separation of church and state. In fact, he had sanctioned priests as campaign managers for the Liberal Party in the first election held after Newfoundland won responsible government in 1855, claiming that priests, too, paid their taxes and had the same rights as other British subjects in the political process. Mullock died in 1869, before the crucial general election on Confederation,[76] but the anti-Confederates tried to capitalize on the fears of the Newfoundland Irish and the sense of local patriotism that Mullock had championed.[77] Thomas Talbot of County Kilkenny, Ireland, who arrived in Newfoundland in 1837 to eventually settle in St. John's, was a fierce anti-Confederate, and he captured those sentiments in the St. John's *Morning Chronicle*. The union of Newfoundland and Canada, Talbot warned, was of a "small and comparatively

CHAPTER 1

powerless country with a large and more powerful one," and it was bound to produce "evils" that in the case of the union of Ireland and Britain "have manifested themselves in almost total destruction of the Irish people as a Nation. The Trade and Commerce, the manufacturing and agricultural industries of the people sank beneath the blighting influence of this Union."[78]

Without a doubt, the leading role in the 1869 election fell to Charles Fox Bennett, as he donned the mantle of nationalist to rally the forces against joining Confederation. Born at Shaftesbury in Dorset, England, he was sent to St. John's as a clerk in 1808, at the age of fifteen. Within a decade, he and his brother Thomas had established themselves as leading general merchants. They supplied outport planters (fishermen who employed other fishermen), engaged in the import of European merchandise and the export of fish, and joined the ranks of the St. John's mercantile elite. Bennett became president of the Chamber of Commerce in 1836. He married into Bristol society, where his company had an operation and his wife continued to reside, and he spent some of each year in England himself.[79] Bennett, his opponents often charged, was never a real Newfoundlander but one driven primarily by personal economic interests.

Bennett was unique among St. John's merchants in that he believed that Newfoundland had considerable economic potential beyond that which came from the sea. He used profits from the fish trade to diversify his business interests, including the establishment of a brewery, a distillery, sawmills, and the promotion of farming. He also saw economic potential in mining, establishing a foundry in 1847 and funding mineral explorations along the Island's coast. His greatest success in mining came at Tilt Cove in Notre Dame Bay, where in 1864 production began on a rich deposit of copper ore that employed nearly eight hundred persons. Bennett was also attracted to politics and had been appointed to the Legislative Council in January 1843. He had opposed the introduction of responsible government in 1855, but that campaign would pale in comparison to his crusade against joining Confederation.[80]

Bennett became a Newfoundland nationalist, vowing to protect Newfoundland from the rapacious Canadians. He voiced his opposition to union in a series of letters to the local newspapers in 1864 and 1865, when the 72 Resolutions were first published in St. John's. Perhaps the fact that he owned about a million acres in mineral rights, which would have been transferred to the federal government under the proposed terms of union, figured into his dislike of Confederation—but self-interest has not necessarily stood in the way of good public policy. He argued that union with Canada would bring no benefit to Newfoundland: "The sending of Delegates to Canada, apart from the proportional amount of revenue which we should have to contribute towards the support of the Confederate Government," Bennett wrote in 1865, "would entail a very heavy expense, and not the least disadvantage that we should suffer." The greatest loss, he continued, "would be the sacrifice of our independent legislation and the control of our own rich colonial resources for the benefit of that nationality which, so far as I can at present conceive, can confer but few and trifling benefits on us."[81] Bennett insisted that Newfoundlanders would be lost in the Canadian Parliament: "What influence could our atom of representatives in so large an assembly of delegates exercise in obtaining for us that amount of legislation our necessities may require?"[82]

To a people who had won their right to self-government in 1855 and had exercised their franchise four times since then, this was a powerful message. Bennett called upon the community to fight against Confederation and prevent the union that would surely result in higher taxes, a constant dread to most Newfoundlanders. Governor Musgrave had complained to Cardwell earlier that "it is a feature entirely peculiar to this Colony that there is no local Revenue or fund of any kind, Municipal or Parochial." There is a "morbid apprehension of any direct Taxation," even in St. John's, he wrote, and so much so "that the state of affairs described in other places as being taxation without representation is often reversed in Newfoundland and appears as representation without taxation."[83] Bennett also played upon the fears of Newfoundlanders against Canada and appealed to their patriotism. In 1864 and 1865, he had been too busy to take on the leadership of the anti-Confederate forces, but even then he insisted that the economic crisis of the mid-1860s was "a temporary but painful malady," and if the colony were only governed wisely and prudently, and its vast resources from the ocean and the land sufficiently developed,

CHAPTER 1

Newfoundland would be a prosperous place and its population able to secure a decent living. He did continue to insist, however, that responsible government had been a mistake for Newfoundland, particularly as it had led to higher taxation. So opposed was he to taxation that he supported Newfoundland reverting to the status of a Crown colony without responsible government, which to his mind was much the better choice than Confederation.[84] Bennett might not have been a democrat, but in 1869 he was the most capable campaigner out on the hustings in Newfoundland. He also campaigned on many of the same issues as the anti-Confederates had in the Maritime provinces several years earlier.[85]

At seventy-six years of age in 1869, Bennett was an unlikely leader for an independent Newfoundland, but he embraced the task with vigour, relish, and zeal. He cast aside thoughts of retiring to his beloved England and returned to St. John's from his annual winter sojourn there at the end of July that year. He bought a 140-ton steamer to allow him to campaign in the outports, purchased a newspaper in St. John's, and launched an energetic and enthusiastic campaign. Within a month, his *Morning Chronicle* was claiming that the Anti-Confederate Committee, which had been established in 1866 at a meeting of fifty merchants and politicians in St. John's, was rejuvenated and working effectively in all parts of the Island. In early September, Bennett, accompanied by Walter Grieve, another St. John's merchant who came out of retirement in England to carry the anti-Confederate message, left St. John's to visit the outports along the northeast coast and organize the commercial operators there against joining Confederation.[86] Following that tour, Bennett and several of his colleagues travelled the south coast to complete their canvass of the Island.

Throughout the campaign, Bennett and his supporters embraced the rhetoric of classical liberalism about intrusive states and warned that the Canadian government would have the "power to extract the youth, both married and unmarried, of the able-bodied men of the Colony to shed their blood and to leave their bones to bleach in a foreign land, in defence of the Canadian line of boundary and that of any other province."[87] Newfoundland had all the protection it needed in the Royal Navy, Bennett insisted, repeating a claim he had made earlier. The Bennett party warned repeatedly of the increase in taxation and the draconian measures from Canada that would irrevocably alter Newfoundlanders' way of life:

> There would be taxes on everything even on the panes of glass in the windows: and in a country where coal was not mined, and wood the sole fuel supply, they were told that no man would be allowed to cut wood, with the result that many people went out, fearing this dreadful thing would befall them, and cut wood enough to last for years, and men dressed in soldiers' coats were sent about to represent Canadian press gangs.[88]

Such mistruths were rampant and powerful. In fact, in the case of cutting wood, Canadian negotiators explicitly stated that Newfoundlanders would be able to continue to freely cut wood on Crown lands for their own use. Bennett also exploited the fear of taxation among fishermen, telling them that Canada would impose taxes on their boats and gear. Above all, he insisted, they did not need to look to Canada to develop any of Newfoundland's bountiful resources.[89]

The Bennett party created a narrative that included stirring up prejudicial feelings that had long marked Newfoundland society. Much of this was directed at French Canadians in Quebec, who the anti-Confederates insisted were still linked to France, which continued to have considerable jurisdiction over large swaths of western and northern parts of the Island. It was always easy to stir up bitter feelings against the French, who had laid waste to fishing stations and other premises throughout much of Newfoundland's history. Newfoundland fishermen often quarrelled with fishermen from Nova Scotia and Prince Edward Island, especially along the Labrador coast, and Quebec and Maritime fish provided serious competition to their salt cod in the Caribbean.

The Irish in Newfoundland were encouraged to compare joining Confederation with the union of Ireland and Britain, thus "bringing to life in the new world the political hatreds of the old." Two of St. John's leading newspapers, the *Patriot* and the *Newfoundlander*, both edited by Roman Catholics—though the latter supported Confederation—realized as early as the autumn of 1865 that the Irish analogy would be the most effective campaign tactic aside from taxation.⁹⁰ Bennett forged a strange coalition in 1869, linking the St. John's Protestant oligarchy—which traditionally voted Conservative, and some of whom feared commercial competition from Canada—with Irish Catholics, who harboured a profound dislike of the British and traditionally supported the Liberals. The alliance worked splendidly. From the outset, Bennett convinced Newfoundlanders that union might be beneficial to the mainland colonies, but it offered nothing to them. The excitement over transcontinental expansion and railway construction held little promise for them, he told Newfoundland voters. He also warned that with union Canada would assume control of Newfoundland's resources to finance all sorts of projects on the mainland, and there would be nothing they could do to stop the Canadians once they surrendered their legislature and the right to make independent legislation.⁹¹ They would also be severing the ties with Britain, he cautioned, appealing to a nascent Newfoundland nationalism. Newfoundland's ambivalence towards Canada and many of the nationalistic and patriotic sentiments that Bennett and other anti-Confederates expressed during the campaign were captured in "The Anti-Confederation Song":

THE ANTI-CONFEDERATION SONG

Ye brave Newfoundlanders who plough the salt sea,
With hearts like the Eagle so bold and so free,
The time is at hand when we'll have to say
If Confederation will carry the day.

Men, hurrah for our own native Isle, Newfoundland,
Not a stranger shall hold one inch of her strand;
Her face turns to Britain, her Back to the Gulf,
Come near at your peril, Canadian Wolf!

Cheap tea and molasses they say they will give,
All taxes taken off that the poor man may live—
Cheap nails and cheap lumber, our coffins to make,
And homespun to mend our old clothes when they break.

If they take off all taxes, how then will they meet
The heavy expenses on Army and fleet?
Just give them the chance to get into the scrap,
They'll show you the trick with pen, ink and red tape.

Would you barter the right that your fathers have won?
No! let them descend from father to son
For a few thousand dollars Canadian gold
Don't let it be said that our birthright was sold.[92]

A tired government promoting Confederation entered the fray in 1869. The Conservative Party had held power since 1861 and had implemented unpopular policies, especially in areas that most significantly affected voters. To deal with the fiscal crisis of the 1860s, it had taken the unpopular steps of abolishing poor relief for the able-bodied and curtailing road work, which was but a thinly disguised way of providing relief during the period of economic distress and depression. Poverty was so widespread in St. John's in 1867 that some of the wealthier families established the Poor Relief Association, a private charity that had more than four thousand persons seeking assistance in the first week of its operation. During the winter of 1868–69, starvation posed a real threat. Reports from around the colony warned of dire conditions. The *Newfoundlander* noted on January 8, 1869, that "we cannot conceal from ourselves that there is a large proportion of the poor at this moment so prostrated by want both of food and clothing, as to be wholly incapable of work, at least for the present, or until they have been fitted for it by the necessary supply of food."[93] The magistrate at Harbour Grace reported that destitution in the area was "appalling," and Thomas O'Reilly, a member for the constituency of Placentia–St. Mary's, claimed in the House of Assembly in February 1869 that six people in his district had died from starvation and that many others were in desperate need of assistance.[94] Perhaps Premier Carter had a point when he said, "I have seen . . . the decadence of the country for the years past, which no effort of ours, unaided, can control."[95]

Yet the electorate had grown weary of Frederic Carter. When he attempted to carry the Confederation banner against such a determined and vigorous opponent as Charles Fox Bennett, he faced an almost insurmountable task. Voters had experienced difficult times, and they turned to an optimistic leader, who promised them that they had the ability to manage their own recovery while at the same time protecting them from the Canadians who, some charged, had been invited by Carter to take over their affairs and their independence. Ambrose Shea, who had been at the Quebec Conference and was one of a few Newfoundland Catholics supporting union with Canada, was of little help to the Confederate cause. He attempted to counter the fears about taxation that were being fanned by the anti-Confederates by insisting that taxes were, in fact, beneficial and when spent on public goods brought a "ten-fold" return to society. To a tax-averse populace like Newfoundlanders at the time, such rhetoric did little to aid the cause of joining Confederation.[96]

Shea also was deemed a traitor by many of his own ethnic group. His departure from the Liberal Party in 1865 to support Carter's predominantly Protestant Conservative Party did not win him any support in Catholic and Liberal circles, even if the views on Confederation crossed party lines. To aid the Confederate cause and to deal with unemployment in Newfoundland, Shea arranged in 1869 for several hundred men to work on the construction of the Intercolonial Railway being built from Quebec to Halifax. Some of those who travelled to the Maritimes failed to secure employment on the railway and sought jobs elsewhere in Canada, never returning to Newfoundland. Many others returned, disenchanted with the whole process, and their experience was used to ridicule both Shea and Confederation:

> Their leader, sly Ambrose, beware of,
> And keep his past conduct in view,
> Remember his trick with the Navvies,
> He'll try the same treatment with you.[97]

During the 1869 campaign stop at Placentia, a predominantly Catholic community, Shea was "met by a priest and people bearing pots of pitch and bags of feathers, and the moaning of cow bells."[98] Placentia was also Bennett's constituency, and he reminded voters that Shea and other Confederates only wanted to "continue to fatten on the taxes they unmercifully wring from your hard toil and keep you, your wives and children, who are but half fed and clothed, in poverty and wretchedness."[99] It was an effective message.

The Confederate campaign was lacklustre in comparison with that of the anti-Confederates and a complete reversal of what would happen in 1948. Supporters of union in 1869 spent much of the campaign trying to refute the allegations of Bennett and his supporters, but they were never able to properly communicate the benefits of union or create a Confederation narrative that was credible or convincing.[100] Still, many merchants and members of St. John's mercantile elite had, by 1869, come to favour joining Canada, as did a good number of the local newspapers, including the *Express*, the *Newfoundlander*, the *Public Ledger*, the *Telegraph*, and the *Harbour Grace Standard*. Many St. John's merchants, who had opposed the introduction of responsible government, thought that union with Canada would result in a less expensive local government and a better system of public administration. The newspapers, however, appeared only two or three times a week, were centred primarily in St. John's, and—given the low literacy rates and limited circulation, especially in the outports—had little real influence.[101] In October 1867, several leading Confederates commenced holding weekly meetings to promote joining Confederation and obviously had some success among some of the merchants. After the election was called in 1869, the Confederate campaign in the outport constituencies was left in the hands of the local candidates, and Premier Carter and the governing party failed to provide any leadership to them. Moreover, the campaign for joining Confederation was handicapped by the continued opposition to union in the other Maritime provinces. Prince Edward Island had decided that it would not join the union in 1867, and Nova Scotia mounted a determined secessionist movement at about the time that Newfoundlanders were to vote on union with Canada in 1869. It has been suggested that Nova Scotia fishermen on the Labrador coast were helpful to the anti-Confederate cause in Newfoundland.[102]

Governor Hill was rightly worried as the campaign wound down. He wrote to Secretary of State for the Colonies Earl Granville on October 22, 1869, that the outcome of the election was very much in doubt. In a lengthy memorandum, Hill noted that there were three classes of people in Newfoundland: merchants, small traders, and fishermen.

CHAPTER 1

The merchants were all decidedly in the Confederate camp "with the exception of one or two selfish men who fancy that their interests may suffer by Union of this Country with Canada, and who have done much and are still doing all in their power to poison the minds of the poor and easily deceived fishermen against it," he reported. Similarly, the small traders, "intelligent and thrifty people," saw the benefits of Confederation, and "they advocate Union with unusual rigour." The fishermen, who would decide the outcome of the election, wrote Hill, "have had their minds so prejudiced by the Selfish Anti-Confederates that they either hesitate or shrink from accepting a change in their prospects the good effects of which they are too ignorant to comprehend." Normally, he admitted, these men were

> guided by the views of their Masters and Employers—the Merchants into whom they are as a rule always in debt, but this year, owing to a good catch of seals and an unusually large cod-fishery, they are more or less free and in consequence in many instances adopt opinions in opposition to the Merchants, yet so fickle are these poor men that they change from one side to the other, as they are solicited for votes so that opposite candidates are in turn promised support.

It was impossible, Hill admitted, to know how they would vote, but he acknowledged that the anti-Confederates had frightened fishermen with warnings of significantly higher taxes in the event of union: it had "great weight, and the Anti-Confederates, observing such to be the case, have not failed to make 'No Taxation' their Party-Cry, with a result, I fear, detrimental to Union." Hill suggested, too, that the taxation rhetoric had been so successful that "many deluded Fishermen have been led to believe that under Confederation their children would be taxed." He also attributed some of the credit for the animosity towards Confederation to the Canadian fishermen and traders who brought their "persistent opposition to Union ... to our shores ... [and] the primitive people of this colony have had their minds quite impregnated with the bitter animosity of the Nova Scotians with results." Given the power of the anti-Confederate campaign, the "result of the coming General Election is not so certain as was presumed, yet I sincerely trust that intellect and energy may crush ignorance and delusion, and that I may soon have the gratification of reporting to Your Lordship that the present local Government have a majority of votes in the House of Assembly."[103]

It was not to be. The election on November 13, 1869, generated great public excitement because the stakes were huge. Yet, surprisingly, nine candidates—eight anti-Confederates and one Confederate—were elected by acclamation with the anti-Confederates being unchallenged in overwhelmingly Roman Catholic constituencies. The Confederates had nominated only twenty candidates, while the anti-Confederates contested all thirty seats, with the exception of Burgeo-LaPoile, which they conceded to the pro-union Conservatives. The anti-Confederates won twenty-one of the thirty seats. All of the Catholic constituencies voted against joining Confederation, but so too did twelve of the twenty Protestant ones. The result, then, was hardly determined by ethnicity or sectarianism, although Newfoundland's Orange Order expressed concern about Bennett's playing to Irish nationalist sentiments.

The Catholic vote was decidedly anti-Confederate, but so too was the Protestant. A majority of the anti-Confederate constituencies were Protestant. Reverend Edward O'Keefe, who had been administering the Catholic diocese of St. John's since the death of Bishop Mullock and perhaps had reservations about Confederation, had instructed his priests to refrain from getting involved in the campaign in order to maintain peace at voting time. It was indeed a peaceful vote, although as a precautionary measure, troops had been dispatched to several communities in Conception Bay. Frederic Carter had the support of a few merchants, but he was unable to win over enough voters to remain in office and carry Confederation.[104] Bennett won election in the Catholic district of Placentia–St. Mary's, where Shea was embarrassed, capturing only a hundred votes. Carter won his own seat, by five votes, but the defeat was so overwhelming for the Confederates that they quickly abandoned the idea of union. As soon as the results were known, "the fishermen and mechanics of St. John's put together a large coffin labelled 'Confederation' which was placed on a vehicle draped in black [and paraded] through the town, headed by a band playing the Dead March, and escorted by an immense crowd" to a grave where a funeral oration was delivered:

CHAPTER 1

And now Confederation a shameful death has died,
And buried up at River Head beneath the flowing tide.
And may it never rise again to bother us, I pray,
"Hurrah, me boys!!" for liberty, the Antis gained the day.[105]

Scottish-born Protestant Thomas Glen, who was re-elected in the predominantly Catholic constituency of Ferryland, also praised the outcome: "The Electors of Newfoundland will, I feel assured, never barter away the glorious liberty they and their children now enjoy, and permit their free country to be ruled by Canadians 'as a mere Outport of the New Dominion.'"[106]

Governor Hill was confident he knew the reason for the failure of the Confederate cause, although his arrogance and disappointment had corrupted his judgment. His assessment assumed, incorrectly, that only the elites were capable of rationally analyzing the issues in the campaign and rendering a logical and judicious decision. He did not consider the ordinary voter as having the capacity for making independent decisions. Yet James Murray, a political neophyte who ran in a southwest coast constituency in the 1882 general election, admitted admiration (after his unsuccessful campaign) for the outport fishermen for their independence. Despite the hardships they faced, Murray claimed that if he were to seek "true sterling independence of character, such as can stand unflinching before all the forces of heaven and hell, where should I look for it?" Not among the merchants like himself, he said, "but among the brave, starving fishermen of Newfoundland who, for that quality at least would in the scale of Heaven, weigh down a whole Island full of us.... Let us go to these brave, honest, hardy Out-harbormen to learn what INDEPENDENCE means."[107] Yet the governor refused to countenance such an idea of the humble fisherman. A week after the votes were tallied, he wrote to Earl Granville, stating that

> the mass of voters in this colony, as already stated by me in a former Despatch, are an ignorant, lawless, prejudiced body, the majority of whom living as they do in the Outposts in almost a primitive state of existence, are unfit subjects for educated and intellectual men to attempt to reason with on the advantages of Confederation. I therefore consider that it was a fatal error to have

submitted to such a population the decision of such an important undertaking as the Union of this Country with Canada.

He reminded Granville that the anti-Confederates had frightened voters with slogans that union meant "Selling the Country" and "Drafting the youth of the Colony to carry arms in the Defence of Canada." "The limits of a Despatch," he wrote, "would not permit me to enumerate to Your Lordship the many falsehoods preached by the Anti-Confederate party to our ignorant population, against which it was impossible for honest Confederates to reason." Still he acknowledged, somewhat reluctantly, that many voters had sought a change in government and believed that a new administration would provide better patronage.[108] He could have added that voters had also weighed the options presented to them in the campaign and then made a rational decision to reject joining Canada. Newfoundlanders, after all, saw themselves as British men, and that meant they were free to choose their own path forward. As the debate on taxation, trade, and the possible coercive power of the state demonstrated, they also embraced classical liberal values such as free trade, limited government, and low taxes. What Hill failed to realize was that Newfoundlanders had also refused to join Canada until they were ready to do so despite the pressure that the Imperial government had brought to bear on them. There were limits to Imperial authority on the issue of Confederation.

But Governor Hill—and many commentators since—would never concede that such a possibility might have existed. Although he acknowledged Bennett to be a "respectable merchant," he scorned others in his party as being "of no position or status whatever." Beyond that veneer of respectability, Hill still described Bennett as an opportunist—and one who, he pointed out, lived in England for some of the year and "has heretofore opposed every measure that he considers detrimental to his own interests no matter how advantageous the same might have been to the advancement of Newfoundland." Clearly angered by the outcome, Governor Hill reminded Granville that

> the men of position, the leading merchants, the people of intellect, the small traders and shopkeepers, etc., [were] all in favour of Confederation and of immediately accepting the very

CHAPTER 1

Sir Stephen Hill, Governor of Newfoundland (1869–76), was a strong advocate of Confederation and suggested, after the 1869 vote, that Confederation be imposed on Newfoundland. John A. Macdonald and the Colonial Office dismissed his suggestion.

advantageous terms now offered by Canada and of endorsing the wishes of the British Government, while the opponents of Confederation [were] an ignorant mob totally devoid of judgement, and persuaded by selfish men whose sole desire [was] to gain power, and who occupy no position in the Country.

For Hill, there was only one logical course of action: "I respectfully submit to Your Lordship the expediency of incorporating Newfoundland with the Dominion of Canada, by an Order in Council." Those who would be angered by such an act, Hill believed, "would in a short time after Union on finding that no great taxation was imposed, not only be satisfied but thank those who had urged such a wise course." Prime Minister John A. Macdonald, who favoured Canada's territorial expansion, realized of course that in Newfoundland the Confederation issue was dead for the time being. After reading Governor Hill's dispatch, he lamented, "The terms offered by us and acceded to by the Government of the Island were so liberal, that, in a pecuniary point of view, we made a bad bargain." He added, "The acquisition of the Island itself is of no importance to Canada," and "we can wait, therefore, with all patience for the inevitable reaction that must take place in a year or two."[109] Hill wanted union as soon as possible, however, but when he opened the new session of the House of Assembly on February 3, 1870, he acknowledged that "the current of opinions and events has strongly set in towards Union." Yet he remained optimistic "that nothing will occur to check, turn, or divert Newfoundland from gliding onward, and that the advance already made may be continued until this Colony joins the Dominion, thus completing the Great End so anxiously desired by the Imperial Government."[110]

Charles Fox Bennett, who had become the new premier (1869–74), saw things differently. He reminded the House of Assembly in his reply to the Governor's Address on February 17, 1870, that Newfoundland was "firm in its adhesion to the fortunes of the Mother Country" and saw nothing in any union with Canada to "inspire hope" but "much to create apprehension."[111] The voters had defied much of the press, the pressure of the British government through the governor, and many of the merchants of influence, particularly those in St. John's, to reject Canada. The vanquishing of the proponents of Confederation was so overwhelming that Conservatives immediately abandoned any hopes for union. Yet Newfoundlanders had won a major victory in the battle over Confederation. They had gone to the polls as citizens of a distinct national entity and as British people, and they had decided that they would continue to chart their own independent course in the North Atlantic world, or at least until they, the people—largely fishermen in outport communities—could be convinced it was in their interest to embrace union with Canada.

CHAPTER 2

THE NATION TURNS INWARD, 1870–1901

THE REJECTION OF UNION WITH CANADA IN 1869 SIGnalled the desire of Newfoundlanders to chart their own course. For the time being, their orientation would remain east towards the Atlantic world rather than west to the North American continent. When they did look to the continent for trade and investment, it was usually to the United States and not to Canada. Yet in the decades that followed, when the cod fishery experienced severe declines, Newfoundlanders sought employment opportunities in Canada and the United States in equal measure. By 1900, there were more than ten thousand Newfoundlanders working in the United States and more than twelve thousand in Canada. Nevertheless, there was little hope of reviving any notions of union with Canada, as opposition to joining Confederation remained strong, and the mercantile community, especially, became solidly anti-Confederate. Merchants and politicians grew increasingly worried about Canadian competition in the fishery and Canada's interference with their aspirations for a free-trade arrangement with the Americans. They believed prosperity and economic security were possible if Newfoundland embraced nationalistic policies such as free trade with the United States, new and aggressive measures in the fisheries that included limiting the influence of foreign fishermen and manufacturers on the French Shore, and a trans-island railway to facilitate the development of the interior. Riled by these policies, politicians and officials in Ottawa and London were regretting deeply that the vote on Confederation in 1869 had not gone differently. Newfoundland's new policies, however, were designed precisely to escape what many in the colony had come to fear were the looming clutches of Canada—by finding economic and social security for themselves as an independent entity. Ironically, by the beginning of the twentieth century, Newfoundland found itself not with greater independence from Canada but increasingly drawn into Canada's sphere of economic and financial influence.

The early years of the government of Charles Fox Bennett (1869–74) had convinced Newfoundlanders that rejecting Canada had been a prudent and wise decision. A succession of good fishing seasons bathed Newfoundland in a new-found prosperity. Taxes on food and clothing were reduced, and the annual vote for public services was increased to include funding for, among other items, an improved coastal steam service and the inauguration of a direct steam operation from the Island to England. Increased public expenditures contributed to the strengthening of the sense among Newfoundlanders of their national state. In 1870, the Imperial garrison withdrew from the Island, fulfilling a long-time wish of the British government to have Newfoundland, Canada, and other colonies that had been granted self-government shoulder the burden of their own defence. Newfoundland, like Canada, protested the British withdrawal, but as Charles Stacey argued long ago, the departure of British troops was a major milestone towards that "genuine spirit of nationality which recognizes the burdens of sovereignty as well as its privileges."[1] The government subsequently organized its own police force, the Newfoundland Constabulary, modelled after the Royal Irish Constabulary.[2] This, too, could be considered a manifestation of nation building and certainly helped foster a sense of independence. Newfoundland Governor Stephen Hill (1869–76) wrote his counterpart in Canada, Governor General John Young (Lord Lisgar), that while the supporters of Confederation were ready for another battle when an opportunity arose, they understood that "the people having had good fishing seasons are in good circumstance, averse to change, and contented with their present Government, to

CHAPTER 2

whom they are disposed to give credit for good management and the prosperity which exists."³

Bennett retained political support by continuing to label the Opposition as Confederates and by courting the Anglican vote, which, combined with his Roman Catholic base, assured him a second majority in the November 1873 general election. It was a slim, four-seat margin, however, as Frederic Carter had increased his party's representation, primarily by playing the sectarian card and exploiting Protestant fears of Catholic domination of the government. The anti-Catholic movement was led by the nascent but growing influence of the Orange Order, a Protestant political and religious fraternal society that feared Roman Catholic interference in civic affairs; it was established in Newfoundland in 1863 from Canada. Carter's supporters were advised to organize Orange societies; otherwise "they may on some unexpected night be all murdered in their beds."⁴ Carter avoided the issue of Confederation, except to stress his opposition to it, and together with sectarianism, they were the predominant wedge issues of the period. Bennett labelled Orange politicians, such as William Vallance Whiteway, a supporter of union in 1869 and a future premier, "scheming Confederates."⁵ In fact, during a rally in the predominantly Catholic constituency of Ferryland, Bennett's supporters displayed a pink, white, and green flag (that would later be promoted as Newfoundland's native flag) with the words "No Confederation" written on it. The *Morning Chronicle* noted that the message was "conspicuous to all."⁶

Bennett's second majority was short-lived, however, as he bungled his lead, allowed his slim majority to disappear, and soon handed the government back to Frederic Carter. Bennett's troubles began when one of his party's elected members retired and another defected to the Opposition after marrying Carter's daughter; two others sought safety in the magistracy in return for past services,⁷ leaving Bennett with an unworkable Assembly. He chose to resign instead of meeting the House, and Carter formed a new administration. In the general election later that year, Carter won a majority victory in a highly charged sectarian campaign that saw political parties returning to their traditional ethnic and sectarian bases. The opposition Liberals captured all the Catholic seats and Carter all the Protestant ones. Carter assured a suspicious Protestant electorate that joining Confederation was no longer an option for him, but Governor Hill happily wrote London that with Carter in the premiership again there would be another attempt at union.[8] But it was not to be. Carter did not stand in the election of 1878 but followed the path of many of Newfoundland's political leaders and traded the uncertainty of politics for the safety of the bench. He turned his Conservative Party over to St. John's lawyer William Whiteway, who won that election, and won again in 1882, remaining premier of Newfoundland until 1885. Whiteway, too, would wax and wane on the issue of Confederation, but some candidates, such as James Murray, who ran in Burgeo-LaPoile as an independent, actively campaigned against union. At a rally in LaPoile, Murray made it clear that he opposed Confederation as it would not benefit Newfoundland and result only in the loss of its political independence. Moreover, it would lead to higher taxes, and he did not expect Canada to put into Newfoundland "one penny more than she got out of it." The issue of Confederation remained a divisive one, and when Murray sensed that "a tense altercation was brewing" because of it, he closed the meeting. In 1869, the constituency had gone to the Confederates when Prescott Emerson, a St. John's lawyer, won by acclamation, though Murray later wrote in the *Evening Telegram* that "the name of Mr. Charles Fox Bennett—our deliverer from Confederation—was universally venerated and beloved." He was also asked by some "why Mr. Bennett was not out leading the van against the present Confederate Government."[9]

DETERMINED INDEPENDENCE: THE CANADIAN MODEL OF ECONOMIC DEVELOPMENT

Newfoundland's population increased by 35 percent in the generation after 1869, and it reached nearly two hundred thousand by 1884. "The question of the future of our growing population has, for some time," a report of the Newfoundland legislature observed in 1880, "engaged the earnest attention of all thoughtful men in this country, and has been the subject of serious solicitude." The report's prognosis was dire. It acknowledged that the fisheries, the mainstay of the economy since earliest colonization, had been prone to "periodic partial failures" and had created "recurring visitations of pauperism." It also realized that

CHAPTER 2

Sir William Whiteway was premier of Newfoundland on three separate occasions (1878–85, 1889–94, and 1895–97). He was generally sympathetic to Confederation but rarely campaigned aggressively for it.

"no material increase of means is to be looked for from our fisheries," as the population growth far outstripped the resource capacity. Change was the only option, and the report advised that the state "direct [its] attention to other sources [of economic activity] to meet the growing requirements of the country." There was "no remedy" except in the diversification of the economy, it claimed.[10] Joining Confederation might be an option if Newfoundlanders were willing to consider it, as Prime Minister John A. Macdonald was still interested in union. He had written the British chancellor of the exchequer, Sir Stafford Northcote, of the importance of adding Newfoundland to the Dominion of Canada. Although it might be a "burden" in terms of establishing naval defence for the Island, Macdonald had said, it would simplify negotiations with the United States over fisheries matters. He suggested sending Governor General Lord Dufferin (1872–78) to Newfoundland to promote union. Nothing came of this suggestion, although Dufferin continued to advocate for Confederation.[11]

Premier Whiteway, earlier a proponent of Confederation, accepted the legislative report's recommendation. He favoured Canada's strategy for economic development and diversification and hoped to replicate it for Newfoundland. Easily winning a general election in 1878, Whiteway embraced a "Policy of Progress"—not unlike Canada's National Policy—and promised to build a railway to facilitate the development of the Island's terrestrial resources. Buoyed by optimistic government surveys from the mid-1860s on the agricultural and resource potential of Newfoundland, his Conservatives believed that great wealth lay in the Island's interior, and it was simply waiting to be developed.[12] Such thinking represented an important turning point in Newfoundland's economic history as the state and most of the colony's economic elite had finally come to realize that an economy based solely on the cod fishery had reached its limit. Future development lay not in the sea but with the exploitation of land-based resources. Emigration was the answer to any surplus labour.[13] The strategy to achieve this new nation-building project was two-fold: (1) attract foreign capitalists to exploit major forestry and mineral resources; and (2) encourage Water Street merchants to invest in local marine-related industries behind a protective tariff wall, just as the Canadians were doing on the mainland.

Whiteway considered two options for the construction of the railway that would run through the unsettled part of the Island and away from where people actually lived. One was from a Canadian syndicate fronted by Edmund W. Plunkett, who proposed a broad-gauge line with the government guaranteeing 75 percent of the cost and providing to the contractor land grants of five thousand acres per mile. In 1881, however, Whiteway chose the second option: an American capitalist

CHAPTER 2

syndicate led by Albert L. Blackman that proposed to construct a more economical narrow-gauge line, as well as a dry dock at St. John's. This project was not without its detractors. When surveyors began plotting a route for the railway in the Conception Bay area, rumours quickly spread that the workers were, in fact, Canadians who had come to build the railways. Some local citizens believed that Queen Victoria had given Newfoundland to Canada and that their taxes were about to increase greatly to finance the railway project. Moreover, playing on the fears that had been generated in the 1869 anti-Confederation campaign, it was also rumoured that a toll gate would be placed on the road to St. John's—to force people to use the railway to help finance its construction. Tax-averse residents were convinced, too, that the red flannel rags on the surveyors' posts were really Canadian flags, and they quickly intervened to prevent further surveying work. In this episode, which came to be known as the "Battle of Foxtrap," the police were summoned from St. John's under the guidance of St. John's then-magistrate Daniel Prowse to convince a crowd of about six hundred, many of whom were women, to disperse.[14] The event shows the mistrust that some Newfoundlanders had towards Canada and its supposed propensity for taxes.[15]

Once it was clear that Canada was not behind the railway, tensions eased, and the railway was soon embraced as a nation-building project. The urban working classes of St. John's, the professional elites, merchants, and politicians—all of whom hoped to benefit from railway construction—were all enthusiastic. Those who advised caution, like Robert Thorburn, an anti-Confederate businessman who had been appointed in 1870 to the Legislative Council by Bennett, were dismissed. Daniel Prowse, then a member of the House of Assembly and an avowed Confederate, reflected the new sense of optimism and warned against the "wooden obstinacy" of the local mind: "Local prejudice, local obstinacy, and local stupidity have always been the greatest obstacles in the way of progress," he said in the Assembly, urging others to break down the "impenetrable walls of obstinate ignorance."[16] The railway also fuelled the emerging sense of nationalism that was taking hold in Newfoundland, as citizens came to believe that the construction of a railway, together with other technological marvels such as the telegraph, marked their colony's arrival into the community of progressive nations. Like Canada, Newfoundland, too, could claim to be an independent and self-governing entity with many of the appurtenances of a nation. After all, it was the link between the Old World and the New when the cable-laying ship ss *Great Eastern* successfully laid a telegraph cable from Valentia Island, Ireland, to Heart's Content, Newfoundland; the government also planned to link much of the colony with a public telegraph system by the 1880s.[17] The railway not only brought a new economic dynamism and a sense of nationhood but also became a symbol of Newfoundland's entry into the age of modernity. As Kurt Korneski has recently observed, the railway was a "symbol of civility, one of the accoutrements of an 'advanced' or British society."[18]

Whiteway easily won re-election in 1882 on his "Policy of Progress" platform, although he was to face a new opposition party, aptly named the New Party, led by St. John's merchant James J. Rogerson. Whiteway portrayed Rogerson's supporters as being against industrial and economic progress, but in fact they were simply worried that the railway construction was beyond the colony's financial means and would certainly lead to bankruptcy.[19] The *Evening Telegram* agreed and mocked the introduction of the "wonderful civilizing factor of the Railway" (as Whiteway and others promoted it), as well as other "progressive measures" such as dockyards, as "disastrous to the Masses," who would ultimately have to shoulder the cost. It chastised Whiteway and Shea as the "greatest rogues in Christendom."[20] There had been earlier warnings that the railway and the debt it would bring would have the same effect in Newfoundland as it had had in Prince Edward Island—and force Newfoundland into Confederation, as had been the case with that colony in 1873.[21] The Blackman Company did, indeed, soon experience serious financial difficulties. It declared bankruptcy in the autumn of 1884 after completing only a 135-kilometre line from St. John's to Harbour Grace. Merchants opposed to the railway then reorganized as the Reform Party, and to achieve political power they shamelessly manipulated sectarian antagonisms.[22] During the 1885 legislative session, they succeeded in forcing the Roman Catholic Liberals to leave government ranks and sit with the Opposition. Then later that year, they convinced Whiteway to resign the premiership with the promise of a judgeship in favour of Robert Thorburn. Thorburn won the general election held on October 31, 1885, as leader of an all-Protestant Reform Party, endorsed by the Orange Order, against an opposition of Catholic Liberals led by the old Confederate Ambrose Shea.[23] The next year, Shea too resigned his St. John's East seat and accepted a position as governor of the Bahamas—perhaps finally realizing that his hope for a more civil and non-sectarian discourse in Newfoundland politics, which he envisioned possible with joining Confederation, was not going to happen. He had also been passed over to be governor of Newfoundland.

MORINE'S CONFEDERATION INITIATIVES, 1887–1888

Given the shambles of Newfoundland politics and the return to sectarianism, it was not surprising that the question of Confederation took centre stage once again. This time Alfred Bishop Morine, a Nova Scotian–born journalist who had come to St. John's in 1883 for a position with the *Evening Mercury*, which at that time supported Premier Whiteway, was its leading proponent. Morine would be associated with union for the next half-century and was described by James Winter, Grand Master of the Newfoundland Orange Order, as the "greatest scoundrel who ever entered the Narrows of St. John's."[24] Possessing an acute legal mind, Morine was a Machiavellian political strategist determined to bring Newfoundland into Canada. He was active in local politics until the 1920s and never far from the centre of controversy.[25] Having won the by-election for Bonavista District in 1886, aligned with Whiteway's Conservatives, he wrote his supporters the "Greenspond Letter," advising them to launch a rumour that his opponent had contracted a venereal disease from a Greenspond woman.[26]

Although perhaps a scoundrel and troublemaker, Morine also had powerful friends. In Ottawa, he was already well known as a journalist before relocating to Newfoundland. From the time he arrived in St. John's, he was in regular correspondence with John A. Macdonald on the state of Newfoundland political affairs, notably Newfoundland's hope to pursue reciprocity with the United States. Confederation was one way to prevent a Newfoundland-US trade deal, and Macdonald wrote Morine that the terms offered for union at the Quebec Conference in 1864 could still be the basis for any fresh negotiations. It was up to Newfoundland to offer any suggestions for change if it wished to pursue talks.[27] In October 1887, Morine invited Ottawa's minister of finance and high commissioner to the United Kingdom, Sir Charles Tupper, to St. John's, perhaps in another attempt to stymie plans that were being considered to launch discussions on securing a reciprocity treaty with the United States. Tupper raised Confederation with members of the Thorburn government and with independent members of the House of Assembly, including Robert Bond, an independently wealthy young legislator,[28] and Whiteway, who was out of politics at the time but still influential. Although Premier Thorburn remained sceptical of union, Tupper was convinced that both Bond and Whiteway were interested.[29] He even suggested Canada might offer terms more generous than those in 1869, and he believed that if Whiteway's supporters could be brought together in a coalition with the Confederates in the Reform Party and be convinced to unite behind Attorney General James Winter, a long-time supporter of Frederic Carter who had first proposed joining Confederation, then union might be possible.[30] Winter met Tupper in Washington in early 1888 while representing Newfoundland at a fisheries conference and returned to Newfoundland a "zealot confederate," complete with a "scheme," as Morine informed Bond on March 20 that year. Morine added that if union were consummated, Whiteway "could be made Lieutenant-Governor," and "you [Bond] taken into the local government of the colony, which he would lead until he could be made Chief Justice." Bond asked that Morine keep their conversations private until "something definite had occurred" concerning the Canadian invitation.[31] Meanwhile, Bond and the other Opposition members were deciding how to reorganize the political opposition to Thorburn. They hoped Whiteway would publicly declare his willingness to return to electoral politics and lead the forces for union.[32]

Ottawa was hopeful that its proposal for Confederation might work as it believed that Winter was ready to break with Premier Thorburn and lead the Confederate movement. The Canadians were ready to announce a formal conference on union once Winter gave his approval that all was in order in St. John's. The formal invitation to Premier Thorburn came on March 6, although the government and the Reform Party were very much divided on the matter. Morine was apprised of the background negotiations, but he did not discuss them with either Bond or Whiteway. As attorney general, Winter tabled in the House of

CHAPTER 2

Assembly the Newfoundland government's correspondence concerning the invitation from Canada, which also included a request for "representation of the opposition party upon the proposed deputation."[33] The Executive Council decided in late March to accept Canada's invitation, but it was not until June that they agreed to send a delegation, as considerable opposition to union remained.[34]

The delegation never went to Ottawa. In May, Whiteway had written to Bond that "whatever our views as individuals upon the question of Confederation," the party's policy as a "political organization should be clearly defined before the delegation leaves for Ottawa." Whiteway acknowledged that any party going to the polls favouring Confederation "would go to certain defeat," and he wanted no part of that. Any party that he led, he said, would be expected to "have a policy founded on a firm belief of the possibility of Newfoundland doing for itself." Although he claimed that as a fishing colony Newfoundland "stands without an equal," he realized that Confederation might be seen by the people as "immediate relief from depression." Even so, Newfoundland would still be "subject to the vicissitudes of fortune [and] dependent on the winds and weather," and even if Confederation provided some periodic relief from their economic troubles, Newfoundlanders "depended as heretofore on our own surroundings and exertions."[35] In other words, Newfoundland would have to fend for itself within the Canadian federation, a point echoed in a letter to the local press that warned Newfoundland would be "a prey to the gluttonous appetites of Canadian wolves."[36]

Meanwhile Bond, highly ambitious and nationalistic, was worried about union and how it might impact his political career. When Thorburn asked him to be a member of the proposed delegation to Canada, he equivocated. He was against taking a position until Canada made public the terms of union with Newfoundland, and ultimately Bond "declined the honour of becoming one of the delegates" who had been scheduled to leave for Ottawa on September 13. Premier Thorburn was increasingly worried about the Confederation initiative, as the anti-Confederates in his government were not prepared to give the delegation any real power to negotiate. They were willing to explore what terms Canada might offer but nothing more.[37] On September 18, Tupper informed Macdonald that he had learned from Ambrose Shea and Ambrose's brother Hugh, who had visited him in Washington, that the Newfoundland government only "really intended to get an offer [on Confederation] in order to refuse it." This was unacceptable to Ottawa, and Canada would not negotiate under such circumstances. Tupper reminded Macdonald that the Newfoundlanders were anxious for a trade deal with the Americans, and that information, he added, "impressed me more than ever with the great importance of having N.F. a part of the Dominion." Moreover, Ambrose Shea was still an ardent Confederate and was willing to commit himself to "the work [of union]," Tupper reminded Macdonald, "if you can show him that it is certain to advance his interests."[38]

This would not be the last time that a situation would arise in which politicians, sympathetic to Confederation, would flirt with the idea of union and then quickly retreat because, as historian James K. Hiller observes, "Few Newfoundland politicians [were willing to] risk their careers for the sake of union with Canada."[39] In December 1888, Macdonald wrote Morine that he regretted his "hasty" decision both to extend an invitation to Thorburn and to burden the Canadian taxpayer by assuming Newfoundland's debt. Nor was Macdonald prepared, it seemed, to resume negotiations with Newfoundland simply to present a united front in Canada's trade discussions with the United States. He remained worried, however, that Newfoundland might enter into separate negotiations with the United States over free trade, which indeed it did in 1890.[40] Morine continued his regular contact with Canadian politicians, especially those from Nova Scotia then in Ottawa, including cabinet minister and future prime minister Sir John Thompson, in hopes of reigniting an interest in union. Yet, as St. John's journalist Moses Harvey observed in the *Montreal Gazette*, any "proposal to confederate would be sure to encounter a powerful and determined opposition" from the business community and from Newfoundland's Roman Catholic leadership. Opponents of union were taking no chances. They created the Anti-Confederate League to ready themselves to fight union whenever it arose.[41] Confederation continued to have its determined critics in Newfoundland some two decades after 1869. Yet, as the *Evening Telegram* noted, merchants might implore citizens to maintain their independence but ask "the mechanics or labourers what they think of independence" when the "slightest hope they have of improving their condition . . . is by leaving the colony for Canada or the United States."42 Merchants and working people had different views on the virtues of an independent Newfoundland.

THE CONTINUED STRUGGLE FOR ECONOMIC GROWTH

When he failed to secure the promised judgeship, William Whiteway returned to active politics and, as leader of the Liberal Party, won the 1889 general election by a landslide. It was the first vote held under a reformed electoral system that included the secret ballot and extended the franchise to all male householders who were either owners or tenants for a two-year period prior to the date of the election. Whiteway united a new generation of young Protestant and Roman Catholic politicians dedicated to the completion of the railway and the promotion of industrial and economic development—all, it was hoped, could be realized through foreign capital.43 The 1889 Liberal election manifesto was written by Robert Bond, who had emerged as a key player in Newfoundland politics and would remain so for the next two decades. The manifesto championed the rights of the working people and promised railway construction and resource development but rejected Confederation. It accused Premier Thorburn's "Fish-Flake Party" of governing only for themselves and making such a mess of things that it would invariably lead to union with Canada. Whiteway charged that people were becoming so desperate that they would soon demand such change that Thorburn would be forced to "hand over our liberties to the Canadian Government" as the only way out of the problems he was creating.44 As one Whiteway candidate reminded voters in St. John's, it was "Sir Wm. Whiteway's and Mr. Bond's refusals to go on that delegation [to Ottawa] that saved the country from having a sale ticket pinned to it. Whiteway would not touch Confederation," he promised, "without an appeal first to the people."45 Whiteway won a commanding majority, capturing twenty-eight of thirty-two seats. On December 17, 1889, at the age of just thirty-two, Robert Bond was appointed to the senior post of colonial secretary, determined to build not only an independent nation but also a vibrant British society in Newfoundland. Both goals required developing land-based resources and constructing a modern railway system.

To fulfill Newfoundland's nation-building aspirations and achieve its industrial and agricultural potential, Whiteway and Bond sought greater control over the French Shore, the area from Cape St. John in the east to Cape Ray in the southwest that had initially been granted to France by the Treaty of Utrecht in 1713.[46] Since the 1860s, successive Newfoundland governments had attempted to exert their control over the area as they pressed the Colonial Office to remove French fishing rights there. Premier Thorburn had been particularly aggressive as he wished to limit the French from competing with Newfoundland fish in the European markets and wanted, among other things, a reduction in the subsidies provided to French fishermen visiting Newfoundland. In an effort to protect Newfoundland's national interest in the fishery, he had enacted legislation in 1886 to prohibit the catch, sale, and export of bait to French fishermen without a licence from the Newfoundland government.[47] The *Bait Act* received approval, after considerable reluctance from the Imperial government, and was put in force in 1888. By 1893, however, the colony had abandoned its effort to eliminate the bait trade with French fishermen because it was incapable of curtailing the long-standing and illicit practice carried on by residents on the south and west coasts. Fishermen along the south coast had mobilized "mass protest and crowd actions" in response to these attempts by the colonial government to intervene in the trade in bait that had become for them an essential part of their livelihood. Simply put, they refused to comply with colonial and Imperial law, and the colonial and Imperial authorities were too weak to do much about it. The wishes of the governing elite in St. John's frequently clashed with the realities of economic life in the remote outports that, in the case of the trade in bait, saw fishermen benefitting greatly from the illicit trade with the French. The governing elites saw the matter only as an extension of their control over the hinterland and cared little about the welfare of the outport fishermen. Korneski claims that

> Such efforts did have major consequences for how people thought about themselves. Whether through intense upheaval or the lower-level, intermittent harassment they experienced as they pursued trade with the French, south coast residents came to understand and to articulate their interests by reference to

place. Increasingly they understood and spoke about themselves as a distinct group whose interests did not correspond to the aims of the Newfoundland state, a government that over the nineteenth century they came to call the "government of St. John's."[48]

When the authorities in St. John's attempted to extend their influence to the St. George's Bay area on the west coast, residents there drafted petitions to Canada's governor general asking that the western region of Newfoundland be joined to Canada![49]

The colony of Newfoundland included more than just the region of St. John's, and the division between St. John's and the rest of the colony was real. Regionalism was an important reality in the colony from the early nineteenth century. It is important to note the diversity of regional views, for instance, on the problem of the French Shore. The economic and political elite in the capital wanted to be rid of the French presence in Newfoundland, but many Newfoundlanders living along the French Shore, especially those engaged in the lobster industry, had established a suitable working relationship with Canadian and French proprietors as well as with those from the St. John's mercantile sector operating in the region. In their quest to live as "British men," they were eager to be employed regardless of the nationality of their employers, because "work meshed well with prevailing ideas about independence, masculinity and Britishness."[50] Attempts to exert the powers of the Newfoundland state, centred primarily in the capital, were frequently resisted in the regions outside St. John's. Along the French Shore, as well as in other regions outside the Avalon Peninsula, there was emerging a different way of thinking about Newfoundland, a phenomenon that would grow and intensify throughout the twentieth century.

The colony's disputes over the nature of French fishing rights in Newfoundland continued to dog the Whiteway government. By the late 1880s, the issue of who had the right to carry on a lobster fishery on the French Shore was the main concern. The Thorburn government had been unwilling to restrict the activities of Newfoundland and other British (mainly Nova Scotian) operators constructing lobster factories on the west coast. Since the establishment in 1873 of the first factory, they had a total of twenty-six factories compared with a single

French factory by the late 1880s. Although sympathetic to French protests of encroachments by Newfoundlanders in the lobster trade, the Government of Great Britain had no statutory authority to enforce the provisions of the treaties granting French fishing rights on the west coast, as its authority had lapsed by mid-century through the non-renewal of Imperial legislation. The Colonial Office, cautiously optimistic that Premier Whiteway would be more accommodating than Premier Thorburn in settling the French Shore problem, invited him to London to discuss possible proposals for settlement. Before Whiteway reached London, however, Britain and France agreed to a modus vivendi—an arrangement between disputants pending final settlement of a dispute—that had France accepting the status quo regarding the establishment of lobster factories. The British government had hoped that once the modus was accepted by all parties concerned, it could continue indefinitely and the government could avoid having to reach a permanent settlement, which it knew would not satisfy all concerned. It had also hoped that Whiteway could be convinced to accept the arrangement, since he was seeking Imperial financial assistance to help complete the construction of the railway to the west coast.[51]

The announcement of the modus vivendi set off an immediate political storm in St. John's. A public meeting at the Athenaeum attracted several thousand people, some wielding placards that read "Down with the French," but both France and Britain were being condemned. The British government had once again victimized and oppressed Newfoundland with yet another uncaring policy. The European governments, people believed, were clearly standing in the way of Newfoundland's economic development. As the *Evening Telegram* had noted a few years earlier about another incident on the French Shore, many believed that "had we had manliness enough to stand up for our rights before we wouldn't now have our necks under the foot of strangers."[52] To capitalize on the public anger with the modus and ride the patriotic wave, the Opposition party rebranded itself the Patriotic Association. Premier Whiteway, too, publicly criticized the modus, much to the consternation of the British government, and launched a highly public protest against distant governments—which would be embraced by twentieth-century Newfoundland premiers after 1949. Whiteway claimed that he had not been consulted and that the British had conceded too much to the French and, hence, had interfered with Newfoundland's territorial rights. He dispatched a strongly worded protest to the Colonial Office, partly to head off the growing chorus of opposition to the modus being organized in St. John's and the outports by the Patriotic Association. It was soon revealed, however, that Whiteway had, indeed, been party to the initial talks concerning the modus, and he responded to that revelation by adopting an even more nationalistic stand that rivalled that of the Patriotic Association. As with their public opposition to Confederation, both political parties matched each other in their condemnation of the British policy on the French Shore.

Nationalistic frustrations were further riled in 1890 when Sir Baldwin Walker, the British commodore on the Newfoundland naval squadron, closed a lobster factory owned by James Baird, a prominent Tory merchant.[53] Baird sued Walker to recover damages, claiming that Walker had no statutory authority to enforce the treaties. His claim was likely to succeed, and because Newfoundland refused to pass the necessary legislation, the British government introduced legislation in the House of Commons in 1891 authorizing its naval officers to enforce the treaties on Newfoundland's west coast. Outraged, the Newfoundland government sent an all-party delegation to London to protest. Eventually, Whiteway agreed to a compromise, passing a temporary enforcement bill to uphold the treaties to the end of 1893 in return for the withdrawal of the "Coercion Bill" (as the modus vivendi was called in Newfoundland) by Parliament. The matter remained a source of tension between London and St. John's and was driven by local defiance and nationalism until 1904, when the French Shore problem was eventually resolved to Newfoundland's satisfaction. A series of Anglo-French agreements—an *entente cordiale*—was designed to end the antagonisms between Great Britain and France and pave the way for their greater cooperation against a growing German threat. France agreed to relinquish the fishing privileges granted in Newfoundland by the 1713 Treaty of Utrecht in return for financial compensation to French fishermen adversely affected by the change and for territorial concessions in West and Central Africa. Newfoundland saw the agreement as another step forward in constructing its own nation within the British Empire.[54]

SEARCH FOR AN INDEPENDENT TRADE POLICY: RECIPROCITY WITH THE UNITED STATES

The strains of Imperial obligation and local nationalism again conflicted in 1890 and '91, when Colonial Secretary Robert Bond attempted to secure a reciprocal trade agreement between Newfoundland and the United States. Believing that Newfoundland had little likelihood of negotiating such an arrangement, the British government had given it permission to try. Julian Pauncefote, the British ambassador to the United States, who was to preside over the talks, was instructed by London to ascertain if Canada could be included in any final agreement reached between the United States and Newfoundland. When the American secretary of state, James G. Blaine, refused such a notion, Pauncefote arranged for both Newfoundland and Canadian negotiators to begin simultaneous but separate talks with the Americans. Bond arrived in the United States with a proposal for a trade treaty that had been submitted to the British Colonial Office in July. On October 7, 1890, he met with Secretary Blaine and subsequently travelled to New York, Boston, and Gloucester, Massachusetts, to explain "Newfoundland's case and capabilities" to various business groups. On October 18, Pauncefote submitted a draft document for Blaine's consideration. In the meantime, Bond had returned to Newfoundland, but he was summoned back to Washington in late November to meet with both Pauncefote and Blaine, where they made great progress towards an agreement. His private negotiations with Blaine lasted four days, and when they ended on December 19, Bond believed they had an agreement that he later claimed in the House of Assembly "could not but be acceptable" to my "bitterest opponent . . . in the island."[55]

Bond returned to Newfoundland flushed with triumph, but bitter disappointment soon followed. Despite their promise, the Imperial authorities decided not to sanction or proceed with the Bond-Blaine Convention. London claimed the talks in Washington had been unofficial and that, moreover, Canada had not been properly consulted. In effect, London was allowing Canada a veto on a trade agreement that Newfoundland valued highly. Canada, unable to consummate its own deal, felt its economic prospects were jeopardized and threatened by a trade pact between the Newfoundlanders and the Americans.

But more importantly, given the secessionist sentiment in Nova Scotia, where Premier W.S. Fielding had won the 1886 provincial election promising to take the province out of Confederation, Newfoundland could not be seen as achieving more outside of union than Nova Scotia was inside it.[56] Further, Ottawa feared that if Newfoundland became economically dependent on the United States—which the Bond-Blaine Convention would likely have fostered—it might end all hope of bringing the Island into Confederation; worse still, it might encourage in Newfoundland a movement in favour of union with the United States. These concerns were not misplaced, as Blaine indeed hoped that his agreement with Bond would have a disruptive effect on Canada.[57]

Canada's interference with the Bond-Blaine Convention soured relations between St. John's and Ottawa. In the spring of 1891, Premier Whiteway retaliated, denying Canadian fishermen licences to purchase bait in Newfoundland. A bitter round of mutual reprisals followed.[58] Although Newfoundland had enacted new rules on the sale of bait to Canadian fishermen in the hope of forcing Canada to drop its objections to the Bond-Blaine Convention, it succeeded only in escalating tensions between itself and Canada. Canada demanded that the Colonial Office repeal the *Bait Act*, as the Newfoundland government did not have, it claimed, the right to discriminate against British subjects. Newfoundland countered with a high tariff on Canadian flour and Canada with a prohibitive tariff on Newfoundland fish, but Newfoundland's capacity for retribution was limited as it depended heavily on Canadian imports. Moreover, punitive tariffs would only raise prices for Newfoundland's hard-pressed citizenry and make an already difficult situation more arduous. What goodwill had existed between the two seems to have evaporated, although both Canada and Newfoundland perhaps realized that they shared a similar destiny. John A. Macdonald had written to Alfred H. Seymour, a resident of Harbour Grace who had contacted him at the time, that Newfoundland would "involve pecuniary loss" for Canada, but he believed the loss could be more than compensated for if the two could come together under a common government.[59]

On June 25, 1891, while still sparring over trade matters with Canada, Colonial Secretary Bond mused to Premier Whiteway about

Newfoundland's long-term future. Revenue was falling, the government was having trouble floating loans, and the level of migration from the colony was distressing. Unless the government could borrow to "initiate at once a settlement scheme in connection with the railway extension [like the Canadians were doing]," its new policy of economic development would likely fail. The Liberal Party needed a new approach, Bond advised, if it "intended to face the country again." He preferred reciprocity with the United States "apart from the Canadians." If this could not be achieved, then the colony should seek a financial guarantee from the Imperial government; it had to do so, however, without "handing over the control of our affairs to them." If those options failed, Bond realized, the only other possibility was Canada: "I have always been opposed to Confederation," he insisted, and "I am still, if we can obtain other help." Like many other political leaders who came before and after him, Robert Bond, too, would turn to Canada when no other option was possible. Given that the United States seemed willing to arrange a trade deal with them, Bond believed Newfoundland was "in a position . . . to obtain exceptionally good terms" from Canada. The threat of a reciprocity agreement with the United States could be "used as a lever," he suggested, as could the application of the Newfoundland *Bait Act*, under which Canadian fishermen, especially those in the Maritimes, were now "suffering a considerable loss." Bond encouraged Premier Whiteway to raise the matter in London with Canadian High Commissioner Sir Charles Tupper, who had visited St. John's a few years earlier to advance the prospects for union. He cautioned Whiteway, though, not to bring the rascal Morine into the discussions and, for the moment, not to raise the matter with the Imperial authorities. Bond knew the difficult history of Confederation in Newfoundland and never imagined proceeding without a plebiscite after terms of union had been negotiated with Canada.[60]

As a way of lessening the tension between Canada and Newfoundland, Prime Minister Macdonald was also thinking about union. He had asked Prince Edward Island senator George William Howlan to broach the matter with delegates from the Whiteway government who were on their way to London in 1891 to protest the enforcement of the 1890 modus vivendi with France. Senator Howlan joined Whiteway and Bond on their transatlantic voyage, and he informed Macdonald later that his discussion with the Newfoundlanders went well. Whiteway wrote Macdonald on May 3, 1891, that all existing disputes would have to be settled first, however, and then time allowed for the ill feelings towards Canada in Newfoundland to subside.[61] Augustus Harvey, a member of the Newfoundland delegation and a prominent St. John's merchant,[62] however, wanted nothing to do with Confederation. He was extremely worried about the impact of Canadian imports on the Island's small manufacturing sector, how Canadian financial institutions would disrupt the local banking sector, and how the transfer to Ottawa of customs duties—which remained Newfoundland's primary source of income—would impact the general revenues of Newfoundland as a province. At the same time, and despite Bond's efforts to keep Morine on the sidelines of the Confederation issue, Morine was reporting positively on political conditions in Newfoundland to his long-time friend, Sir John Sparrow David Thompson, minister of justice and later prime minister. Morine attempted to create a pro-Confederate group consisting of James Spearman Winter (who would be Newfoundland's premier from October 1897 to March 1900), merchant and politician Moses Monroe, merchant James Pitts, and lawyer Donald Morison, all Orangemen associated with the previous Thorburn government. According to one historian, Morine hoped to "ride into Ottawa at the head of a pro-Confederation party."[63] He informed Justice Minister Thompson, however, that until the Canadian government outlined the terms of union, his group would not be able to declare publicly for Confederation. Morine sought an invitation for his colleagues to visit members of the Canadian Cabinet, but when Thompson's response came in late 1891, the businessmen were too busy with the fishery to travel to Ottawa. They did agree, however, that Winter should go to discuss terms and try to secure financial assistance for the next general election in case the issue of Confederation was on the ballot. What Winter encountered in Ottawa was a group of Canadians more concerned with Newfoundland's refusal to grant bait supplies to Canadian fishermen than they were with union. Canadian-Newfoundland relations had deteriorated over trade issues, and especially over Whiteway's determination to have the Colonial Office approve the proposed trade agreement that Bond had negotiated with the Americans over Canadian objections.[64]

St. John's, 1890.

In April 1892, however, Canada suggested that the two parties meet to discuss the lingering issues over fisheries and trade. When they convened in Halifax that November, it was against the backdrop of the Great Fire that had ravaged St. John's the previous July, leaving eleven thousand people homeless, destroying $13 million in property, and creating a sudden and devastating economic downturn while the government attempted to deal with the crisis.[65] Although the Canadians—and Americans too—had been generous in their assistance to Newfoundland in the wake of the fire, Ottawa showed little inclination to give Newfoundland any trade advantage with the Americans that Canada itself did not have. For nearly a week, Whiteway, Bond, and Harvey for Newfoundland and Sir Mackenzie Bowell, government leader in the Senate and minister of the newly created portfolio of trade and commerce, Joseph-Adolphe Chapleau, minister without portfolio, and Sir John Thompson, who would become prime minister less than a month after the conference, tried to resolve their countries' differences.[66] Canada strenuously objected to Bond's determination to have the Colonial Office ratify the deal he had arranged with the United States. Moreover, the Imperial government had earlier ruled in Canada's favour that Newfoundland could not deny Canadian fishermen bait licences, effectively denying Newfoundland the use of bait

CHAPTER 2

St. John's after the Great Fire, 1892. This view from Duckworth Street East shows the extent of the destruction.

as a lever in its diplomatic relations with Canada.[67] Although Newfoundland and Canada were essentially constitutional equals, each largely managing its own domestic affairs with its own responsible government, in practice they were often unequal when mutual matters came before the Colonial Office. One was clearly more equal than the other despite, theoretically, having the same rights and privileges within the Imperial family. In most confrontations between the two that ended up on the steps of Whitehall in London, Canada would win out because of its greater stature and influence. It had become not only a dominion in 1867 but also the senior dominion in the Empire, and Newfoundland, despite the legalities of the matter, was still regarded as a colony even if it was self-governing. In Whitehall, Newfoundland was seen to have lesser importance than Canada.

At the Halifax conference, the Canadian delegation proposed union as a solution to the problems dividing the two countries, but it did not press the matter largely because of a lack of enthusiasm from the

Newfoundland representatives. Even so, Confederation was never far from the formal discussions, often propelled by Morine's behind-the-scenes manoeuvrings. He wrote Minister Thompson that union was highly possible, but to rally the pro-Confederates in Newfoundland, support from Thompson's party was critical. Ever the rascal and political opportunist, Morine warned Thompson that if he, Morine, had no voice in the negotiations then he would oppose any attempt by Canada to complete the union movement that had begun in 1864.[68] Morine told Thompson that the Whiteway government was "doomed to overwhelming defeat at the next election, unless some revolution-making question comes to the front to completely change the aspect of affairs." Moreover, he reported, "Bond hates all things Canadian, especially the present Government," but was ambivalent more generally on the matter of Confederation, although he likely had a "tendency" to go to the anti-side. Whiteway, on the other hand, "would be a confederate if he dared, but hasn't backbone enough to fight for the cause." His frankness on the matter, Morine confided to Thompson, came because "where Confederation is concerned I am a fanatic."[69] From the conference, Trade and Commerce Minister Bowell had written Morine that Bond wanted a definite offer from the Canadians, but Canada had become reluctant to provide any offer until it "knew whether the people of Newfoundland were desirous of entering the union."[70] The delicate dance on Confederation continued. Unlike Morine, who believed in Confederation almost as an act of faith, the more nationalistic Bond was willing to entertain only such terms of union that he believed would advance Newfoundland's general well-being. Proposals and counter-proposals had been exchanged at Halifax, but in the end no agreement could be reached. Newfoundland continued to lobby the Imperial government to ratify the Bond-Blaine Convention of 1890, and Bond had not yet given up on advancing Newfoundland economically through reciprocity with the Americans.

Even so, Canadian influence in Newfoundland accelerated as Premier Whiteway continued his efforts to extend the railway line to the west coast. In 1890, the government had signed a contract with Canadian promoters Robert G. Reid of Montreal and G.H. Middleton of Toronto to complete the railway to Halls Bay in Notre Dame Bay. The Canadian contractors agreed to a price of $15,600 per mile, payable in government debentures. Two years later, Reid negotiated a new contract to extend the railway line from the Exploits River to Port aux Basques. A second contract signed in 1893—an election year—gave Reid the right to operate the Placentia branch line and the trans-island railway, once completed, for a ten-year period in return for a land grant of five thousand acres per mile operated. He refused a longer period, fearing that "operating losses would become too onerous when they could no longer be offset by the profits of construction."[71] Reid's insistence on a limited term was an ominous sign but a shrewd move on his part, as railway building in the 1890s placed a considerable strain on the colony's finances and probably exacerbated the economic and fiscal problems that characterized the period.

During the early 1890s, Newfoundland experienced serious domestic political and financial problems that brought the colony, once again, to the verge of bankruptcy—and union with Canada. Although the fishery had recovered in the late 1860s and the colony was doing reasonably well, the 1880s saw the return of major difficulties in the sector. With increased competition from French and Norwegian fishermen, the international trade saw a decline in prices and a reduction in profits for Newfoundland merchants and lower prices for fishermen. Many outport fishermen were squeezed by the credit system and fell further into debt to the local merchants who also had their own credit problems. Fishermen, whose number had increased dramatically during the period of prosperity in the 1870s, attempted to relieve their distress by selling directly to foreign buyers who travelled to Newfoundland or by delivering to merchants an inferior product of poorly cured fish, further aggravating the situation while also creating a terrible reputation for the Newfoundland product. Merchants responded by securing millions in loans from the colony's three banks. The Union and Commercial banks were both privately owned and dominated largely by the St. John's fish merchants who also oversaw operations of the two institutions. The Newfoundland Savings Bank had been operated by the Newfoundland government since 1834 as a colony-wide savings business. By 1894, the two private banks had a total of $5.1 million in outstanding loans, of which $2.1 million went to their directors, but they had only $4.8 million in deposits on hand. There was little possibility that their loans could be repaid in the foreseeable future given the turmoil in the fisheries. The banks were also operating without any external audits or much regard for the current economic crisis, and they had reportedly falsified their annual reports to the government. As those banks saw their own cash reserves diminish, they borrowed heavily from the Newfoundland Savings Bank and the London and Westminster Bank in London, which had long financed the Newfoundland fish merchants.[72]

The financial and economic crisis was exacerbated by a political culture that Frederic Carter and Ambrose Shea had hoped would change had Newfoundland joined Canada in the 1860s. Re-elected in late 1893 under the Liberal Party banner, the Whiteway government soon found itself the victim of a carefully planned strategy devised by Morine that had a number of defeated Tories filing petitions in the Supreme Court under the 1889 *Corrupt Practices Act*, charging seventeen government members with illegal use of public funds during the recent campaign. When the first judgment—heard in February 1894 by James Winter, former Tory premier and now judge—found against two Liberal members representing the District of Bay de Verde, Whiteway feared that the remaining fifteen defendants would receive a similar fate and be forced to resign. He attempted to save his government through a series of political machinations that included seeking Governor Terence Nicholls O'Brien's approval to have the legislature repeal the 1889 *Corrupt Practices Act* and requesting an immediate dissolution and a new election—both of which were denied. Whiteway threatened not to pass any supply and revenue bills and prevent any minority government from doing so if his majority government were forced out. On April 11 that year, however, despite having a majority in the House of Assembly, Whiteway tendered his resignation, and O'Brien invited Tory leader A.F. Goodridge (April–December 1894) to form a minority government. Goodridge then prorogued the Assembly.[73]

Although Premier Whiteway and his Executive Council had resigned, the new government had not removed the Liberals from their positions as directors of the Newfoundland Savings Bank, which was essentially run as a government department. In early December, when word spread quickly that the Commercial Bank was in deep trouble, the Liberal directors did little to help. The London Bank had suspended credit to Commercial, refused to honour any further banknotes, and requested payment on some of its loans after a major London-based commission broker suspended its operations. The firm Prowse, Hall and Morris, which represented several prominent St. John's merchants, had suspended operations after the death of partner Henry Hall; the trustees of his estate then demanded immediate cash payments from the St. John's merchants to settle their debts. The Commercial Bank was unable to meet these demands. Short of cash reserves, it called on its clients to immediately repay their debts, which they were unable to do. On December 10, which became known as "Black Monday," the Commercial Bank closed its doors, and depositors, worried about their savings, rushed to withdraw their deposits from both the Union and the Savings banks. The government-run Savings Bank had priority on all funds at the Union Bank, and the Liberal directors demanded their deposits to meet the demand from its clients. This allowed the Savings Bank to remain solvent but forced the Union Bank to close permanently just hours after the Commercial Bank shuttered its doors. Financial panic ensued, as crowds filled the streets looking for exchange for their worthless banknotes. The crisis resulted in a devaluation of Newfoundland's currency, forced several large merchant firms to suspend operations, and in short order left thousands of people unemployed.[74]

The Newfoundland Savings Bank was in grave trouble, as its assets were tied up in unmarketable colonial debentures and notes of the two failed banks. It faced bankruptcy and threatened the solvency of the government itself. The mercantile community was in chaos with the year's catch still in storage and with limited access to credit and cash. Moreover, the political wrangling over the past year had effectively undermined the confidence of foreign investors and bankers in the colony's economy and future. Indeed, the government's railway contractor, Robert G. Reid, had problems selling his railway debentures in Britain, and the prices of outstanding government debentures of all issues dropped precipitously. And while confidence outside Newfoundland was eroding rapidly, locally it was learned that the Whiteway Liberals had encouraged a run on the Commercial and Union banks by telling people not to accept their banknotes. Such activities only added to the political chaos in Newfoundland, and the whole banking crisis accentuated the growing divide between its urban and rural areas. Fishermen and their outport suppliers believed they were the backbone of the economy, but the Water Street merchants reaped all the benefits from their labour, and moreover, it was the Water Street merchants who had created the turmoil and robbed them of the little cash they had held in the failed banks.[75]

The Conservative Goodridge government, failing to secure financial assistance from the Imperial government, resigned on December 12, 1894.[76] When the government needed an experienced hand, none was available. Whiteway had been unseated, and St. John's lawyer Daniel J. Greene (December 1894–February 1895) was appointed to lead a Liberal ministry. Financial stability was restored in part through the establishment of Canadian banks in the colony and the legalization of Canadian currency as a medium of exchange—adding to the growing influence of Canada that was already evident in mining, forestry, and, of course, the railway.[77] The Bank of Montreal, which had close connections to Reid, became the colony's financial agent, acquiring the position by loaning the Newfoundland government $400,000, enabling it to meet the semi-annual interest owing on its bonds and debentures due on January 1, 1895.[78]

If not for the resignation of the Goodridge government, Morine might have been able to fulfill his ambition of leading a delegation to Ottawa to negotiate Confederation, but his plans were thwarted when William Whiteway resumed the premiership in February 1895.[79] In another quirk of Newfoundland politics, Premier Greene had introduced legislation to reinstate the disgraced politicians who had been disqualified over the election fraud. Nevertheless, once back in government, Whiteway, Bond, and the Executive Council faced a bleak situation.[80] The Colonial Office at that point was willing to provide financial assistance, but only if Newfoundland agreed to a royal commission to investigate its financial and constitutional situation. Whiteway refused such an arrangement because he feared the suspension of responsible government and the relegation to the status of a Crown colony that would follow if he accepted the British investigation. Joining Confederation was a more palatable choice.[81] Some people in Newfoundland, particularly the Tories, would have welcomed the revocation of responsible government.[82] Morine, who had been agitating for union with Canada, thought the government had dithered for too long. For a "believer in the benefits of confederation [and]

CHAPTER 2

Canadian banks opened in Newfoundland and Labrador following the 1894 bank crash. The Royal Bank of Canada, n.d.

convinced that it would do great good to the masses of our people," Morine wrote in the *Evening Herald* of January 5, 1895, the opportunity for a good negotiated deal with Canada had "gone by." Confederation was now "out of the question," he lamented, "for the colony has reached a condition" in which union would "only be consented to by Canada, if at all, upon terms so bad that the Colony could not with advantage or honour accept them." The opportune moment had been in 1888, claimed Morine, when "our credit was good" and when "Canada wanted the Colony, and the Colony could have commanded its own terms." At that time, the original Father of Confederation "was at the helm of affairs in Canada—then was our golden time," but at that moment, "prejudice, ignorance and misrepresentation gained the day, and the opportunity was lost."[83]

William Whiteway was much more optimistic about a renewed relationship with Canada, even if it did not include union. On January 12, 1895, he wrote to the new prime minister, Sir Mackenzie

Bowell—whose own government was in disarray over proposed remedial legislation to continue publicly funded separate schools delivering French-language and Catholic instruction in Manitoba—asking for $550,000 in loans. The Canadian government had no parliamentary authority to authorize such a loan, and Bowell immediately denied the request by telegram. With Newfoundland teetering on financial collapse, and the interest payments on its loans due on July 1, options were narrowing quickly. Premier Whiteway told his Liberals that he had always been a Confederate, and he was committed to getting the best terms possible for Newfoundland. Given the circumstances and given that Confederation was a better option than what the British had proposed, Whiteway encountered no dissension within his party. They did agree, however, that any terms of union negotiated in Ottawa would have to be put to the electorate.[84]

On February 5, 1895, Premier Whiteway proposed to Prime Minister Bowell that they begin talks on Confederation. Bowell agreed, as did the British government. "One of my principal reasons for wishing to see Newfoundland united to the Dominion," wrote the Marquess of Ripon, secretary of state for the colonies, to Governor General Lord Aberdeen (1893–98) that February, "is that in Canadian Ministers we should deal with men of a higher class, of wider minds, and of more statesmanlike vision than the men who have misgoverned and ruined Newfoundland."[85] Since at that time Whiteway was in poor health, Robert Bond led the delegation to Ottawa, together with fellow Liberals Edward Morris, George H. Emerson, and William H. Horwood. Whiteway refused to send an all-party delegation as the government had done in the 1860s. The departure of the delegation on March 27 by steamer raised the ire of the St. John's anti-Confederates. One press report notes that thousands gathered on the waterfront to express their opposition to union with "their grave and silent demeanour."[86]

At a public dinner during the negotiations, Bond thanked the Canadians for their assistance to the residents of St. John's following the 1892 fire and expressed delight that "the feeling in Newfoundland was growing warmer towards Canada. It had not always been thus," he declared, "but there was more chance at present of the two peoples becoming united than there had ever been before." As Gordon Bradley would do in 1948, as leader of yet another such delegation, Robert Bond insisted

CHAPTER 2

Canadian and Newfoundland Confederation delegates, 1895. Robert Bond, William H. Horwood, George H. Emerson, and Edward Morris were members of the Newfoundland delegation who met with the dominion delegates in Ottawa to reopen talks on Confederation.

that Newfoundland was not a beggar nor a financial or economic catastrophe, despite its recent difficulties. He stated that Newfoundland was not "a kind of worthless fragment of creation . . . that was left over after this great continent was formed" but a nation with abundant resources of land and sea and a proud and vibrant people who "hardened by the storms that rage along our coast would be able and willing to defend our common country should occasion ever require it. . . . Newfoundland has been the nursery for the [British] navy and there are just as [many] brave and true hearts beating in the fishery hamlets of Newfoundland to-day, and just as strong British national sentiment as there was a century ago." "We are anxious," said Bond, "to learn what Canada is prepared to offer us" to join the Confederation; if suitable terms can be negotiated "which will enable us to build up a community that will withstand the winds and storms of the future, then Newfoundland will . . . join you, and aid you too, in completing a structure which, bound together by the bonds of patriotism, will add greater prestige to that Empire upon which the sun never sets."[87]

Given the political uncertainty in Ottawa over the Manitoba schools question and the lingering dispute between English and French Canada over language and education, Ottawa's attention was perhaps elsewhere when the Newfoundlanders arrived. The last thing it wanted was to assume responsibility for the French Shore, which Secretary Ripon had insisted would become a federal responsibility. Moreover, the mid-1890s were troubling economically and fiscally for Canada, and Ottawa was embroiled in a series of disputes with the provinces, including Nova Scotia, which had been agitating for redress from the articles of Confederation for a decade. Ottawa certainly could not be too generous with Newfoundland without further alienating the existing provinces. The earlier turmoil over trade that had resulted from the Bond-Blaine Convention had passed, but at that time, Canada's interest in union had been largely rebuffed by Newfoundland. There was no real urgency for Canada to rush into the negotiations this time.

The Canadians offered less than what the Newfoundlanders were prepared to accept. Because of the expense it had incurred in railway construction, Newfoundland could no longer claim to have a minimal debt, which then stood at $15.8 million, and this became the major issue in the talks, which lasted for twelve days. Newfoundland asked

CHAPTER 2

that Canada treat the railway portion of the debt ($9.5 million) as an asset to be transferred to the federal government, which, in the event of union, would assume full responsibility for it. If Ottawa provided a debt allowance of $50 per person, as it had done when Prince Edward Island entered Confederation in 1873, then Newfoundland would have a credit of $10.35 million against a debt of $6.27 million. Canada would pay annually to Newfoundland 5 percent interest on the difference, for an annual payment of $203,674 to be used as general revenue. Additionally, Canada would provide an annual subsidy of 80 cents per head ($165,000), a fisheries bounty of $150,000, and various subsidies totalling $862,858. The issue of compensation for Crown land emerged, as it had in 1869, and Newfoundland insisted that Canada provide $250,000 annually, although as a province it would retain control over all precious metals. The federal government would assume responsibility for the Newfoundland Constabulary, fisheries expenditure, all major public works, and a steamship link from Port aux Basques to Nova Scotia once the trans-island railway was completed, a link between St. John's and Liverpool, and a coastal steamship service. Newfoundland's demands came with a hefty price tag: annual federal payments of approximately $1.5 million and federal expenditures of about $740,000 on services in Newfoundland.[88] What Newfoundland requested was too much for Canada. It offered to assume the Newfoundland debt up to $10.3 million and pay an annual allowance of $465,000, including a subsidy at 80 cents per person, interest on the debt of $100,000, an allowance for Crown lands of $150,000, and an additional annual grant of $50,000. The cost to provide federal services was several hundred thousand dollars more than expected. Canada maintained that it was being generous—as it would argue again in 1948—and being any more generous would certainly cause trouble in Parliament and with the other provinces. As a province, Newfoundland would have four senators and ten members in Parliament.[89]

The Newfoundland delegation considered the financial offer inadequate. With the loss of its customs duties, its major source of revenue, it could see no way to service its share of the public debt and provide a range of services, including the completion and then operation of the railway. It maintained that Canada stood to benefit greatly from union. Newfoundland would open its fishery and bait trade, for instance, to Canadian fishermen without compensation, but Canada was steadfast in the terms offered. Still, the delegation seemed poised to accept the Canadian offer, perhaps because there was hope that London might step in to supplement what Canada was providing. Governor General Aberdeen wrote the Colonial Office on April 11 that there was a "prospect of reaching [a] basis of agreement," but "much ... if not everything, will depend on whether HM's Gov[ernmen]t will supplement [the] allowance to be given by Canada to Newfoundland." Lord Aberdeen also warned that if union were not consummated, the United States might try to lure Newfoundland with a loan to help it out of its fiscal crisis: "I am informed," he wrote in an anxious dispatch, "that overtures have been made from a U.S. source to Newfoundland suggesting a loan of about $3,000,000. The Delegates from N.F. do not speak about this," he added, "but of course whether this story has any significance or not, there can be little doubt that there might be trouble in that direction, esp. in the present absurd temper of a certain section of American politicians, e.g. Senators Fry, Lodge, Morgan and others."[90] Although Britain had long desired union between Canada and Newfoundland, it was unwilling to provide any assistance to bridge the financial differences between the two parties.[91] At that time, Great Britain was willing to see Newfoundland declare bankruptcy rather than expend large sums of money on it. With no other lifelines, the issue of Confederation was dead for Newfoundland. Whiteway notified Prime Minister Bowell on May 1 that his government could not accept the financial terms unless the Canadian government assumed the full Newfoundland debt, completed the railway, and provided a subsidy of $650,000.[92] Canada countered with a grant of $6,000 per mile towards the cost of the railway and a subsidy increase of $35,000, but this was still too little for Whiteway.[93] Canada was reluctant to add to its own public debt, especially at a time when the Conservatives, then led by Sir Charles Tupper, were to face the electorate within weeks.[94]

The advantages and disadvantages of joining Confederation had been widely discussed in the local press while the delegates were in Ottawa, and articles from Canadian newspapers about the negotiations were reprinted in the St. John's dailies. Even if the Newfoundland delegation had returned to St. John's with favourable terms, it would still have faced a determined opposition. The opponents of union had mobilized, and much of the opposition came from outside the House of Assembly.

CHAPTER 2

Both Opposition leader Donald Morison, a former Grand Master of the Orange Order (at the time the member representing Bonavista) and Alfred Morine supported union. James Murray, merchant and former politician, was one of the primary leaders of the Anti-Confederate League. He had founded the *Anti-Confederate* newspaper, and he and other opponents reignited the old shibboleths of conspiracy and local nationalism, arguing—as had the anti-Confederates in 1869—that Newfoundland's economic and financial distress was merely temporary and that union would disrupt Newfoundland's trading relations, increase the cost of living, give away Crown lands to strangers, and lead to massive emigration. Moreover, Newfoundland and Canada had nothing in common, they insisted. They were joined in their condemnation of union by the Political Reform and Labour Association, which was strong in St. John's but also had nine branches and more than seventeen hundred members in outport communities. Farmers, labourers, fishermen, and mechanics all were worried about taxation, and they opposed union "under any circumstances." The *Daily News* warned its readers "Your fate as a free country trembles in the balance."[95]

There were few clamouring for union, and the Whiteway government needed much more than Canada was offering if it were to take the issue to the people.[96] Bond had hoped for a better outcome and was disappointed that Canada had tried to capitalize on Newfoundland's fiscal difficulties and had driven such a hard bargain. He had expected something better from the Canadians and would now treat them in the future, he said, with a greater measure of "mistrust."[97] Morine, on the other hand, insisted that, given the situation in Newfoundland, Canada had been more than generous.[98] When his critics confronted him for failing to achieve union, Prime Minister Bowell reasoned that Confederation with Newfoundland had merely been delayed, not defeated. That might have been so, but the 1895 negotiations certainly did little to create goodwill towards Canada in the minds of many Newfoundlanders. With the prospects of union diminished, Newfoundland had to look elsewhere to avoid bankruptcy. With the help of the railway promoter Robert Reid, Bond secured in London a long-term loan of £550,000 floated by Coates, Son and Company and Morton, Rose and Company, with Hanson Brothers of Montreal acting as intermediaries. He also negotiated a short-term loan of $150,000 through Hanson

Brothers to keep the Savings Bank solvent. It was backed in the first instance by colonial debentures and by a guarantee of $100,000 from Bond himself.[99] Bond thus used his personal fortune to help save Newfoundland from bankruptcy.

As Newfoundlanders breathed a sigh of relief that with Bond's munificence they had escaped a calamity, Judge Daniel Prowse's *A History of Newfoundland* was published to considerable acclaim.[100] Prowse, an advocate of Confederation who did not see any incompatibility in being a Confederate and a Newfoundland nationalist, constructed a narrative of Newfoundland's triumph over adversity and struggle that he believed stimulated a great sense of nationalism.[101] In an 1898 review, Queen's University principal George Grant observed that it was "now impossible for Newfoundland to isolate itself much longer from the general life of British North America. In spite of its mistakes and the mistakes of Canada, especially the blunder of 1895," concluded Grant, "Confederation with the Dominion is sure to come."[102] Prowse shared that view, but it would certainly take considerable time to realize his dream. In the meantime, Newfoundland continued to celebrate its national heritage and its British connections. In 1897, Newfoundlanders proudly commemorated the 400th anniversary of John Cabot's landfall on behalf of the English Crown and the laying of the foundation of the British Empire.[103] Those bonds with the United Kingdom remained strong, evidenced perhaps by a small number of Newfoundland volunteers serving in the British and Canadian contingents in the Boer War (1899–1902). That some Newfoundlanders served in the 1st Canadian Contingent in South Africa was also an indication of the growing connection between these two colonies.[104]

After the 1895 Confederation debacle, Newfoundland's politicians and their journalistic supporters generally kept their feelings on Confederation to themselves, although they often accused their political opponents of secretly being Confederates. P.T. McGrath, editor of the opposition St. John's daily *Evening Herald*, was, for example, a Confederate supporter in 1895 and wrote a series of articles that positively approved of life in Canada. His writings about Canada and Confederation thereafter became more circumspect and he never disclosed his actual beliefs, although as a political strategist he often played the Confederate card against his political opponents.[105]

CHAPTER 2

THE 1897 GENERAL ELECTION AND THE
REID RAILWAY DEAL OF 1898

Given what had transpired since the previous election, it was no surprise the Whiteway government had fallen out of favour. When Newfoundlanders went to the polls in 1897, during another severe depression in the fish trade, and after the failed Confederation talks, they handed control to Tory party leader James Winter. The Tories had emphasized the failure of William Whiteway's "Policy of Progress" to provide the much-heralded promise of greater employment and prosperity. By 1899, markets for local fish had revived, and after a year of retrenchment that resulted in cuts to the civil service and an increase in the tariff to raise additional revenues, the government successfully floated a $350,000 loan. Minister of Finance Alfred Morine restructured government departments along the Canadian model with similar departmental responsibilities. A Department of Marine and Fisheries was established, and the Receiver General's Office became the Department of Finance and Customs.[106]

The Newfoundland government disposed of its ownership of the recently completed railway and handed its operation to the Reids for fifty years in return for additional land grants of five thousand acres per mile of railway operated, bringing the company's total holdings to about four million acres. At the end of that period, the railway would become the property of Reid's successors should they pay $1 million to the government and return twenty-five hundred acres per mile of the original grant. Reid also agreed to operate a coastal steamship and the Gulf of St. Lawrence ferry, providing his own vessels, in return for subsidy payments. Additionally, Reid was contracted to take over the government's telegraph lines and to purchase the St. John's dry dock. Other clauses in the agreement awarded Reid the right to build a street railway in St. John's and to supply the town with electricity from a power plant that it would construct at Petty Harbour.[107]

The Winter administration was confident that it had transferred the cost of the railway from the state to Reid. The deal was to resolve the financial crisis facing the colony and provide much-needed employment, particularly in St. John's. On the other hand, Robert Bond, who replaced Whiteway as Liberal leader, wanted no part in the deal.

Ever a strong nationalist who blamed outside interests for Newfoundland's slow economic development,[108] Bond vowed to fight the passing of control to Reid, claiming that Winter had sold Newfoundland's assets for much less than their market value while giving control over the colony's economic development to a Canadian monopoly. The matter momentarily split the opposition Liberals, although they circulated petitions throughout the Island calling on the Colonial Office to disallow the legislation. Altogether, 22,774 signatures were obtained by January 1899, but the Imperial authorities refused to interfere. In the meantime, word leaked out that Morine had acted as Reid's solicitor during the drafting of the Railway bill and was forced to resign from Cabinet. The government lumbered on for a few more months, but it, too, was forced out on a vote of no confidence, and Robert Bond became premier (March 1900–March 1909).[109]

Like many political leaders in Newfoundland, Bond donned the mantle of a nationalist determined to protect the interests of Newfoundlanders against predatory outside interests. He sought to amend the railway contract, rather than seek its repeal, in an effort to win over fellow Liberal Edward Morris and his supporters.[110] Later, in 1900, Bond faced the electorate with the pledge of "no further concession to R.G. Reid" and with a promise to amend the 1898 *Railway Act*.[111] Stressing the need to escape the clasp of the Reid monopoly, Bond asked whether the House of Assembly was to be "Reid's House" or the "People's House."[112] Moreover, the Liberals once again raised the old bogeyman of Confederation, charging that Morine was determined to bring about union with Canada. Yet McGrath at the *Evening Herald*, an avowed supporter of the Bond-Morris alliance, noted that the accusation of Morine and his supporters "harbour[ing] confederation sentiments" was scarcely likely to be seriously considered by the intelligent public. After all, he asserted, there are so "many of our public men with confederate views nowadays" that one could "scarcely throw a brick, as Mark Twain says, without hitting some of them; and all the electors are aware of the fact."[113]

Bond won an overwhelming victory, with a Morine-led Opposition financed by the Reids winning only four seats. Bond's victory was a vote of confidence in local nationalism and a determination to seek economic prosperity independent of Canadian control through the pursuit of renewed trade talks with the United States. Bond kept his promise on the Reid contract, and in July 1901 a new contract was signed. Robert Reid gave up his reversionary interest in the railway after fifty years of operation and control of the public telegraph system. The Newfoundland government returned to him his $1 million with interest. For a payment of $850,000 from the state, Reid also gave up approximately 1.5 million acres in land grants, but was permitted to form the Reid Newfoundland Company, which had responsibility for managing his landholdings and for operating the railway, the coastal steamship services, the St. John's dry dock, and the St. John's streetcar and electrical systems.[114]

With the completion of the Newfoundland trans-island railway to Port aux Basques in October 1897, the Reid Newfoundland Company steamer *Bruce* began a regular steamship service to North Sydney later that month. Robert Gillespie Reid crossed on the initial voyage and was welcomed in North Sydney with considerable enthusiasm. There he joined Andrew George Blair, Canada's minister of railways and canals, and the local Board of Trade to celebrate the launch of the Port aux Basques–North Sydney ferry service as "hands linked across Cabot Strait." It would be another decade before Canada extended financial assistance in the form of a subsidy to that ferry service, but Sir Charles Tupper, a long-time proponent of union, lobbied hard for it. The Reid Newfoundland Company also lobbied the Canadian government for a subsidy on the Nova Scotia–Newfoundland steamship service. It engaged Joseph Wood, a shipping agent and commission merchant of Halifax, to lobby Canadian Minister of Trade and Commerce Richard Cartwright. In late 1897, Thomas George Shaughnessy, vice-president of the Canadian Pacific Railway, approached Cartwright on Reid's behalf, suggesting that Canadian mail be sent through North Sydney as Port aux Basques was now the terminus for the Newfoundland Railway's trans-island route. That December, Shaughnessy reminded Cartwright that the completion of the Reid line across Newfoundland would provide a "service which cannot fail to bring the merchants of Newfoundland into very much closer communications with the merchants of Canada with the result that this country would receive a very considerable portion of the trade of Newfoundland which heretofore went to New England."[115] By 1906, the Canadian government instituted a $20,000 subsidy to promote direct steamship communications between Canada and Newfoundland out of North Sydney and alternative ports in the case of ice, and it continued this subsidy until 1923. Malcolm MacLeod argues that the subsidy arrangements were never a part of an expansionist Canadian strategy for Newfoundland, as Canada was rather "indifferent" to the needs of Newfoundland, and Newfoundland "frequently assumed a posture of self-reliance, [and] when necessary [it] mount[ed] campaigns of pressure and persuasion against the Dominion government." Yet it cannot be denied that Canadian support through the provision of subsidies to the Newfoundland Railway brought Newfoundland further into the Canadian orbit.[116]

Still, as the Newfoundland correspondent for the *London Times* observed, for "30 years our people have refused to unite with Canada, the main reason advanced against confederation being that it would be 'selling our country.' "[117] Yet the issue of Confederation remained part of the public debate. A supposedly private visit by former prime minister Mackenzie Bowell to St. John's in August 1900 raised, once again, the question of union. Reid, who made no secret of his sympathies in favour of union, arranged a dinner that was attended by many of the city's leading citizens. Bowell insisted his visit was strictly a holiday and that he had no wish to fuel the debate on Confederation. When quizzed by journalists, he refused to discuss the prospects for union, saying only that he hoped the whole of British North America would soon be united.[118] His words were sufficient to worry those who feared union with Canada and sufficient to rekindle the hopes of those who wished to see Newfoundland become a province of Canada. After all, in the past two decades, Canada had increased its hold on Newfoundland, and that influence would continue to grow.

CHAPTER 3

PROSPERITY, CONFEDERATION, AND THE DOMINION OF NEWFOUNDLAND BEFORE AND AFTER THE GREAT WAR, 1902–1927

THE FIRST DECADE OF THE TWENTIETH CENTURY IN Newfoundland was relatively prosperous. Under the leadership of the new country's first prime minister, Robert Bond (b. 1857, d. 1927), the goals and hopes for the nation, it seemed, were finally being realized. The country's natural resources were being developed and new employment opportunities soared, as many had indeed believed possible when in 1869 they had voted against union with Canada. The economic expansion was fuelled largely with foreign capital, notably from the Canadian investor Robert G. Reid, once described as a man of "inestimable value to the colony."[1] In the capital, the Reid Newfoundland Company had constructed a street railway system, a new railway terminus including freight and storage sheds, roundhouses, general stores, and machine, locomotive, car, and dock shops. At Grand Falls, the Anglo-Newfoundland Development Company Limited opened a new pulp and paper mill. The continued development of iron ore at Bell Island, primarily by Cape Breton steel companies, contributed greatly to the national prosperity, highlighted for instance by a budget surplus of $125,000 in fiscal 1908.² Another sign of economic prosperity and diversification was increasing unionization, as workers joined Canadian and American trade unions and participated in strikes for higher wages and better working conditions.³

The optimism was acute. Nevertheless, many throughout the country realized that vigilance was still necessary to protect their native land, especially from outsiders. Those sentiments were best demonstrated, perhaps, by the instant and immense popularity of the "Ode to Newfoundland." Written by Governor Sir Cavendish Boyle—knighted in 1899 for his service to the British Empire—and performed for the first time to great applause on January 21, 1902, at the Casino Theatre in St. John's, the "Ode" evoked the Island's natural beauty in all seasons and all weather and called on its people not to forget their ancestors. Above all, it exhorted them to stand on guard to defend their beloved land.⁴ This chapter explores this desire as Newfoundlanders wrestled with the challenges of economic development and diversification in the opening decades of the new century. As we will see, political allegiances remained fluid and union with Canada continued to be an issue, especially at election time. The Fishermen's Protective Union, a new social and economic movement that morphed into a major political force, had a significant disruptive effect on Newfoundland politics and society as it reminded citizens that their situation could be different. As with so many societies, Newfoundland too saw change and upheaval during the Great War, and it inspired a new sense of nationalism and a yearning for a modern way of life.

Although long rejected, talk of Confederation refused to die, and Newfoundland politicians seemed eager to raise the issue with their Canadian counterparts whenever their paths crossed. At the Colonial Conference in London in 1902, just after the Boer War, Premier Bond and Canadian Prime Minister Wilfrid Laurier found time to discuss union. Laurier's minister of finance, Nova Scotian William Stevens Fielding, followed up shortly after and wrote to Bond inquiring about the state of support for union. Bond was not optimistic: "I am convinced that our people are strongly hostile to Confederation," he replied.⁵ Yet in the general election held two years later, the Opposition cast Bond as a Confederate. Fully cognizant of how the issue usually played out in such contests, Bond countered by including in the

Liberal Party's 1904 election platform a declaration of "No Confederation" and then castigated the Opposition as Reid-backed Confederates.[6] Perhaps A.F. Goodridge (b. 1839, d. 1920), former Conservative Party leader and premier from April to December 1894, gave the best appraisal of the public debate on Confederation when he noted that Bond, in particular, though other politicians too, used union with Canada to suit their party's political ends. Bond might have declared "his opposition to Confederation, but he may change his mind as he did in 1895," reported the *Free Press* of St. John's.[7] The United Opposition Party candidates were unequivocal, however, and they signed a joint statement emphasizing their opposition to union: the "cry that Confederation with Canada is aimed at by us or any of us in this election, is wholly and wilfully false, and has been concocted and is being circulated for the purpose of alarming the electorate into supporting the Government." Among the signatures to the pledge was the party's leader, Alfred B. Morine, who had been a long-time proponent of joining Canada.[8] On October 31, 1904, Bond easily won re-election, capturing thirty of thirty-six seats, with the duplicitous Morine being re-elected as well. The campaign showed that being anti-Confederate was a good strategy, at least at election time.

ROBERT BOND, TRADE WITH THE AMERICANS, AND INDEPENDENCE

Even if Bond harboured some sympathy for union with Canada, his particular goal was reciprocity with the United States. Like many Newfoundlanders, he believed that closer economic ties would allow access to the huge and growing American market of all exports from throughout the colony and encourage American investment in Newfoundland. Moreover, it might stem massive emigration, a particularly worrisome issue. That his success in the Bond-Blaine trade agreement in 1890 (see Chapter 2) had been thwarted by the Canadians and British should have been reason for caution, but Bond, a committed nationalist, was convinced that reciprocity was critical, both for Newfoundland's independence and its prosperity.[9] Over the past decade Canadians had had sufficient time to forge their own reciprocity with the Americans, and surely they would not again blame Newfoundland for their failure if Bond were successful in working out a trade deal with the United States.

Upon becoming premier on March 6, 1900, Robert Bond set to work on a new draft reciprocity agreement with US Secretary of State John Hay. Like his predecessors, Hay mischievously hoped that an arrangement with Newfoundland might strengthen American influence there and just possibly cause some consternation and discomfort in Canada. The impediment for Bond this time, though, was not the Canadians or the British but influential Massachusetts fishing lobbyists and the state's important senator, Henry Cabot Lodge, who convinced the powerful Senate Foreign Relations Committee not to ratify the Bond-Hay Convention. Bond learned, once again, the limitations of a small British colony like Newfoundland, but he was not deterred; he attempted to pressure his New England opponents into accepting Bond-Hay by disrupting their fishing operations in Newfoundland. He wrote to Lodge, hoping to convince him that he preferred a trade arrangement with the Americans to union with Canada, as free trade would mean "greater benefit to the people of the Colony." Under Confederation, wrote Bond, "Canada would monopolize the whole trade of the Colony and also command the North American fisheries through the bait supplies which would then be vested in her." Bond vowed to continue the pursuit of reciprocity and was "opposed to Confederation with Canada, believing that reciprocity" would be of "far greater benefit" to Newfoundland."[10] For Robert Bond, like other Newfoundland leaders, Confederation was a last resort.

By the time of the Bond-Blaine Convention of 1890, American activity in Newfoundland had been confined to the winter herring fishery in Bonne Bay and Bay of Islands on the west coast of the Island. Americans were accustomed, through the Anglo-American Convention of 1818, to fishing within the three-mile limit and purchasing bait on the same terms as Newfoundlanders, in addition to having the right to trade in Newfoundland ports. Americans hired Newfoundland crews for their vessels and often completed their season by buying the catch of local fishermen. Bond was determined to change those arrangements to force reciprocity with the Americans. After all, Newfoundland was a British colony, thus a member of the Empire, and Bond believed that status brought Newfoundland considerable standing and influence to

CHAPTER 3

Drying fish at Greenspond, early twentieth century. Women were largely responsible for curing the salt cod in addition to their many other duties, including caring for children, tending to the gardens, and managing the household.

manage its own affairs. When he introduced in the House of Assembly a draft treaty to regulate the Newfoundland fishery, Bond claimed to have secured for Newfoundland "that dignity, recognition and right that had been accorded to the other colonies of the Empire." It had earned the right "to direct negotiations with the United States," and London had recognized Newfoundland's "equality with other colonies of the Empire as regards trade negotiations" in permitting it to do so.[11] Even if London was not yet willing to accept such independence from its colonies, Bond used the trade agreement to usurp the role of nationalist for the local crowd.

To disrupt American operations in Newfoundland, Bond amended the *Foreign Fishing Vessels Act* of 1893.[12] It ended licensing for the Americans, gave Newfoundland customs officials sweeping authority to board foreign vessels, and stipulated that the presence of anything previously obtainable under licence would constitute prima facie evidence of illegal purchase. Bond claimed that the American right to fish in Newfoundland, given in earlier conventions, did not include the liberty to fish in bays, creeks, and harbours, as had been previously assumed. His provocative actions were strongly condemned in Washington and immediately disavowed in London. The administration of

President Theodore Roosevelt, which aggressively protected American interests abroad, defended its fishermen, and London saw no reason to jeopardize its developing friendship in the "Great Rapprochement" with the United States, then well under way, to accommodate the questionable behaviour of the leader of a minor colony. During the 1905–06 fishing season, trouble was avoided when American vessels engaged Newfoundland crews and made their purchases outside the three-mile limit. Bond soon paid for his miscalculation, however. In May 1906, he sought to close that loophole by a further amendment to the *Foreign Fishing Vessels Act*, but after vehement protests from Washington, the Government of Great Britain refused assent to the change. Worse still, from Bond's perspective, was the British decision to arrange a modus vivendi with the United States for the 1906–07 fishing season, negotiated without his participation or consent. It assured American fishermen of the benefits they had enjoyed before 1905. Bond challenged the modus vivendi, dismissing as nonsense the notion that Newfoundland could not supervise and regulate American fishermen operating within the three-mile limit. To make his case, Bond launched an action against two Newfoundland fishermen who had joined American vessels, but to little avail. The men, although convicted, had their fines paid by the Imperial government, and the Americans skilfully managed to avoid further retaliatory action by Newfoundland while the 1906–07 fishing season ran its course.[13]

The British had decided that the only way out of the tangled situation in Newfoundland was to refer all outstanding issues under the Anglo-American Convention of 1818 to the Permanent Court of Arbitration at The Hague. At first Bond stubbornly refused, but while attending the Colonial Conference of 1907 he gave way on the matter. Laurier, similarly angry with the British for failing to protect Canadian interests in the Alaska boundary decision of 1903, only reluctantly agreed with the British decision to seek a final interpretation of the 1818 Convention, which also allowed Americans access to Canadian waters. With Bond's eventual agreement to have the issue referred to The Hague, the Court's award, delivered on September 7, 1910, generally favoured the British position.[14] Despite their hopes, both Newfoundland and Canada learned that they could not unilaterally change their fishery regulations agreed to in historical treaties if such changes impacted the United States.

CHAPTER 3

As a result of his quarrels with Ottawa and Washington and his defiance of London over his various trade initiatives with the United States, Robert Bond had made many enemies, none more so than Newfoundland Governor William MacGregor (1904–09), who found Bond's foreign policy initiatives not only "ambitious, [and] vindictive," but also objectionable.[15] MacGregor was, moreover, sympathetic to the fishermen on the west coast of the Island, who enjoyed a profitable trading relationship with the Americans, and he resented Bond's interference in their livelihood. MacGregor was a medical doctor who also took a passionate interest in the social and economic welfare of the local population. He visited Labrador in 1905 and 1908 to examine the living conditions of Indigenous Peoples there, and he subsequently published reports highlighting conditions in the area. He also studied the Newfoundland economy, publishing a report on its foreign trade and commerce.[16] MacGregor was also interested in Confederation. In June 1906, he began a three-week holiday tour of Canada, including visits to observe the hospital system in Montreal, where he met Harbour Grace native Dr. Thomas Roddick, dean of medicine at McGill University. He chatted with officials at the headquarters of the Bank of Montreal and attended a dinner hosted by the son-in-law of former Liberal premier Sir William Whiteway (1878–85, 1889–94, and 1895–97). From Montreal, MacGregor travelled to Ottawa, where he met Governor General Earl Grey, Prime Minister Laurier, Minister of Finance Fielding, and Leader of the Opposition Robert Borden. MacGregor was optimistic about Canada's future, and he praised Laurier for proclaiming that the "twentieth century is Canada's." Following stops in Toronto and Niagara Falls, he returned to Newfoundland and spent a week on the west coast salmon fishing with one of the sons of Robert Reid, who was then a director of both the Canadian Pacific Railway and the Bank of Montreal, as well as owner of the Newfoundland Railway—and an avowed Confederate.[17]

Bond also visited Canada that June. He too combined "private business" and "pleasure" and visited the Agricultural College at Guelph, Ontario. Interviewed in Toronto by a reporter from the Toronto *Mail and Empire*, he "spoke very freely and off-handedly in regards to Newfoundland." Newfoundland was politically very quiet, Bond insisted, and there was nothing of any great importance to stir the people.

The question of entering Confederation, he claimed, was "never mentioned now, as there was absolutely no sentiment in regard to it. Annexation to the United States," he suggested, "was an equally dead issue, and even less heard of [as] a strong Imperialistic sentiment thoroughly pervad[es] the people." Indeed, Newfoundland was "in the most prosperous condition it had ever reached, its mining, lumbering, fishing and other industries being in a very satisfactory state,"[18] Bond reminded the press. Apparently, he saw no reason to join Canada.

When Bond's interview was reprinted in the local press, the *Evening Herald* countered with an article from the *Montreal Star* that featured an interview with Alfred Morine, who had been visiting Montreal. He was soon to depart Newfoundland, after having run afoul of the Reids and the Tories, who saw Morine as "the greatest obstacle to party unity."[19] Morine did not accept exile to Canada cheaply, however, as Reid agreed to pay him an annual salary of $12,000 until 1912, or as long as he agreed to stay out of Newfoundland.[20] At a public meeting on May 24, 1906, in saying his goodbye to his constituents in Bonavista and friends in the capital—and as he later observed in an unpublished part-memoir—"I always found myself more in sympathy with the people of the outports than with St. John's people."[21] They were the ones who stood to benefit most from Confederation, Morine had told the *Montreal Star*. There was "no price" that the Dominion of Canada could pay "to meet the reasonable demands of Newfoundland [that] would be too great," as Newfoundland "is valuable intrinsically and politically," said Morine. Union would benefit Canada immensely. Canada, according to Morine, would "monopolize the trade" with Newfoundland rather than having to share a $12 million asset with the Americans. Through the Bell Island mines, Newfoundland already supplied the iron ore for the Cape Breton steel industry, and union would certainly increase the amount of capital investment in Newfoundland's mineral resources. Union would also provide an improved lighthouse service that would "be beneficial to Canada, as well [as to] Newfoundland [which] is in the mouth of the St. Lawrence." With union, Newfoundland would cease paying customs duties, lowering the cost of living to the consumer. Opposition to Confederation, Morine insisted, came from two sources: "those interested in manufacturing who fear loss of capital, through competition, and the poorer class, who fear direct taxation."

CHAPTER 3

Local manufacturers had no reason to oppose union, however, as they would retain their advantages of position and trade connections. As for taxation, he pointed out that the Newfoundland government "would control the direct taxation the same as it does now." Moreover, if the subsidy from the dominion were large enough, there would be no need for local taxation. On the lingering trade dispute with the United States, Morine submitted that the fisheries of Canada and Newfoundland should be under one control, as "any partial settlement of the question with the United States might be to the disadvantage of the Dominion and the Island." Morine acknowledged the lingering dispute between Canada and Newfoundland over the Labrador-Quebec boundary (discussed below), but he claimed that with joining Confederation, the "rights of Newfoundlanders would be protected in this region, and the colony's claim could be considered when the question of subsidy came up."[22]

Governor General Earl Grey shared Morine's view on Confederation, and he too was another of Bond's detractors. Grey saw Bond's feud with the United States and the Colonial Office as possibly providing an opening to bring Newfoundland into Canada. He readily accepted an invitation from MacGregor to visit Newfoundland in late July 1906—ostensibly for a holiday and salmon fishing—which he saw as an excellent opportunity to assess personally the support for Confederation. Grey attended a number of public events in St. John's, including the annual St. John's Regatta, North America's oldest annual sporting event. At a luncheon at Government House, with Premier Bond in attendance, Grey insisted that there should be no political importance attached to his visit, as he had come merely to enjoy Newfoundland and his old friend William MacGregor. His impression of Bond was not flattering though, and he wrote Laurier on his return to Ottawa that Bond was "jealous, suspicious, avariciously tenacious of all patronage, a strong and unforgiving hater and most vindictive," though he had "the strength which a touch of madness brings."[23] Grey acknowledged that in Newfoundland Confederation was not a "blessed word," and given the opposition, the push for Confederation could come only from Newfoundlanders.[24]

Inside the walls of Government House in St. John's and in the corridors of power and influence in Ottawa, the Confederation issue was regarded differently and with greater urgency. At St. John's, Governor MacGregor had a genuine dislike for Bond and regarded his policies with the United States and Canada as detrimental to the interests of the British government.[25] One way out of the mess, he believed, was Newfoundland joining Confederation. Grey—an Imperialist like MacGregor—shared those views, and his visit to Newfoundland had been arranged not only to assess support for Confederation but also to encourage it, especially with Bond and the anti-Confederate manufacturers, who Grey described as "the few two penny ha'penny industries at St. John's." Those in Newfoundland who supported union were an influential group that included, besides MacGregor, Roman Catholic Archbishop Michael Howley, representatives of the Bank of Montreal and the Canadian iron ore companies doing work in Newfoundland, and the Reid Newfoundland Company. Upon his return to Ottawa, Grey also informed the Colonial Office that union could be achieved in either of two ways: (1) by persuading Robert Bond that Confederation was essential to his political survival; or (2) by encouraging Edward Morris, another leading politician, to break from Bond and become the leader of a Confederation movement. Morris was, in Grey's assessment, "much liked and respected" and a "confederationist.... He has the power of knocking out Bond and winning the island to confederation," especially "if Bond remains obdurate." Of that, Grey concluded, "I feel pretty certain."[26] Of course, Grey must have known that he could count on the support of the powerful Reid Newfoundland Company, which had a long-simmering dispute with Bond. By 1906, it was lobbying the government to buy its Newfoundland holdings for $9.5 million; it was anxious to be rid of the Bond government and to have Newfoundland join Canada.[27]

In August 1907, Morris made his political move, as Grey had hoped he would, and broke with Bond in a disagreement over wages paid to road labourers in his constituency community of Kilbride. Many regarded this as flimsy grounds for the rupture, but Morris had the tacit support of both the Colonial Office and Governor MacGregor.[28] With Morris sitting as an independent, P.T. McGrath, the politically well-connected journalist, resigned the editorship of the *Evening Herald* and launched the pro-Morris *Evening Chronicle*—with funding from Reid. Within months, Morris announced the formation of

CHAPTER 3

the People's Party, which prominently included former Tories and a group from the well-heeled economic elite who were allied with the Reid Newfoundland Company and hoped to attract foreign capital to industrialize Newfoundland.[29] McGrath had published in late 1906 an article—"Should Newfoundland Confederate with Canada?"— in the Canadian popular magazine, *Westminster*. "The question of confederation transcends immeasurably all others of public interest in Newfoundland," McGrath asserted. Moreover, it had "figured in numerous election contests and made or marred the careers of many of our politicians," and to the "masses it is as the proverbial red rag to the bull." McGrath pointed out that Lord Grey's recent visit forced the Newfoundland government to deny that the visit was part of a plot to "sell the country." Even so, McGrath could not resist the opportunity to review Newfoundland's role in the Confederation talks in the 1860s and discuss the advantages and disadvantages of political union to both Canada and Newfoundland, thus helping to keep the issue alive.[30]

The general election held on November 2, 1908, resulted in a tie: the Bond and Morris parties each elected eighteen members in the thirty-six-seat House of Assembly. This created a constitutional crisis. Bond had attempted to make the vote a referendum on his personal performance.[31] The situation, however, was no longer favourable to him—particularly as the price of fish came under pressure from overproduction, poor quality, and competition in the foreign markets, and the price of imports, particularly flour and other staples, increased. Realizing the strength of the People's Party and its leader, Edward Morris, Bond tried "to gull the country with the 'Confederation cry.' " He accused Morris of trying to orchestrate political union with Canada. His Liberals and their supporters insisted that the "combination" now "posing as the 'People's Party' " would facilitate the domination of Newfoundland by the Reid Newfoundland Company and lead to bankruptcy, and then Confederation. Bond pledged to resist such a path, promising voters that only when they, themselves, "demand" Confederation at the polls would he consider it. He promised to defend Newfoundland's constitutional interest, reduce taxes, and spend prudently. He announced his support of old age pensions.

In his political manifesto, Morris left no doubt of his stand on union. In fact, his emphatic opposition to Confederation was the first item in the platform of the People's Party; every candidate running under the party's banner, Morris insisted, was "solemnly bound by this pledge."[32] To capitalize on the anti-Confederate sentiment among the populace, Morris went to great lengths to rebuke those who embraced Confederation: "All my life, [I have been] a staunch, unwavering opponent of Confederation on any terms. I was not old enough when the question was before the country in '69 to vote against it, but as a boy I attended its funeral."[33] And to defend his position in the 1895 delegation that went to Ottawa to explore terms of union, Morris swore that he had strongly opposed the terms Canada had offered. Newfoundland's "true mission," he affirmed, was to "work out her own destiny, independent of Canada, for, in my opinion, all that the most ardent Confederate might hope to obtain from union with Canada can be accomplished by ourselves as an independent Colony." Declaring that Newfoundland could be one of the great colonies of the British world, he affirmed his "unyielding resistance to every claim" that Canada might make for any portion of Labrador.[34]

It might be a tad bizarre, given that both parties had stated unequivocally their opposition to union with Canada, that, in the constitutional chaos that the 1908 election had created, those who hoped for Confederation were optimistic. This was especially true of Harry Crowe, another Nova Scotian who, like Morine, had come to Newfoundland as an enthusiastic supporter of union with Canada. Crowe arrived around 1902 to enter the timber trade, and immediately he became enthralled with the industrial potential of the Island. He befriended Robert Gillespie Reid and his two sons, William and Harry. In 1903, he established the Newfoundland Timber Estates Company Limited with William Reid, Henry Melville Whitney[35] of Boston—founder of the Dominion Coal Company and the Dominion Iron and Steel Company in Sydney—and Benjamin Franklin Pearson, a Halifax financier and politician. The Newfoundland Timber Estates Company Limited conducted lumbering operations in central Newfoundland and worked with the Reids and others—including Premier Bond, who had provided a ninety-nine-year lease to large tracts of forested land with generous provisions for mineral and water, as well as timber rights to the London-based Harmsworth newspaper and publishing interests—to establish the Anglo-Newfoundland Development Company

CHAPTER 3

Limited in Newfoundland, which later established a pulp and paper mill at Grand Falls. Crowe was also instrumental in convincing a second British firm, A.E. Reed and Company Limited, to establish a pulp mill at nearby Bishop's Falls, where construction began in 1911.[36]

Crowe was also a friend of Bond and apparently visited him regularly at The Grange, Bond's country estate in Whitbourne, ninety kilometres west of the capital, St. John's. In the political turmoil created by the election deadlock, Crowe hatched a scheme whereby he believed that if Bond could be maintained in power, he might be persuaded to accept union with Canada.[37] First, Crowe tried to convince Joseph Downey, a member of the People's Party for St. George's District and a former employee, to join Bond's Liberal Party. Following a meeting at Grand Falls, Crowe was convinced that Downey would abandon Morris, and Bond had agreed to offer Downey the speakership in the House of Assembly. Downey, however, eventually decided to remain with Morris. The Crowe-Bond Confederation scheme was exposed during the 1909 campaign (see below) to the great advantage of Morris.[38] Crowe was in Ottawa when he learned of Downey's decision not to cross the floor, and he immediately tried to arrange a political accommodation between Bond and Morris that could lead to their mounting a common front to bring Newfoundland into Confederation. Under such an arrangement, Morris was to eventually become prime minister, and Bond's reward would be a seat in the British House of Lords.[39]

Apparently, Archbishop Michael F. Howley supported Crowe's initiative. Howley had spent more than two decades as a priest on the west coast and in Fortune Bay, areas of Newfoundland that were among the Island's most isolated and underdeveloped. He witnessed first-hand the difficulties that the people of those regions experienced and felt that the Newfoundland government was not providing sufficient support to such neglected areas. Both areas, incidentally, interacted economically and socially in numerous ways with Nova Scotia. Howley was a frequent visitor to the Canadian mainland and saw there—as had Frederic Carter and Ambrose Shea in the 1860s—the advantages the people had over those in Newfoundland. Confederation, he believed, was a solution to the problems that those regions of the country endured.[40]

Crowe informed Governor General Earl Grey of his proposed arrangement. Bond, it was suggested, would turn to Confederation because it was a better alternative for Newfoundland than having it ruled by the "Tammany Hall" politics of Morris and the Reids, and because, like many career politicians entering their twilight years, he thought that carrying Confederation might provide for an auspicious and remarkable ending to a fine political life.[41] Crowe also believed that Morris could be persuaded on Confederation, if necessary, by the Reids and his Canadian friends, such as Sir Edward S. Clouston, the first vice-president of the Bank of Montreal, and Sir Thomas Shaughnessy, president of the Canadian Pacific Railway, who allegedly had provided Morris with funds in the 1908 campaign. Grey even visited Clouston in Montreal to promote the idea of union. On February 12, 1909, Crowe wrote Bond from Halifax of his discussions with Morris: "I found him a very sympathetic listener in my attempt to point out the advantages of Union with Canada, and the opportunity the present political deadlock offered in bringing it about without any formidable opposition." Morris, Crowe added enthusiastically, was willing to "sacrifice his present prospect of becoming Premier in order that it may be accomplished." "He agreed," Crowe chortled to Bond, "that you were the only one that could submit this question to the people at the present time." As for the political deadlock, Crowe proposed that two or three strong anti-Confederates would be out of the country and absent from the forthcoming session of the legislature. It was Crowe's plan, too, that nothing be said about union publicly until Bond had received Prime Minister Laurier's best terms; the matter would be taken up in the Newfoundland House of Assembly only at the end of the session, ostensibly to allow limited time for any of the antis to mobilize. If Bond approved of the arrangement Canada offered, then Morris would provide no opposition, and the terms would be submitted to the people as a united effort of the two parties. All Morris required from Bond, Crowe pointed out, was that he (Bond) was satisfied with the proposal, and then Morris "would pledge his word that nothing more would be heard of it directly or indirectly from him." Crowe felt confident Canada's terms would be "liberal."[42]

Intrigued by Crowe's coalition idea, Grey informed both Governor MacGregor and the Colonial Office of the proposal. MacGregor held little hope of the plan coming to fruition, believing that neither Bond nor Morris, together or separately, was strong enough to carry joining Confederation in an election. Moreover, he seriously doubted the two could work together.[43] Laurier, meanwhile, was willing to accept the proposal if Bond supported a Morris platform for political union with Canada. Bond was not interested in working with Morris, however, and asked MacGregor to dissolve the legislature and call another election. When MacGregor refused on the advice of London, Bond resigned on March 3, 1909, in favour of a Morris government, and Crowe's scheme fell apart.[44] Historian James K. Hiller contends that the plot failed because none of the principals understood Bond, who had an intense dislike and distrust of Morris; Bond was not prepared to compromise himself in some half-baked scheme.[45] Moreover, as the November 1909 election campaign made abundantly clear, there was such scepticism about Confederation that it would have been foolhardy for any politician in Newfoundland to attempt to bring it about in an underhanded manner. Crowe remained committed to Confederation nonetheless and never missed an opportunity to preach its benefits, especially to Canadian audiences. In March 1914, he said to the *Halifax Chronicle*, "he was more and more convinced that it would be in the best interest" of Newfoundland to unite with the "young, rich nation" of Canada. Indeed, his Confederate views were part of his wider belief that all Anglo-Saxon countries should forge closer relations.[46] He had long advocated union of the English-speaking countries, including the United States, and the creation of a commercial arrangement between Canada, Newfoundland, Great Britain, and the United States. In 1915, when Crowe visited the British West Indies, he even became an advocate of its political union with Canada and Newfoundland, an idea that received the endorsement of the London *Times*.[47]

In the re-run election, held on May 8, 1909, Confederation was the dominant issue. Both party leaders renounced Confederation and promised to build an independent Newfoundland, casting considerable doubt on Crowe's intrigues. Bond touted his long-standing anti-Confederation credentials and characterized Morris as a "Confederation schemer," not to be trusted. Bond asserted himself to be the Newfoundland nationalist and the only "obstacle" to Morris in working with Crowe and Downey to bring about Confederation. Morris was just like Morine, charged Bond, and people should hold a "wholesome fear and distrust" of him because of his Confederation views. The Liberal *Evening Telegram* went further and labelled Morris as Morine's "legitimate heir and successor" and warned that "eternal vigilance is the price of freedom!"[48] Moreover, Morris reaffirmed the promise he had made in 1908 at the founding of the People's Party that he would never stand for Confederation with Canada, and he accused Bond of deliberately raising the Confederation cry to discredit him and mislead voters.[49] Morris took his anti-Confederate sentiments to a sitting judge and swore "I am and have been all my life opposed to Confederation," adding for good measure that he had never accepted "one cent" from business interests outside the country to support his party, as Bond's Liberals alleged.[50] Bond also derided Morris as the "tool of the Reids," while Morris's supporters countered with "Bond's Day is Done" and "No More Bondage!"[51]

The decisive moment of the 1909 campaign was a press report of correspondence revealing Bond's engagement in secret talks with Canadian officials and ministers to bring about Confederation. Crowe was identified as the intermediary, and letters published late in the campaign showed that Bond and his Cabinet were, indeed, involved in talks with Canada. Anger erupted when the news broke, and candidates for the People's Party could not believe their good fortune. Although Bond termed the story a "base fabrication," he struggled in the final days of the campaign to present himself as a defender of the Newfoundland nation.

Bond was continually interrupted and hectored during his campaign speeches, but the low point came on April 30 at Western Bay. Arriving by water from Carbonear, Bond had to land by a smaller craft, as the community did not have a wharf large enough to accommodate the steamer—a regular occurrence in many outport communities. As he approached the dock, he was advised to return to the steamer as he was not welcome in Western Bay, a community about twenty-five kilometres southwest of Harbour Grace. Among the assembled crowd jeering the former prime minister was John C. Crosbie, St. John's merchant and successful People's Party candidate.[52] The fifty-two-year-old Bond, undeterred, began to ascend the stagehead rails, one of a number of wooden poles fastened one above the other to form a type of ladder. One of Crosbie's supporters, fisherman Alfred Bishop, became increasingly agitated, took a few steps down the rails towards Bond, and kicked him swiftly and viciously in the chest, knocking him into the water. It is not known if Bishop was encouraged by the local candidate, but panic ensued. Bond could not swim. Disaster was averted, however, when those in the landing craft retrieved him from the water. Bond, soaked and angry—and no doubt embarrassed—roared at Crosbie that he would be held responsible for the assault; however, it was Bishop who was charged with aggravated assault and sentenced to six months of hard labour. Bond requested that Bishop's sentence be reduced, claiming that the poor fisherman had also been a victim of others—presumably he meant Crosbie. Bond decided not to bring charges against Crosbie.[53]

As former governor Ralph C. Williams (1909–13) observed of Bond, Morris, Morine, and other politicians, the great majority of Newfoundlanders were opposed to Confederation, and union was never a plank in the platform of any political party. "A politician may, at election time, level a charge of 'confederation' against his opponent," Williams wrote, but "he does it, not because he really fears confederation as a living issue, but simply to score a political point against his adversary ... as a Judas who would sell his country."[54] In the 1909 campaign, the news of Bond's alleged treacherous, duplicitous behaviour on Confederation was costly. Morris, already having the advantage of the prime ministership (since March 2), turned the campaign into a rout, taking twenty-six seats to Bond's ten. Once again politicians learned that being associated with any scheme to bring Newfoundland into Confederation would prove costly.

PROSPERITY, RURAL PROTEST, AND REFORM

The prosperity associated with the first Morris government (1909–13) was in many ways, and ironically, the fulfillment of Bond's dream for economic diversification. The Grand Falls pulp and paper mill for which the grounds had been laid under Bond's leadership began operations and contributed greatly to an increase in the country's exports. Much of Newfoundland's prosperity came from the politically popular but financially unsound branch railway line policy that Morris pursued with almost reckless abandon. The government spent $7 million for branch lines, 50 percent more than Morris had promised, but it also introduced, in 1911, Newfoundland's first old age pension scheme of $50 per year for men aged seventy-five years and older who could prove they required financial assistance. The policy had been actively discussed since at least 1907, when the Bond government appointed a royal commission to investigate old age pensions in response to lobbying from Alfred Morine, then leader of the Opposition, who argued for universal coverage for men. Both Bond and Morris made granting old age pensions a feature of their political platforms in both 1908 and 1909. Newfoundland's was the first state-operated old age pension scheme in North America.[55]

Edward Patrick Morris had attempted to create a populist appeal, but the real force for social and economic change, and a new relationship between state and citizen, came not from the People's Party but from outport fishermen. It was with a touch of irony perhaps that St. John's–born William Coaker, who was farming on an island in Dildo Run in Notre Dame Bay, launched the Fishermen's Protective Union (FPU) on November 2, the night of the 1908 general election. Both Bond and Morris had portrayed themselves as standing for ordinary Newfoundlanders, but Coaker and fishermen throughout the country knew that neither political leader really understood the deep and profound disillusionment fishermen had with Newfoundland's economic and social system. Simply put, Coaker and his supporters demanded a greater share of the wealth that came from their labour—that had sustained the country since European settlement. Not surprisingly, the FPU grew rapidly, especially in the northern bays. It laid the foundation for a monumental shift in Newfoundland politics and created hope among its citizens, although it would take more than three decades to bring those hopes and new ideas to fruition. The FPU might have had some undertones of class conflict,[56] but it was essentially a quest for social citizenship. It made no attempt to unite the labouring class, only to secure a better life for fishermen. Coaker campaigned for an ambitious social welfare program that included old age pensions, insurance policies for injured fishermen, and other initiatives that were being embraced as social rights and social citizenship by progressives who advocated similar demands in the United States and across much of the British world, especially in the settler

CHAPTER 3

William Ford Coaker in 1904, a year after he formed a telegraph operators' union. In 1908, he held the first meeting of what would become the Fishermen's Protective Union at the Loyal Orange Lodge at Herring Neck and changed the political landscape of Newfoundland.

colonies of New Zealand, Australia, and Canada at that time. The formation of the FPU and the founding of the Newfoundland Board of Trade (which Coaker described as a Merchants' Union) a year later in 1909 were two different responses to long-standing problems in the salt cod fishery, as Coaker believed that fishermen, not merchants, should determine the price of fish. He was appalled at the substantial gap that existed between what merchants paid for fish and what they received in the foreign markets. The merchants collected the rewards and the economic rents from the fishermen's toil. In 1907 and 1908, when overstocked markets once again depressed prices despite above-average catches, Coaker capitalized on the growing disillusionment among fishermen and decided it was time to alter how the Newfoundland economy operated.[57]

The original anthem of the FPU, "Forty Thousand Strong" (or "We Are Coming, Mr. Coaker"),[58] embodied the rallying cry for change and was a reaffirmation that fishermen saw themselves as British people who deserved a better fate in Newfoundland than they had ever experienced. It acknowledged that fishermen had been "misruled" by "both merchants and by governments for too long," and they vowed to alter the situation. The anthem acknowledged fishermen as British men, derived from the blood of the "Saxon and the Celt." They were also "free men" and committed, as "valiant" Britishers mythically always are, to "rightify each wrong." The fight, they insisted, was "the fight for freedom," an optimistic note that would be echoed in 1941, at the lowest ebb of the Allied struggle against Nazi Germany, by British prime minister Winston Churchill and American president Franklin D. Roosevelt in signing the Atlantic Charter, incidentally in Placentia Bay in Newfoundland. The FPU's anthem and its platform were an articulation of widely accepted British principles of freedom, justice, and equality, and as British people, Newfoundlanders believed they deserved better and a standard of living to which British citizens were entitled. This message was also encapsulated in 1910 in the FPU's newspaper, the *Fishermen's Advocate*. There Coaker asked his followers if each received his "own" when

> he boards a coastal or bay steamer, as a steerage passenger and has to sleep like a dog, eat like a pig, and be treated like a serf? Does he receive his own at the seal fishery where he has to live like a brute, work like a dog...? Do they receive their own when they pay taxes to keep up five splendid colleges at St. John's... while thousands of fishermen's children are growing up illiterate? Do they receive their own when forced to supply funds to maintain a hospital at St. John's while fishermen, their wives and daughters are dying daily in the outports for want of hospitals?[59]

Coaker and his supporters demanded a different country than the one to which they had been accustomed for generations. As one admirer of Coaker wrote privately to a friend, in 1924, like "so many other social movements in history," the FPU had been "born out of a condition or situation—the culminating point of a long period of poverty and oppression among the fishermen, a sense of being downtrodden on their part." The admirer was the journalist Joseph R. Smallwood.[60]

CHAPTER 3

Inspired by labour parties in the United Kingdom, Australia, and New Zealand, and by the progressive and social gospel movements in the United States and Canada, Coaker and the FPU decided in 1910 upon independent political action, with the object of holding the "balance of power" in the legislature to advance their agenda of cooperation and fairness to the country's fishermen. FPU proposals were embodied in the Bonavista Platform of 1912, a radical program calling for new ways of managing the fishery. It wanted cooperative marketing of fish and government-controlled grading, for example, so that a greater share of the economic rents from the catch went to fishermen and not fish merchants. It demanded that the state provide greater security for its citizens, especially through social programs and lower customs duties on the staple foods on which fishermen and their families depended. It also advocated greater democracy in governance, notably the use of recall of members who lose the trust and support of their constituents as well as higher pay for members of the House of Assembly to ensure their independence and to lessen the likelihood of their being beholden to the country's mercantile elite.[61]

William Coaker and the Fishermen's Protective Union were advocating radical transformation in Newfoundland politics. It is not clear, however, that the political elite understood the changes Coaker and the FPU were seeking throughout the country and in Newfoundland's political culture. William Frederick Lloyd, the editor of the St. John's Liberal *Evening Telegram*, saw in the FPU a political advantage for his Liberal Party and a way to defeat Morris. As a way for the Liberals to regain power, he attempted to broker a deal between Bond and Coaker, who had been a political supporter of Bond in the 1890s. His overtures failed because of the deep division between the two leaders. Harry Crowe, the avowed Confederate, also tried to bring the two together, first by addressing the issue of leadership and party loyalty. In a letter to Coaker, on November 27, 1912, Crowe advised Coaker that Bond's reticence on an alliance stemmed from Bond's concern that FPU candidates for the upcoming election, already chosen by FPU district councils, had sworn their allegiance to Coaker. Bond felt it would be "embarrassing and humiliating for him to have a power within his party that would not recognize him as the only leader." Coaker refused to turn his organization over to one of the traditional political parties.

Crowe's real motive, however, was joining Confederation, and he tried to persuade Coaker how beneficial it would be for fishermen. It would provide better and new public services, as well as lower or eliminate the tariff on fishing supplies and provisions.[62] Crowe later wrote Prime Minister Robert Borden that Coaker and the FPU were an "important factor" in any campaign for joining Confederation. Moreover, there was hope on another front: Crowe had spoken with Bond on a recent visit to London and had secured his "unquestioned support" for union. He had, Crowe wrote, "confided in me his present convictions, namely, that the sooner the old colony is united with the Dominion, the better, and he is sanguine of being able to bring it about." Given what had happened in the 1909 election, Crowe ended his letter to Borden with "I would thank you to treat this in strict confidence."[63]

Meanwhile, another advocate of joining Confederation was about to make a return to Newfoundland. Alfred B. Morine, who had been "exiled" to Canada for several years, attracted considerable press when he arrived with his wife in St. John's, on July 4, 1912, for a six-week holiday that included salmon fishing, of which both were "fond."[64] The *Fishermen's Advocate* reported that "rumour has it that he is likely to take up his abode in Newfoundland again and not unlikely to play a prominent part in the next election."[65] Coaker also noted the presence of the "Eminent Visitor" and observed that Morine "is somewhat changed. Seven years absence in a city like Toronto [or] Ottawa has considerably expanded his views and taught him many lessons that could not be learnt in Newfoundland." "Politicians," he noted, "are very shy of him, and fear his return. If he does return he will be a power they will have to reckon with, whether he becomes active or passive." Coaker also acknowledged Morine's strengths as a lawyer: "He would stand supreme," he noted and welcomed him as a "popular fighter . . . to lay bare the government's wrongdoings."[66] Coaker had indeed made overtures to Morine to become the FPU's solicitor. Liberals were hopeful of such an arrangement because they believed Morine could encourage Coaker to support Bond at the next general election, to be held in 1913.[67] Morine returned permanently in mid-November and established a legal practice in the Board of Trade Building on Water Street.[68] He could not run for the House of Assembly until he had been a resident in Newfoundland for at least two years,[69] but in January 1913

CHAPTER 3

he became solicitor for the FPU.[70] Like Coaker, Morine believed that the outport people had not shared in the country's wealth.

For Prime Minister Morris, any coalition of Morine and Coaker with Bond was worrisome. Just before the 1913 general election, held on October 30, Coaker and Bond forged a Liberal–Union alliance that, although shaky, provided a formidable opposition.[71] Morris's response was to once more burnish his anti-Confederate credentials: I "will not consent to union with Canada on any terms; and before the question will be taken up by me or by those associated with me," he vowed, "I shall resign my seat in the Legislature."[72] For Bond, Morris's railway branch line policy and other extravagant and reckless expenditures had created a "grave peril" for Newfoundland. Yet the railway had become all the rage in Newfoundland, a symbol of modernity and progress, especially for the new class of self-made men and professionals who supported Morris. Moreover, it was being demanded by the larger communities even though it would add to the colony's burdensome debt that already stood at more than $22 million. Bond saw it differently, however.[73] Railway expansion was threatening "the very vitals of the community and sapping our existence as an independent State of the Empire," he warned. It is "a peril so grave and so insidious that it must be faced, investigated, and overcome," Bond said. He promised in his election manifesto that if elected, he would appoint a "thorough Expert Examination into the financial condition of the Colony, with a view to establishing its finances on a sound basis," and the "re-establishment of the credit of the Colony both at home and abroad by a sane and judicious expenditure of the Colony's revenues."[74] When the votes were counted on October 30, 1913, the People's Party prevailed, with twenty-one seats to the FPU's eight (all in the outports) and the Liberals' seven.[75] Bond realized the jig was up. To flee the indignity of his third-party status, he resigned both the leadership of the Liberal Party and his seat in the House of Assembly,[76] intoning, "I am not prepared to aid the policy of the President of the F.P.U., which he has declared to be the seizure of the Government of this Colony by the Union over which he presides."[77] "What an ignoble ending to a public man, who at one time was the darling of the people," Coaker lamented.[78] Bond's humiliation was made complete when Coaker was elected by acclamation in the by-election to fill Bond's Twillingate seat. Coaker had vacated his own Bonavista District constituency to allow Morine to return to elective politics in late 1914.

Morine's intention to push Coaker on joining Confederation was interrupted by the Great War. As tensions mounted in Europe in 1914, Governor Sir Walter E. Davidson (1913–17) and Prime Minister Morris worried about the impact a conflict might have on Newfoundland's economy, particularly its submarine cable connections to Europe. They worried too about the potential of German cruisers off their coast. But in St. John's, as in Canada, the declaration of war was greeted with tremendous enthusiasm, as thousands paraded "singing patriotic songs." Newfoundland was ill-prepared for war, however, as it had no standing military force and only six hundred reservists in the Royal Naval Reserve who trained on an old Admiralty vessel in St. John's harbour.[79] Yet Morris moved quickly when war was declared. On August 7, he authorized Davidson to dispatch a telegram to London, promising to raise by the end of October a naval force of a thousand men to serve abroad for one year, with Newfoundland meeting all expenses, and a land force of five hundred to be raised within a month. The first group of naval reservists left on September 6 to join HMCS *Niobe* to hunt for German vessels off Canada's east coast. The Blue Puttees,[80] as the first army contingent was known, arrived in England on October 14 and were initially placed under Canadian control with the First Canadian Contingent at Salisbury Plain. Later, the Newfoundland Regiment in early 1915 was attached to the 88th Brigade of the 29th Division of the British Army.

Newfoundlanders feared throughout the war that they would be regarded as Canadian, and as renowned soldier Owen Steele noted, "The larger Canadian presence at the camp created many occasions for mistaken identity." Newfoundlanders were conscious of their national identification, and the Newfoundland Regiment created for them a strong sense of community and a feeling of nationhood.[81] By November 1918, almost twelve thousand Newfoundlanders had enlisted for overseas service, the majority joining the Newfoundland Regiment, with others joining the Royal Naval Reserve and the Newfoundland Forestry Corps. Some thirty-two hundred served in the Canadian Expeditionary Force,[82] and a few Canadians, such as banking clerk Sydney Frost, enlisted in the Newfoundland Regiment. An unknown

CHAPTER 3

but likely much smaller number served in the American armed forces.[83] Many middle- and upper-class young women also volunteered in nursing units in the Canadian and British forces, primarily with the British Voluntary Aid Detachment. Others served as nurses' aides and ambulance drivers and on hospital ships.[84] Most of them, like the young soldier in the Newfoundland Regiment who wrote home from Salisbury Plain, were "all very particular here that we should not be classed as Canadians."[85]

Governor Davidson had organized Newfoundland's war effort, supposedly to keep it unified, non-partisan, and non-political. At a public meeting in St. John's on August 12, 1914, attended by three thousand citizens, Davidson approved the appointment of a committee of fifty-five prominent St. John's citizens (with power to add to its number) to oversee the raising and equipping of land and naval forces. The committee quickly became known as the Newfoundland Patriotic Association (NPA), under Davidson's chairmanship. From the start, it was St. John's–led, with half of the executive being Water Street merchants and the remainder representing the major religious denominations and political parties. It subsequently appointed committees and subcommittees with responsibility for recruitment, training, equipment, transport, officer selection, and finance. The legislature passed a *War Measures Act* (based on existing British and Canadian statutes) in early September that authorized the government through orders-in-council or through a third party, such as the NPA, to manage the war effort directly. While Prime Minister Morris never formally gave the NPA the authority to conduct the war, in practice Governor Davidson did so for nearly three years, although the government was responsible for the pay of the members of the regiment as well as all expenses associated with the regiment while it remained in Newfoundland. The government also covered the costs of the regiment's transport to Britain and committed to cover future pension benefits.[86]

Eventually Prime Minister Morris had to contend with a growing discontent as citizens became increasingly suspicious of the Newfoundland Patriotic Association. People openly complained that Water Street merchants, who essentially controlled the NPA, benefitted from rising prices for coal, salt, and other staples and that the major Water Street merchants had quickly sold many of their steel-hulled steamers for tremendous profits when those very vessels were integral to the economic life of the country, notably in the seal hunt, in the marketing of salt cod and other exports, and in the maintenance of communications and trade around the coast. Citizens also criticized the mismanagement of the recruitment process and of the money raised to support families of soldiers serving overseas. All of this pointed to the need for the state to play a greater role in managing the war effort and, more generally, provide better management of the economy for the well-being of citizens. The government should, many insisted, assume control of the marketing and distribution of basic staples to end profiteering by the country's mercantile elite and provide better supports for citizens impacted by the war, including pensions for widowed mothers and separation allowances for married troops. The divisions over the war reflected the long-standing schism between St. John's and the outports.[87]

Certainly, the growing number of war dead also contributed to the government's problems. The Newfoundland Regiment had seen its first action in 1915 in the Gallipoli campaign, where 1,167 men joined the fighting. Its casualty rate, at 55.4 percent, was high and included 41 dead, 84 evacuated because of wounds, and another 522 who suffered various illnesses, including dysentery, frostbite, and trench foot. The regiment's first "baptism of fire" was costly,[88] but it would pale in comparison to the Battle of the Somme. It was July 1, 1916, that 721 members of the regiment serving with the 29th Division of the British Army advanced on well-fortified German lines under the barrage of heavy machine gun fire near the village of Beaumont Hamel. Just thirty minutes out of their trenches, and without firing a single shot, 386 Newfoundlanders had either been killed or gone missing in action. Another 396 were wounded. All 25 officers were either killed or wounded; only 68 men reported later for duty call. It was a senseless moment in a destructive and demoralizing war, although the British Army and the Newfoundland government attempted to reassure Newfoundlanders that their losses were not in vain by emphasizing the heroic sacrifices at the Somme.[89] The British commander, Brigadier-General Douglas Edward Cayley, wrote Governor Davidson that he regretted that Newfoundland's only regiment "has made such sacrifices [and] should suffer such a fate .... I cannot sufficiently express my admiration for their heroism ... nor my sorrow for their overwhelming losses, which

CHAPTER 3

Opening of the war memorial in St. John's, 1924.

admiration and sorrow will be all shared by Newfoundland." Field Marshal Sir Douglas Haig, commander-in-chief of the British Expeditionary Force, similarly wrote Davidson: "Newfoundland may well feel proud of her sons. The heroism and devotion to duty they displayed on July First has never been surpassed."[90]

The country could hardly recover from the senseless and futile loss of so many young men in just a few moments, but it vowed to keep the regiment at full force and in the field through active voluntary recruitment. On July 17, 1917, shortly after the first anniversary of the Beaumont Hamel disaster, Prime Minister Morris invited William Frederick Lloyd, leader of the Liberal Party, and William Coaker of the Fishermen's Protective Union to join him in a coalition government. If they accepted, Morris agreed to resign later as prime minister and to hold elections in 1918. Both joined with Morris.[91] Coaker became a minister without portfolio, turning down the opportunity to be minister of marine and fisheries to "protect the interests of the Fishermen as President of the FPU and Manager of the Union Companies." However, he was keen to implement some of the FPU's policies and insisted he had joined a "National Government" that was to be non-partisan rather than a coalition; he believed he was ushering in a "distinctly new" government through the creation of a national party[92] and fulfilling one of the aims of the FPU to change how the country was governed. As Morris spent much of the remaining months of the war in London at the Imperial War Conference, Lloyd, in effect, ran the government. Morris resigned in early 1918, with an appointment to the British House of Lords as Baron Morris of Waterford, and Lloyd became prime minister on January 5, 1918.[93] The National Government established a militia department to assume the work of the Newfoundland Patriotic Association, imposed for the calendar year 1917 a tax of 20 percent on net business profits in excess of $3,000, and restricted the powers of the Legislative Council in money matters.[94] Coaker insisted on a guaranteed price for fish to fishermen by setting a floor and warning merchants that the government would not issue insurance policies to exporters purchasing fish below the set price.[95]

The government's most immediate problem was the shortage of recruits. The Newfoundland Regiment was in danger of being disbanded in April 1918. It needed three hundred men immediately with a guarantee of sixty more each month to continue as a separate unit. More than eight thousand men had already joined the war effort, but nearly as many—6,246 volunteers—had been rejected on medical grounds, an indictment no doubt of the terrible social conditions in the country, as well as the lack of adequate health facilities and the lack of adequate nutrition. Moreover, the casualty rate for the regiment was 20 percent, a figure more than double that of the Canadian army.[96] Conscription, of course, was the obvious answer, but the matter, like so many others, divided the outports and St. John's. In the city, there was general support for both the war and conscription; in the outports, opposition to conscription was strong. For outport fishermen, like farmers in Canada and elsewhere, conscription meant a disruption in their livelihood, especially problematic because prices for fish were among the best in living memory. Fishing remained largely a family enterprise, and losing a son or two to military service had serious economic repercussions, at a time when the industry was enjoying considerable prosperity. Coaker was well aware of the strong outport opposition to conscription, but he faced relentless pressure within the Cabinet to fall in line behind it. His options were limited: he had to either support Prime Minister Lloyd (January 1918–May 1919) or withdraw from the National Government. Coaker reluctantly supported a

CHAPTER 3

referendum on the matter, but the Newfoundland government bowed to British pressure and announced conscription without one, a decision made out of fear of losing a referendum vote.

On April 26, 1918, Coaker announced his support for conscription even though anti-conscriptionist messages had flooded FPU headquarters in the previous months. Not surprisingly, FPU members accused Coaker of favouring St. John's interests over those of the outports. Some reportedly smashed pictures of him hanging in their homes and treated with scepticism his insistence that the National Government had proven itself receptive to union-sponsored measures since its formation in July 1917, and his continued presence in the government was necessary to implement an FPU fishery reform program. To mollify the FPU discontents, the Lloyd government extended the income tax to the professional and middle classes, whose incomes had been exempt from the 1917 business profits tax. Most of that group also lived in St. John's. None of the conscripts saw active duty, but the whole episode of conscription had forced some to wonder where Coaker's interests really lay. The episode also revealed, once again, the bitter divisions between St. John's and the outport communities.[97]

The feeling of nationhood brought on by the Great War was also partly responsible for dropping the designation of "colony" in favour of "dominion." From the date of the Canadian Confederation on July 1, 1867, Canada and Newfoundland were self-governing colonies within the British Empire equal in their constitutional rights but, as we have already seen, in practice often unequal when mutual matters came before the Colonial Office. As historian James Hiller has observed of the late-nineteenth-century relations between the two, in trade disputes with Canada in the early 1890s, for instance, Newfoundland never had the "stature with which to back up its quite valid claims to equality of status." This was because Canada was "too important" for Britain to treat the smaller colony as an equal by favouring Newfoundland over Canada.[98] At Imperial Conferences in London, Newfoundland attended, nonetheless, as an equal along with Canada, Australia, New Zealand, and South Africa. Within the British Empire, the term *dominion* dates from 1867 and its official usage in the *British North America Act* recognizing the "Dominion of Canada."[99] However, over time it also came into general usage in describing the self-governing colonies, and at the 1907 Imperial Conference the British government established a Dominions Department within the Colonial Office and henceforth referred to the self-governing colonies as dominions, which were able, if they wished, to conduct trade negotiations independently of the British Embassy, an important concession highly valued by Canada. The term *dominion*, constitutional expert William Gilmore has argued, could be applied to Newfoundland from that date as it did to Canada and Australia in terms of their relationship to Britain.[100] However, the Newfoundland government never officially used the term *dominion* until early 1918 (preferring *colony* instead in emphasizing its claim to be Britain's oldest colony) when it became part of official government usage in proclamations, for example, following the recognition by the British government of the five self-governing colonies' contributions to the British effort in the Great War.[101]

In 1917 and 1918, Newfoundland prime ministers participated in the deliberations of the Imperial War Cabinet along with the leaders from the other four self-governing colonies.[102] Britain promised they would have input at the forthcoming peace conference once the war ended. When the 1919 Paris Peace Conference was held, both Canada and Newfoundland were participants. However, Canadian prime minister Robert Borden was absent at the official opening meeting on January 18, 1919, offended that Newfoundland had been given precedence over Canada at the event.[103] Subsequently, because of the United States' objections, Newfoundland was considered too small to have its own seat at the negotiations, and its participation was included as part of the British legation. Canada, Australia, New Zealand, and South Africa did have seats at the conference and thus were able to join the newly established League of Nations as a result.[104] Newfoundland did not.

Newfoundland officially used the term *dominion* in 1918 and 1919, but the government stopped doing so at the urging of Governor Sir Charles Alexander Harris. There had been, he pointed out, no changes in its letters patent of 1876 containing instructions to the governors to use dominion.[105] Newfoundland's proper designation was "colony" or "island," as found in its letters patent, E.J. Harding of the Colonial Office informed Newfoundland High Commissioner Sir Edgar Bowring on March 14, 1921. "Newfoundland has been represented at Colonial and Imperial Conferences since 1887," he wrote, and as such it "may be described as one of the self-governing Dominions." However, he considered the term "Dominion of Newfoundland" as an official description of the country to be incorrect, in the same manner that, officially, Australia was known as a *commonwealth*, not a dominion, and South Africa a *union*, even though they were both recognized in Whitehall as dominions. On the other hand, New Zealand and Canada had styled themselves as dominions. Many of the largely self-governing states of the Empire—and later Commonwealth—were dominions in the eyes of the British government, and this included Newfoundland even if its official title was that of colony or island.[106]

Despite the difference in title, Newfoundland never pursued an independent road in external affairs, unlike Canada and South Africa. Rather, in the 1920s, except for matters considering the fishery export markets and in its relations with Canada, Newfoundland used the services of a High Commissioner's Office in London and the British Embassy in its foreign relations as an economic measure. Using British officials was cheaper than maintaining a more costly ambassador and consular service. One exception occurred in early 1921 when Minister of Marine and Fisheries William Coaker attempted to negotiate a commercial agreement with the Portuguese government on behalf of the Newfoundland government without the approval of the British government.[107] Yet there was generally no great desire among Newfoundland political leaders to pursue an independent policy in Imperial affairs. Vincent Massey, a member of the Canadian delegation to the 1926 Imperial Conference, noted that Newfoundland's attitude was "purely Colonial and proud of it," as Monroe indicated in his opening speech at the conference. "We represent such a very small number of people," he said, "that we do not expect to have very much say on Imperial matters." Following pressure mainly from Canada and South Africa for the dominions to have authority to conduct their external affairs independent of Britain, Newfoundland was, however, formally recognized as one of the self-governing dominions under the Balfour Declaration at the 1926 Imperial Conference.[108] On May 27, 1927, Monroe informed the House of Assembly, "we are now an autonomous community equal in Status with the other Dominions of the British Empire. We did not ask for it, nor did we want it, and we did not throw our hats in the air when we got it. It is of no value to us."[109]

CONFEDERATION REMAINS AN ISSUE DURING THE GREAT WAR

Despite the change in Newfoundland's constitutional status, the issue of Confederation refused to lie dormant, and even during wartime it continued to be an issue. Politicians and their operatives in both Ottawa and St. John's continued to discuss the subject. Draft terms of union were drawn up once again, and the subject took further twists and turns and continued to help shape local political developments, although much of the impetus for union this time was driven by the commercial interests of the Reid Newfoundland Company.[110] Not surprisingly, Morine and Crowe were also in the middle of these efforts, as they used their influence in Ottawa to move Canada towards union. Alfred Morine, who had been trying to consummate union for years, had continued his contact with Canadian federal politicians during his sojourn in Ontario, and on his return to Newfoundland in 1912, he intensified those efforts. On January 16, 1914, he wrote fellow Nova Scotian and prime minister of Canada, Robert Borden, of the political situation concerning Newfoundland and Confederation. Both Coaker and Morris were ready to discuss political union, he suggested. Most important, he thought, was Morris, who had been "making close inquiry into general feeling here" on Confederation. Apparently, the prime minister had found "public opinion not so opposed as to make the adoption of good terms impossible," Morine optimistically informed Borden. Bond, who had long been a fixture on the Newfoundland political landscape, Morine reminded Borden, was out of public life for "the present," although he "might return on one side or the other of a Confederation campaign." It was difficult to know Bond's feeling, he admitted, but he thought that Crowe "would be the right man to discover it."[111] Morine was so excited about the prospects that he had drafted potential terms of union for Borden. He had not discussed them with Morris, he cautioned Borden on February 5, 1914, as "I want first to have some assurance from him that he proposes to move in the right way."[112]

Crowe had also spoken to Borden about union. On May 2, 1913, he wrote privately of his earlier conversation in London with Bond, who, Crowe claimed, was now giving Confederation his "unquestioned support." Apparently Bond had become so concerned about Morris's fiscal policies that Confederation seemed the best option for getting rid of Morris, although the former prime minister had certain pre-conditions that Crowe needed to discuss with Borden.[113] On October 23, 1914, just days after the declaration of war, Morine again wrote Borden that Edward Jackman, a St. John's businessman and former Bond politician but now a Cabinet minister supporting Morris, was instructed by Morris to meet Borden on an upcoming visit to Ottawa.[114] Jackman had Morris's "complete confidence," he insisted,[115] and did in fact meet members of Borden's Conservative government to discuss possible union. Jackman also had several conversations with the prime minister. Borden wrote Morris, on November 20, 1914, that before further discussion ensued he would require more financial information about Newfoundland.[116] Morine felt confident of union, and perhaps to aid the cause he gave a public lecture on Confederation in St. John's on February 10, 1915. It was the "best audience both in size and quality which has ever assembled in St. John's," he subsequently informed Borden.[117]

Businessmen with commercial interests in Newfoundland were also promoting union. Sir Thomas Shaughnessy, president of the Canadian Pacific Railway, a director of the Bank of Montreal and of the Reid Newfoundland Company, pursued the matter with Canadian officials on behalf of the Reids, who were particularly interested in how the federal government would take over ownership and management of the Newfoundland Railway System in the event of union.[118] In June 1915, William Reid appointed Jackman his company's representative, and he quickly achieved the outlines of an agreement between Ottawa and the railway company.[119] Jackman told Thomas White, the federal minister of finance, that the "crux of the situation" in any negotiations on union was the Reid Railway; White saw the Reid motive for union immediately and wrote Borden, on June 10, 1916, that except "for the position of this railway, Newfoundland would not be seeking admission to Confederation." "Reid evidently controls the Government," he added for good measure. Despite having secured generous land grants from the Newfoundland government, the Reids were swamped in debt and found the operating "deficit too heavy to be borne." "In a word," White wrote Borden, "Reid and the Railway Company may be upon the brink of insolvency. He desires to unload upon the Government of Canada the railway and its annual deficit.... Reid therefore desires to bring Newfoundland into Confederation for the personal reason that his own fortune will be saved, or at all events that he will sustain no further loss."[120] However, all parties involved in these negotiations soon realized that the key to any successful Confederation effort was no longer Bond but securing the crucial endorsement and support of William Coaker.

In early 1916, William Reid began efforts to bring Coaker around to his side. Reid hoped to accomplish this by promoting a fresh fish industry in Newfoundland, a development in which Coaker took considerable interest. Coaker believed that a new sector in the fishery would diminish the control of the St. John's mercantile elite. Reid arranged for Coaker to visit Ottawa while on the mainland, where he met both Prime Minister Borden and his predecessor, Liberal Party leader Sir Wilfrid Laurier.[121] Coaker also visited the House of Commons, where he was accorded a great honour as a visiting parliamentarian. He later informed readers of the *Mail and Advocate* that "several of the leading men [he had met] asked about Confederation and assured me that both parties [in Canada] would be ready to grant Newfoundland any terms within reason that the Colony stipulated . . . . If I wanted to arrange terms of Confederation," he boasted, "I have no hesitation in asserting that I could have secured terms that would make all former offers a mere flea bite in comparison." Coaker, however, valued independence for Newfoundland: "I assured all that Newfoundland was not willing to seek Confederation with Canada and the general opinion of Newfoundland was that the Colony could yet paddle her own canoe." The Canadians were not deterred, and according to Coaker, they agreed there "could be no Confederation with Newfoundland except through the free will of the people expressed at the polls." Laurier and Borden agreed too that the decision had to be Newfoundland's. "I was glad to learn this," Coaker acknowledged, "for it removes the chances of plotters and schemers to turn the Colony over to Canada by an act of Parliament unless submitted to the electorate and approved by a majority of the electorate."[122]

William Coaker had apparently been willing to listen to possible discussions on proposed terms of union with Canada because he was extremely concerned with Newfoundland's financial situation.[123] He also believed that Borden, who was surely aware of the plight of Nova Scotia fishermen, was determined to protect the interests of all

CHAPTER 3

fishermen, including those within the FPU.[124] However, the terms that were being loosely discussed—which Governor Davidson had observed in his report to the Colonial Office in March 1916—were not as generous as those offered by Canada in 1914 because of wartime conditions. Nonetheless, Coaker, Morris, and William Reid all seemed agreeable to them.[125] Before leaving Ottawa, Coaker had invited Laurier to visit Newfoundland during the summer of 1916 and to be a guest of Governor Davidson, who generally favoured union between Newfoundland and Canada. The governor believed that Laurier wished to visit Newfoundland so that he might claim to have helped promote union and the rounding out of Confederation as envisioned in 1864 rather than see Borden take all the credit for bringing Newfoundland into the union.[126] By mid-1916, however, Newfoundland's politicians became preoccupied with the on-again, off-again negotiations between Prime Minister Morris and the Opposition to establish a National Government, and the issue of Confederation was relegated to the proverbial back burner. Yet by April 1917, Governor Davidson observed that public opinion was "practically unanimous in favour of Federation with Canada," largely because of the interest on borrowing necessitated by wartime expenditures and the pension charges for disabled veterans (adopted at the same level as in Canada). Both items resulted in higher levels of taxation than Newfoundland could possibly afford. In a "private and personal" draft letter to Walter Long, secretary of state for the colonies, Davidson observed that he would not be surprised if, when the House of Assembly met in May, a committee was appointed to go to the Canadian government "asking for the formal offer of those terms which have been indirectly conveyed to individuals from statesmen on both sides in the Canadian Parliament. However," he pointed out, "the issue rests with Sir Edward Morris."[127] But as noted earlier, Morris left the colony shortly thereafter for London. This fact, along with a libel suit related to Coaker's involvement in the Confederation attempt in 1916 (discussed below), effectively derailed any plans for union.

Coaker was also implicated in an internecine feud within the management of the Reid Newfoundland Company. One of the combatants, William Reid, wrote to Lord Shaughnessy that he (Reid) had orchestrated a conspiracy that had Coaker travelling to Ottawa in 1916, where

Coaker allegedly discussed draft terms of union. The letter was circulated among the People's Party members of the National Government to get them to support William Reid in his feud with his brother Harry and to embarrass Coaker, in hopes of forcing him to leave the government. When part of this letter dealing with Coaker was published in the press, Coaker filed a libel lawsuit against William J. Herder, the publisher of the *Evening Telegram*, for Reid's comments about Coaker's efforts to bring about Confederation in 1916. A grand jury found Reid's claims were not libellous, and Robert Borden pressured William Reid to let the matter drop.[128]

POLITICS FOLLOWING THE GREAT WAR

Politics in Newfoundland were more fluid than usual following the Armistice. Roman Catholic Archbishop Edward Roche was particularly hostile to the Fishermen's Protective Union, and he hoped to restore the old alliance of Roman Catholics and the Liberal Party under Bond's leadership. Michael Cashin, the leader of the People's Party and a member of the National Government, hoped to win Roche's support to strengthen his own position in Roman Catholic districts, which, together with the support of the Water Street merchants, would have given him the prime ministership. Cashin even moved a successful vote of non-confidence in his own government, after which Governor Sir Charles Alexander Harris (1917–22) called upon him to form a new administration, which included former Liberal Albert Hickman, former FPU John Stone, and Alfred Morine.[129] Richard Squires, a protégé of Morris, had left the National Government in the final year of the war and, in August 1919, launched the Liberal Reform Party. He immediately forged an electoral alliance with Coaker.[130] They turned their attention to the Reids, who they claimed dominated the Cashin government, and to Morine and his constant scheming to promote Confederation.[131] They warned that the Reids were Confederates out of pure financial self-interest, not out of principle or interest in creating a better life for ordinary Newfoundlanders. They embraced Newfoundland nationalism, claiming that the Squires party consisted of a "body of young, enthusiastic Newfoundlanders who are prepared to go 'Over the Top,' and 'Do their bit' for the country in which they live, just as our fellow-countrymen, the boys of khaki and blue did their bit on field and flood for Homeland and Empire."[132] In contrast, Cashin promised voters sound management of the dominion's finances and its natural resources, and he made a point of reminding voters that in 1916 Coaker had visited Ottawa to "sell" the country to Canada.[133] Cashin also accused Squires of being in the pocket of William Reid, highlighting Coaker's charges from 1918 that Squires, as minister of justice, had received money from Reid.[134] The general election was held on November 3, 1919. The Liberal Reform Party, an alliance between the Liberals led by Richard Squires and the Fishermen's Protective Union of William Coaker, formed the government, having won twenty-four of the thirty-six seats. The People's Party, with twelve elected members, became the Liberal-Labour-Progressive Party following the election and formed the Opposition. Squires served as Newfoundland prime minister, and Coaker became marine and fisheries minister.

Coaker was now in a strong position to impose order and regulate Newfoundland's chaotic fisheries industry and to address the pressing problems that he felt threatened the fisheries and Newfoundland society more generally. But the wartime prosperity in the fishery soon evaporated, as the Scandinavian countries returned to the European markets. Moreover, Western governments imposed tighter restrictions on currencies and their banking systems in the face of a growing shortage of foreign currency. In September 1918, the Italian government sought to deal with its currency shortages, particularly in fish buying, by creating a monopoly popularly known as the Consorzio. Coaker acted swiftly to bring order to the chaos in the marketing of fish, and he issued a series of proclamations under the *War Measures Act* to regulate the marketing of fish exports, whereby minimum prices were set for each major market, and exporters were threatened with the loss of their licences for breaching the regulations. English fish broker George Hawes, who represented several large Water Street fish exporters, was retained to negotiate with the Consorzio, and the Newfoundland government established an advisory board for consultations regarding the fish trade. It also allowed for the setting of a price that exporters would demand, which could fluctuate upward or downward according to the supplies on hand and individual market conditions. The policy was a success for the 1919 season, and Coaker was applauded by the Board of Trade for his initiative.[135] Subsequently, Coaker introduced a legislative program that embodied most of those measures. The 1920 *Codfish Standardization Act* provided for a commission to regulate all aspects of catching, processing, culling, warehousing, and transporting fish with a goal of improving the quality of the Newfoundland product, increasing its value, and providing for higher incomes for fishermen. These various measures, known popularly as the "Coaker Regulations," were a progressive and economic means to provide for a viable fishery. Most of the exporters and fishermen were supportive, but there was hostility from the Canadian banks with their restrictive tight monetary policy, certain powerful merchants worried about a credit squeeze, and a few politicians.[136]

There was no postwar boom in Newfoundland. Like Canada and other Allied nations, the Dominion of Newfoundland faced economic difficulties following the Great War. With a depression in trade and decreased demand for Newfoundland codfish, the unemployed of St. John's protested their grave situation, and once again, Confederation emerged as a potential solution to Newfoundland's lingering economic problems. The plight of the large number of unemployed was evident in the spring and summer of 1922, when emigration from the outports surged. Indeed, in May, the Red Cross passenger liner *Rosalind*, which sailed regularly between New York, Halifax, and St. John's, experienced its largest boarding of passengers on a single day in the company's history: over 250 passengers embarked in St. John's hoping to find work in Canada or the United States. The *Free Press* observed that the "exodus" had assumed "serious proportions," as "by train and steamer men and women are leaving at every opportunity."[137] The *Daily News* of December 31, 1921, had earlier quoted former prime minister Robert Bond saying that it was "necessary, I submit, to do a 'stock taking,' to the preparation of a correct balance sheet so that we may know whether our Country is solvent or insolvent."[138]

Nevertheless, Coaker wanted no part of Confederation as a possible solution. Speaking to the annual convention of the Fishermen's Protective Union that December, he lamented that some of his countrymen had come to see joining Confederation as the solution to Newfoundland's current economic problems:

CHAPTER 3

> I cannot see how Union with Canada can benefit Newfoundland.... Canada's economic position is today even worse than ours; she will not purchase fish, oil, paper or pulpwood from us, because she possesses them in abundance. She does not require our lumber or minerals, except iron ore used at Sydney Steel plant. She competes with us in the fish market. She has no spare capital to develop our natural resources.... What is to be gained by political union with Canada under such circumstances?

Coaker bemoaned the attitude of those Newfoundlanders who were too often "prone to ally [sic] our anxieties by the belief that we can always fall back on union with Canada." He called on FPU members and fellow Newfoundlanders to "fight out our own battles, and resolve that we can build up a country that will maintain a population of a million and will develop our dormant resources." The FPU's daily newspaper, the *Evening Advocate*, declared that the country now knew exactly where William Coaker stood on the matter; he had put himself on an "undeniable record as being an anti-Confederate." Coaker's stand "kills forever the hope of those spineless Newfoundlanders whose eyes seem to be eternally gazing toward Canada," the article concluded.[139]

Like earlier Newfoundland politicians, Coaker believed that industrial development was necessary if the country was to succeed. Unlike many of them, however, he believed that the development of Newfoundland's land-based resources had to be pursued together with fisheries reform. Such diversification was to supplement the fisheries and provide an outlet for the Island's growing number of unemployed and, hence, reduce the rising cost of relief expenditures. After the failure of his cherished fisheries regulations, Coaker was kept from quitting politics by his enthusiasm for a new pulp and paper project being proposed by the Reids. Since 1915, they had been attempting to secure financial backers to build a paper mill on the Humber River in western Newfoundland, where they held extensive timber and power concessions. After several unsuccessful attempts, Coaker and Attorney General William Warren remained steadfast in their support of the project, believing that it was better to expend money on industrial development to create employment than to raise large loans simply for relief. Both ministers were prepared to recommend that the government should, if necessary, support the Reids with financial guarantees of $15 million if they decided to go it alone with the Humber project. By 1922, the Reids and a British firm, Armstrong Whitworth, had put together a new proposal projected to cost £4 million, with the loan guarantees backed equally by the British and Newfoundland governments. With a general election pending in 1923, the Humber proposal, with its promise of hundreds of jobs and the influx of millions of dollars into the local economy, was an attractive symbol of industrial progress. The Reids, however, made their participation in the project dependent on the Newfoundland government buying their money-losing railway. In June 1920, the Reids had threatened its closure unless the government immediately offered financial assistance. Faced with a shutdown of the railway, the Squires government arranged a loan of $1.5 million for capital expenditures and agreed to assume any losses over the amount of $100,000 on operating expenses for a one-year period. Following a report by R.C. Morgan, a Canadian railway consultant, the government appointed a public board to supervise the Reid Newfoundland Company's running of the railway for another year. In April 1922, the Reids' request for further assistance from the Newfoundland government was refused, and the following month the railway suspended operations for a week. In July, the government of Newfoundland bought the railway, the dock in St. John's, and Reid's steamships for a total of $2 million—after having earlier in the year given its approval of a guarantee for the Humber development. On May 2, 1923, Squires went to the electorate yet again, this time seeking public support for his plans on the Humber River.[140]

With the public debt mounting, the financial situation for Newfoundland was rapidly becoming untenable. This time, Newfoundland turned to Canada—not for union but with the offer of Labrador for the price of the country's national debt. If such an arrangement could be had, Coaker told FPU members in a private circular dated February 9, 1923, "our taxation would be reduced $3,000,000 yearly as that is the interest paid yearly on our public debt. This is the God send that we should seek, [and] if accomplished Newfoundland's taxation would not be more than it was in 1910." Any transfer, of course, would not interfere with Newfoundlanders' fishing rights on the Labrador coast.[141] Governor William Lamond Allardyce (1922–28) considered the remark, "to say the least, injudicious" as a general election was due soon. The Opposition

CHAPTER 3

View of the town of Corner Brook and the Corner Brook Pulp and Paper Mill, late 1920s. The mill opened in 1925 as the Newfoundland Power and Paper Company, owned by the Reid Newfoundland Company and other financial backers, but was later purchased by the New York–based International Power and Paper Company.

vigorously denounced the "Coaker Plan" for selling Labrador.[142] On the hustings, William J. Higgins, long-serving St. John's member of the House of Assembly, noted the difference between earlier talk of Confederation and the selling of Labrador to Canada. "In years past the Confederation issue was brought up periodically at election times," he told supporters at a rally on April 3, 1923, but it was "looked upon more as a bugaboo, or an election kite. Now it has taken a different change." Since 1869, when the electorate rejected a government on the Confederation issue, "our motto was Newfoundland for Newfoundlanders," said Higgins. "No Government or party since that time had the audacity or brazenness to undertake that policy again, until Coaker and Squires got control, and then they brazenly announce what is the first step towards Confederation." The Newfoundland government's consideration to sell Labrador was seen as a great betrayal, especially as it was being considered "without the voice of the people being consulted." Higgins wondered if such discussion on Labrador would result in joining Confederation and reminded voters of the case of Nova Scotians—who woke up one morning and found they had been "sold into Confederation with Canada."[143] William Smith (1859–1932), historian and deputy archivist at the Public Archives of Canada who had been in St. John's a few months earlier collecting material on the Labrador boundary dispute, wrote W.S. Fielding, Laurier's minister of finance, that "the feeling as regards Confederation is not more favourable than it ever was." He also confirmed what many in Ottawa suspected: "When it is desired to stigmatize a man as unworthy of any confidence, he is called a confederationist." Yet, he reminded Fielding, there was reason to be optimistic about the prospects of union, and "the admission is freely made that they [Newfoundlanders] may be compelled to seek terms with Canada, and, while they are still jealous of their independence, I do not think the old bitterness against Canada exists, and they look at the prospect [of union] with more equanimity than they did."[144]

The Liberal-Labour-Progressive members joined to become the conservative (Tory) Opposition and were led into the 1923 general election by John R. Bennett, a former Morris associate.[145] The Tories criticized the Squires government for policies that in the past three years had "dragged down this country from the heights of prosperity to the depths of adversity and reduced our people from a state of comfort and contentment to one of abject misery and utter distress." They warned that Newfoundland, which "four years ago was comparatively independent," was now on the "verge of insolvency, and a people then reasonably prosperous and happy are now looking wide-spread destitution in the face." The Opposition took direct aim at the public debt, which stood at $60 million or $240 per person. Servicing the debt amounted to more than $3 million per year or nearly $15 per capita. "About one-third of the whole earnings of the people must be sent out of the Colony every year to pay interest upon the public debt alone," it charged. The money, claimed Bennett, had been spent on works of "no general public benefit or reproductive value, or else to paying off large annual deficits on the railway and on the current accounts. It has been expended upon a scale of unbridled extravagance, the main object being political corruption, which there has been no attempt to conceal." Bennett promised "our utmost to save the country from the catastrophe towards which the present Government has sent it speeding."[146] But rhetoric did not, however, convince voters. The Squires-Coaker Liberal Reform Party won the election with twenty-three of the thirty-six seats. The Opposition captured but thirteen seats, all in predominantly Catholic areas.

Squires would not long remain as prime minister. Within weeks of his re-election, he resigned amid allegations that he had misappropriated public funds for electioneering purposes. William Robertson Warren took over as prime minister (July 1923–May 1924), and with the support of the Dominions Office, British barrister Thomas Hollis Walker was appointed to examine public expenditures in several departments. In his report, Hollis Walker cited examples of "gross mismanagement," noting that "relief was provided at prodigious cost, far in excess of what was necessary," and "politicians exploited the situation and improperly scattered public money to further their political aims."[147] The Warren government had Squires arrested on April 22, 1924, on charges of larceny, which two days later prompted a vote of non-confidence in the government, which Warren lost. A new election was to be held on June 2. Meanwhile, on May 3, Warren formed a new Cabinet consisting mainly of Opposition members, including its leader, William J. Higgins, former leader John Bennett, and only one of his own former members, Matthew Hawco. When Hawco withdrew his support for Warren, the prime minister resigned, and Albert Hickman (May 10–June 24, 1924) formed a new government from members of the Liberal Reform Party that had previously been led by Richard Squires. William Coaker decided not to run in 1924.[148] Businessman H.R. Brookes, perhaps not surprisingly given the state of local politics, wrote in a local monthly trade magazine, "The outstanding feature of the present situation is the terrible dearth of political leaders. In past years Newfoundland has had great leaders on both sides of party strife."[149] He could have added *but not anymore*.

In a March 20, 1924, lecture to the Methodist College Literary Institute (MCLI), Alfred Morine echoed similar concerns: "Government of the Colony since 1917 has been composed of discordant elements, having no common platform, and no centralized leadership. It has not had independent supporters in the Assembly to check it, nor competent criticism to warn it. I am persuaded that much we deplore in the conduct of public affairs since 1919 is due to absence of team work." Morine's outlook was dire: democracy, he wrote, "has failed to justify its existence" in Newfoundland. He then called for the substitution of self-government by an autocracy, a "government by an overlord, in which the governed people should have no voice." It was not a failure of a governing system, Morine lamented, but "it is the people who have failed, their representatives who have failed, to maintain the integrity of our system as by law established, and have created in its stead an odious and incapable autocracy, contrary to the spirit of our laws."[150]

The future most certainly did not look promising, but Joseph R. Smallwood believed that things could be different with a "new" Liberal Party. In 1926, the twenty-five-year-old Smallwood set out his plans in an extensive political manifesto in the St. John's *Globe* to revive the Liberal Party, which he believed should be the great friend of labour. Smallwood had earlier worked as a socialist journalist on newspapers in New York and had been active with the Socialist Party of America. One of the staff members with the union-operated Rand School of Social Science in New York remembered Smallwood as someone "not interested in socialism as a means to an end in itself, but as something that might be good for Newfoundland." He was well acquainted with Christian socialist and liberal thinking then current in American and British circles and in the British press, as were many others in St. John's. Smallwood then identified as a "working class activist," and his plan for the Liberal Party revival covered a wide range of issues from Newfoundland's pressing financial situation to education reform. One item that stands out, especially in light of his later campaign for Confederation, was his commitment to social reform. He claimed that liberalism's greatest feature was its championing of social reform, which he described as "a general attempt to reform and abolish the evil conditions under which the masses of the people are compelled to live." The rights and interests of people, he wrote, had to be protected by the state against the "greed of greedy employers." These were embryonic ideas in the mid-1920s, but they were ones that Smallwood would promote aggressively in his campaign for union with Canada some two decades hence.[151] In the meantime, the Newfoundland government had other issues to deal with.

CHAPTER 3

Joseph R. Smallwood in 1921 with Camilla Coaker, daughter of William Coaker, and Nellie Clouter. Smallwood was then a journalist.

MORE DISSATISFACTION WITH CANADA: SUBSIDIES AND LABRADOR

One of them came with the nationalization of the Newfoundland Railway in 1923, as it raised questions in Canada about the subsidy it had provided to the Reids to maintain a daily steamship service between Port aux Basques and North Sydney. The steamship subsidy had been an important part of the diplomatic contact between Newfoundland and Canada for more than three decades. In 1892, Ottawa had provided its first subsidy to promote steamship service between Canada and Newfoundland. By 1906, it was supporting the Port aux Basques–North Sydney route with a $20,000 subsidy to the Reid Railway. In 1911, Newfoundland's prime minister at the time, Edward Morris, convinced Laurier to raise the subsidy to $35,000 per vessel, and by 1914, the Reid Railway Company was collecting $65,000 from Ottawa for the Cabot Strait ferries. In 1923—after the Newfoundland government took over the railway—some members of Parliament, including Prime Minister Mackenzie King and his minister of trade and commerce, Thomas

Andrew Low, began asking whether Canada should continue providing the subsidy. The following year, the steamship subsidy was no more.[152] As Low told the House of Commons: "We found that the Newfoundland government had taken over the service and on account of that ... we decline to continue" the subsidy.[153] He added, "We paid a subsidy when the service was under private ownership, but when the government took it over we dropped the subsidy feeling that it was not proper to pay a subsidy to another government."[154]

Newfoundland was both disappointed and angry with Ottawa's decision. It lobbied immediately, and for many years thereafter, to have the subsidy restored. Indeed, the "subsidy became the most important dispute in Newfoundland's relations with Canada after the Labrador boundary was settled in 1927."[155] At one point, Newfoundland's Colonial Secretary John R. Bennett attempted to play the American card to force Ottawa's hand, warning Low that much of Canada's trade with Newfoundland, which had been shipped through Port aux Basques, might be lost to the United States if a regular St. John's–New York service were established. Bennett added, "We really think it would be to the advantage of Canada to assist us in making the route to North Sydney as popular and as profitable as possible, and the payment of a yearly subsidy by your Government will certainly give us heart and assist in the provision of a better service." Moreover, Bennett reminded Low throughout 1925 and 1926 that the Railway Commission in Newfoundland operated the railway and steamship service not as a regular department but at arm's length from the government, clearly addressing Low's concern that the ferry was operated by the government. "At the present time," he wrote to Low on January 30, 1926,

> the Government are paying to the Management [of the Newfoundland Railway], the subsidies and Post[al] Grant exactly as during the time the road was leased to the Reids, and a strong endeavour is being made to make ends meet, and to keep the proposition on a commercial basis. Under these circumstances you will appreciate that the loss of the subsidy granted by Canada to the Straits Steamer, is an important matter, and in view of the larger boat, and the greater expense, the $35,000 means that much more.

CHAPTER 3

Moreover, he pointed out, both Canada and Newfoundland benefitted from the Port aux Basques–North Sydney ferry service, and "I really think that the amount of the subsidy is a small sum, as compared to the advantage that Canada will reap from this connection."[156]

In 1926, when James Malcolm, an Ontario MP, replaced Low as minister of trade and commerce, Bennett reminded him immediately of the subsidy. He pointed to the increase in trade between the two countries and to the fact that "the Canadian Government gives no subsidy whatever to the steamer plying between North Sydney and Port aux Basques." Bennett was clearly frustrated with Canada's refusal to reinstate the subsidy, as Newfoundland was bearing the full cost of the operation of the ferry: "As the vessel is performing work that is a benefit both to Canada and to Newfoundland, I submit that this ship deserves a subsidy from the Canadian Government." He reminded Minister Malcolm that Canada had eliminated the subsidy in "the time of stringency" but asked "if it would not be possible to arrange for the Vote of $35,000 to be paid to the S.S. *Caribou* in respect to the services which she is carrying out. Your subsidy at one time," he wrote, "was $70,000 per annum, there being two steamers plying the trade. There is now a larger and a better boat for which we would ask the subsidy of $35,000 per annum. Might I bespeak your favourable consideration of this matter?" Bennett dispatched Herbert J. Russell, the general manager of the Newfoundland Railway, to deliver his letter to Malcolm. The minister replied that if Newfoundland and Canada could complete a trade arrangement, he would be prepared to recommend to Cabinet that it provide a subsidy of $35,000 to the operation of the SS *Caribou*.[157] However, the government of Newfoundland rejected the proposal from Ottawa, because the revisions to the tariff that Canada sought would have cost Newfoundland more in lost customs duties than it would have received in the subsidy. The issue did nothing to build goodwill between the two countries.

The one bright spot for Newfoundland was its victory over Canada in the Labrador boundary dispute. The question of precisely where in Labrador lay the boundary between Newfoundland and Canada was first raised in 1888 by Newfoundland Supreme Court Judge Robert Pinsent. Once raised, however, this issue would take more than three decades to be resolved. Judge Pinsent had worried that the uncertainty over Newfoundland's jurisdiction in Labrador raised a problem of "practical and essential significance." Under the letters patent dated March 28, 1876, Pinsent stated that Newfoundland's jurisdiction in Labrador was "all the coast of Labrador, from the entrance of the Hudson's straits (Cape Chidley) to a line to be drawn due north and south from Anse Sablon, on the said coast, to the 52nd degree of north latitude, and all the islands adjacent to that part of the said coast of Labrador."[158] Pinsent wanted the British government to provide a clear definition of Newfoundland's relationship to Labrador, leaving "no doubt as to the jurisdiction of its Courts and authority of legal officers." The boundary matter came up in an 1892 conference held in Halifax between Canada and Newfoundland, and it was decided that each would appoint a geographer to consider all material concerning the boundary and report to their respective governments.[159] Neither Newfoundland nor Canada at the time acknowledged that under the Royal Proclamation of 1763 most of the disputed area had been designated "Indian Territories."[160]

Nothing came out of this suggested initiative, and the matter remained dormant until 1902 when the government of Quebec contested the legal right of a Nova Scotian timber speculator, Alfred Dickie, to develop timber reserves in the Hamilton Inlet area under licence from the Newfoundland government.[161] Quebec protested, claiming that federal legislation in 1898, which extended its provincial boundary, gave it control over Labrador.[162] When Dickie appealed to Newfoundland for help in his defence before a Quebec court, Premier Robert Bond responded favourably. The case was never tried, as the Quebec and Canadian governments decided to seek a referral to the Judicial Committee of the Privy Council (JCPC) in London, and Newfoundland agreed to do so in 1907.[163] As we can see, the issue moved slowly, and in February 1914, Prime Minister Morris updated the House of Assembly, saying his government had been negotiating with Ottawa the terms of reference to be submitted to the Privy Council. "We have put forward what we are told is the correct question," said Morris, but the Canadian government refused the "proper question," which was "What is the boundary between the two countries?" The Canadians, he concluded, "wish us to agree to ask the Tribunal to find a boundary; in other words, to make or draw a boundary. We believe we have a good case."[164] The outbreak of the Great War, however, prompted further delay, although Quebec did attempt to find a resolution during the war.[165]

By November 1920, the two sides had worked out the question to be presented to the JCPC. Attorney General of Canada Charles J. Doherty and Attorney General of Newfoundland William R. Warren agreed to the following: "What is the location and definition of the Boundary as between Canada and Newfoundland in the Labrador Peninsula, under the Statutes, Orders in Council and Proclamations?" The agreement was further amended two years later, when both governments agreed to present a petition to His Majesty, "praying him to refer the said matter to the said Judicial Committee to hear and consider the same and to advise His Majesty thereon."[166] Although Newfoundland and Canada had researchers building their legal arguments, they also sought to settle the dispute through informal negotiations. In November 1922, Warren visited Quebec City to discuss the matter with Premier Louis-Alexandre Taschereau. "While I have laid the seeds of a settlement," he wrote to journalist P.T. McGrath, Newfoundland's historical researcher on the case, "nothing can be done unless Squires is here & there will have to be considerable negotiation. Please regard all this as confidential and between you and me." Warren laid down three principles for a settlement. The first was "free and open fishing" for all Newfoundlanders on the Labrador coast and "no duty to be levied on goods going there for fishing from Nfld. and no taxation on Newfoundlanders of any sort." Taschereau and Quebec Deputy Attorney General Charles Lanctôt agreed to this. The second principle, that all those having titles in Labrador from Newfoundland authorities be given the same from Quebec, was also acceptable. The third principle, that Quebec "take over" the Newfoundland national debt "staggered them" so much that "Taschereau nearly fell off his chair." The parties continued the conversation and "finally agreed that we had made progress, and that it was more or less a question of [what] amount [was to be paid to Newfoundland in exchange for Labrador] and what the Federal Government would do." Later, Warren admitted to Taschereau, "I was merely breaking the ground."[167] Apparently, Newfoundland wanted $50 million, but Warren told Prime Minister Squires that "personally I think if we get $25,000,000 we shall be well out of it."[168]

Matters remained in abeyance until another effort was made in 1924. It came via McGrath, who reported that he had encountered Lanctôt on a voyage from London, who had told him there was a strong sentiment among members of the Quebec government to settle the dispute with a cash purchase. They were "quite willing that every safeguard desired by Newfoundland in regard to her fishery interests would be agreed to." He added though "that Canada could not afford to pay a large 'indemnity' for the territory." Premier Taschereau and Lanctôt were anxious for a settlement and were willing to visit Newfoundland during the summer of 1924 "to discuss the question of purchase in all its details."[169] Quebec even attempted to settle the matter without the knowledge of the federal government in late November 1924 when Canadian timber speculator Joseph de Champlain intervened on behalf of Premier Taschereau.[170] In the meantime, there had been a general election in Newfoundland on June 2, and Premier Taschereau invited the new prime minister, Walter Stanley Monroe (1924–28), to send a delegation to Quebec. The St. John's *Evening Telegram* reported that the delegation had no authority to finalize matters, but only to gather information to put before the full Cabinet for discussion and approval, and the public were assured that the government entertained no consideration of selling Labrador to Quebec.[171] Monroe and Taschereau agreed on protections for Newfoundland fishermen along the Labrador coast, but the question of money remained.[172] The "difficulty lies in the question of the price to be paid to Newfoundland," Taschereau later wrote Monroe. He continued, "I would therefore suggest that even in a very confidential way, you might inform me of the minimum amount which you would ask. And, if we agree on this, I believe that the other difficulties may be overcome." Monroe wanted $30 million but told Taschereau his government colleagues felt that "unless the price was a big one," they could not bring a proposition before the legislature conceding the sovereignty of the coast to Canada.[173] By March 4, 1925, Monroe offered a compromise. Newfoundland would accept $15 million for all its "rights, title and interest whatsoever to Labrador" but retain an exclusive right to use the area within three miles of the high-water mark. It was too much. Quebec informed Ottawa that, as future negotiations would not likely result in an agreement, it was recommending that the boundary question be left to a decision of the Privy Council. The federal government concurred, and that July a joint petition was sent to the Privy Council.[174]

Almost two years later, on March 1, 1927, Viscount Cave handed down the report of the JCPC on the question of Labrador, deciding in Newfoundland's favour.[175] One St. John's newspaper regarded March 1, 1927, henceforth as one of "Newfoundland's Red letter Days [if] for no other reason than it marks the ending of a thirty years' dispute, and two decades of uncertainty which have done much to retard development and to cause capitalists to remain aloof" in Labrador.[176] The Privy Council report was widely heralded as a great victory for Newfoundland. McGrath emphasized the future economic value Labrador had to Newfoundland, especially the enormous hydroelectric potential of Labrador's inland. Expatriate Newfoundlanders in Boston immediately celebrated that "Newfoundland has at last come into her own," and imagined the verdict being "hailed with satisfaction by every Newfoundlander."[177] The Canadian reaction was carried extensively in the local press, especially the disappointment in Quebec over the decision, which sowed the seeds for future disharmony between Newfoundland and Quebec.[178] Given the long-standing impression among Newfoundlanders that the Dominion of Canada's interests had always prevailed over theirs, they were delighted with the 1927 decision on the boundary of Labrador. Newfoundland had won a major legal battle against Canada, although the JCPC decision gave Canadians one more reason to pursue union with Newfoundland.

CHAPTER 4

DESPAIR, GOVERNMENT BY COMMISSION, AND A SLOW REBUILD, 1928–1941

Q UEBEC EXPRESSED GREAT DISSATISFACTION AND anger with the British Law Lords' decision on Labrador, but emotions in Newfoundland were more muted. Even with Labrador's huge potential, many people in Newfoundland were finding that the dream of industrial development and prosperity through exploitation of new natural resources that they had hoped for since 1869 was proving quite elusive. Even with the opening of a new mine at Buchans in 1928 and the promise of a third pulp and paper mill on the Gander River, prosperity still seemed a long way off. Signs of serious trouble for the country might have tempered any jubilation over finally, unequivocally winning Labrador. Despite decades of promoting economic diversification, Newfoundland still had the fishery as the mainstay of its economy and its largest employer. The fishery accounted for $16 million of the country's $22 million export trade, and like exports everywhere else, this sector would collapse in the early 1930s. Since 1920, the government had been running annual deficits to finance its obligations. Doing so for capital expenditures was nothing extraordinary, of course. Borrowing, however, to repay maturing loans and to finance relief was neither a good omen nor a sound way to manage the affairs of state. Meanwhile, the world economy had recovered significantly from the recession immediately after the Great War, and modern technology had vastly improved the livelihood of the urban middle class and of most workers everywhere. In 1928, the Newfoundland government raised $10 million to retire a $7.5 million war loan and to cover public spending. The following year, $6 million more was borrowed to redeem a 1905 loan. This practice continued, and in 1930, the country returned to the credit market for another $5 million for similar purposes.[1]

The dominion seemed to be racing towards the financial precipice, a state of affairs closely watched by the St. John's Methodist College Literary Institute, the city's premier debating club. So concerned was it with the mounting public debt that on March 3, 1927, the MCLI debated whether Newfoundland had borrowed beyond its means, and if so, how much retrenchment was needed in public expenditures to keep the country solvent. The number of people fleeing Newfoundland in the late 1920s in search of employment and a better life elsewhere had reached new and historic levels, and this too was further evidence of the morass enveloping the country.[2] Many people were wondering if the source of the malaise was the lack of good governance and an inept system of party politics, which had been seriously discredited by the Squires scandal and the subsequent Hollis Walker Report that detailed the investigation of the fiscal mismanagement (see Chapter 3). The MCLI returned to the topic of political affairs again at its March 25, 1927, gathering and debated whether parliamentary governance and the party system—the very essence of being British and democratic—should be replaced by an elected non-partisan commission. William Coaker, the president and founder of the Fishermen's Protective Union, had popularized such a notion at the annual convention of the FPU at Port Union in December 1925.[3] Of course, the subject was a controversial one, and it could be argued that, like other controversial topics such as Confederation with Canada, it was debated simply as a hypothetical question for the amusement of the city's educated elite. Yet the hypothetical, like humour, is sometimes an undemanding way to reveal the truth. By all accounts, many people in Newfoundland believed that the country needed a rest from politics. Such discussions were an indication of the depth of despair hanging over Newfoundland.

CHAPTER 4

And as had happened previously, it was wondered if union with Canada was the best path forward.⁴ Few thought it was, but be that as it may, Canada would continue to extend its reach into Newfoundland's economy and society in the years ahead.

As leader of the cumbersomely named Liberal-Conservative Party, Walter Stanley Monroe was sworn in as prime minister in June 1924. Monroe promised to right the country's public finances. He failed, however, and was unable either to control the spiralling public debt or to bring honesty and efficiency to government. At the end of fiscal 1928, Newfoundland's debt stood at more than $77 million, compared with $43 million in 1920–21. Moreover, the Monroe government itself had contributed more than $16.5 million to that total.⁵ Monroe had found it impossible to curb the practice, initiated by Squires, of borrowing both to pay the interest on the national debt and to fund current expenditures. Nevertheless, some of the new loans did improve public services—such as the improvment of a dry dock at St. John's and expanded railway and marine services, including the purchase of the newly built ss *Caribou* (which served the Port aux Basques–North Sydney route that connected Newfoundland to Canada from 1928 to 1942).⁶ Average annual borrowing during Monroe's tenure (1924–28) approximated $4 million, but 40 percent of all government revenues went to meet interest payments on existing debt.⁷ Finance Minister John Crosbie had privately warned Monroe, in December 1926, that borrowing to make interest payments on Newfoundland's enormous debt had to be curtailed if bankruptcy was to be avoided. "My one thought since the 1919 general election," wrote Crosbie, was "that bankruptcy was before us."⁸ He had tried unsuccessfully to impose some restraint on public expenditures but was opposed at every turn.⁹ Political maverick Peter Cashin, for instance, had resigned from the government in 1925 after winning his father's old district of Ferryland to protest Crosbie's fiscal restraint, which had also included raising the tariff. Cashin charged that the measure "will bleed the people white." It was, moreover, "class legislation of the rankest kind," especially since the income tax "had been expunged" for the wealthy.¹⁰ The country had few options.

The uncertainty and divisions within the Monroe government—including a series of defections led by F. Gordon Bradley, who was already entertaining notions of Newfoundland joining Canada—provided an opportunity for the 1928 resurrection of disgraced former prime minister Richard Squires, who was now promising prosperity and what journalist Joseph R. Smallwood was calling the "New Newfoundland." Smallwood, working in Corner Brook as a journalist at the time, was a known opponent of Confederation with Canada, as he frequently reminded the local press, and he saw Newfoundland's future inextricably linked to industrialization, as had others for decades. Newfoundland was "upon a new march ... towards modern, large-scale industrialisation," he optimistically wrote, and the whole dominion was "industrial minded."[11] Bradley and others switched their loyalty to Squires, who, despite his earlier humiliation, was eager to return to active politics. Squires had been elected Grand Master of the Orange Order in July 1925, and by the end of that year he had tempted Coaker with another coalition,[12] a combination that Governor Sir William Lamond Allardyce observed "would seem to have considerable chance of winning the next election." In writing to Leo Amery, the secretary of state for dominion affairs, Allardyce lamented the current state of Newfoundland politics, noting that there was "no indication so far of any pronouncedly strong man of integrity and independent status emerging from the present situation. In Newfoundland," he added, "with few exceptions men enter politics for what they can make out of it," and none of the current lot "realize the gravity of the existing financial situation and care less." He did not see any way of enforcing any measure of retrenchment, as the "electorate have no wish for any such drastic measure."[13]

Before election day on October 29, 1928, Monroe had turned the government over to his cousin, businessman Frederick Alderdice (August 16–November 17, 1928).[14] Coaker had re-entered the fray, running successfully in Bonavista East.[15] Alderdice and his supporters had issued a "call to arms" to prevent the "election of the Coaker-Squires-Cashin outfit," which they pronounced would be "absolutely a national catastrophe." The choice, as they put it, was "Alderdice and Prosperity, and Sane and Safe Rule" or a "further period of mismanagement, and corruption of the worst possible kind." On March 9, 1925, the government extended the franchise to women twenty-five years of age and older and allowed them to stand for election (although men

CHAPTER 4

This photograph of the Women's Franchise League was taken c. 1920, probably in Carbonear. Standing second from left, Fannie McNeil; seated left, Agnes Ayre; seated right, Janet Ayre. Women won the right to vote in 1925.

needed only to reach the age of twenty-one to vote); Monroe's party then campaigned for the women's vote, citing Squires's dismissive attitude towards women in the early 1920s, when they had initially sought the franchise, as well as his terrible record as prime minister.[16] Squires attempted to rekindle the dream of industrialization and reminded voters that he had put the "Hum on the Humber." He spoke of further industrial development should he be elected and avoided addressing the Hollis Walker Report's findings of mismanagement. He circulated a gramophone recording, made in New York, giving an inspirational message that included a litany of promises lampooned by his critics as the "Gramophone Manifesto."[17] Squires's approach to the campaign was reflected in a telegram to Liberal candidate Ken Brown in

Twillingate District: "Lay aside every weight and the annoyances of misrepresentation and abuse which so easily discomfort us and run with patience toward the price of the high calling of Statesmanship."[18] It worked. Squires won twenty-eight of the forty seats. Ninety percent of eligible women (52,343 voters) turned out to cast a ballot—and they probably propelled Squires to victory.

Newly re-elected Prime Minister Richard Squires (1928–32) would shortly have to confront the worst global economic downturn in the history of humankind. Newfoundland's exports, like those the world over, collapsed. Total exports for its primary products of fish, pulp and paper, and minerals fell in value from $40 million in 1930 to $26.6 million two years later; fisheries exports declined from nearly $17 million in fiscal 1928 to $6.3 million in fiscal 1932.[19] Finance Minister Peter Cashin spoke "frankly" in his 1929 budget speech of putting "all my cards on the table." The country had been "living in a fool's paradise," he admonished, and people had to realize the dire financial conditions they faced as a country. For too long, people had been told that "money can be found for every purpose and that the Government exists solely to spend money here, there [and] everywhere, without any thought of where the money is to be got or how it is to be repaid." The Liberals promised a balanced budget by 1931 and asked all Newfoundlanders "to stand behind us in the endeavour to restore the country's financial stability." The Dominion of Newfoundland had to break its bad habits, reorganize, reconstruct, and pursue industrial development.[20] Despite his earlier protests against restraint, Squires imposed an income tax on residents and revised upward the existing schedule of customs duties.[21] Borrowing was kept at $6 million to provide for public works, fisheries development, and railway reconstruction and to cover the railway operating deficits—which, alone, accounted for half the amount of the loan. Retrenchment became the new normal.[22]

None of this worked. Support for Squires quickly eroded. Coaker, the former FPU leader who had promised social and economic change to fishermen nearly two decades earlier, was happy with none of what he was seeing, and he was soon in open revolt against his prime minister's management of the country's affairs. In his 1930 New Year's message to members of the Fishermen's Protective Union, Coaker renewed his call for an elected commission of six men to govern the country for ten years

CHAPTER 4

Prime Minister Richard Squires and his wife Lady Helena Squires in Italy, 1921.

as, in the words of one historian, "Newfoundland politics were in need of purification."[23] "There is, in my opinion," wrote Coaker, "no hope of essential change by changing a Liberal Administration for a Tory. Each new administration is a little bit worse than its predecessor."[24] Coaker had retired from the presidency of the FPU in 1926, and it was clear to him that the FPU legacy had not been great: its political influence was minimal and its support among fishermen was declining. The only solution to the social and economic turmoil facing the country, he believed, was a Commission of Government,[25] similar to the National Government he had joined during the Great War.[26] Nor did Squires get any support from the two major St. John's dailies: both the *Daily News* and the *Evening Telegram* had been his fiercest critics since 1919. By late 1930, Squires was looking to escape the difficult situation brought by the Great Depression. He even attempted to sound out the possibility of following his mentor, E.P. Morris, who had been Newfoundland's prime minister for much of the Great War but had abandoned the country as the wartime situation deteriorated. Morris was elevated to the House of Lords as Baron Morris in 1918, but when Squires sought a similar path to a baronetcy while visiting London for the Imperial Conference in December 1930, nothing came of his efforts.[27]

LABRADOR FOR SALE, AGAIN

As the difficulties mounted in Newfoundland, union with Canada and the sale of Labrador emerged once more as policy options for the dominion. These two issues had never gone away, not even after the 1927 decision by the Judicial Committee of the Privy Council to award Labrador to Newfoundland and earlier failed attempts at union. In fact, when Albert Hickman attempted to hold on as Liberal leader after Squires made it known that he wanted his old job back, he did so by emphasizing his opposition to Confederation and by reaffirming his loyalty to an independent Newfoundland.[28] His anti-Confederate stance had also been precipitated by a resolution in the Canadian Senate urging Canada to purchase Labrador, after which the *Montreal Star* reported that exploratory talks between Canadian and Newfoundland officials were to be held on March 22, 1928. Prime Minister Monroe had unequivocally denied such claims at the time, insisting that the matter had never been considered by his government and had certainly not been discussed with Canadian officials.[29] Hickman expressed to the *Evening Telegram* his opposition to Confederation, as he had "every hope for the future of our country," and he insisted that if the government were "properly handled," Newfoundlanders could be "the happiest in the world."[30] One press report noted that Confederation was a subject that has "been revived more or less at every election since the battle of 1869."[31] The *Evening Telegram*, however, blamed Canada's manipulation of the media for the revival of interest in Labrador, noting that the "Canadian press has been used to set a baseless rumour afloat with the hope that it may influence local political opinion."[32]

But it was more than a rumour. Just before the 1928 election, Quebec businessman Joseph de Champlain, who held vast timber rights in Labrador, had in fact been authorized by the Newfoundland government to enter into negotiations with Canada for the sale of Labrador. Minister of Justice Ernest Lapointe had suggested to Alderdice (Newfoundland's prime minister at the time) that Newfoundland take up the matter of selling Labrador with the Canadian government directly rather than through de Champlain. Alderdice agreed, and he suggested a conference on the matter "at any time suitable to your Government," provided that Newfoundland's fishing rights on the coast

CHAPTER 4

were protected.³³ The Alderdice government had reportedly sought $100 million for Labrador; before the matter could be pursued, however, Alderdice was defeated in the general election.³⁴

Shortly after Squires became prime minister, the matter surfaced once more. He asked de Champlain to explore options for the sale of Labrador to Canada, but when word of the discussions leaked out, he denied having engaged in any talks about Labrador. Squires insisted that his government wished to have Labrador developed under the British flag—an obvious admonition directed at the predominantly French-speaking province—and that he hoped to secure British and American capital to do so. Quebec premier Louis-Alexandre Taschereau also denied involvement in any plans for Labrador, but the *Daily News* reminded readers that in 1925 Taschereau had similarly denied that de Champlain had been involved in negotiations over Labrador on his behalf with Monroe. It was also claimed that Colonial Secretary Arthur Barnes had asked de Champlain to explore the possibility of launching negotiations separately with Quebec.³⁵

In 1931, Squires led an unofficial delegation made up of himself, Peter Cashin, and Harris M. Mosdell, minister without portfolio, to Ottawa to discuss the potential sale of Labrador with Prime Minister R.B. Bennett. Although Squires was unable to attend the September 25 meeting as planned, Bennett agreed to submit the matter to his Cabinet to determine whether Canada was interested in initiating more official talks. Indeed it was; in St. John's, the Squires Cabinet also agreed. An official delegation consisting of Squires, Cashin, Mosdell, Coaker, and Barnes was authorized by Cabinet to begin formal negotiations with Canada. Labrador would not be disposed of cheaply, however, as Squires hoped to use the proceeds from any sale of the vast territory to eliminate Newfoundland's debt. He asked Prime Minister Bennett on October 7 for a purchase price large enough to retire Newfoundland's debt of approximately $87 million, plus an additional $13 million at the end of successful negotiations, bringing the total ask to $100 million. Moreover, the request included the stipulation that Canada deposit $10 million in trust with a chartered bank in Montreal to settle any dispute that might arise from Newfoundland's issuing of timber licences in Labrador. Newfoundland also wanted all rights and privileges of its fishermen recognized and preserved in perpetuity by the Government of Canada. Once all conditions were met, Newfoundland would pass legislation giving Canada clear legal title to Labrador. But the price was too much for Bennett and his Cabinet. "Under present economic and financial conditions," he wrote Squires a week later, "it is not feasible for us to favourably consider your proposal." Bennett did not shut the door completely, suggesting that "probably under more favourable conditions we may be able to reconsider the situation."[36]

CANADA EXTENDS ITS INFLUENCE OVER NEWFOUNDLAND, 1931–1932

Despite the mounting fiscal and economic crisis shrouding the Dominion of Newfoundland during the late 1920s, much of it caused by the indebtedness of the Newfoundland Railway and the expenses incurred to participate in the Great War,[37] its government had found buyers for all debentures floated in the international markets. It had done so even though it had not established a sinking fund for the retirement of its debentures as they matured. Newfoundland's borrowing had become a severe crisis by 1931, resulting in financial oversight measures that the country found both limiting and embarrassing. The Canadian banks had long financed Newfoundland's borrowing, but they now refused to advance further credit—as Newfoundland's revenues dwindled and more of its borrowing went to servicing its debt. By early 1931, the national debt stood at approximately $100 million, and interest payments consumed 65 percent of current revenues.[38]

Squires petitioned the Canadian banks to reconsider their decision and to allow his government to meet its interest payments due on June 30, 1931. When the banks refused, Squires appealed to Prime Minister Bennett, who was wrestling with his own pending fiscal crisis, to intervene. The banks subsequently agreed to a temporary loan of $2 million to allow Newfoundland to meet its end-of-June obligations. This loan, however, came with several conditions. Newfoundland had to seek from Great Britain the appointment of a financial adviser to monitor and supervise its finances. As part of those external controls, the Canadian banks insisted that Newfoundland agree to a full investigation of its entire financial structure, implement further revisions to its customs duties and other sources of revenue to provide for a more substantial and sustainable income, and reorganize and better coordinate its various public services. The banks also demanded that Newfoundland accept the financial adviser's recommendations for strengthening its finances to allow for a balanced budget, the creation of a sinking fund for outstanding and future bond issues, and the establishment of a plan of long-term financing for short-term indebtedness. Squires had no option but to accept the conditions; he set out immediately for London to discuss the selection of a British expert.[39]

The Canadian banks were in no mood for further accommodation, however. Even once Newfoundland had appointed Sir Percy Thompson, deputy chairman of the Board of Inland Revenue in the United Kingdom, as financial adviser in August 1931,[40] and Canadian businessman Robert J. Magor to oversee reorganization of the railway, dry dock, telegraph system, and other public utilities, Squires was kept on a very short leash by the Canadian bankers. When he and Thompson met bank officials in Montreal at the end of September, they refused to advance any further short-term loans unless Thompson made an interim report by the middle of December, indicating how Newfoundland would move towards financial solvency. The interim report came on December 1, and Thompson's message was simple: increase revenues while continuing to impose reductions in public expenditures as the means of controlling the budgetary deficit. He urged an immediate reorganization of departments and stricter financial accounting controls. The Department of Finance, he recommended, must assume greater control over the daily expenditures of public funds through the creation of a British-style Treasury Board and impose administrative efficiencies in all departments. The government had to meet the interest payments due in January 1932 without further borrowing from the banks and balance the budget through increased taxation, which Thompson acknowledged would "impose a heavy strain on the community."[41] Even with further retrenchment, Governor John Middleton (1928–32) confided to the secretary of state for dominion affairs, James Henry Thomas, that they had no way to forecast the attitude of the Canadian banks to the changes, although he was hopeful that Newfoundland could remain solvent. After all, Thompson's retrenchment reforms and Magor's recommendations for public infrastructure reform had the support of Opposition leader Alderdice and leading members of his team.[42] Still, Governor Middleton was worried that the increasing difficulty faced by the Newfoundland Savings Bank, which had insufficient credit to guarantee Newfoundland government bonds already issued, might aggravate the situation, especially if local depositors withdrew their savings. The whole situation was further complicated by Newfoundland's dependency on the Canadian banks. By law, Newfoundland's legal tender was gold, but since 1894, the customary currency operating in the country had been the bank notes of the four major Canadian banks. These banks had an obligation in law to redeem their notes in gold and to pay depositors in gold, but with the depreciation in the value of the Canadian dollar, exporters in Newfoundland who made payments abroad were frustrated that they had to buy foreign currency with depreciated Canadian dollars instead of being allowed to obtain gold and ship it abroad for payment.[43]

Despite implementation of the financial and fiscal controls mandated by the Canadian banks, by the end of 1931, Newfoundland's inability to make its debt interest payments remained a real concern. Default was a prospect that neither the British nor Canadian government welcomed, as it threatened irreparable damage, they believed, to both the reputation and the credit rating of the whole British Empire. Prime Minister Bennett believed that if Newfoundland defaulted, it would be "very injurious to Canada."[44] With Squires, he again appealed to the Dominions Office for more assistance to Newfoundland. Bennett made it clear that his country's own financial commitments made it impossible for Canada to provide any further help.[45] The Canadian bankers came through one more time, however, and another conditional loan of $2 million was provided, but it came with the Squires government agreeing to even more stringent conditions imposed by the bankers. Newfoundland agreed again to balance its budget and make provisions for a sinking fund, but this time the Canadian controls went further. The banks insisted that the total proceeds collected from customs duties in Newfoundland be deposited daily into a special account at a bank to be nominated by the four Canadian banks. The special account could not be accessed by the Newfoundland government but was to be in the joint names of

CHAPTER 4

Sir Percy Thompson (the appointed financial adviser) and the comptroller of the Treasury. Each week, the revenue collected was to be placed in the consolidated revenue fund to maintain public services at the minimum scale necessary for their continued functioning. Any surplus funds were to go to the payment of interest on the public debt. Essentially, spending was removed from the control of the Newfoundland government, and the Canadian banks insisted this procedure was to continue until Newfoundland had a balanced budget. In essence, this amounted to the removal of democratic government in the small dominion and recognition that Newfoundland was now under the control of the Canadian banks.

The Canadian banks authorized the Newfoundland government to enact legislation requiring the repayment of existing temporary loans through new temporary loans and endeavoured to raise an internal loan. The banks were looking out for their own shareholders, too, and forced the Newfoundland government to float a bond as early as possible and use the proceeds to repay the Canadian banks the temporary loans that had been advanced.[46] All of this came with a dire warning: there would be no further loans after June 30, 1932, and the Canadian banks expected the Newfoundland government to meet the interest payments on its national debt. In accepting these authoritarian and austere conditions, Squires found that the "last door of orthodox finance, forcibly held ajar for more than a year, had now been shut."[47] Despite the severe and deep cuts to both public services and expenditures, the Squires government was unable to balance the budget for fiscal 1932. Instead, the deficit became the largest to date in Newfoundland's history. At the same time, moreover, the number of people receiving "the dole," or able-bodied relief of 6 cents a day, rose sharply. During the depths of the Great Depression in the winter of 1932–33, one-quarter of the population of Newfoundland was dependent on the government for the necessities of tea, flour, pork, and molasses, which increased expenditures on relief, further exacerbating the debt crisis. The number of unemployed resulted in a further decrease in revenues. By 1933, Newfoundland's debt remained at more than $100 million, with total railway-related expenditures accounting for $34.5 million of this amount.[48] The national income was about $30 million.[49]

THE DOMINION OF NEWFOUNDLAND'S DESCENT INTO CHAOS

Even in the midst of the financial crisis, the Newfoundland legislature accepted the *Statute of Westminster* on May 15, 1931, in an Address to His Majesty the King; Great Britain had requested that the dominions approve or reject the statute by December 31. Section 1 recognized Newfoundland as one of the dominions to which the statute would be applicable. Section 11 of the statute abolished the term "colony" as it applied to the dominions, and this, too, was applicable to Newfoundland. In the address the legislature enacted legislation reserving the right that no section of the statute would apply to Newfoundland unless its legislature agreed to it, but given the financial situation at the time, the Squires administration reserved the right to adopt the various provisions of the statute at a later date.[50] At the same time, the legislature also passed legislation declaring the "Union Flag or Union Jack" to be the "National Flag of the Dominion of Newfoundland" and establishing a Department of External Affairs, whose responsible officer—the prime minister—would "deal with all matters arising between this Dominion and His Majesty's Governments in Great Britain and in other Dominions, and the Governments of foreign countries."[51] Newfoundland's willingness to assume the greater responsibility of its new-found status was subsequently hampered by the whirling financial crisis that was enveloping Britain's "Oldest Colony," as it liked to be called at that time. Its new status could do little to help the government avoid seeking financial help from Canada and Britain to prevent bankruptcy in the coming months or protect it from embarassing constitutional change in 1934.

Even as it was dealing with the new constitutional niceties, the Squires government realized that it could not navigate the Great Depression alone. Moreover, all of the bluster, swagger, and audacity of its 1928 election campaign that had promised sound fiscal measures and economic growth through industrialization had evaporated completely. The Dominion of Newfoundland was now vanquished. The Speech from the Throne in February 1932—opening one of the last sittings of the House of Assembly for a generation—admitted failure. We have "deemed it advisable," Governor John Middleton intoned, "to obtain outside assistance and advice in the rehabilitation of the country's finances."[52] A series of new restraint measures followed, but

CHAPTER 4

citizens had already had enough. The volatile situation, especially in St. John's, was exacerbated by allegations of corruption in the highest echelons of the government that embroiled even Squires himself. Three days before the opening of the legislature, on February 4, Minister of Finance Peter Cashin resigned without public comment, his silence adding fuel to the proverbial fire. When the House of Assembly reconvened, Cashin rose from his seat on a point of privilege to accuse the prime minister of falsifying the minutes of the Executive Council to cover up certain legal fees he had been paying himself out of public funds. Cashin, however, was not done after dropping that bombshell. He then accused other members of the Cabinet of similarly misusing public funds, notably Dr. Alex Campbell, the prime minister's closest political friend, who had been investigated a decade earlier by Hollis Walker for corrupt practices and for failing to file his income tax return.[53]

The charges, sensational and inflammatory, incited to action the poor and unemployed of St. John's, who were struggling with the worst of the Great Depression. The state had not been able to provide the help that would have allowed for their subsistence, they had been told, because there was simply no money in the government's coffers. It was not fear they had to confront—as President Franklin Delano Roosevelt would warn Americans the following March, in his first inaugural address—but corruption and crooked politicians. On February 11, several hundred people collected outside the prime minister's office and demanded relief assistance that was eventually granted but only after they had forced their way into Squires's office.[54] Five days later, a larger crowd gathered at the Colonial Building, the seat of government since 1850, to hear Peter Cashin, who had promised details on the charges he had made against the government. Squires, meanwhile, had convinced the House of Assembly to appoint the governor to conduct an inquiry into Cashin's allegations that the minutes of the Executive Council had been tampered with to cover up the prime minister's misdeeds. Middleton, who essentially was asked to investigate whether he had been duped and deceived by his first minister, found no evidence of the allegations against Squires. He reminded the Assembly that it had no constitutional right to question the accuracy of the minutes, but such admonishing only added to the anger both inside and outside the Assembly. It mattered little to the increasingly discontented what the governor said, as many believed that he was no better than the politicians, especially as information—or misinformation—filtered out that public funds had been misused when they had to live on 6 cents a day. On April 4, a large meeting was organized in the city by the St. John's elite, and opponents of Squires demanded a full, impartial inquiry. Public confidence in the government and the democratic system was as scarce as jobs in Newfoundland at the time.[55] Writing to his business partner in Greenock, Scotland, on April 22, 1932, St. John's businessman Tom Collingwood observed that "intelligent people are sick of politics and what I would like to see personally would be a suspension of the Charter for a period of 8 or 10 years, and the Country governed by a Commission from the Old Country with the aid of a few local men."[56]

Angry citizens grew angrier. They expected more of their leaders and their state. What they received, instead, was more bad news. In the middle of the growing crisis, Squires passed new legislation increasing, once again, customs duties—which accounted for 80 percent of public revenues. Everything increased in price, including essential food items. Squires also cut public expenditures, including pensions for veterans, a particularly galling development, as it was alleged that he had absconded with $5,000 a year for his role as chairman of the War Reparations Commission. Three members of his government resigned in protest. But those moments of contrition among a few members of the Executive Council made little difference to the people who were being asked to endure short-term pain for no discernible gain. The situation exploded on April 5, as the frustration and anger of the unemployed towards the Squires government coalesced into a mob of ten thousand demanding higher relief payments and jobs. They stormed the doors of the famed Colonial Building against which the mounted police were helpless. Inside, legislators (in session) barricaded the door to keep the angry throng from the floor of the Assembly, but the citizens took possession of the remainder of the building, looting and destroying public documents in the process. Fearing for his life, Squires scampered away with his wife and a few colleagues through a secret passage and remained in hiding for a day. Accompanying the detested prime minister was a future premier, Joseph R. Smallwood, one of the political

CHAPTER 4

An angry St. John's crowd marching on the Colonial Building, the Newfoundland seat of power, during the Great Depression, 1932.

advisers who secretly helped Squires skirt the angry multitude.[57] It was rumoured that Squires would resign immediately, but he emerged the next day to dismiss such intelligence as nonsense. He would appeal to the people. A general election was set for June 11. By then, William Coaker had had enough, and with the prospect of making the lives of fishermen better—his life's goal since he created the Fishermen's Protective Union in 1908—evaporating quickly, he escaped into retirement. Longing for the strong, non-partisan leadership that the National Government had provided from 1917 to 1919, Coaker again said, "What is required for Newfoundland and what is most essential for the present conditions is a Mussolini." While he still preferred an elected Commission of Government, Coaker remarked that "if a man with a soul encased in steel, experienced and not under forty years old, appeared on the political horizon in this country today as a Mussolini I would support him with all my strength."[58]

Squires must have realized the futility of his efforts even as he insisted that the public protests were organized by his political opponents. Only a handful listened as he campaigned on that elusive goal of balanced budgets, bonuses for the fisheries, and industrial and agricultural development, as he had in three previous campaigns. Meanwhile, Alderdice promoted himself, as he had in 1928, as a plain man of business. Supported by Water Street merchants, he promised to "repair the damages wrought by the misgovernment, misconduct and tragedies of the past few years, and give the country a safe and sane administration of its affairs, with fair play to all and favor to none." Alderdice promised voters that, if elected, one of his "first acts will be the appointment of a committee, the members of which will serve without remuneration, to enquire into the desirability and feasibility of placing the country under a form of commission government for a period of years." To maintain a measure of democratic legitimacy, he assured voters that if the committee were to make such a recommendation, he would then ask the electorate for its "approval." "No action will be taken," he explained, "that does not first have the consent of the people." It was a policy that the recently departed Coaker strongly advocated.[59]

The election was Alderdice's in a landslide, with his party capturing twenty-five of the available twenty-seven seats (the House of Assembly having recently been reduced from forty seats as an austerity measure).

Most of the members of the new government were Water Street merchants, elected by voters in the hope that they could better avoid the impending financial collapse of the country than Squires had. Squires went down to defeat in Trinity South; his wife, Lady Helena Squires, who had won a by-election in 1930 as the first female to contest elected office in Newfoundland, fell in Twillingate. The 1932 general election was to be Newfoundland's last for nearly two decades.[60]

APPOINTMENT OF THE AMULREE COMMISSION

Despite getting a new government, Newfoundland continued to careen towards the debt precipice. It avoided default on interest payments on June 30, 1932, but only because Squires had awarded the Imperial Oil Company a monopoly on all petroleum products, either imported or manufactured and sold in Newfoundland, in exchange for $1.75 million in government bonds and payment to the government of a minimum annual royalty of $300,000 for fifteen years. Default was avoided once again six months later when Canada and Great Britain provided a joint loan of $1.5 million to allow Newfoundland to pay its creditors. Britain had already decided that under no circumstances would Newfoundland be allowed to default. A condition of the loan was the acceptance of an Anglo-Canadian commission of investigation into the Island's political and economic affairs and future prospects.[61] Businessman Tom Collingwood noted, on December 23, 1932, that "it is said that should Canada or the Old Country advance us further monies, they are to have a lien on the Labrador." As things were, Collingwood wished that "England would take us over as a Crown Colony for a period of say 20 or 25 years. By that time we would be on our legs again, and all the professional politicians would have passed out" of the political system.[62]

Nor was there any help coming from throughout the British Empire. After assuming office in 1932, Prime Minister Alderdice attended the Imperial Economic Conference in Ottawa in July, where he sought Canadian and British assistance on trade relations to improve Newfoundland's economic situation. He failed to achieve support for greater use in Britain of iron ore from Bell Island, where in normal times the mine employed 2,200 people, but during the early

1930s wage cuts and substantial layoffs had reduced the work force by half. The mine would return to substantial productivity in the late 1930s only because of increased demand from Germany, which was building up its military arsenal.⁶³ With Canada, there were still some outstanding contentious issues between the two dominions. One was Canada's continued unwillingness to renew the annual subsidy for the steamer service between North Sydney and Port aux Basques, which was not restored until union was completed in 1949.⁶⁴ Another was Canada's efforts to control immigration from Newfoundland, which since the early 1920s was becoming more regulated and restricted. This was quite a change from before the Great War, when Newfoundlanders moved relatively freely to Canada for employment. The situation became expressly difficult for those Newfoundlanders who went to Canada for part of the year to work, especially in the Nova Scotian fishery and the Sydney coal mines, and returned home for the remainder of the year. ⁶⁵ It was only after 1939 that Canada relaxed its regulations as labour was greatly needed for its factories and farms during the Second World War.⁶⁶

In his opening statement to the Imperial Economic Conference, Alderdice said that Newfoundland's trade traditionally consisted of fish exports to the countries of southwestern Europe and the Mediterranean and more recently to South America and the West Indies. New exports such as iron and copper from Buchans were also mainly to foreign countries. What the conference promised Newfoundland and other dominions was "preferred trade" within the Empire. Alderdice was able to claim a victory in tariff protection for cod liver oil and salmon, but it was not enough to help Newfoundland deal with its pressing debt situation nor helpful in balancing its budget.⁶⁷

On February 17, 1933, the British government appointed the Newfoundland Royal Commission to "examine the future of Newfoundland and in particular the financial situation and the prospects therein." William Warrender Mackenzie, Baron Amulree, a Scottish lawyer and former Labour politician, was made chairman, and the commissioners commonly bears his name. He was joined by Canada's representative, banker Charles A. Magrath. Newfoundland's nominee—perhaps an indication of the control of the Canadian banks over the country—was another Canadian banker, Sir William Stavert, who had also been an adviser to the Newfoundland government. Peter Alexander Clutterbuck, who in the 1930s became the leading "Newfoundland expert" at the Dominions Office and was later, in 1946, appointed to Ottawa as British high commissioner, was made secretary of the Commission. The commissioners began their investigation with an open session in St. John's on March 13, 1933. All other meetings, however, were held in camera "in order that all those who wished to give evidence might speak their minds freely with the assurance that their confidence would be respected." As Amulree noted, "In this way we would most quickly and certainly arrive at the facts and ascertain the true current of public feeling."[68] The commissioners met mornings and afternoons for four weeks and occasionally heard evidence in the evenings. They left St. John's by train on April 17 and, over a two-week period, visited the larger outports from Harbour Grace to Channel and collected evidence from communities in northern Newfoundland and Labrador. Then they went to Ottawa to meet with Canadian government officials to hear "evidence from witnesses there who could not travel to St. John's." Bennett's finance minister, Edgar Nelson Rhodes, told Amulree that he opposed bringing Newfoundland into Confederation because Newfoundland "would really in effect become another Ireland—not in the racial sense, but a nuisance and always grumbling and wanting something." And he saw no attraction in Labrador: "not worth possessing," said Rhodes.[69]

The commissioners also interviewed bank officials in Montreal and Halifax, then returned to St. John's on May 29, where they held approximately a hundred formal sittings in camera with 260 additional witnesses.[70] Many subjects were discussed in those sessions, but the opinion sought most often by the commissioners was on Confederation, even when witnesses had no interest in discussing the matter.[71] While the Commission was doing its work, Alderdice warned Amulree that Newfoundland could not meet its upcoming interest repayment commitment,[72] and he urged the commissioners to recommend a course of action that would "enable us to meet, at least in part, our obligations to our Bondholders, and at the same time, relieve the desperate conditions under which so many thousands of our people are now labouring."[73] In his testimony to the commissioners, Prime Minister Alderdice stated that as a "result of the maladministration of recent years," the people had "lost all sense of self-reliance and now looked to the Government to supply all their needs. It would probably take eight years or so to educate them out of this attitude." He advised Amulree that if a Commission of Government were introduced, its members should be Newfoundlanders "chosen for their known integrity and devotion to the country's interests."[74] The Commission concluded its hearings at the end of June.

Many of the witnesses had suggested to Amulree that Newfoundland's problems stemmed in part from the absence of a strong tradition of democratic local government outside St. John's. Harris M. Mosdell, a medical doctor and deputy minister of public health, and formerly also a politician and journalist, typified that view: "We had set up a system of responsible government," he said to the commissioners, "that did not bring responsibility to the average man ... the voter, [who] has never been put in a position where he has had to carry a full measure of responsibility of citizenship." He was simply asked every four years, Mosdell lamented, to go to the polls and vote for a particular candidate, and "then all further interest or further connection with practical affairs ceases.... In my opinion you will have to organize this country from the bottom up before you remedy a condition that exists and prevent a recurrence of that condition again." The solution, suggested Dr. Mosdell, lay in the setting up of local government boards or councils, as was the case in Canada, to promote community spirit and a sense of political responsibility—because then people would realize that the money governments spent came out of their own pockets.[75]

It was no surprise that on October 4, 1933, the report of the Amulree Commission to the British House of Commons recommended the suspension of democratic government in the Dominion of Newfoundland in favour of a special Commission of Government, presided over by the governor until the time the country became self-supporting again. The proposed Commission would have full legislative and executive authority and take the place of the existing legislature and Executive Council. Composed of six members, exclusive of the governor, the Commission would draw three each from Newfoundland and the United Kingdom. Each commissioner would be responsible for a reorganized government bureaucracy and one of six departments, although the Commission's proceedings would be subject to supervisory control by the British government. The governor-in-commission would be responsible to the secretary of state for dominion affairs, and London would assume general responsibility for the country's finances until Newfoundland became self-supporting.

The Amulree Report was widely welcomed by the general population and by special groups, including the Great War Veterans' Association, which believed such constitutional change was in "the best interests of the Country and the welfare of our people."[76] The Board of Trade offered similar support; at a special meeting on November 24, President Raymond Gushue suggested that they regretted

> the loss, even temporarily of the proud privileges and principles of Responsible Government, but [we] feel that our exercise of these principles has of late years been accompanied by such confusion and chaos that a respite from party politics as provided by His Majesty's Government in the United Kingdom can be to the advantage of the people of this country, and better prepare them for a return to financial stability and to the proper re-assumption of these privileges and principles.

Board of Trade member Peter Cashin expressed support but wanted the people consulted on the change,[77] a sentiment echoed by St. John's merchant and board member Chesley Crosbie, who noted, "We had two choices in the matter. One was to accept the recommendations, the other financial collapse." Crosbie too would have preferred a referendum, even though he admitted that the people would likely agree with the decision already made. Edwin John Godden was the only Board of Trade member to register dissent.[78] Squires and Coaker both disagreed with the announcement, as they too wanted a plebiscite to obtain the public's approval.[79] The *Fishermen's Advocate*, remaining true to its roots, feared that the proposed government would combine "Dictatorship and Oligarchy" to rule Newfoundland in the interests of the political and economic elite.[80]

With the suspension of responsible government in 1934, Newfoundland's constitutional position was that of a "dominion with suspended status" with a British-appointed Commission of Government responsible for both its domestic and foreign affairs, which were subject to approval of the Dominions Office.[81] In the words of one Bank of England official, Newfoundland was "now neither a Dominion nor a Colony, but just a place."[82] This change in status took the form of an address from the Newfoundland legislature to His Majesty the King asking that the letters patent of March 28, 1876, and July 17, 1905, which "would provide for the administration of the Island," be suspended "until such time as it may become self-supporting again," on the basis of the recommendations of the 1933 Newfoundland Royal Commission.[83] The Commission appointing the Commissioners of Government on January 31, 1934, recognized the "Island of Newfoundland and its dependencies."[84] From 1934, the High Commissioner's Office in London was reorganized as the Trade Commissioner's Office because Newfoundland no longer had dominion status, but official letterhead of the Trade Commissioner still symbolically continued to use the "Dominion of Newfoundland" in correspondence. Before Newfoundland's Confederation with Canada in 1949, Newfoundland reverted to its pre-1934 constitutional status in order to facilitate its entry into union. However, the exact nature of Newfoundland's pre-1949 constitutional status became a major point of contention in Newfoundland's dispute with the federal government over the ownership of offshore mineral rights in 1978, with the Supreme Court of Canada ruling that Newfoundland had never held the same dominion status as Canada.[85]

The Commission of Government assumed office on February 16, 1934, with three Newfoundland members (Alderdice, William R. Howley, and John C. Puddester, all associated with the previous government and representing the religious diversity of the country) and three British members (Thomas Lodge, Sir John Hope Simpson, and E.N.R. Trentham).[86] Sir David Murray Anderson (1932–36) was governor. Ensconced in the government-owned, stately Newfoundland Hotel, the Commission held its meetings in camera and had full legislative and executive powers. The Commission of Government's financial management avoided the crisis experienced by the previous, democratically elected government, as the Dominion of Newfoundland's outstanding debts were now guaranteed by Britain at a lower interest rate, thereby saving more than $2 million annually in interest charges. The Commission did not have to face the fiscal precipice which had so occupied previous administrations, and it hoped to turn

CHAPTER 4

Newfoundland governor Sir David Murray Anderson speaking at the inauguration of the Commission of Government, 1934.

to the "rehabilitation" of the Newfoundland economy and society. At a stopover in Halifax on their way to St. John's to assume office, Hope Simpson and Lodge declared that rehabilitation could occur only if "prosperity" returned "first to the producer... [as] it is no use to start at the top and hope for prosperity to sift downwards."[87]

Immediately the commissioners, especially Hope Simpson, set out to rehabilitate the fishing industry through legislation they hoped would both raise the standard of the Newfoundland product and force fish exporters to work together for the common good. They hoped that fishermen would embrace the advantage that cooperative societies offered and that the industry would provide those employed in it, finally, with a decent standard of living.[88] Others, such as Lodge, believed that the rehabilitation would come from the development of agriculture; in January 1935, he wrote (not without some racist implications) of Newfoundland that "with the possible exception of Russia and a couple of Balkan States, I doubt whether there is any purely white community in the world on such a low cultural level or where complete ignorance of anything outside the daily task is so wide spread." Lodge blamed the fishery and the manner in which it operated.[89]

What emerged from the Commission of Government was an attempt to deal with unemployment, low literacy rates, and destitution. Government departments were reorganized, the administration of public relief and the dole was revamped, and the training of teachers began to improve literacy levels in the country. Roads were constructed to end isolation, tourism was encouraged, and exploration was undertaken for new minerals. An experimental farm and an agricultural community were planned for Markland, some sixty kilometres from St. John's. The Commission of Government hoped to launch a social experiment and march Newfoundland into a better and more prosperous future. But the initiative had scant success. Nevertheless, it was an attempt to break the hold that fish merchants had over the country.[90]

ATTITUDES TOWARDS THE GOVERNMENT BY COMMISSION[91]

Some in Newfoundland saw in the Commission of Government considerable hope and wanted to help. St. John's businessman and journalist Albert Perlin welcomed the new government and launched, on January 20, 1934, a weekly publication titled the *Observer's Weekly*, promising to provide an "accurate and concise interpretation of events at home and abroad" while offering a "constructive" editorial policy aimed at "explaining the new government to the people and explaining the needs of the people to the new government."[92] It was a noble venture, and Joseph Smallwood, a defeated Liberal candidate from the 1932 general election, was among the first to offer his constructive advice. He had embarked on a two-month tour of the northeast coast in an attempt to organize a fishermen's cooperative, and he believed the Commission deserved to hear about what he had seen.[93] He wrote Governor Anderson and the *Observer's Weekly* even before the Commission was formally in place about the conditions he had witnessed in rural Newfoundland. Writing from Cape Freels Cove, on February 6, 1934, Smallwood expressed his ardent conviction "of the soundness and necessity for the Commission," and he claimed to have "quite unreservedly and enthusiastically" campaigned in 1932 for constitutional change. He was a friend of the Commission, he asserted, and he was "closely in touch with the people in this part of the Island." There was, noted Smallwood, a "lamentable and pathetic lack of information concerning the Commission," and that had to change if it hoped to rehabilitate the country. Smallwood was always an operator, and of course he had a solution for "informing *the people*, that is, the masses of fishermen whose intelligent and informed conscious support is necessary of the week-to-week work of the Commission, and generally of the kind of sympathetic and statesmanlike treatment that they may expect by the Commission of the Island's problems." As a journalist, not surprisingly, he suggested that the publication of a *"very simply worded* bulletin or report periodically, addressed to the people, and posted in every post office, telegraph and telephone office, Court House, etc., would, I think, prove a cheap and effective medium of such information."[94]

No doubt, Smallwood saw himself as the editor of that bulletin. When the Commission ignored him, he fired a salvo of criticism against it in the November 24 issue of the *Observer's Weekly* for its "deep silence [and] for not communicating to the public its attitude toward, or philosophy of the fundamental problems of our country." The people needed to know, he insisted: "What do they [the commissioners] really think of Newfoundland? Of Newfoundland's future? Along what road do they consider Newfoundland should go? What do they think the Newfoundland picture will be when at length their work is done, assuming their efforts to be successful? Is it unreasonable to suppose that they have such a picture in mind?" And he made it clear that such silence from the Commission was "exasperating"; it was also "irritating to be treated like children, as children who are to be seen but not heard." He pleaded with the commissioners to "take us into their confidence, treat us as grown-ups" and "come out from behind that thick, asbestos-lined, sound-proof screen and meet us frankly, face to face."[95] Smallwood would be one of several regular critics of the Commission during its tenure.

The unemployed people of St. John's, who had played a pivotal role in chasing Squires from office, were among the first to organize against the Commission of Government. They held several public meetings during the winter of 1934–35 calling for work and better dole assistance.[96] In a meeting with John C. Puddester, commissioner for public health and welfare, members of the Committee of the Unemployed warned that their living conditions had become so "deplorable and inexcusable" that they wanted action in the form of work, not dole. When the Commission refused to meet their demands, hundreds marched on the Colonial Building, throwing stones and hurling abuse at the police protecting the building. Several of the protestors were arrested and charged but later acquitted by jury. St. John's remained a city on edge, as people grew increasingly angry with their plight.[97] The situation might have been even worse in the outport communities, where it was reported in 1935 that thirty thousand families "have nothing" and where, out of a population of two hundred and ninety thousand, by the winter of 1938, there were eighty-five thousand receiving public relief at the rate of 6 cents a day.[98] On a tour of the south coast in 1936, Commissioner Hope Simpson described the situation in Grey River, an isolated fishing community of about 130 people situated approximately forty-seven kilometres east of Burgeo: "A nightmare settlement, Clothing appalling. Saw girl in school in cotton nightshirt & bare legs. Houses dilapidated. Everyone short of trawls and nets but all have dories .... No potato seeds. Very little work done in gardens. People not fit to work." Of the young girl, Lady Hope Simpson wrote, "Bare legged & bare footed in a grimy white nightgown, snow on the hill side behind her."[99] Those desperate people who confronted the government were motivated by their own plight, but they would come to represent too an emerging voice, not only in Newfoundland but also throughout the developed world for a more activist government. They were part of a movement that wanted their state not merely to control aspects of the economy but also to ensure a better standard of living for all citizens. They were waiting for a political leader to embrace their cause.

William Coaker was also critical of the Commission. In August 1934, he wondered in the *Fishermen's Advocate* "What has been done by the Commission Government so far?" and chastised them by saying more could have been done "by any six senior school boys, who possessed the power of the Commission and the backing of the British Treasury."[100] A month later, he again demanded political reform and the restoration of responsible government as soon as the "country is out of the woods, the budget balanced and the Fishing Industry placed on an

CHAPTER 4

even keel and a class of politicians produced that is determined to place country first always." Coaker wanted the reformed state he had first envisioned when he created the Fishermen's Protective Union, a state that would have established greater control over the means of production and provided a measure of social security for the people. He also sought a system of governance that protected the public interest by advocating public improvements and allowing citizens a full voice in the creation of policy and the scrutiny of public expenditures. As a first step, Coaker suggested that four of the six commissioners be elected. Like Smallwood, he wanted fishermen and other workers involved in the political process to create a better, more equitable society.[101]

Peter Cashin was another critic. Following his resignation from government in 1932, he had reached out to Canada and established an insurance agency for a Canadian company. He also created an export and import business that shipped coal from Canada, and in 1934 he became involved in the fish and timber export business in Placentia Bay.[102] Cashin also flirted with the dubious lottery and sweepstakes sector, perhaps playing on his popularity and oratorical skills, hoping to generate revenue for the government and lucky ticket holders, as well as the Canadian bankers he tried to entice into the business.[103] More than twelve hundred citizens filed into The Majestic Theatre in St. John's on October 30, 1935, to hear Cashin demand a return to responsible government. Police reports pegged a similar number listening outside by loudspeaker.[104] The event was organized by a committee that styled itself "Crusaders," and Cashin boasted that he had the financial support necessary to re-enter the political realm as soon as "a favourable opportunity presents itself." Even then, Cashin demonstrated a proclivity for conspiracy, charging both Lodge and Alderdice of graft and declaring that he could prove that the Commission of Government was brought about "by bribery and corruption."[105] The meeting ended with the singing of the "Ode to Newfoundland." Shortly thereafter, Cashin decided to leave Newfoundland for Canada, but before doing so, he wrote Governor Sir Humphrey Walwyn (1936–46) that "Russia is Paradise compared to Newfoundland at the present time."[106] In expressing those sentiments, Cashin, like others, demonstrated his belief that the state had to be reformed and become more responsive to the needs of its citizens.

The opposition to the Commission of Government continued, but the Dominions Office in London never saw the criticism as interfering with their plans for Newfoundland. "Newfoundland expert" Peter Clutterbuck observed from London that Ken Brown, the new president of the Fishermen's Protective Union, and Longshoremen's Protective Union President Michael Coady were the only two in Newfoundland "capable of working up any serious agitation against the Commission." Clutterbuck accepted Lodge's view that Squires and Cashin were both politically "dead."[107] Even so, Secretary of State for Dominion Affairs Malcolm MacDonald, wishing to avoid any danger of "local political agitation," suggested that Governor Walwyn establish an advisory council composed of prominent Newfoundlanders to advise the Commission.[108] Walwyn immediately began compiling a list of "eligibles" from outside St. John's. When, however, he presented the list to the commissioners, they decided that the "admitted value and usefulness of such a Council would be completely outweighed by the difficulties and dangers associated with its creation and functioning." Instead, they opted to use the press and radio to better inform the public and to keep magistrates fully informed of the Commission's work, and these magistrates would then pass information along to those living in rural Newfoundland.

The radio became an important feature of Newfoundland society and politics in this period and later, as it did throughout North America. The Commission of Government created the Broadcasting Corporation of Newfoundland and eventually purchased the private radio station VONF (Voice of Newfoundland). Radio broadcasting was to be a part of the Commission's plan for economic and moral reform in Newfoundland, but the outbreak of war again in 1939 and the return of prosperity helped to derail those plans. Radio broadcasting began in St. John's, but it grew to serve the needs of all Newfoundlanders as new stations were established in Corner Brook and Gander. In a country that was largely isolated, the Commission used radio broadcasting to try to mould culture and society across the Island. Although radio ownership was largely concentrated in St. John's, citizens in outport communities often gathered in the homes of those who owned the devices to listen to various broadcasts, including news and messages posted for specific communities as well as announcements from the

Commission on its various policies. Such gatherings undoubtedly spawned dialogue and discussion of national events, and, as we will see later, the radio was pivotal in the 1940s during the debates over Newfoundland's constitutional future.[109] The Commission took a number of additional steps to aid communication with the people of Newfoundland, including (1) publishing pamphlets to explain government activities; and (2) proposing legislation that would foster the development of rural local councils and use ad hoc advisory bodies to confer with the commissioners on proposed legislative and executive measures.[110] The Board of Trade, nonetheless, suggested this was too limited and continued to push for an advisory council.[111]

Expectations for the Commission of Government had been high. People had put much faith in it hoping for immediate improvements to the economy and their lives, but they saw little evidence of that, at least until the outbreak of war in 1939.[112] Many of those who had promoted the Commission soon became disenchanted with it as well because of its failure—like governments elsewhere—to deal adequately with the economic problems created by the Great Depression. Yet the Commission, particularly the British-appointed commissioners such as Thomas Lodge, Hope Simpson, and John H. Gorvin worried many of the St. John's mercantile and professional elite with their ideas for change. Hope Simpson later wrote of the prosperity of the mercantile community, who lived in luxury and seemed to have money for everything they wanted, in contrast to the poverty of the fishermen. Even more startling for him was the attitude of those wealthy merchants. He wrote Sir Edward Harding, permanent undersecretary at the Dominions Office, that he had raised the issue of the plight of fishermen at a dinner party in St. John's attended by several leading merchants: "The three merchants were agreed that the standard of comfort was very low but that the fisherman wanted nothing more, and was happy struggling along in the circumstances in which he found himself." Hope Simpson claimed that he was warned that the British commissioners "must be careful not to attempt to create in the minds of the people of this country a demand for a higher standard of comfort." Such an attitude was typical among the Island's elite, he noted.[113] Lady Hope Simpson expressed a similar view: "The merchants here had put nothing they could back into the island: they have taken their fortunes abroad—spent their money in England." Yet she was simultaneously more charitable to the merchant class than her husband and more critical of Newfoundland, where she saw little enlightening during the 1930s: "Can you blame them?" she wrote of the fish merchants. "Who would invest their money in an island where government was so corrupt!" She had no higher view of Newfoundlanders themselves, labelling St. John's "a dirty foul-smelling slum" and the rest of the Island "a farm that has been ruined and left." She went on to write, "The bad farmer impoverishes his land—the good farmer enriches it."[114]

Commissioner Gorvin, too, hoped to create in outport communities new economic and social institutions to deal with the pressing problems of low wages, illiteracy, and inadequate public services. He wrote to Whitehall that the British commissioners were in Newfoundland "to achieve reforms and the economic administration of the Fisheries is high on the list of reforms to be effected."[115] Although his plans were derailed by the outbreak of the Second World War, they show that some in the Commission of Government were not content to leave things as they were. The Commission frequently adopted a "populist stance common in Newfoundland politics and appealed to the unemployed and the underemployed over the heads of the elite which, as usual, had proclaimed its interest as the national interest."[116]

The view of the British government by early 1938 was that the Commission of Government had made "substantial social and economic progress." Dominion Affairs Secretary Malcolm MacDonald reminded the British House of Commons that the process of recovery would be gradual, however: "The Island cannot immediately expect to be self-supporting and without being so, there can be no return to self-government. The Commission was determined," he said, to "keep in close touch with local opinion both in day to day administration and on major questions of policy."[117] This would matter little to the unemployed, and in mid-1938, when the economy worsened, Governor Walwyn informed Harding that he was worried about a "more surly and 'bolshie' spirit that was emerging as there was little prospect of any improvement in their economic condition." There was more than an "undercurrent of discontent" among some "seven to eight hundred men without a chance of employment" in St. John's, and Walwyn feared that "conditions in this country are the subject of much press controversy usually leading to a condemnation of the Commission for not providing employment regardless of economic difficulty." He was, however, confident of relative tranquility, because a number of prominent men, particularly lawyers and merchants, were still opposed to any return of self-government, although there were signs they, too, were becoming "restive."[118]

The Commission of Government could no more solve the crisis of the Great Depression than any other government around the world. Nevertheless, it can be argued that the surrender of responsible government and the appointment of a Commission of Government in 1934 were done for the purpose not only of dealing with Newfoundland's fiscal situation but also of ushering in a new way of managing affairs in the country and making the necessary changes to ensure that the state was sustainable. The Commission of Government might also be seen as a step in the pursuit of a new relationship between state and citizenry. Albert Perlin, one of Newfoundland's most prominent and influential journalists at the time, advised the Commission in 1934 that its responsibility was "grave": "You will find a country stricken with poverty, its morale broken," he wrote, and out of the "wreck" the commissioners had to "reconstruct a new Newfoundland."[119] Education had long been recognized as a prerequisite for change, and even before the suspension of responsible government, the high levels of illiteracy bred "a sluggish intellectual life and an unimaginative and inefficient debate about the goals of the society and how they might best be realized," according to scholar David Alexander. He goes on to argue that "anyone who surveys the economic and political history of Newfoundland cannot escape the impression of a political culture which was sunk in a mediocrity which the country and its people did not need."[120] He submits, "Literacy and education are essential to a lively intellectual life wherein the goals of a country are effectively debated, defined, and efficiently implemented."[121]

Thomas Lodge pointed out early in the Commission's tenure that education was "the most important question of all" and that compulsory education was necessary in the school system. "Whatever the difficulties the Commission Government will fail in its task," Commissioner Lodge wrote, "[and] will deserve to fail, if it cannot raise very substantially the general level of education in this island."[122]

In Canada at the time, governments spent $11.00 per capita and $53.00 per pupil per year to educate their children, but in Newfoundland these amounts were much less: $3.60 per capita and $17.40 per pupil. Although the Commission was unwilling to confront the Roman Catholic hierarchy and other religious leaders over the denominational control of education, it worked within the existing structures to improve the levels of education in Newfoundland. It proposed reforms in curricula and examinations, introduced higher salaries and better training for teachers, established better methods of inspection for schools, created a system of adult education to deal with low literacy rates, and, of course, made school attendance compulsory. In 1935, for instance, more than fourteen thousand children aged six to fourteen years were permanently absent from the country's schools. The Commission of Government encouraged school attendance by providing nutritious supplements for children, through the provision of milk to schools in St. John's and cocoa malt to outport schools, where milk was not generally available.[123] Health outcomes for Newfoundlanders were no better than those in education. Approximately 60 percent of the population had no access to health care when needed, and the mortality rates for children were abysmal. In Canada, the infant mortality rate was 73.1 per 1,000 live births, but in Newfoundland, it was 102.8. The Commission proposed the training of midwives and the establishment of universal child welfare services to deal with infant mortality. It also proposed to expand the limited hospital facilities and add capacity at the sanatorium for tuberculosis patients. Additionally, it hoped to create district nurses, which the Commission believed might "contribute more than almost any factor to the rehabilitation of the people and especially to the raising of the standard of home life and conduct."[124]

The British government, of course, wanted to prevent a recurrence of the 1933 fiscal situation in Newfoundland once the country returned to self-government. It asked the Commission of Government in late 1936 to prepare a long-term program "ultimately to make the Island self-supporting again, and to train and equip the people of Newfoundland so that they are then in a position to administer their own affairs unaided once again."[125] The Commission considered an ambitious plan for economic development, notably in the fishery and agriculture sectors, in what it termed "economic reconstruction" that would rehabilitate the country's economy and foster self-reliance and raise income levels for fishermen. Thus, the Commission proposed major reforms in health care, education, public services, local government, broadcasting, and the general improvement in living conditions throughout the country. It paid particular attention to education. It was an ambitious but expensive plan, estimated to cost the British Treasury between $7 and $8 million. Although London initially agreed with the plan, it was derailed by a downturn in the economy in 1938–39, when Newfoundland's revenues declined and its deficit rose to nearly $4 million, the highest since the Commission was imposed. The British provided a subsidy to cover any deficit. The number of people on relief mushroomed—by April 1939, nearly eighty-five thousand were on relief, the most since early 1934.[126]

Everything changed for Newfoundland and for many other countries when, on September 1, 1939, Nazi Germany invaded Poland. Two days later, Great Britain and France declared war on Germany, marking the beginning of the Second World War, which would not end until August 1945 in Europe (and later in Asia). The downturn in the economy and then the outbreak of war claimed a plan by Gorvin to radically reform the economy and reinvigorate the society of rural Newfoundland. His draft "Act to Facilitate the Economic Development of Special Areas of Newfoundland" was intended to have the state provide assistance for the cooperative development of the fisheries to minimize the control exercised by fish merchants and to increase the agricultural capacity of the country. The Act would also have launched a program of road construction to open up new areas for agriculture and development and to end the curse of isolation that had long plagued Newfoundland. Gorvin had hoped that his initiatives would encourage industrialization, especially through manufacturing, and introduce technical and vocational training for adults.[127] Wartime spending became the priority, and plans for reconstruction became a casualty of the war. However, the acceptance by London in 1939–40 of those reconstruction plans suggests that the British government was intent on remaking and reconstructing Newfoundland. Even if the British government would not lead in those reconstructive efforts in Newfoundland, the Second World War, which brought American and Canadian dollars and prosperity to the Island and Labrador, would lay the seeds that would radically transform Newfoundland into a modern society. Once the war turned in favour of the Allies, the Commission of Government once again laid out a plan for the social and economic reconstruction of Newfoundland, and by then the people, too, were demanding not only a new relationship between themselves and their state but also a new type of society.

In the last days of peace in 1939, the old Confederate Alfred B. Morine paid his final visit to Newfoundland. At eighty-two years of age, he no longer advocated union between Canada and Newfoundland. The "time is most inopportune," he told the *Evening Telegram*: "They don't want you and you don't want them."[128] He helped create a non-partisan, non-sectarian committee to consider the restoration of responsible government that included as members Walter Monroe (although he disassociated himself from the committee within a week), Chesley Crosbie, J.M. Devine, Jesse Whiteway, and Michael Gibbs, a former mayor of St. John's. Even though he attracted the St. John's elite around him, Morine insisted that those people had contributed to the cleavages and insolvency that marked the country. Moreover, the large number of destitute people, he insisted, stemmed from an "infamous supply system long practiced in the fisheries, enforced upon the fishermen by greedy and stupid merchants, and persistent misgovernment by corrupt and incapable politicians." What was needed to restore prosperity and democracy, he stressed, was a change in the system of trade and honest governance.[129] Then, with the outbreak of war and the return of prosperity in Canada and Newfoundland a few years later, Morine would drop his pessimistic attitude on union and once again become an advocate of Confederation.[130] He had always believed that Canada would "never be complete" until Newfoundland became part of it but had also insisted that the timing had to be right for both parties for union to happen.[131]

By the time of the Second World War, Sir Richard Squires was also openly promoting union with Canada. While visiting Winnipeg, after the royal visit of King George VI and Queen Elizabeth to Canada and Newfoundland in 1939, Squires said it was the opportune moment for Canada to take Newfoundland into Confederation and fulfill the intention of the founders of Canada in 1867.[132] Squires would be dead by March 1940, and with Coaker's death two years earlier and Cashin

CHAPTER 4

Royal Visit of King George VI and Queen Elizabeth to St. John's, 1939.

living in exile in Montreal, the Newfoundland political scene had lost many of the prominent figures who might have challenged the authority of the Commission of Government. The Coaker-Squires political legacy, however, lived on in one political figure who continued to grow in prominence: Joseph R. Smallwood.

By 1939, Smallwood was a radio host on the Voice of Newfoundland's popular *The Barrelman*, as well as a struggling farmer on the outskirts of St. John's.[133] His radio program was sponsored by Francis M. O'Leary, a strong anti-Confederate and member of the business community. Smallwood also edited O'Leary's newspaper, in which he promoted Newfoundland's rich cultural heritage.[134] In one 1938 column, Smallwood ascribed Newfoundland's political problems to the lack of communication, the "means to enable people to communicate with each other, both physically and intellectually." "That's where we've fallen down," he lamented, "and that's the main cause of our backwardness as a people and as a country!"[135] Within a few years, Smallwood would use his communication skills—especially on the radio—in hopes of changing all of that and would bring himself to the pinnacle of power in Newfoundland.

The outbreak of war in Europe in 1939 and the Commission's mobilization of the Island's human and natural resources for the Allied war effort not only silenced the Commission's critics but also rocketed Newfoundland into a different world economically. Among the major developments was the arrival of the Americans after Britain granted the United States ninety-nine-year leases, in 1941, for the construction of military bases in Newfoundland. The Americans quickly erected major facilities, including an army base at St. John's, a naval base at Argentia, and an air base at Stephenville. They also shared with the Canadians and British use of the Gander and Goose Bay air installations, mostly built by the Canadians. By 1943, American expenditures for construction alone totalled $105 million, and the number of military personnel stationed in Newfoundland peaked at nearly eleven thousand. At the height of the American and Canadian military construction boom, nearly twenty thousand Newfoundlanders were employed, earning higher wages than they had ever thought possible. By then, the average annual income was $1,500, compared with $333 in the fishery just nine years earlier, in 1933. There was employment for all who wished to work, and in droves men left the fishery that for decades had failed to provide a living wage. There was such a shortage of labour that the Island's paper mills at Grand Falls and Corner Brook reduced newspaper production for several months in 1943 and 1944. Women, too, found increased opportunities for employment and higher wages.[136] Increased demand for Newfoundland's resources and foreign military expenditures ended the Commission government's budget deficits, which had peaked at $4.8 million in fiscal 1940. Budget surpluses became the norm during wartime, and by fiscal 1946, Newfoundland had accumulated surpluses of more than $28 million. It even provided interest-free loans of $12.3 million to Britain.

Flush with cash, the Commission of Government was finally able to undertake further improvements in public services. It had begun to lay the foundations of a welfare state in Newfoundland with several modest initiatives. Moreover, salaries were increased for teachers, twenty-five regional libraries were established, including one at Pushthrough, free and compulsory education was instituted in 1944, and a program of adult education was launched to deal with the country's abysmal literacy rates. The Commission of Government attempted to reform health and welfare, increasing the number of cottage hospitals and adding a 270-bed wing to the St. John's sanatorium to confront rampant tuberculosis. It successfully encouraged the growth of local government outside St. John's through a system of grants and incentives to communities with limited revenue bases. By 1948, eighteen communities were incorporated.[137] The Commission also embarked on a program for the development of the frozen fish industry to modernize the sector that continued to employ thousands. It was hoped that a modernized fishery would raise the standard of living of a large segment of the Newfoundland population. Finally, it seemed Newfoundland had found prosperity, even if it was induced by the war. The march towards progress had begun.

On August 14, 1941, British prime minister Winston Churchill and American president Franklin D. Roosevelt met in Placentia Bay aboard HMS *Prince of Wales* to discuss possible British-American cooperation during both the war and postwar periods. Following their meeting, they issued the Atlantic Charter, which was a statement of "common principles" embodying their hopes for a "better future for the world." One of the sections in the statement expressed their wish "to see sovereign rights and self-government restored for those who have been forcibly deprived of them."[138] How self-government and the restoration of a nation's sovereign rights would work out in Newfoundland would be hotly contested over the next several years, but one thing was certain: by the end of the war in 1945, Newfoundland would be a different place than it had been when the war began in 1939. Six years of war would in many ways complete Newfoundland's reorientation from Britain to North America, especially to Canada. This shift was represented perhaps more prophetically by a change in the traffic laws requiring automobile owners to drive on the right side of the road, like all North Americans, rather than the left, as was done in Britain.[139]

CHAPTER 5

THE NATIONAL CONVENTION, SOCIAL CITIZENSHIP, AND NEWFOUNDLAND'S FUTURE, 1941–1946

FOR MANY WHO HOPED AND BELIEVED THAT ONCE NEWfoundland had achieved financial stability and a measure of prosperity, Great Britain would restore democratic government and constitutional independence, Tuesday, October 28, 1946, was their day of infamy. On that day, Joseph R. Smallwood rose in the historic Colonial Building and before a stunned National Convention, recently elected to consider the country's constitutional future, pronounced that Newfoundland was, in fact, not a nation. "The history of this island is an unbroken story of struggle," he exclaimed. He let it be known that he would be introducing a motion that the Government of Canada be informed that Newfoundland was interested in a federal union and that it wished to send a delegation from the National Convention to know what terms and conditions it might offer to facilitate such an arrangement. Smallwood further declared that Newfoundland could not survive as a separate constitutional entity and that he was not prepared to see it struggle on as an independent nation. In fact, he asserted, Newfoundlanders "view the future now with more dread

Joseph R. Smallwood was elected to the National Convention from Bonavista Centre, which included the military town of Gander. He quickly became one of the dominant figures in the Convention, promoting the union of Newfoundland with Canada. He was already a household name from *The Barrelman*, a fifteen-minute radio program on the Broadcasting Corporation of Newfoundland intended to promote knowledge and pride in Newfoundland's history and culture.

than they felt a century ago." The situation was more precarious than in the eighteenth century when Europeans first landed to fish and settle, he lamented. The citizens of Newfoundland had also finally come to realize the great gulf that separates "what we have and are from what we feel we should have and be." Smallwood reminded his audience that in recent years Newfoundlanders had learned from radio, newspapers, and visitors "something of the higher standards of well-being of the mainland of North America; we have become uncomfortably aware of the low standards of our country.... Compared with the mainland of North America we are fifty years, in some things a hundred years behind the times."[1]

CHAPTER 5

This stunning speech exposed Smallwood's perspective on Newfoundland's challenging history, its struggles, its economic failures, its legacy of despair—and its position in the post–Second World War milieu. For him the past was appalling, a place from which to escape, not to seek a return. "In the North American family Newfoundland bears the reputation of having the lowest standards of life, of being the least progressive and advanced of the whole family," Smallwood maintained, issuing a clear indictment of the failure of the country's previous governments and its leading elites. Although Newfoundlanders had the right, he acknowledged, to pursue independence, to return to the pre-1934 constitution, such a course would be costly to ordinary people. To "turn away from North American standards of living and from North American standards of public services" would result in a lower standard of living for everyone. Let Newfoundland, a small country with a limited population, not nurse "delusions of grandeur," he advised. He then scratched the wound he had so dramatically exposed, saying, "We are not a nation. We are merely a medium size municipality, a mere miniature borough of a large city." For Smallwood the choice was simple: "continue in blighting isolation or seize the opportunity that may beckon us to the wider horizons and higher standards of unity with the progressive mainland of America." Confederation with Canada was the only option. It would, he professed, "raise our people's standard of living," give them "a better life," provide "our country stability and security," and furnish it with "full democratic responsible government under circumstances that will ensure its success."[2] Smallwood's speech that infamous day, according to some, was a clarion call for the "New Newfoundland" that he had been promoting for nearly two decades. The issue was not about constitutions, he concluded, but about the social and economic well-being of the citizens of Newfoundland.

Many people at the time, and some ever since, were embarrassed, even horrified, by Smallwood's portrayal of their beloved land— even if they, too, must have realized its past economic struggles and persistent poverty had condemned very many Newfoundlanders to a standard of living far below what was by then commonplace in North America. Still, many of the members of the National Convention recoiled at Smallwood's depiction of their country, especially as, at that particular time, Newfoundland rivalled Canada in terms of economic prosperity and buoyant labour markets. They were angered by the portrait of failure and despair he painted. To some Newfoundlanders, Smallwood's rhetoric was not simple hyperbole but a betrayal, bordering on treason. Not surprisingly, the motion put forward generated considerable anger and dismay, as well as debate. Nevertheless, on that day, the issue of joining Confederation—and Smallwood himself—not only stepped onto the national stage in Newfoundland but in fact arrived at its very centre. Both Smallwood and the issue of union with Canada captured the attention of the National Convention like nothing else ever had or would. Some members argued that the motion was premature, introduced before the Convention had even begun its work; others accused Smallwood of trying to sell the country to the Canadians. Still others, intent on securing the return of responsible government and independence, which they believed had been so shamefully surrendered in 1934, dismissed all other constitutional options, including Confederation, until the injustice of 1934 had been rectified and democracy restored.

Peter Cashin, a member of the National Convention representing St. John's, immediately saw in Smallwood's speech notions of conspiracy. He charged that London and Ottawa were behind Smallwood's brazen attempt to force Confederation onto the Convention's agenda, dismissing it as having as much legitimacy as seeking terms with Moscow.[3] Indeed, as ensuing events were to show, Smallwood had reignited once again an old quarrel: Newfoundland's relationship with Canada. As political scientist S.J.R. Noel pointed out nearly half a century ago, Smallwood had stirred the hornet's nest, being the first person since labour leader William Coaker, in 1908, to tell Newfoundlanders that the conditions and hardships they endured were not ordained by Providence but were the result of an exploitative economic and political system that they, themselves, had the power to change.[4]

In the debate that Smallwood unleashed in 1946, many things would be different from what they had been when union with Canada was debated in the 1860s—including, of course, the outcome—but as Charles Fox Bennett had learned then, the question of how Newfoundland would deal with Confederation would be resolved largely by voters in the outports. Their world view and their interpretation of the campaign to come, limited though it may have been in the estimation of the country's elite, would once again determine how the debate on joining Canada would be settled.

THE FUTURE CONSTITUTIONAL OPTIONS

What Smallwood did on that October day in 1946 was not how the narrative of Newfoundland's constitutional future was supposed to unfold. The Second World War had created prosperity unlike anything that any living Newfoundlander could recall and budgetary surpluses rarely seen in Newfoundland's long history. The St. John's elite, especially, had already turned their thoughts to the country's constitutional future. They envisioned the restoration of the suspended constitution that would allow Newfoundland to reclaim its dominion status and make it, once again, the constitutional equal of New Zealand, Australia, Canada, and even Great Britain itself—and of course they saw themselves once again assuming the leading role. Their representatives had created, in July 1940, the Newfoundland National Association to promote greater public debate and "to inculcate and develop a sound public opinion" that would enhance democratic institutions.[5] Their plan was to promote good citizenship among civic-minded individuals that would improve "the science of Government within the country in consonance with those Democratic principles and for which their origins in the British tradition and for which the British Commonwealth of Nations stands." They considered themselves very much a part of the British world. The Newfoundland National Association's board of governors, which included Newfoundland luminaries such as lawyers Philip J. Lewis and Eric Cook and businessmen Francis M. O'Leary, George Crosbie, Ronald Ayre, and Silas Moores, had no interest in union with Canada.[6]

Nonetheless, in the early 1940s, there had been growing debate about Newfoundland's future. Through his short-lived weekly newspaper, *The Express*, Smallwood had given voice to a public discontent in satirizing the non-elected Commission of Government. At this time, he, too, favoured the restoration of responsible government, and in his first issue, Smallwood launched a seven-part critical history of the Commission. He had once "welcomed" the Commission with the "greatest fervor," he claimed, but by 1936 he had been "driven to acceptance of the conclusion that the system had broken down and that it did not contain within it the seeds of success." Smallwood's history, adopting the view of Daniel Prowse (see Chapter 2), was intended to "reveal the tragedy of Newfoundland" and to "reveal the bleak, unrelieved failure of Dominions Office rule."[7] Like Prowse, Smallwood had hope, and in subsequent issues of his newspaper, he laid out Newfoundland's future constitutional options: advisory council to the Commission of Government; elected Commission; representative government; group government; and responsible government. He himself made no mention of union with Canada at that time, certainly no favourable mention of Confederation that he would later embrace with great passion and enthusiasm. The newspaper also contained articles analyzing government policy by lawyers F. Gordon Bradley, Eric Cook, and John B. McEvoy, all of whom, incidentally, would eventually support joining Canada. There were also interviews with leading citizens on public issues of the day, as well as with business owners on the issue of Confederation with Canada. Whether "the time is now opportune" for Newfoundland to join Canada had also been the subject for two of St. John's debating clubs in March 1941.[8] Within a year, the Board of Trade also joined the ranks of those criticizing the Commission and called for greater public consultation in governing Newfoundland. The Board of Trade demanded the appointment of a public body of representative citizens to advise the Commission and provide for some kind of formal process to engage public opinion, although not for union with Canada.[9] A year later—and largely out of self-interest—it unanimously called for the restoration of responsible government and the appointment of a Royal Commission of Enquiry to consider a new constitution. This move was propelled by the Commission's proposal in mid-1942 to increase the taxes on income and excess profits, retroactive to 1942. Finance Commissioner Ira Wild had declared in a radio address that additional revenues were necessary to avoid calling on the British government, hard-pressed because of the war, for financial assistance. At an emergency meeting convened to discuss the proposed changes to taxation policy, board member Peter Cashin proclaimed that the new tax would be the "most vicious that ever were produced by a Government" and argued that both taxes and expenditures be reduced.[10]

CHAPTER 5

The British War Cabinet also monitored the situation in Newfoundland. In March 1943, Dominions Secretary Clement Attlee had proposed sending a bipartisan parliamentary committee to "see something of its [the Commission's] many activities and the way of life of the people, and form some idea both of the potentialities of the country and of the capacity of Islanders to take charge of their own affairs." A three-person "Goodwill Mission" was dispatched in 1943, consisting of British MPs Charles Ammon, Sir Derrick Gunston, and Alan Herbert, to travel the Island and Labrador. Personal conflict plagued the mission, and each member presented his own report. Yet all three found that there was little appetite in Newfoundland for a return to pre-Commission days and scant support for union with Canada; it seemed that Newfoundlanders were not sure exactly what they wanted. Nevertheless, all three parliamentarians also agreed that the people themselves should decide their constitutional future when they were ready to do so—in a national referendum. Independent MP Herbert suggested a National Convention, comprising Newfoundlanders from all backgrounds and regions, to enable the people to decide for themselves their constitutional future.[11] The British government accepted this recommendation and on December 2, 1943, announced that after the war ended, the necessary mechanisms would be provided to allow Newfoundlanders to decide their own path forward.[12] Attlee himself had also travelled to Newfoundland to get a first-hand view of the situation there.[13]

In the 1860s, the British government had encouraged Newfoundland to join Confederation, and by the early 1940s it was even more convinced that that was the best option. Newfoundlanders would have the final word as to their political future, of course, but the British would leave "themselves considerable leeway" in the coming months to shape the options from which Newfoundlanders might choose.[14] One of the developments that persuaded Britain that union with Canada was the best option was the huge cost associated with a proposed post-war reconstruction program that the Commission of Government had drawn up for Newfoundland. In September 1944, the cost for reconstruction, which included plans for economic development, improved communications, new and improved social programs, and the construction of new government buildings and other infrastructure, was projected to be $100 million.[15] When the British Treasury saw the proposal, it quickly informed the Dominions Office that an amount of such magnitude simply did not exist to rehabilitate Newfoundland. Britain was already borrowing heavily from Canada, and elsewhere, including from Newfoundland, to fund its own postwar reconstruction, and given the currency crisis with Canadian and American dollars, it could ill afford to finance reconstruction in Newfoundland. John Maynard Keynes of the Treasury, who thought the $100 million was a misprint for $10 million, advised his government that even if "we were stuffed with money, this [amount] would seem to be out of proportion." And for Britain to borrow even greater amounts than it already was to finance reconstruction in Newfoundland, he suggested, would "make her look extremely silly." Keynes accepted the long-held British position on Newfoundland and advised that the "right long-term solution is for Newfoundland to be taken over by Canada." Yet he noted, "the argument seems to be that the Newfoundlanders will overcome their reluctance to leave us and put themselves in the hands of Canada if we give them these great sums." "It would have been natural to conclude the exact opposite," he surmised, "namely that, after this signal mark of our favour, the Newfoundlanders would be still more reluctant to part company with us."[16] It was time, in his view, for the United Kingdom to free itself of the responsibility for the small dominion.

On May 10, 1940, Britain's Labour and Conservative Parties had formed a coalition government led by Winston Churchill. By September 1943, Lord Cranborne had replaced Attlee, now deputy prime minister, as dominions secretary, and he too favoured Confederation. Cranborne was following in the path of earlier British colonial and dominions secretaries, who had long believed that Newfoundland's future lay with Canada. If anything, after Newfoundland's suspension of responsible government in 1934, the British became even more convinced that Newfoundland could not thrive as an independent state: its only recourse was either to be absorbed into the United Kingdom, along the lines of Northern Ireland, or to become a province of Canada. Cranborne realized, however, that union with Canada would take some further time given the apparent opposition to Confederation in Newfoundland. He proposed waiting until the end of the war to initiate plans to have Newfoundland once again govern itself, but in the meantime, he recommended taking steps to improve local government and educate the people in the democratic process. All members of the War Cabinet agreed with Cranborne's proposals, except the Canadian-born minister of information, Lord Beaverbrook, who believed that Newfoundland was a "valuable strategic jewel in the Imperial crown," and self-government for the struggling dominion would maintain that close connection.[17]

Of course, union had also been Canada's objective since the Quebec Conference in 1864, and with the outbreak of the Second World War, Prime Minister William Lyon Mackenzie King had unequivocally said so on a number of occasions. He had announced in 1939 that Newfoundland would be included in Canada's defence preparations. Later, in 1943, in a reply to a question in the House of Commons from Newfoundland-born CCF MP Joe W. Noseworthy, King praised the attachment between the two countries and said that the door was always open for Newfoundland to join, and "should they make their decision clear and beyond all possibility of misunderstanding, Canada would give most sympathetic consideration to the proposal."[18] Ottawa was concerned that the 1941 Leased Bases Agreement between Great Britain and the United States, which gave the Americans a ninety-nine-year lease to construct and operate several military bases there, might shut Canada out of Newfoundland and create an Alaska on Canada's eastern flank. In 1941, Canada had appointed its first high commissioner to Newfoundland to clearly signal its growing interest in the country and increase its influence there. When Nova Scotian Charles J. Burchell left Ottawa to take up that position, King reminded him of Canada's military, strategic, and long-term interests in the Dominion of Newfoundland and instructed him whenever possible to "emphasize Canada's special relationship with Newfoundland."[19] A normally cautious and nervous politician, King always feared that admitting Newfoundland might give rise to political turmoil and damage his Liberal Party, especially in the Maritime provinces, particularly if Ottawa offered terms to Newfoundland that Maritimers considered more generous than the arrangements they had forged within Confederation. But such worries and fears never prompted King to bury the idea of union. David MacKenzie suggests that, nevertheless, the question of Newfoundland's future "was not the kind of problem that inspired much

The relationship between Newfoundland and Canada had been growing since the mid-nineteenth century, but it became closer during the Second World War. Pictured here is a dance at the opening of the Women's Division Lounge, RCAF Station, Gander, Newfoundland, March 3, 1945.

conversation in the halls of the East Block or informally in the cafeteria of the Chateau Laurier." Yet the prospect of losing Newfoundland to the Americans (even if the United States had never expressed an interest in annexing Newfoundland) prompted some discussion both inside and outside Ottawa. It led, for example, to the publication of the influential book *Newfoundland: Economic, Diplomatic, and Strategic Studies*, edited by Robert A. MacKay, who had been recruited from Dalhousie University to the Department of External Affairs in 1943.[20]

Great Britain was soon forcing Canada to make up its mind about its relationship with Newfoundland. In 1943, Whitehall was anxious to know Ottawa's real thoughts about Canada's future with Newfoundland. Malcolm MacDonald, now the British high commissioner to Canada, raised the matter on several occasions with Norman Robertson, who became undersecretary of state for external affairs in 1941 and who, with others in the department, believed union would be best both for Newfoundland and for Canada. Over a lunch in August 1943, MacDonald told Robertson that the Dominions Office wanted a "preliminary exchange of views" on Newfoundland before his government would make an official statement concerning Newfoundland's future. When Robertson pursued the subject with King, he reminded the prime minister, "My own feeling is that 'somehow, sometime' Newfoundland should become part of the Canadian Confederation. I think that, in the long run, both political and strategic consideration make this inevitable."[21] Further informal discussions on Newfoundland between Canadian and British officials followed in the autumn of 1943, and the Department of External Affairs began developing background papers. MacKay prepared two memoranda outlining his views on Newfoundland's economic and strategic position and warned that, as a province, Newfoundland would likely be an economic and political liability. King's Cabinet War Committee subsequently discussed Newfoundland but did not come to any final decision.[22] Meanwhile, the British were growing increasingly anxious for Ottawa to formulate a policy on Newfoundland, largely because the Treasury had made it clear that it was in no position to assist Newfoundland after the war, especially for any large-scale reconstruction that would be required. The Dominions Office, moreover, was hoping to soon establish a National Convention, as MP Alan Herbert had earlier suggested, to consider Newfoundland's constitutional future.

AFTER THE WAR, A RENEGOTIATION OF CITIZENSHIP

The Second World War in Europe ended on May 8, 1945, but the war in the Pacific would continue for another three months, until the bombing of Hiroshima. On July 5, 1945, a general election was held in Britain, which Labour leader Clement Attlee won by a landslide, replacing Winston Churchill as prime minister of the United Kingdom, a position he held until 1951. That same month, Hugh Dalton, chancellor of the Exchequer in Attlee's new government, told Dominions Secretary Lord Addison that there was no money for Newfoundland reconstruction and that if money were to be provided "it will have to come from Canada."[23] The crucial role of Clement Attlee in those discussions cannot be discounted. Attlee had great hope for social citizenship in Newfoundland, as indeed he did for the United Kingdom itself. He had visited Newfoundland as deputy prime minister and dominions secretary in 1942, not to review the strategic importance of the Island, but to consider the question of "how best and how soon Newfoundlanders could be led back to a truly democratic way of life and what form their new institutions should take."[24] The War Cabinet's senior officials were of the opinion that Newfoundland's destiny lay within the Canadian Confederation and that British policy should be formulated to help achieve this goal. Attlee himself remained uncommitted initially but wanted a first-hand view of the Island.[25] During that 1942 visit, he became convinced that Great Britain should continue with the Commission of Government until the end of the war, when there would likely be a strong local demand for a return to self-government. Britain should, in the meantime, prepare Newfoundlanders for the constitutional change that would occur, but Attlee saw three possible options in the immediate postwar period: a continuation of the existing system of government by Commission; the return to self-government; or a constitutional half-way house with Britain retaining some financial control over Newfoundland affairs. Confederation with Canada was considered unacceptable, Attlee had believed in 1942, because there did not seem to be any public support for it in either Canada or Newfoundland. Attlee was very much aware that a "contract" had been made with the people of Newfoundland whereby a general demand from the people for self-government would have to be acknowledged.[26] Yet he wondered if Newfoundland could stand on its own with the return of peace, and he told Newfoundlanders in a radio broadcast from St. John's during his visit that "nothing could be more foolish than to imagine that the exceptional conditions of war make a solid foundation for a post war economy." He insisted, too, that Newfoundland, like Britain, had to "win the peace ... [and] build a new and peaceful world." Nothing was more important, he said, than to rid the world of want and "never again must we have a return to the conditions of the years around 1930."[27] The Commission of Government had warned him in January 1943 that Newfoundland likely could not survive economically in the postwar period as an independent nation and prosper. The best

CHAPTER 5

option for Newfoundland, according to the Commission, was "political incorporation of this country in a larger unit."[28]

By 1945, when he was still a member of Churchill's Cabinet, it had become obvious to Attlee, and indeed to most of the British Cabinet, that Newfoundland would not fare well on its own in the aftermath of the war and that union with Canada was the best option. Lord Beaverbrook—the former Max Aitken of New Brunswick—who then held the ceremonial post of Lord Privy Seal and who, according to the prominent war historian A.J.P. Taylor, "had no political following," disagreed with Attlee on Newfoundland.[29] But Attlee refuted Beaverbrook's claim that Newfoundland was self-sufficient and able to stickhandle the tricky and uncertain period that was to follow. It was true, Attlee reminded Beaverbrook, that Newfoundland had accumulated a wartime surplus, but between 1934 and 1940, "the Island required considerable financial assistance from this country [Britain]," and there was considerable uncertainty about Newfoundland's future. He also cautioned his Cabinet colleagues that no decision on Newfoundland should be based on the extraordinary circumstances of wartime. Attlee dismissed Beaverbrook's claims that there was a "clamouring in Newfoundland for a return to responsible government."[30] Beaverbrook was a great Imperialist and he had no wish to see the British Empire diminished, which he felt would happen if Newfoundland joined Canada.

Clement Attlee was, foremost, a social democrat, even after he became prime minister. He had been active at the London School of Economics with socialist Sidney Webb and in the left-wing Fabian movement, believing that capitalism had created an unjust and inefficient society. His sympathies lay with the "political underdog" and their problems "invariably received his full attention." A major proponent of improved social welfare measures and of using the power of the state to improve conditions for Britons, Attlee wanted the same for Newfoundlanders. A strong and enthusiastic promoter of the influential 1942 Beveridge Report, which spelled out a set of principles necessary to banish poverty from Britain, Attlee laid the intellectual foundation for a system of social security in the postwar period that, indeed, was partially implemented in many countries, including Canada.[31]

Addison dispatched Peter A. Clutterbuck, another old hand from the British civil service and well-known "Newfoundland expert" (see

Chapter 4), to Ottawa. Clutterbuck met with officials from the Department of External Affairs, including Robertson, MacKay, Hume Wrong, and J. Scott Macdonald, Canada's high commissioner to Newfoundland (appointed May 4, 1944). "I did not conceal my disappointment," Clutterbuck reported to London, when the Canadians told him that there was little interest in Newfoundland and, given the likely cost of union, that Canada had little interest in bringing the beleaguered country into Confederation. Clutterbuck even tried nudging the Canadians towards union when he reminded them that there was a "substantial movement of opinion" in Newfoundland on Confederation, a point that Macdonald confirmed. Clutterbuck reminded MacKay that Canada's social security legislation, particularly the family allowance, was "beginning to penetrate Newfoundland consciousness,"[32] but those comments seemed to make little difference in Ottawa.

Perhaps the Canadians were playing coy with Clutterbuck, because on several occasions in 1945, both King and his officials suggested to London that if the British withheld financial assistance, it might "assist Newfoundlanders to turn their thoughts to Canada." King continued to insist, however, that nothing should be done to "compel Newfoundland to come into Confederation or to show a desire to have them come in." King continued to say, as he had for a number of years, that Newfoundland should know that if it saw its future with Canada, then Canada would look most favourably upon its wish.[33] Undersecretary for External Affairs Robertson seized on King's words and followed up with the prime minister in a memorandum dated September 25, 1945, outlining the benefits of union. A few days later, King himself discussed the matter with British High Commissioner Malcolm MacDonald and suggested that it might be best to deal with Confederation before it became an issue of "party politics" in Newfoundland. The British were delighted. They were then convinced that Canada desired union, even though King instinctively continued to waver, reminding Dominions Secretary Addison in late October 1945 that "we are simply thinking aloud and are committing no one to anything."[34] The British Cabinet ignored King's obvious indecision and moved forward on its Newfoundland policy.

Yet Attlee was worried that the St. John's mercantile and professional elite might control the proposed National Convention that he was planning, unless some safeguards were established to ensure that bona fide residents in the districts stood as candidates and represented the views of all sections of the country. If vested interests controlled the process being established to return democratic government to Newfoundland, those necessary social reforms and a form of social citizenship that he considered essential might not come to Newfoundland. For Attlee, it was not simply a matter of deciding a constitutional arrangement.[35] He noted in a Cabinet meeting on November 1, 1945, that because of "special conditions obtaining in Newfoundland," Britain had to ensure that measures were taken to guarantee that "the Interests of the Islanders themselves" would be properly represented in the Convention.[36] Attlee's Labour government subsequently imposed a residency restriction on candidates for election to the National Convention to facilitate the participation of a wide representation of citizens from throughout Newfoundland that he hoped might lead to an improvement in social conditions in the country. He was determined that Newfoundland, too, consider and implement some of the newer notions of social citizenship that he was attempting to promote in the United Kingdom. Yet Attlee realized that Newfoundland itself would have to decide its own future.

On December 11, Addison informed Parliament that Newfoundlanders would elect a National Convention of forty-five members, each of whom would have to have been resident for two years in the district in which election was sought. This Convention would

> consider and discuss among themselves, as elected representatives of the people, the changes that have taken place in the financial and economic situation of the Island since 1934, and bearing in mind the extent to which the high revenues of recent years have been due to wartime conditions, to examine the position of the country and to make recommendations to His Majesty's government as to possible forms of future government to be put before the people at a national referendum.[37]

This announcement, observed Charles Granger, editor of the *Fishermen's Advocate*, "comes like the first faint drawn-ray of freedom" and must "arouse in the hearts of all patriots sentiments of inspiration and sobriety, and a strong desire for sound decisions."[38] Governor Walwyn, soon to leave Newfoundland after a decade-long tenure, reported, however, that the announcement had "produced little reaction. It was really what most people expected although there is a certain element that appears disappointed in the absence of financial assistance." "Generally speaking," he added, "there is a feeling of alarm that the baby is now being handed to them [Newfoundlanders] and they don't know how to handle it." Walwyn was perturbed that "some of the old politicians are already creeping out of the jungle and appealing for the support of their old constituencies."[39]

Joseph Smallwood, who was by then living in Gander as the manager of a hog farm at the airport and active in local political discussions with his fellow Newfoundlanders on the base, was excited about the news. In 1944, he had written in the *Evening Telegram*, calling on Newfoundlanders to be fully "awake to their political future." He said he wanted to "arouse" in them an "intense interest and activity and enthusiasm" and demonstrate to everybody their "absolute determination" to "control their own national destiny." One practical solution, Smallwood suggested, was the formation of political parties and to "be done with shadow-boxing—straw ballots and the like, and similar evidences of political insolvency." Such an intervention into the public sphere, he believed, was the only way for the people to be "taken seriously by London and Ottawa" and get the "respect" they deserved. And he urged immediate action rather than waiting for the war to end. He also called upon some "outstanding Newfoundlander" with faith in the country to "throw his hat in the ring" and announce that "he is not only willing but frankly eager to become Prime Minister."[40]

Smallwood was on a business trip to Montreal in December 1945 when he read in the *Montreal Gazette* of Attlee's proposed plans for Newfoundland. Walking the city streets for hours, an excited Smallwood debated with himself what political options Newfoundlanders should adopt. He was already determined to be part of the forthcoming political campaign—"all of my work and my training up to that moment made my entry inevitable," he later recalled, but he was not sure what he preferred other than it was not to be a continuation of the Commission of Government. Memories of a conversation with Gordon Bradley in 1930, in which the latter claimed that Confederation was the

CHAPTER 5

only salvation for Newfoundland, prompted Smallwood to consider union with Canada as a viable political option for his beleaguered country. Right then and there, Smallwood became a Confederate.[41] Returning to Gander from Montreal the following day on an RAF bomber, he immediately decided to update his knowledge of recent Canadian political developments. Perhaps he was about to fulfill the destiny some had seen possible for him two decades earlier. In 1926, when Smallwood outlined his plans to make the Liberal Party a party for the worker and recommended that it "commit itself to principles and policies of social reform nature," prominent St. John's lawyer George Ayre wrote, "Mr. Smallwood, if he plays his cards well . . . has a great opportunity for good. He has already shown his rare organizing ability, his capacity for leadership, his ability as a speaker, a debater. He is young and wonderfully energetic. He seems to have all the qualifications for one who in time will become one of the leading men of the country. What a glorious prospect."[42] The constitutional debate that was about to begin would reveal just how prophetic Ayre's claim really was.

Writing to the *Daily News* a few weeks later, on January 20, 1946, Smallwood told Newfoundlanders that they must immediately "put out of mind" any hope for a continued form of Commission government or affiliation with the United States as a feasible solution to the "Newfoundland problem." Instead, Newfoundland must have responsible government "either with or without Confederation." "It seems to me," he wrote, that this "whole question of Confederation will have to be investigated very thoroughly. We shall have to discover exactly what we lose, and exactly what would we gain by entering Confederation. Would it be a net loss, or a net gain? There must be plain facts that will answer that question and these facts will have to be got and studied by all of us."[43] He immediately wrote Prime Minister King and the nine provincial premiers for information on the federal–provincial system. The materials poured in, and Smallwood assiduously mastered the workings of the Canadian federal system. Convinced that union with Canada was the best option for Newfoundland, he published in March 1946 a series of eleven articles in the *Daily News* arguing the merits of Confederation.[44]

Smallwood understood that for most Newfoundlanders the real issue was not which specific constitutional arrangement or which form of government would eventually replace the Commission of Government but how their personal lives could be improved once that process was complete, views he had long held—since the 1920s and his support for Coaker and the FPU. Smallwood, like Attlee, realized that there had been a major shift in recent years in what citizens expected of their governments. The new dynamism was one where governments pursued policies to rid the world of poverty and adversity, want and misery, and such objectives were to be accomplished through an interventionist, activist state. Governments should build a new social order to eliminate the fear of unemployment and the sense of economic insecurity that workers encountered when their capacity to meet the needs of their families was threatened or failed. That Smallwood came to these conclusions is not surprising, of course. Canada, Australia, Great Britain, and the United States had already engaged—and were engaged still—in similar debates about new social priorities such as family allowances, veterans' benefits, national health programs, unemployment insurance, and pension plans. Indeed, throughout much of the modern world, but especially in the Allied nations that had participated in total war to defeat Nazi Germany and Japan, citizens were demanding a new relationship with the state that would eventually usher in a new form of citizenship. Why would Newfoundland be any different?

Smallwood and his supporters came to believe that the enactment of social rights was necessary to enable individuals to actually enjoy civic and political rights. The expansion of social rights became an important aspect of twentieth-century citizenship in Newfoundland. These were important instruments of statecraft, especially in Western countries following the Second World War, to maintain political solidarity, to build sustainable and vibrant communities, and to achieve social cohesion.[45] Social citizenship addresses central questions of obligation and entitlement in society, and in Newfoundland these notions and ideals were played out, first in the National Convention and then in two referendum campaigns. When combined with the more traditional and long-standing political and constitutional rights, such as the right to vote, these social rights provided for a full and complete integration of the citizen into the wider social and political order. The citizen was no longer simply the abstract voter but, instead, a flesh-and-blood individual with material needs and with the expectation that the state would consider those needs, not only in circumstances of deprivation or disability but also in the normal course of life.

In some jurisdictions, gender and race have been central to contestations about the dimensions and meanings of citizenship. In Newfoundland, this dynamism was shaped primarily by economic and social well-being as well as by gender—especially the appeal to women as mothers—that defined the new approach to citizenship, although the issue of class also needs to be brought under the historian's gaze.[46] Evidence of the emergence of these dimensions can be seen in an analysis of Newfoundland society in the early twentieth century.[47] Indeed, it can be argued that the emergence of William Coaker—and his attempt to organize fishermen in 1908, then lead the Fishermen's Protective Union into national politics in 1913—was motivated by a quest for social citizenship. Coaker made no attempt to unite working people in Newfoundland; rather, he was determined above all to gain a greater share of the economic rent from the fishery and, for the most part, to provide greater economic and social security for fishermen and their families. He advocated an ambitious social program that included old age pensions and insurance policies for injured fishermen, as well as other initiatives that were being embraced as social rights and social citizenship by progressives who advocated similar demands in the United States, Canada, and elsewhere at the time. Similarly, the collapse of responsible government in 1934 stemmed, in part, from a population demoralized by long-term neglect by the state. This is an aspect of Newfoundland history that the Amulree Report noted when it investigated Newfoundland's financial affairs in the early 1930s (see Chapter 4). The Commission of Government that governed Newfoundland from 1934 attempted to make the state more meaningful in the lives of ordinary Newfoundlanders. The Commission understood the importance of social and economic reform and, especially during the Second World War, saw reconstruction in much the same light as the British and Canadian governments. The Commission's ambitious reconstruction plans embraced the extension of public services and improvements in civic infrastructure, as well as the provision of a measure of social security as a central tenet of its postwar objectives for Newfoundland.[48]

On June 29, 1946, Newfoundland's new governor, Sir Gordon Macdonald (1946–49), informed Dominions Secretary Lord Addison that he was satisfied that the people were "beginning to take a more active interest in the affairs of their own country" and noted the "growing support for the restoration of responsible government." He proceeded to point out that "this is evident amongst the younger section of the electors. There are others who, though most sympathetic to the restoration of responsible government, are somewhat apprehensive and definitely doubtful as to whether *immediate* restoration is likely to be the best thing for the country."[49] "There are those who give vigorous as well as vociferous support to Confederation with Canada," Macdonald's predecessor Walwyn had noted several months earlier, but there is "no doubt that at the moment they are in a minority. To what extent the deliberations of the National Convention will influence public opinion, time alone can tell."[50]

Yet less than 50 percent of eligible voters cast a ballot for the National Convention election on June 21, 1946, although the turnout was much higher in St. John's, the country's largest urban centre. In many ways, the election was a popularity contest, and voters had to select from a group of men and women, who for various reasons had gained some prominence in their ridings. Eight representatives were acclaimed; thirteen were merchants, the single largest occupational group; three were cooperative workers; two were trade unionists; and three were former members of the House of Assembly. Of the members returned, the largest religious denominations were well represented, with sixteen of the members from the Church of England, thirteen from the Roman Catholic Church, and eleven from the United Church. Despite the residency requirement to ensure the whole population was represented, not a single fisherman was elected; and of the two women nominated, neither was successful. Among the elected was Smallwood, who campaigned on Confederation with Canada and won 89 percent of the vote in Bonavista Centre—the largest majority of any of the members. Other notable members included Gordon Bradley (Bonavista East), Ken Brown (Bonavista South), Peter Cashin, and Chesley Crosbie (both from St. John's West).[51] The National Convention met for the first time on September 11, 1946, and would continue sitting until January 30, 1948. Its deliberations marked the official beginning of the

CHAPTER 5

The National Convention, September 1946.

process of returning democratic government to Newfoundland, more than a decade after it had been suspended.

It was decided that the debates in the National Convention would be recorded and broadcast each evening over the Broadcasting Corporation of Newfoundland, the government-owned broadcasting network that reached all parts of the Island.[52] That momentous decision by the Commission of Government brought to Newfoundlanders everywhere not only the debates and goings-on in the Convention but also discussions about the role of the state and the changing nature of citizenship. Those discussions and debates engaged voters in the electoral process as they had never before been engaged. Once the debate became argumentative and entertaining, the *Evening Telegram* reported that "thousands of people listened keenly to the debates each evening."[53] Members of the Newfoundland Rangers, the country's police force, later reported to St. John's that there was considerable interest throughout the country in the debates in the National Convention, especially when social programs such as the family allowance and old age pensions were discussed.[54] That the role of citizenship emerged in the National Convention demonstrates that

Newfoundland, too, was aware of how notions of citizenship were changing widely at that time.[55]

The Convention had the effect of awakening Newfoundlanders generally to some harsh realities. Some commentators, such as *Daily News* columnist A.B. Perlin (who wrote under the name "The Wayfarer"), had noted as early as 1943—two years before the establishment of the National Convention—the difficulties Newfoundland would have finding social and economic security after the end of the Second World War. Perlin wrote that while other countries were turning their attention to planning for ways the state might ensure social and economic security, Newfoundland was the exception in postwar planning: it had no industries to convert to peacetime production or wealth out of which to create markets. The prospects were bleak and the way forward challenging, he noted, although (as we have already seen above) the Commission of Government had laid out an ambitious and costly program of reconstruction. Perlin then suggested that Newfoundland had as much claim on the great and wealthy nations for help with postwar reconstruction as the peoples of Europe "which are going to be helped with billions of invested capital after the war."[56] In his view, Newfoundland needed outside assistance if it were to establish a secure future in the postwar era.

The debate on the changing understandings of citizenship began in Newfoundland in the National Convention, where members were in fact engaged with the emerging notions of social citizenship, notions that were central to how Newfoundlanders were seeing their place in the future. For many citizens, such ideas came to them nightly through the radio broadcasts of the taped Convention debates. Newfoundlanders, like citizens elsewhere, were interested in how their country would make the transition from war to peace, as well as how the constitutional situation would be resolved for their benefit and how they might find in the post-Commission era economic, political, and social security and stability. Such rhetoric inspired a spirited and heated debate about the type of society that members of the National Convention—and citizens more generally—hoped for in the years ahead. Two dominant groups emerged in the National Convention: one argued primarily for the restoration of democracy and the return of responsible government, and the other, a smaller group, favoured union with Canada—which, its supporters pointed out, also brought a return to responsible government and democracy. The Confederates rallied around the tangible benefits of being Canadian, arguing that responsible government had collapsed, in part, because the government's chronic neglect had left the people of Newfoundland entirely disillusioned.[57]

Smallwood was elected to the National Convention promoting union with Canada, and he was, perhaps, among the few candidates elected with a clear set of ideas for the future. In August 1946, even before the Convention began, Smallwood had visited Ottawa, where he met with a number of Canadian ministers and officials, including Minister of Justice and Attorney General Louis St. Laurent, to gather information about Canada. This was Smallwood's first meeting with St. Laurent, and the two would, over time, establish a good working relationship, although St. Laurent would realize after 1949 that as premier Smallwood would demand more than Ottawa could provide.[58] Smallwood did not have much success in Ottawa in 1946, although he did meet with Jack Pickersgill, Prime Minister King's private secretary, and this, too, would eventually blossom into a long-time political relationship, especially after Newfoundland became a province.[59] Canada's high commissioner to Newfoundland, J. Scott Macdonald, had reportedly—and ironically—informed his superiors in Ottawa that Smallwood was "of slight consequence and without political following."[60] What Macdonald and others could not have known at the time was that Smallwood had a steely resolve and the power of a charismatic leader. His approach made him leader of his group, and together with Bradley, a respected politician from the pre–Commission of Government days and a former Grand Master of the Orange Order, they believed that their objectives for Newfoundland could be achieved only through joining Canada. Together with a small group of similarly minded members within the National Convention, they became imbued with the political discourse on social security and the expansion of social rights to all citizens. They focused on the problems facing the country and demanded that after the referendum—whatever the outcome—the state introduce a series of programs to address citizens' social and economic needs.[61] They knew they offered in union with Canada an attractive option to many, especially to fishermen and mothers in the outports.

As part of the National Convention's process to gauge the changes that had occurred in Newfoundland since 1933, it appointed a number of committees to inquire into aspects of Newfoundland's economy and society. Each committee presented its report to the Convention and stimulated, in turn, considerable debate in the Convention, and indeed throughout Newfoundland. The reports also helped set an agenda for future policy directions in the country. From the British point of view, the Commission of Government reports were "harmless, if somewhat windy, and at times, ungrateful and wrong-headed exercises, that allowed some steam to be vented politically without threatening either normal Commission [of Government] rule or their own grand design," which, as we have seen, was Confederation with Canada.[62] Radio audiences were interested in how Newfoundland would make the transition from war to peace and, at the same time, find economic, political, and social security and stability. The Convention debates, especially those that focused on people's well-being, created a sense among Newfoundlanders of frustration and hopelessness about their plight, but also awakened in them the prospect of new possibilities. The broadcasts made people aware of their situation, the lack of state support, and the absence of public services in their country compared with those of the rest of North America and various other Western political communities.[63]

Many of the committee reports in the National Convention called for a new form of engagement between citizen and state. The Public Health and Welfare Report was particularly instructive. Noting that the public's perception of the role of the state had changed enormously since 1933, the report said that the country could not return to a time when the state took little interest in the people's well-being. "The modern concept of the state is that of the 'social welfare state,'" the report noted, and "we agree upon the practical impossibility of Newfoundland evading acceptance of that modern concept." Thomas G.W. Ashbourne and Lester Burry, chair and secretary, respectively, of the Public Health and Welfare Committee, and under whose pens the report was undoubtedly written, seem to have been fired up with a vision of social justice as a strategic and practical necessity for Newfoundland: "People now expect their government to provide social services and we agree that this responsibility must be assumed by our modern government."[64]

The Report of the Fisheries Committee similarly called upon the state to adopt a social security scheme for fishermen.[65] Many of the ideas raised in these and other reports, and in the debates in the National Convention more generally, had a huge impact on the people listening each evening, oftentimes sitting together around the radio in the home of whoever had one—listening and talking to each other about what they were hearing. Newfoundlanders soon came to understand that some members of the National Convention, particularly the Confederates, seemed genuinely concerned about their well-being and were proposing something quite revolutionary in what governments should and could guarantee to protect ordinary citizens against want, squalor, ill health, and economic distress.

The question in the minds of many listeners was how the country would be able to pay for new social programs. The Report on the Financial and Economic Position of Newfoundland, prepared by G.W. St. John Chadwick and E. Jones in the Dominions Office in June 1946 for the National Convention, offered some good news. The report noted that even though financial difficulties had been a mainstay of the first years of commission government, the war had brought a period of prosperity, "which enabled the country to become self-supporting and to build up surplus balances." Yet the report's authors also warned that Newfoundland continued to present "complex administrative and distributive problems." With a population of only 316,000 dispersed among thirteen hundred communities scattered along an extended coastline—and only three of which had more than five thousand inhabitants—the challenges posed by geography, isolation, and climate were immense. They "impose a heavy burden on the central government and lead to a duplication in administration such as would be avoided in a more centralized community," the authors concluded. Moreover, the fishery and the pulp and paper industry, the two principal primary industries, "suffer from an inability to provide continual employment [, which] leads to a considerable mobility within the available labour force." The budget surpluses had come from large-scale spending by foreign governments on defence projects, not from any changes in economic rents collected from Newfoundland's resource or manufacturing capacity. The report reflected the widespread fear that the prosperity during the war might be fleeting.[66] With the war over and American and Canadian spending largely gone, it was quite likely that government revenues would be significantly reduced, and Newfoundland might again find itself in financial difficulty. If that turned out to be the case, any new social spending would be very unlikely. There was no denying the fragility of the Newfoundland economy.

During the debate on the Chadwick-Jones Report, some members of the National Convention, particularly those whose views aligned with Smallwood and Bradley's, were raising questions about the expansion of social and economic rights in the postwar period.[67] Isaac Newell, a cooperative organizer with the International Grenfell Association and member for White Bay in northern Newfoundland, and one of the self-described "junior members of this Convention," said he "was much more concerned about how the people of this country are going to eat during the next 50 years than with how they are going to vote." That, he added, "was the thought of the people who sent me here." Peter Cashin had led the debate on the Chadwick-Jones Report by chastising the British government for revoking responsible government. In response, Newell reminded Cashin that to declare himself "as a 100% advocate of responsible government [and to] focus on wartime budgetary surplus and the wrong perpetrated against Newfoundland [by Whitehall]" was simply avoiding the real question of whether or not Newfoundland's "economic system was economically sound." Newell maintained it was not, although he mixed his metaphors badly in making that assertion: "We are still cranking the old Model T economic system that Cabot left us when he went back to claim his ten pounds. It's archaic.... It's almost medieval. Certainly our economic setup has all the earmarks of the old feudal system, with its lords and villains," and, he asserted, "war, which uprooted so many things, has failed to dislodge it." "There are too many instances of tuberculosis and beri-beri" in Newfoundland, he claimed, noting that "they are the by-product of malnutrition. We need a state that can spend more on public health and provide economic prosperity." Newell did not believe Newfoundland could do so as an independent dominion.[68] Later, in the National Convention, he remarked that "the Convention's search for political constitutions will be ineffectual if it is not allied to a desire for social justice."[69]

Others offered similar arguments. United Church minister Lester Burry, the sole delegate from Labrador, told the National Convention that the people he represented "are not concerned with constitutional government, but with a government that will give them a decent living for the labour they put into their work."[70] William Keough, another young member of the National Convention, from the Port au Port area in western Newfoundland, added there was a certain minimum standard of living that was consistent with human dignity, and Newfoundlanders "cannot be satisfied in conscience with less than that minimum." Reflecting notions of Britishness often associated with a progressive and advanced society, Keough said the real question was "whether this land we live in can support a community of civilised men in such a fashion as civilised men expect to be supported in the mid-20th century": it is not a "constitutional" matter, he asserted, but an economic one. The Convention would have to decide, he said, if the "last forgotten fisherman out on the bill of Cape St. George, or down on the bill of Cape Norman," would have "a certain minimum standard of living consistent with human dignity" and "walk the ways of a more prosperous land in happiness, peace, and dignity." For Keough, it was "three square meals a day, a decent suit of clothes on the back, and a roof that doesn't leak over the head"[71] and, as he wrote later, a "capacity for compassion for the common people."[72] Bradley, representing Bonavista East, added, "Our government has not always functioned for the welfare of the people. In too many cases the people's welfare has been the last consideration."[73] He and others wanted a new role for the state, one that would bring greater social and economic security to Newfoundland. Their voices found a receptive audience, especially in outport Newfoundland, where the people were avidly listening to the debates and discussions over the Broadcasting Corporation of Newfoundland.

Smallwood praised Newell, Keough, and Burry as the "authentic voice of the people of Newfoundland," as they were "almost continuously into intimate touch with the real people." The voice of the people of the outports was finally being heard in St. John's. There would be some, he charged, that would try to focus the attention of the National Convention "on politics and constitutions," but there were "bigger things" than that, as Newell and others had pointed out. Smallwood claimed that the Newfoundland people were "completely uninterested in far-fetched and high-faluting questions of types and forms of government. . . . They are tremendously preoccupied with questions of

After studying at Mount Allison University in New Brunswick, Lester Burry became an ordained minister and spent much of his career in Labrador. He worked to improve the standard of living there and believed that Confederation with Canada was the best way to achieve that goal. Elected to represent Labrador in the National Convention, he favoured Confederation from the beginning.

bread and butter."[74] Daniel Hillier, another of the members who would support joining Canada, echoed similar sentiments: "The great thing that worries many of our people is not so much the form of government we set up, it is the fact of being able to maintain their families and give them decent meals and clothing."[75] Thomas G.W. Ashbourne, the member from the northeast coast district of Twillingate, told the Convention that "people long for freedom from want and a sense of security, so that they will not only have three meals a day, but there will be that dignity and that prestige which we as Newfoundlanders desire."[76] Just a year earlier, Reverend John Watkins, the parish priest in Hermitage, wrote to the *Evening Telegram* that fourteen children had died within seven months on the south coast because of lack of medical facilities.[77] But it was not only in the outports that such tragedies were occurring. In June 1944, the *Evening Telegram* also reported on the death of Mary Ellen Hutchings, a ten-year-old girl from the "slums of St. John's" who showed signs of frostbite, gangrene, and other verminous diseases,

CHAPTER 5

William Keough, elected from St. George's District on Newfoundland's west coast, was a member of the delegation to London and a strong Confederate. In one of the most memorable speeches of the Convention debate, he told members they would have to decide if the "last forgotten fisherman out on the bill of Cape St. George, or down on the bill of Cape Norman" would have "a certain minimum standard of living consistent with human dignity" and "walk the ways of a more prosperous land in happiness, peace, and dignity."

although the cause of death was determined to be starvation.[78] Not surprisingly, then, some of the members of the National Convention who favoured a return to responsible government also realized the world had entered "an age of social reform, and no government will try to impede progress" in the direction of social improvements. Alfred Watton, for instance, said that voters in his district of Fogo wanted "a government that will give us the greatest measure of economic and financial stability," or what he called "rights."[79]

The dire social situation in parts of Newfoundland was real. It was noted later that Newfoundland's health services, despite advances during the Commission era, were backward compared with those of the Canadian provinces. In the treatment of tuberculosis in 1948, for instance, Newfoundland was where "England and Wales were in 1910," it was suggested. The comparative mortality rates of Newfoundland with the Canadian provinces were also startling. Newfoundland's were very much higher: the Newfoundland annual death rate per 100,000 population was 122.0, while Ontario's was 25.7. The only province even close to Newfoundland was Quebec, at 72.4 per 100,000, and Nova Scotia's rate was 62.4 per 100,000. A 1948 Newfoundland memorandum also noted that upward of twelve thousand Newfoundlanders were suffering from tuberculosis, but the country could accommodate fewer than four hundred in its sanatoria.[80] Other health indicators also placed Newfoundland far behind the Maritime provinces, which, Leonard Miller, the director of medical services in Newfoundland, pointed out, lagged behind the rest of Canada. For instance, infant mortality in Newfoundland was much higher than in the other Maritime provinces: in the period from 1941 to 1945, infant mortality per 1,000 live births in Newfoundland was 92 compared with 52, 58, and 74 in Prince Edward Island, Nova Scotia, and New Brunswick, respectively. While Newfoundland compared somewhat favourably in the number of hospital beds per 1,000 population (4.0 for Newfoundland, but 3.8, 5.5, and 4.9 for PEI, Nova Scotia, and New Brunswick, respectively), total public hospital expenditure in 1946 for Newfoundland ($1.6 million) paled in comparison with New Brunswick ($4.1 million) and Nova Scotia ($5.0 million), although it was greater than what was spent in PEI ($712,341).[81] Given such a situation, several letters to the editor of the *Western Star* of Corner Brook in 1946 made absolute sense. They demonstrate that people wanted to move beyond the present state of affairs in Newfoundland. One letter, signed "Newfie," noted the "backwardness" regarding the state of roads and communication in western Newfoundland, while Canada "looks after such public needs." The letter writer saw greater security in union with Canada. A letter from Baxter A. Smith, dated March 8, 1946, questioned how Newfoundland could manage with a return to responsible government and independence and asked of soldiers returning from the war, "What have they to look forward to?"[82]

One could not ignore that question given Newfoundland's fiscal difficulties throughout much of the first half of the twentieth century. Yet many of those elected to the National Convention who demanded the immediate return of responsible government believed that the wartime surpluses meant that the future would be different than the past had been. The Report of the Committee on the Financial and Economic Position of Newfoundland—a committee chaired by Peter Cashin and whose members were largely supportive of a return to responsible government—was sanguine about the postwar period. It claimed that "our country is not the same today as it was before the war." The economy "has undergone something akin to a revolution in our geographical importance [especially in relation to aviation]," even though the international community had agreed that nations could not use their geographical position to trade landing rights for the emerging airline sector, for instance, for economic advantage. Moreover, most governments realized that such a strategic advantage was fleeting, as technological advances would soon diminish the importance of places like Gander. Still, the report optimistically concluded that "a change from a deficit to a credit is not to be regarded as anything abnormal," suggesting that Newfoundland had become a fiscally sound state.[83] As Cashin noted when he tabled the report, "All the debating in the world won't change the figures [showing a wartime surplus]." The report, written largely by Cashin himself, drew selectively from other committee reports and was essentially a piece of "political propaganda," historian Jeff Webb has observed. It was also obsessed with the public debt.[84]

So disgusted was Keough with the tone and optimism of Cashin's report that he resigned from the finance committee, although he had by then aligned himself with the supporters of Confederation. Robert Job, a scion of a long-established St. John's merchant family and a keen advocate of closer trade relations with the United States, also resigned. Keough opened the debate on the financial report disagreeing with Cashin's assertion that Newfoundland was self-supporting. In a lengthy speech, Keough acknowledged that he had been called a communist and a Confederate, and he wondered why "insisting upon the importance of three square meals a day" for the people of Newfoundland had made him such. He reminded delegates that Cashin and others liked to point out that Newfoundland's per capita debt was $237 compared with $1,387 for Canada and $1,853 for the United States. However, their economies, Cashin argued, were better able to manage their debts than Newfoundland. Moreover, during the Second World War, both the United States and Canada had made major advances in their industrial capacity, while Newfoundland had not. Further, he

Peter Cashin, speaking in the National Convention, was minister of finance from 1928 to 1932 and became one of the fiercest proponents of a return to responsible government. Often unpredictable and always keen to speak his mind, he was not trusted by others who advocated a return to responsible government in the 1946–48 constitutional debates.

suggested, Newfoundland had to face new demands from throughout the whole country. In the past, the government operated on the principle that "the best government was the government that governed least," but going forward, Keough pointed out, the state had to provide public services for the whole country and not only for the Avalon Peninsula. Things had started to change by the 1920s, he said, and "when the boys came marching home the first time [from the Great War], they came to a land suddenly aware of the public amenities of the industrial civilisation on the mainland." While the Second World War brought "war jobs and war dollars," it did not bring prosperity but merely made it possible "for a few more Newfoundlanders than ever before [to come] a little closer than ever before to achieving a decent standard of living." Despite the wartime surplus—which Keough claimed was achieved at the expense of keeping living costs down and failing to provide necessary public services—economic activity in Newfoundland was still no more able than it had been in the past to finance public and social services at a level comparable to those in the rest of North America. "What we must look for today," he insisted, "is some fundamental change indicative of an increase in taxable capacity to support the desired social services," because Newfoundlanders should not be expected to "be forever content with decidedly inferior standards of public and social services than those enjoyed by other British and American peoples." The essential characteristics of the economy of Newfoundland have not changed, Keough concluded, in a clear attack on Cashin, and a $30 million surplus could hide that reality. According to Keough, there was no evidence that in normal economic times Newfoundland had the necessary revenue "to support the public and social services that other western peoples enjoy."[85]

Cashin and other supporters of responsible government, however, saw the $30 million budgetary surplus as an indication of Newfoundland's self-sufficiency and demanded democratic government and full voting rights associated with earlier notions of citizenship. They failed to realize how notions of citizenship had changed, as the Confederates in the National Convention pointed out repeatedly. Cashin, finance minister from 1928 to 1932 and chair of the finance committee, criticized Canada's social programs as immoral.[86] His allies in the Convention and outside chastised the Commission of Government for its spending on social and public welfare during the 1930s.[87] Such language was unfortunate for those who embraced a return to responsible government. These members came across to the listening public, especially those in outport communities, as uncaring about the plight of ordinary Newfoundlanders and out of date with the new dynamism that was sweeping Newfoundland and many other countries. The division between Confederates and those advocating a return to responsible government widened after the National Convention sent separate delegations to the United Kingdom and Canada to determine what aid those countries might offer Newfoundland.

CHAPTER 6

CONSTITUTIONAL OPTIONS EXPLORED: DELEGATIONS TO LONDON AND OTTAWA, 1946–1948

ALTHOUGH JOSEPH R. SMALLWOOD'S MOTION IN OCTOber 1946 to send a delegation to Ottawa failed, a second attempt to explore union with Canada was successful. This time, joining Confederation was presented as part of a wider motion, introduced in the National Convention on February 4, 1947, to send delegations (1) to London to ascertain what economic and financial relationships might be established between the Dominion of Newfoundland and Great Britain; (2) to Washington to investigate a trading relationship between Newfoundland and the United States; and (3) to Ottawa to explore union with the Dominion of Canada.[1] Given the large American military presence, there was considerable interest in the United States in Newfoundland. Robert Job, a leading St. John's businessman whose family had built a commercial empire in Newfoundland over three centuries and one of the Convention's most prominent members, was a strong advocate of closer economic ties with the United States. Smallwood, the leading Confederate, claims that he convinced Job he would support the motion to engage in talks with the Americans if Job agreed to send a delegation to Ottawa.[2] As things turned out, Smallwood needed to string Job along only until something turned up to derail the scion's hopes for a special tariff arrangement with the United States. The pin that let the air out of Job's balloon was the Commission of Government. It refused to permit a delegation to Washington, as Newfoundland's relationship with the United States, including policies regarding trade, was a matter "for negotiation between governments through the regular diplomatic channels" and clearly outside the mandate of the Convention.[3] Only two delegations, therefore, were subsequently dispatched: one to London and then one to Ottawa. The outcomes of those meetings added to the bitterness and acrimony that already marred the National Convention.

THE CONVENTION'S DELEGATION GOES TO LONDON

Chaired by Gordon Bradley, the delegation to London left Gander on April 25, 1947, and returned on May 10. Of the seven members, five—Peter Cashin, Malcolm Hollett, Albert B. Butt, Chesley Crosbie, and H. Pierce Fudge—were clearly supportive of a return to responsible government; each was bitterly opposed to union with Canada. Only two—William J. Keough and Bradley—supported Confederation. Newfoundland Governor Gordon Macdonald and Commissioner for Justice Albert J. Walsh were summoned to London to advise Whitehall during the talks.[4] The five delegates favouring a return to Newfoundland's pre-1934 constitutional status were especially optimistic as they headed across the Atlantic. They fully anticipated a warm and generous welcome upon landing in London. After all, Newfoundland had provided considerable assistance to the Allied Forces during the recent conflict, including an interest-free loan to help Great Britain rebuild once the Second World War was over.[5] Surely, the British would show their appreciation when Newfoundland came calling. The delegates were not, after all, seeking a handout from the British; they were only trying to ascertain what financial and trade assistance the United Kingdom might provide once Newfoundland returned to self-government and then only if it required any financial help in the postwar period. They were hoping to return home with an assurance that the British government would guarantee the country's financial security if it ran into some difficulty later, a condition they believed was necessary to convince their fellow Newfoundlanders to vote for independence and

CHAPTER 6

Gordon Bradley was one of the most respected politicians in the National Convention. He assumed the chair of the Convention when Cyril J. Fox became ill, and he led delegations to both London and Ottawa.

self-rule. They were hoping, too, that London might, for instance, consider the loans that St. John's had extended to Britain as partial payment for Newfoundland's sterling debt or, at the very least, consider paying interest on those outstanding loans. Surely, they believed, Newfoundland could count on Britain for development assistance and trade concessions at some time in the future. Perhaps Whitehall would even commit to increasing its purchases of Newfoundland's exports and shoulder a portion of Gander airport's operating deficit given that Britain was such a heavy user of the facility.[6]

The delegates should have known, however, that London was not likely to be very accommodating. Many in St. John's already knew that the Dominions Office was very hesitant about receiving the delegation in the first place.[7] Those selected to go to London should also have realized that Whitehall was not prepared to engage in a freewheeling discussion of any renewed relationship with Newfoundland, despite the fact that it had been one of the dominions that had helped in the fight against Nazi Germany and in England's postwar reconstruction. For starters, the British government insisted on a tightly scripted conversation with the delegation. It had even requested that questions be submitted before the delegates left St. John's; clearly, that was a way to limit and control the discussion once the delegates arrived. The National Convention had obligingly sent several questions to London, notably about the possibility of cancelling or refunding Newfoundland's long-term debt, modifications to the leased bases agreement with the United States, and new trade and tariff arrangements between Newfoundland and the United Kingdom. The delegation received none of the assurances it sought on any of the subjects raised by the Newfoundlanders. Lord Addison, secretary of state for dominion affairs, Glenvil Hall, member of Parliament and financial secretary to the Treasury, together with other British officials who met the delegation, insisted that if Newfoundland opted for independence, it should not expect financial support from the Government of Great Britain. Newfoundland was not doing so badly, Addison reminded the delegation. The United Kingdom, in contrast, was "burdened with terrific debts and we have had," he lectured them, "as you know, to sacrifice all or the greater part of our overseas assets." Further, he declared that nearly half of Britain's shipping lay at the bottom of the sea and that "therefore with the best of goodwill in the world we are not in a position, however kindly may be our disposition, to be generous in these matters [raised]."[8]

Hall also reminded the Newfoundlanders that they had benefitted enormously from the war, that they had in fact emerged from the conflict with surpluses. He maintained that if the United Kingdom provided generous aid, Prime Minister Clement Attlee would surely be

CHAPTER 6

asked by the Opposition, "Why on earth are you doing this [providing assistance to Newfoundland] when our need is so great?" With some finality, Hall added, "We are, as Lord Addison said, in a jam, otherwise we would meet Newfoundland with open arms."[9] If Commission of Government was retained, and Newfoundland remained essentially a ward of the British government, then Britain would continue to be responsible for some of its finances. If, however, Newfoundland opted for a return to responsible government and became again a separate and independent dominion, then it should not anticipate any financial help from the British.[10] Independence, if chosen, meant that Newfoundlanders would have elected to chart their own course among the community of nations.

Smallwood had been very worried about the possibility of continued assistance from Great Britain, especially in the form of the Commission of Government. He was so troubled that before the Newfoundland delegation left for London, he sent a personal communication to Louis St. Laurent. At this time, and until November 15, 1948, St. Laurent was Canada's minister for external affairs; then he became prime minister of Canada, a position he held until 1957. Smallwood urged St. Laurent to advise the British that any financial support for Newfoundland either as an independent dominion or with continued Commission of Government would likely derail hopes for union with Canada.[11] There is no evidence that St. Laurent acted on Smallwood's suggestions, although clearly Smallwood had no idea of the discussions that had already taken place between the British and the Canadians about the future of Newfoundland. Had Smallwood known of these negotiations, he would not have been so concerned.

The meetings in London, not surprisingly, were tense and unfruitful for Peter Cashin and his allies. They returned to St. John's not only disappointed but also angry and bitter over the treatment they had received from the moment they stepped off the plane. They were met at the airport by Rear Admiral Sir Arthur Bromley, who had suffered disgrace for his negligence in the 1922 loss of the British cruiser HMS *Raleigh* at Point Amour on the south coast of Labrador, with the loss of eleven sailors. To add insult to injury, the Newfoundlanders discovered that an error had been made in their hotel reservations, and alternative, inferior accommodations had to be found.[12] It was an ominous beginning, but delegates did hope that things would improve and that London could be counted on to help if Newfoundland opted for a return to the constitutional arrangement that existed in 1933. It was not to be. The five pro–responsible government delegates went home crushed with what they saw as the uncooperative and obstructive attitude of Lord Addison, and of the Attlee government, more generally. And if London's turning its back on Newfoundland was not infuriating enough, Addison even implied that he might not accept the National Convention's recommendations on the options to put before the electorate regarding his promised referendum. He reminded the delegation that he would seriously consider adding to the options to be presented to the people if the recommendation of a substantial minority in the National Convention was not supported by the majority in the Convention. "We could not be more disappointed, annoyed or insulted by the manner of our reception as an official delegation than we are," was how Cashin described his reaction to Addison's comments: Addison was "playing a clever game with our country, and we are not going to let him get away with it," Cashin promised.[13] He and the other supporters of responsible government had been confident that they could keep union with Canada off the referendum ballot because they had a majority in the National Convention. Addison's intimation that he (Addison) would have the last word on the referendum options changed the ground rules completely, although it should have been no surprise to anyone that at that time—with the Commission of Government in place—London had the final say on any jurisdictional issues concerning Newfoundland. The Newfoundland delegation had learned about Addison's intentions almost by accident, however. The Newfoundlanders had raised questions about choices that might appear on the referendum ballot, and when pressed, Addison had asserted that he had "a say as what should go on the ballot."[14]

Had the delegates taken just a little time to understand him, they would have known that Lord Addison, like Prime Minister Attlee himself, was a strong democrat with an impressive record of looking out for the ordinary citizen. Addison had been an early proponent of social legislation in England, notably promoting national health insurance in 1911 and laying the foundations of the British Ministry of Health in 1919. He was its first minister of health and had promoted

CHAPTER 6

The delegation from the National Convention to London to discuss what assistance Newfoundland might receive from the British government if it opted for independence. Peter Cashin, third from the left, was terribly disappointed with the reception they received in London and alleged that London was attempting to "lure our country into the Canadian mouse-trap."

other legislative measures to improve the welfare of workers. In fact, he had often claimed to have entered politics to improve the conditions of the poor and had switched from the Liberal Party to Labour before the 1924 general election in the United Kingdom. Within the Labour Party, Addison continued to further his deep-seated ambition to improve the health and well-being of the general population, and when Attlee made him secretary of state for dominion affairs, Addison played an instrumental role in Labour's early anti-Imperialist policies, although he was a strong proponent of strengthening the British Commonwealth. Moreover, Addison knew the Newfoundland situation intimately, and he had also become friendly with Canada's prime minister, Mackenzie King.[15] It was perhaps inevitable then that Addison reminded the Newfoundlanders in 1947 that it was for the "people to decide the answers" to their constitutional questions, not the members of the National Convention. A vote on union with Canada, he suggested, was not to be "gauge[d] by the vote in the Convention" but by "the vote of the people." Through his ministers, Prime Minister Attlee himself, in fact, had been advising the Newfoundland delegates to exercise prudence, generosity, and discretion in the National Convention when deciding options to place before voters. But many of the delegates in the National Convention, especially the Cashin contingent, did not see it that way at all. They simply fumed at what they regarded as Addison's and London's interference in their affairs. Yet Addison was resolute in his determination that if an "influential minority said, 'We would like this question put as well', it would be my duty to have regard to that wish... that is for the people to decide."[16]

For Peter Cashin and his supporters, Addison's response to the delegation's queries about the referendum, together with his refusal to provide financial support if Newfoundland opted for independence, were simply clear signs of the long-suspected conspiracy on the part of the British government to force Newfoundland into union with Canada. Cashin believed that the Commission of Government, which he accused of supporting Newfoundland's joining Confederation, had undue influence over Lord Addison and the Attlee government. After all, London had summoned Commissioner for Justice Walsh to assist with the talks. Upon his return to St. John's and speaking in the National Convention, Cashin reminded everyone that the delegation did not "seek financial assistance from the mother country," as "Newfoundland today needs no financial help from anyone. Our country is undoubtedly self-supporting." He charged that the United Kingdom was determined for its own benefit to keep control of Newfoundland "as long as there was a dollar left to the credit of our treasury." Moreover, he asserted, Newfoundland had become for the British "nothing more than an international pawn" that they were using "for the purpose of making international deals with both the United States and Canada." And for Cashin the final objective was obvious: Great Britain wanted Newfoundland to become a part of Canada. "I say to you," he told the assembled members of the Convention on his return from London, "that there is in operation at the present time a conspiracy to sell, and I use the word 'sell' advisedly, this country to the Dominion of Canada." He then reminded members that, in 1869, Newfoundland, "as a far poorer country and a less enlightened people," had prevented the British from railroading it into union with Canada. This time, warned Cashin, "attractive bait" will be used once more to "lure our country into the Canadian mouse-trap. Listen to the flowery sales talk

CHAPTER 6

which will be offered you, telling Newfoundlanders they are a lost people, that our only hope, our only salvation, lies in following a new Moses into the promised land across the Cabot Strait." He called upon voters to be as vigilant as their grandparents had been in 1869 and to defeat those "walking amongst us . . . whose burning ambition it is to see this country passed into the hands of strangers; to haul down the flag of our fathers and replace it with an alien one; to make the Ode to Newfoundland a forgotten thing on the lips of our children, and to extinguish the torch which our liberty-loving ancestors cherished for nearly 100 years."[17] Pierce Fudge agreed. He described the London meetings as resembling "an underground conspiracy planning some illegal movement" rather than a meeting with representatives of the British government.[18]

For Bradley and Keough, however, what transpired in London was reason to be hopeful.[19] They had feared that if they had to depend on the National Convention to place union with Canada on the referendum ballot, their cause was surely doomed. As a way to counter that, they had attempted throughout the Convention proceedings to appeal not to the small group convened in the Colonial Building but to the Newfoundland voter through the nightly radio broadcasts over the government-owned Broadcasting Corporation of Newfoundland. The supporters of union in the National Convention fully understood the obstacles they faced in having Confederation with Canada put before the electorate. Bradley and Keough were delighted with Addison's intervention, of course, and on the eve of their departure from London, Bradley told the press that he was not surprised by the reception the delegates had received in the British capital. In fact, he was pleased with the British attitude towards Newfoundland, and he declared that thousands of Newfoundlanders feared the return of responsible government, as their country did not have the capacity to provide a stable economy on its own. It was a "ship in the ocean," said Bradley, dependent upon foreign trade, and "we have to sell what we produce—we have to buy what we consume, and we have no control over the prices of either." There had been, he also pointed out, a swing in opinion regarding Confederation, and all that was needed was for the Canadian government to give acceptable terms and Newfoundland would become the tenth province of Canada. Bradley also told the London press that he would soon lead a delegation to Ottawa. When the referendum was held, it would show, he predicted, union with Canada was the second choice among voters, with a continuation of the commission system first and responsible government third.[20]

Back in the National Convention, Bradley and Keough disagreed "completely" with Cashin's interpretation of how the delegation had been treated in London and how the British had behaved. They were a fact-finding mission, Keough insisted, but some members—alluding particularly to Cashin—attempted to "bargain and negotiate" with British officials. Directing his comments "to the people of this island" listening by radio, Keough added, "I am convinced that Lord Addison and the United Kingdom government have dealt with us in good faith," and that they "will facilitate in every way an expression of your opinion as to the form of government you really do desire." He added, "The British government is not going to try and sell you up the St. Lawrence."[21] As Peter Neary points out, "The British could only get their way if Newfoundlanders would go along with them," and Whitehall had no way to gauge how Newfoundlanders would vote in the upcoming referendum.[22] The British government even had contingency plans in case their desired objectives for Newfoundland failed.

Yet it could by no means be denied that the British had a preferred policy on Newfoundland, even if it had become self-supporting during the war and had such surplus that it could provide financial assistance to weary London. There was considerable concern within Attlee's government that in the postwar turmoil, Newfoundland would likely find itself in a situation where it required financial assistance as it had in the years before the war. After all, there had been no real structural changes in the Newfoundland economy during the war. When the Commission of Government prepared a ten-year reconstruction plan for the country, estimated at $100 million, Britain recoiled. It had neither the appetite nor the ability to provide such funds. Attlee had warned Newfoundlanders when he announced the National Convention that "special difficulties [of Britain's] financial position over the next few years may well preclude us from undertaking fresh commitments."[23] Moreover, the Commission of Government itself had earlier warned London that Newfoundland's surplus should be guarded prudently. Even though revenues were holding up, "the ugly heads of unemployment and relief" had reappeared in the immediate postwar period, and it was anticipated that revenues would soon fall and "substantial payments on account of relief" could be expected. In fact, the number of persons on relief in fiscal 1944–45 had increased by nearly 25 percent over that of just two years earlier when wartime employment had peaked in Newfoundland, and expenditure on public relief had mushroomed from $280,000 to $592,000 in the same period.[24] A permanent solution had to be found to the question of Newfoundland, and Britain believed union with Canada was the most appropriate course of action. Newfoundlanders, however, had long resisted such an arrangement, and they had to be convinced that joining Confederation was in their best interests. One way of doing that—as Peter Cashin pointed out—was to limit the available options on the referendum ballot. Britain liked to point out that Confederation would accomplish what Newfoundlanders surely wanted: the restoration of democracy and the re-establishment of responsible government, revoked during the Great Depression. Union with Canada would also provide Newfoundlanders with a measure of social and economic security that they had long lacked. Even the Irish press, which watched the events in Newfoundland closely, editorialized while the Newfoundland delegation was in London that "Union with Canada would seem to be the most practicable way to a solution of the administrative difficulties that have troubled Newfoundland for a considerable time."[25] Although the British might have worked to make such a union possible, there was still considerable lifting to be done by Smallwood, Bradley, and others to achieve victory for the Confederate cause.

THE CONVENTION'S DELEGATION GOES TO OTTAWA

A keen advocate of Newfoundland's union with Canada was J. Scott Macdonald, Charles Burchell's successor as Canada's high commissioner to Newfoundland. Three months before the election of members to the National Convention, and long before the Canadian government had formally agreed to receive a delegation of them (should Newfoundland even be interested in sending one), Macdonald had dispatched to Prime Minister King a detailed analysis of the attitude in Newfoundland towards joining Confederation. At the time King was secretary of state for external affairs in addition to being prime minister. That document was widely circulated; it was forwarded to Brooke Claxton, minister of national defence, and to Louis St. Laurent, then minister of justice, as well as to other ministers and officials in the Department of Finance and at the Bank of Canada. It was even copied to Canadian embassy officials in Washington and London. Macdonald had given much space in his dispatch to a series of letters Smallwood had written for the local newspapers. He noted that Smallwood had emphasized "the great benefits that would automatically accrue to Newfoundlanders generally through Confederation"—among them the abolition of customs duties on Canadian goods, though they were the major source of government revenue for Newfoundland; the lower tariff against other foreign goods; unemployment relief at Canadian rates; the family allowance and old age pensions; and the right to migrate to any part of Canada. Smallwood had estimated, Macdonald pointed out, that the cost of living for Newfoundlanders following union would drop by about a third. Macdonald also commented on speeches given on Confederation by John B. McEvoy and Peter Cashin, but noted that "there is little genuine sentiment in Newfoundland for union with Canada in the positive sense of desiring to be part of the Dominion and to work together for the building up of a great nation stretching from St. John's to Victoria." The sentiments that existed throughout the Island for joining Canada, he surmised, were "based on the feeling that Newfoundland's economic position is rather precarious and that Newfoundlanders would enjoy greater prosperity and a more assured future in a turbulent world if they were part of the Dominion."[26] It certainly was never sentiment or any feelings of attachment that would bring Newfoundland to Canada, but the wide circulation of Macdonald's document suggests that the interest in Newfoundland throughout the Canadian government was great, although ministers and officials also understood that if Newfoundlanders were to vote for Confederation, it would be primarily to improve their own standard of living. The dreams of 1867 might finally be fulfilled because Newfoundlanders regarded Canada as the best means of achieving a measure of social, financial, and economic stability that it might not find if it opted for independence and a return to responsible government. This did not seem to bother the Canadians very much, if at all.

CHAPTER 6

On October 30, 1946, King's Cabinet made the decision to welcome a delegation from the National Convention to discuss the possibility of union, if members there proposed such a group. King then authorized the establishment of two committees to oversee discussions on the possibility of union between the two countries. The Cabinet Committee on Newfoundland would have decision-making authority, and it would offer recommendations for consideration of the full Cabinet. Chaired by Louis St. Laurent, who became the minister of external affairs on September 4, this committee consisted of King's most senior ministers: J.L. Ilsley, the new minister of justice and attorney general as well as member of Parliament for Halifax; C.D. Howe, minister of reconstruction and supply; Frank Bridges, minister of fisheries and New Brunswick's representative in the Cabinet; Douglas Abbott, minister of finance; Brooke Claxton, minister of defence; and Senator Wishart M. Robertson. John R. Baldwin of the Privy Council Office was appointed secretary. The Cabinet Committee supervised an Interdepartmental Committee on Canada-Newfoundland Relations (ICCNR), which comprised representatives from a number of government departments. Its task was to study the problems and costs associated with union and make recommendations to the Cabinet Committee on possible terms (of union).[27]

Officials in the Department of External Affairs were obviously pleased with the Cabinet's decision. They had been pushing King since the beginning of the Second World War to be more proactive on Newfoundland. Norman Robertson, undersecretary of state for external affairs, had had his special assistant Dr. Robert A. MacKay prepare a detailed memorandum as a basis for discussion in hopes that Canada's policy towards Newfoundland would be more aggressive than it had been in the past. By April 1944, that memorandum had been reviewed by the whole Cabinet.[28] The Interdepartmental Committee saw that Newfoundland would likely experience financial difficulties as a province, and by the time the Cabinet Committee on Newfoundland reported to King, in December 1946, it projected that union would cost Canada between $10 and $15 million annually. The price tag was jarring, but it did not diminish Ottawa's interest.[29] Although King privately worried about the cost of union, he continued to publicly express enthusiastic support for it. He was delighted that it might fall to him to fulfill the original dream of the makers of Canada to unite all the former British possessions in North America. The prospect of joining those illustrious nation builders, he told his diary, might tempt him "to remain a little longer in public life than otherwise I would wish to be."[30] Of course, the addition of Newfoundland and Labrador would, indeed, round out the Dominion of Canada from sea to sea, but there were more practical and tangible reasons why union would be beneficial to Canada. Newfoundland would bring to the dominion considerable resource wealth, including a thriving and expansive fishery, mineral and (potential) hydroelectric resources, especially in the vast Labrador territory, and forestry assets. Union with Canada would also safeguard the Newfoundland market, valued at between $25 and $40 million, for Canadian exporters, and it would assure Canada of its defence and civil aviation privileges in Newfoundland while limiting the American influence in the region.[31]

The delegation from the National Convention arrived in Ottawa on June 24, 1947. Once again, Bradley was chairman, and he told a reporter that their objective was "to see if we can ascertain a fair and equitable basis, fair to both Canada and Newfoundland, by which the colony can enter Confederation." Bradley said he had no real "index of the feelings of the Newfoundland people," but they would decide their constitutional future in a referendum at a later date.[32] Besides Bradley, the delegation of seven included Smallwood, Thomas G.W. Ashbourne, Charles Ballam, and Reverend Lester Burry, all of whom were either sympathetic to or strong supporters of union, and P.W. Crummey and Gordon Higgins, both of whom leaned towards a return to responsible government and independence for Newfoundland. High Commissioner Macdonald had already informed Ottawa that the delegation could furnish "little to the information on Newfoundland which is not already in our possession," adding, "we will... know a good deal more about the economic and financial position of Newfoundland than the delegation themselves." He observed that "the delegation will not be of much assistance, therefore, to the Canadian Government in reaching a decision on the question of whether or not to make an offer of union." Aside from Smallwood, he wrote, the delegation was not well informed on the federal form of government and "are essentially small town men with no great experience of government."[33]

CHAPTER 6

Delegation from the National Convention, which negotiated the entry of Newfoundland into Confederation, Railway Committee Room, Centre Block, Parliament Buildings, June 25, 1947. (Front, l.–r.): Joseph R. Smallwood, Hon. F. Gordon Bradley, Rt. Hon. William Lyon Mackenzie King, Louis St. Laurent, and J.L. Isley (Rear, l.–r.): P.W. Crummey, Rev. Lester Burry, Thomas G.W. Ashbourne, Hon. Douglas Abbott, Gordon Higgins, J.J. McCann, Charles Ballam, and Hon. Frank Bridges.

It was perhaps a tactical error for those who supported responsible government to have controlled the London delegation and to have allowed the Confederates to dominate the Ottawa one. Bradley claimed that he had been a Confederate since his days at Dalhousie University and had once declared "I don't care two straws for Newfoundland as an abstraction." He considered Newfoundland from the perspective of "pessimistic realism." Moreover, he believed that Newfoundland, "small, remote and economically weak ... could not survive and prosper as an independent unit." Like many liberals, Bradley rejected socialism as a political philosophy, but he did believe that "the state had a primary duty to serve the greatest good of the greatest number and to help those most in need."³⁴ For him, joining Canada would permit Newfoundland to address its unique economic and social situation and provide access to new social programs that had become commonplace elsewhere. He was convinced that Newfoundlanders had to be provided with the features of social citizenship that were then widely available throughout Canada. Five of the seven delegates to Ottawa shared Bradley's view.

The outcome of the discussions in Ottawa was never in doubt. Nevertheless, Canada's long-serving deputy minister of finance, William Clifford Clark, took it upon himself to express his opinion to Julian Harrington, counsellor at the American Embassy in Ottawa, that Canada would have a "little Ireland on its hand—a disgruntled people no matter what is done for them."³⁵ Cabinet had already agreed that it would let the delegation know that Ottawa was keen on union, and should the people of Newfoundland indicate such a desire, Canada would be prepared to admit Newfoundland as a province. And it would provide Newfoundland the treatment "accorded other provinces." This meant that Ottawa was prepared to discuss how the instruments and services of the federal government might be extended to the new province and how it might assist the new provincial government over a transitional period to maintain a reasonable standard of public services and balance the provincial budget.³⁶ Ottawa was not, however, prepared to go much beyond that.

The meetings between the two sides were essentially discussions about extending a range of federal services to Newfoundland, with Canada absorbing from the Newfoundland government those areas that fell within federal responsibility. Smallwood was the dominant member of the delegation, and he had clear expectations of what such a union would mean—and they largely aligned with what Ottawa was to offer. Earlier, in November 1946, he had defended Confederation against attacks from several members of the National Convention. Writing in the St. John's *Evening Telegram*, he had pointed out that under its constitution Canada would assume the cost of operating a variety of services then provided by the Newfoundland government at great expense, notably the Cabot Strait ferry service, the railway, and coastal boat services. He let readers know, if they did not already, that the federal government provided to the provinces a federal penitentiary, a demonstration farm, a national park, and national harbours. Ottawa would assume responsibility for Newfoundland's public debt of approximately $73 million and also grant a variety of annual subsidies and transfers. Beyond that, Newfoundlanders would receive Canada's social welfare programs, including old age pensions, the family allowance, and veterans' pensions. In joining Confederation, Newfoundland would continue to make progress on a number of public and social services, including education, health care, and local road-building initiatives.[37] Ottawa did not anticipate any hard bargaining from the Newfoundland delegation, as the federal-provincial arrangement was pretty much set by the practices instituted after Confederation in 1867 and by the *British North America Act*. Newfoundland would simply fit into the existing Canadian framework.

In the first meeting between the Newfoundland delegation and representatives of the Government of Canada, Gordon Bradley tried to present Newfoundland's situation in the best light he could. The impact of the Great Depression, he said, had been "disastrous" for Newfoundland, and the National Convention had been "led, in turn, to the thought that possibly the integration of our Newfoundland economy with that of a much larger, much more diversified, and more stable economy would be the real solution of our country's problems. It is a very small step from consideration of economic integration to constitutional and political federation." Yet, added Bradley, Newfoundland did not want "economic crutches" but "rather the removal of certain economic impediments in our basic industries that are the inescapable product of our economic and constitutional insecurity." He noted, in particular, the hardships caused by import duties. In concluding, he asked, "Is it too much to hope that out of these conversations commencing today there may emerge a fair and equitable basis of federal union which both peoples, Canadians and Newfoundlanders, will willingly, indeed gladly, accept?"[38]

By hosting the delegation, Ottawa had accepted the likelihood of union. As a first step in the discussions, it presented the Newfoundland delegation with an important document titled "Some Notes on the Constitution and Government of Canada and the Canadian Federal System." This was a detailed introduction to Canada's federal system. Extensive in its range of topics, the document included a discussion of the constitution (the *BNA Act*), how the Government of Canada operated, what federal services were provided across the country, and the functions performed by various federal boards, agencies, and offices. It addressed "the classes of subjects in which the Federal Parliament has exclusive jurisdiction." Much of the document was given over to those federal services and under what conditions union could be made to work.[39]

In the talks that followed, the financial situation of Newfoundland generated the greatest attention. Robert A. MacKay was tasked with leading the Interdepartmental Committee on Canada-Newfoundland Relations. He had earlier written to Ira Wild, commissioner for finance in St. John's, inquiring about budget and income tax matters. The subject revolved largely around the expenditures that Newfoundland would have to meet as a province.[40] MacKay also asked J. Scott Macdonald for his view on the financial terms he had been preparing in the summer of 1946, but Macdonald was not much help. He advised that Ottawa consider "offering Newfoundland vastly improved ocean communications with Canada" and build in Newfoundland a trans-insular highway so that people could "drive to the mainland [with a car ferry] in the same way that they do in Prince Edward Island." Such commitments from Canada, he told MacKay, would "be sufficiently spectacular to capture the imagination of Newfoundlanders." Macdonald had earlier described the deplorable conditions—and, indeed, absence—of highways and roads in Newfoundland, suggesting that it would take upward of $40 million to construct an adequate road transportation system in Newfoundland.[41] Isolation was one of the greatest problems facing Newfoundland, and people wanted better transportation facilities within the country and to Canada.

Grand visions of a new transportation infrastructure might be appealing, but the state of Newfoundland's finances remained the critical issue. The Financial Subcommittee, one of eleven that the two sides had created to facilitate the discussions in Ottawa, studied the estimates of federal revenues and expenditures in Newfoundland in the event of union and how Newfoundland would balance its budget as a province. It was soon clear to both sides that there was considerable risk, especially over the financial viability of Newfoundland as a province. Ottawa would have liked to defer discussion of financial

CHAPTER 6

matters until there was some certainty that Newfoundland would, indeed, join Canada. The Newfoundlanders, however, wanted a commitment right then and there that "a fair and equitable basis of union" could be arranged. On July 14, 1947, St. Laurent informed the Cabinet that the Newfoundland delegation "will not be satisfied with an undertaking to discuss financial matters in the event of a Newfoundland vote in favour of union with Canada." The delegates wanted an offer of concrete terms from Canada so that they could return home confident that an arrangement was in place for Newfoundland's entry into Confederation. The delegation also wanted some assurance that union would provide the new province with a reasonably sound financial future. Bradley had made it known that if the terms were beneficial to Newfoundland, he would be a strong advocate for union, but if not, he would retire to Bonavista and watch the proceedings from there. The Canadians had long seen Bradley as key to a successful campaign for union in Newfoundland and believed that without him any hopes for union were doomed.[42]

There was some scurrying in Ottawa in the few days that followed St. Laurent's report to the Cabinet, as officials reminded St. Laurent that the difficult financial question would require a political solution. When St. Laurent discussed the matter with King, the prime minister reminded him that he had warned from the beginning that Newfoundland had the potential to create political problems for the government, but King stopped short of bringing the negotiations to an end. At the Cabinet meeting on July 18, St. Laurent reported that union would cost Canada approximately $15 million more in expenditures than it would gain in revenues. He noted this amount was in addition to assuming Newfoundland's debt, offering a special subsidy to meet an anticipated provincial budget deficit, or the "budget gap" as the two sides started calling the matter, and other anticipated expenditures, such as investments in the Newfoundland Railway to bring it up to Canadian standards. The amounts were troubling. Nevertheless, at that meeting the Cabinet decided to move ahead with the negotiations and make a "serious effort" to complete Confederation with the addition of Newfoundland.[43]

Smallwood, who was waiting outside the Parliament Buildings while King met his Cabinet, was elated when J. Scott Macdonald informed him of the Cabinet's July 18 decision. It was rumoured that he and other members of the delegation were becoming increasingly frustrated with the slow pace of the negotiations and Ottawa's obvious reluctance to confront the issues facing Newfoundland in fear of a backlash from the other provinces.[44] In hindsight, such discussions were a harbinger for Smallwood of how the federal system worked.[45] The situation was further complicated, it seems, by the Newfoundland delegation's insistence on even greater generosity on terms that Ottawa thought had already been agreed to by the Newfoundlanders. The Canadians, it seems, also considered the Newfoundlanders "pretty irresponsible" at times during the negotiations. P.A. Clutterbuck, then the British high commissioner to Canada, reported that the Canadian representatives were also becoming frustrated with most of the delegates who were "pressing for a basis which would in effect have given [the] new provincial government complete freedom to indulge in all kinds of extravagant expenditure while leaving [the] federal government to cover [the] provincial debt."[46]

But both groups wanted to consummate a deal. Thus, the Canadian government realized that a specific offer, including specific financial arrangements to Newfoundland, would have to be made. The negotiations stalled shortly thereafter, however, when on August 10, Frank Bridges, the New Brunswick representative in the federal Cabinet, died suddenly. King had feared all along that the Newfoundland Confederation talks might become embroiled in Canada's party politics, and he refused to finalize the terms and make a public announcement during the forthcoming by-election campaign. Moreover, Quebec premier Maurice Duplessis, still smarting over the 1927 JCPC ruling that awarded Labrador to Newfoundland (see Chapter 3), entered the fray by expressing his reluctance to have Newfoundland join Canada without reopening the Labrador boundary question. Also, Nova Scotia premier Angus L. Macdonald wondered aloud if the provinces should be consulted on the entry of another into the Confederation.[47] King would eventually dismiss all those concerns, since according to Liberal polling, a majority of Canadians, including supporters of all three major parties, favoured union. It was unlikely, then, that the opposition parties would attempt to make political hay out of any proposal to bring Newfoundland into the Confederation. Yet he insisted—despite

CHAPTER 6

objections from St. Laurent and others in his Cabinet—that the political risk of announcing an arrangement with Newfoundland during the New Brunswick by-election was too great. To conclude union, Newfoundland would require special terms, and once they were made public, feared King, "the different provinces would begin to take exception to them," and Canadians, especially those in New Brunswick, would be asking why they were "treating strangers better than our own people and supporters." John B. McNair, the New Brunswick Liberal premier, agreed, telling King that the by-election would be an easy win for the Liberals if Newfoundland were kept out of the campaign. And it was.[48]

The Ottawa talks between the Newfoundlanders and the Canadians dragged on intermittently, awaiting the outcome of the by-election in New Brunswick. Some members of the National Convention became increasingly impatient with Bradley and the amount of time the delegation was spending away from St. John's. In mid-July, five members of the Convention, led by Peter Cashin and Malcolm Hollett, telegraphed Bradley that they had met with Governor Gordon Macdonald, on behalf of some twenty-five delegates, and demanded that the Convention resume immediately. Keough described Cashin and Hollett's intervention as an act of "megalomaniacal conceit" and said that he strongly favoured the "Ottawa delegation taking adequate time to accumulate all information to which the Newfoundland people are entitled in justice."[49] Bradley agreed. He refused to engage with his detractors from a distance, claiming, "I have no comment to make." Then he consulted Governor Macdonald, who advised him to complete his work in Ottawa.[50] The discontented in the National Convention charged that Bradley was simply trying to postpone a vote as the negotiations in Ottawa were going badly. On July 18, Bradley cabled Cashin and the other four delegates, explaining his refusal to return immediately to St. John's to reconvene the Convention. He also declared his intention to continue talks with the Canadians until a deal was complete. A few days later, on July 21, supporters of responsible government responded with the formal establishment of the Responsible Government League (see next chapter) to fight joining Canada. A provisional executive under President Francis M. O'Leary of St. John's was appointed and a list of potential members drawn from both St. John's and outport Newfoundland was prepared.[51] The battle lines in the constitutional struggle were now more formally drawn.

After four more weeks of discussions in Ottawa, Bradley and St. Laurent announced that they would soon reach an agreement, which they hoped would provide a basis for union between the two countries. Bradley assured Newfoundlanders that these terms would then be presented to the National Convention and later to the people in a referendum.[52] Further talks then ensued, much to the dismay of responsible government supporters in the Convention. Bradley's comments had done little to mollify his opponents, however. Again in early September, members of the Convention, on two separate occasions, requested that Bradley bring the delegation home immediately, declaring that he had exceeded the terms of reference given to the delegation. The responsible government faction also expressed grave concerns over press reports of Quebec's continued "antagonistic attitude towards Newfoundland" and its refusal to accept the Labrador boundary decision of 1927.[53] Bradley again dismissed the unease and opposition of his fellow delegates, telling them on September 9 that "his thorough investigation" of union would continue and that discussions were coming to a conclusion. A few days later, he cabled National Convention Secretary Gordon Warren that the delegates would reconvene on October 8, when they would consider the arrangement that had been forged with the Canadians in Ottawa.[54]

A draft working document entitled "Basis for the Admission of Newfoundland as a Province of Canada" was completed by September 23, 1947, and agreed to by the two sides on September 29, the day before Bradley and his delegation finally left Ottawa by train for Newfoundland. During a stopover in Montreal, Smallwood confidently declared that Newfoundland would vote to join Canada when a referendum was held the following spring.[55] Prime Minister King hoped that would, indeed, be the case, but when he first saw the terms his ministers had negotiated, he was horrified. "We were giving Newfoundland pretty much everything that she wanted without adequately weighing what Canada would be getting in return," he fumed.[56] He had refused to have the Cabinet approve the proposed terms with the New Brunswick by-election hanging in the balance, and he was clearly delighted that it had been decided to allow the Newfoundland delegation to return to St. John's without having any final terms in hand. It had also been decided that the two sides would not issue a report on what they considered to be a mutually satisfactory result of their discussions as that would appear to be too much like "negotiations." It was agreed instead that the Canadian representatives who had "negotiated" with the Newfoundlanders would submit a series of proposals to the Canadian Cabinet based on what had been agreed to with the Newfoundland delegation. The Cabinet would then decide what terms they were prepared to recommend to Parliament as the basis for the union of Canada and Newfoundland. The Canadian government would then communicate formally through the governor of Newfoundland to the National Convention on a proposed arrangement for union. The Newfoundland delegation had also insisted that any such communications should include an explanatory statement of various items raised by the Newfoundland representatives.[57] After ninety-nine days in Ottawa, the National Convention's delegation arrived back in St. John's by train on Saturday morning, October 4.[58]

THE PROPOSED TERMS OF UNION

A few days after the Liberal by-election win in New Brunswick, the federal Cabinet quickly approved the draft arrangements for union with Newfoundland.[59] Then on October 28, 1947, Prime Minister King informed Governor Macdonald that the "Proposed Arrangements for the Entry of Newfoundland into Confederation" were "a basis for union ... that would be fair and equitable to both countries." King further added, "I feel I must emphasize that as far as the financial aspects of the proposed arrangements for union are concerned, the Government of Canada believes that the arrangements go as far as the Government can go under the circumstances." King was acutely aware of how the other provinces might view the terms, and he reminded Macdonald that "the Government could not readily contemplate any changes in these arrangements which would impose larger financial burdens on Canada." Yet King was more than willing to reconsider any of the issues that did not involve money. "On the other hand, with respect to those matters which are primarily of provincial concern, such as education," he wrote, "the Government of Canada would not wish to set down any rigid conditions, and it would be prepared to give reasonable consideration to suggestions for modification or addition."[60] In keeping with the original Confederation pact between the federal and provincial governments in 1867, the Canadian government promised Newfoundland in 1947 that it would continue to recognize and accommodate the diversity that existed within the provinces.

The "Proposed Arrangements for the Entry of Newfoundland into Confederation" were presented to the National Convention on November 6, 1947, but not before Bradley resigned as chairman of the National Convention on October 10[61] to avoid facing a non-confidence motion that was being planned against him. He was replaced by John McEvoy, a lawyer and former student of Robert A. MacKay at Dalhousie University. Because the proposed terms had grey covers, they became known as the "Grey Books," and they were immediately published in the local press. Newfoundland was to be admitted as a separate province of Canada, and then all federal public and social welfare services were to be made available immediately to Newfoundlanders. Canada would take responsibility for the Newfoundland Railway, postal services, fishery protection, broadcasting, civil aviation, and customs. Newfoundland's sterling debt would become Canada's responsibility, but as a new province, Newfoundland would retain its financial surplus for development purposes and receive a variety of subsidies. These subsidies included an annual payment of $180,000, plus 80 cents per person (subject to periodic increases), and a $1.1 million special annual subsidy in lieu of various fixed annual payments provided by statute to the Maritime provinces. Additionally, Ottawa would provide a special transitional grant of $3.15 million during each of the first three years of union, which would diminish gradually over a twelve-year transitional period. Within eight years of union, the Canadian government would appoint a royal commission to review the province's financial position and recommend the form and scale of any further additional assistance. Such a review would likely minimize the financial risk to the province, and in Smallwood's understanding, ensure that union would create a secure and stable future for Newfoundland. In Smallwood's recollection, he and MacKay negotiated the transitional grant arrangement in the hot Ottawa summer in 1947: "We two were locked up all

CHAPTER 6

day in a room in the East Block of [the] Parliament Buildings, without air conditioning, in the heat of July and August. I usually stripped to the waist—and still sweated in that oven."[62] Newfoundland would have seven members in the House of Commons and six senators.

Not all matters of concern for the Newfoundland delegation were covered in the "Proposed Arrangements for the Entry of Newfoundland into Confederation," however. They had posed a number of questions of the Canadian representatives on a variety of issues, and because these matters were more practical than constitutional, they were included in the "Summary of Proceedings," published by the Government of Canada as Part II of the "Meetings between Delegates from the National Convention of Newfoundland and Representatives of the Government of Canada" (Black Books). Included in this material were the opening statements of Bradley and King, a summary of the proceedings in Ottawa, and a series of memoranda (prepared jointly by the two sides) that had been used to launch the discussions on union. Clutterbuck, who had watched the negotiations closely in Ottawa, thought that the Canadian offer was "exceptionally generous" and went far beyond "any experience previously entertained." He believed that Newfoundland received a financial arrangement comparable with that of the other provinces, with an additional transitional grant and with the added fiscal assurances of a promise to review the fiscal situation within eight years.[63]

In Newfoundland, there was considerable opposition to the Confederation proposals—both within the National Convention and outside of it. Albert Perlin of the St. John's *Daily News* was particularly concerned with the proposed terms and Smallwood's proposed budget, prepared for the National Convention, for Newfoundland as a province of Canada. Perlin suggested that Smallwood had underestimated both the revenue and the expenditure needs of Newfoundland in Confederation. Like many others, Perlin believed that responsible government should first be restored and then negotiations carried out with Canada. That process would allow the use of experts by both sides and protect Newfoundland's national interest, something Perlin charged had not occurred in the recently concluded sessions in Ottawa. "At almost all of those meetings," he claimed correctly, "the Canadian government was fortified by the presence of technical advisers while at some times the Newfoundland delegation found itself compelled to postpone the consultations while statistical information was procured from the government in St. John's."[64] The proposed terms were debated in the National Convention for thirty-four days, beginning on November 20, 1947, and lasting until January 16, 1948. That debate generated considerable interest across Newfoundland.[65]

Although the National Convention debated each of the proposed terms, it was, in essence, debating the impact of union with Canada on Newfoundland. Smallwood led for the Confederate side and championed union, trying to sell the idea to the people through the daily broadcasts of the proceedings over the Broadcasting Corporation of Newfoundland. His message was simple: as a small nation, Newfoundland could not prosper on its own. Canada promised security and an improved standard of living, as well as a return to responsible and democratically elected government.[66] As Bradley had done in the opening session with representatives of the Canadian government in Ottawa, Smallwood again mixed patriotism with realism in his defence of the proposed terms in the National Convention. He insisted that

> Newfoundland may be described as a country in search of a satisfactory form of government . . . . We believe we possess very great possibilities of development and expansion along industrial lines. We have lacked the capital and the adequate population—and here I am thinking of numbers—to develop our natural resources to anything more than a token of what we believe they might be. We believe we possess at last the basic possibilities of enduring prosperity, if once we come by the type of government that will be a help rather than a hindrance to sound development. We are wondering frankly whether Confederation is that type of government.[67]

For Smallwood, Bradley, and other supporters of union, the debate on the articles of union was about the form of government that would ensure prosperity and social and economic security for Newfoundland.

This view was reflected in Smallwood's final speech in the debate on union in the National Convention. "These terms," he said, "would make a new country of Newfoundland," continuing his narrative from

CHAPTER 6

eighteen months earlier that Newfoundland was not a nation. The new reconstructed constitution, he believed, had to make Newfoundland better for the worker and his family. These terms "would make a new country for the people of Newfoundland—a new country where the poor man would have a chance. A country where the poor man would have a chance to live and breathe, a chance to bring up his family decently. These terms," he insisted, "would give our people a chance, and that is something they have never had yet. And when I say our people," he said, clearly playing to the voters listening on the radio, "I mean the toiling masses of our people, our fishermen and loggers, our miners and millworkers, our railroaders and teachers, our clerks and labourers, all our people who toil by hand or brain to make a living in this country."[68] For Smallwood, Confederation "would be a new charter of happiness for our children." He promised the union with Canada "would mean a happier land, a land of hope and progress. The people would come at last into their own." He claimed that "For the country in general, these terms would mean hitching Newfoundland's wagon to the rising, shining star that we call the great British nation of Canada. It would mean linking our own dear Newfoundland to the third largest land in the world—a land where the common people get a break, where they get a decent chance to live and rear their families." And then, sensing that he was riding the new tide of history that would change the lives of people throughout the country through Canada's new social welfare measures, Smallwood added, "For Newfoundland these terms mean security and political freedom."[69]

Smallwood's message was powerful, and it could not be easily dismissed. Confederation promised Newfoundland the financial and fiscal security and stability that it might not otherwise have, even if it meant rejecting independence as a country. The full range of Canadian social security benefits—from the family allowance to unemployment insurance to increased veterans' benefits—provided a measure of security that Newfoundland workers and families had never before experienced. With the removal of customs duties, Canadian goods would enter free of duty, resulting in a lower cost of living for many. On the issue of the family allowance, for instance, Smallwood spoke directly to Newfoundlanders. In one instance, he noted that if there were 270 children under the age of sixteen in the District of Bay de

Verde, the parents would collectively receive $1,620 a month in family allowance payments. To Smallwood, Canada was the promised land. But his opponents in the National Convention tried vociferously to denigrate the proposed terms. They insisted that parents would have to pay in taxes to the federal government the amount they received in family allowances and other social programs, a point that Smallwood vehemently rejected. In the debate, Peter Cashin, the greater orator and respected politician, demonstrated how out of touch he was with the current thinking in the modern world and how little he understood of the growing demand for social reform and the hope for government intervention to improve the lives of ordinary people. Cashin deprecated Smallwood's visionary talk of championing the working people and transforming Newfoundland society through the introduction of social programs. The supporters of responsible government instinctively favoured the right over the left in the debate over social citizenship. In the final days of the National Convention, Cashin blasted the family allowance as "the most immoral and corrupt enactment that has ever stained the pages of the statutes of Canada." Smallwood responded with a single word: "Nonsense."[70] A few days earlier, Cashin had become so agitated and angry in the National Convention that he left his seat and attacked Smallwood physically.[71] Later still, when Pierce Fudge angered Smallwood, Smallwood "immediately lost his temper," the *Evening Telegram* reported, and shouted out to Fudge "are you trying to scare me, I don't scare easy." He then challenged Fudge to settle their differences outside.[72] Certainly, the debate was very emotional.

The motion to return responsible government to Newfoundland was debated for four days.[73] Then Gordon Higgins, one of the delegates for the City of St. John's, moved on January 19, 1948, that the National Convention formally recommend to the Government of Great Britain that both responsible government (as it existed in 1933) and the continuation of the Commission of Government be placed before the voters of Newfoundland in a national referendum. Confederation was decidedly not among the proposed options. Smallwood, along with about a dozen others, spoke against the motion, stating he agreed with responsible government in principle, but disagreed with it in practice. He felt that a return to the former system was a "terrible gamble to take"

CHAPTER 6

because under responsible government "Newfoundland went broke. This country went on the rocks, people were on the dole in the tens of thousands, children were hungry and naked, standards of health were very low and tuberculosis soared."[74] Yet Smallwood supported the motion. It passed unanimously on January 22.

The next day, Smallwood moved that the referendum ballot also include the option of the union of Newfoundland with Canada based on the proposals from the Canadian government that had been presented to the National Convention. In making his case, Smallwood said that the terms of union had been thoroughly debated in the Convention and that "new hope has arisen in the hearts of our people." They saw in Canada "new hope for the common man ... and new hope for justice and fair play for themselves and their children. They see in it the dawn of a new day for Newfoundland." If the anti-Confederates were so confident that they spoke for the people, Smallwood challenged his foes, then let the people have the opportunity to vote against it in the referendum.[75] Others within the National Convention saw no need of that. "Newfoundland is being bartered away," some cried. Albert Penney, a businessman from Carbonear and an anti-Confederate, said it best: "I have come to believe that there was a planned scheme to try and sell out our country to Canada from the very beginning." He vowed not to be "party to selling out our country."[76] Cashin added that with Confederation, Newfoundland would cease to be an independent country and "Newfoundlanders will cease to be Newfoundlanders."[77] He then branded the Confederates traitors to their country, reminding them "Iscariot had the decency to hang himself."[78] Cashin condemned Smallwood for bringing the "spirit of Trotsky into the Convention, falling back on the soap-box trick of setting class against class," and he declared there was only "one thing lower, and that is setting creed against creed."[79] When the members of the National Convention held their vote, sixteen voted to include Confederation on the referendum ballot; twenty-nine voted against it.[80] The anti-Confederates were jubilant but theirs was a pyrrhic victory as they had obviously forgotten what Addison had told the London delegation: the British government reserved the right to decide the options to be placed before the people. Smallwood immediately labelled the delegates who opposed Confederation the "twenty-nine dictators" for denying ordinary people an opportunity to choose their own constitutional future. In their attempt to keep union with Canada off the ballot, the anti-Confederates had, ironically, given the Confederate cause a great platform from which to launch its campaign.

Bradley and Smallwood pounced immediately. They capitalized on the interest generated in Confederation in the National Convention debates. As J. Scott Macdonald reported to Ottawa, the decision of the National Convention "appears to have given rise to a spontaneous wave of indignation in many parts of Newfoundland." Bradley, proving himself to be the man of the moment, yet again, took to the airwaves on January 31, 1948, urging people to send telegrams of protest to the governor. Macdonald reported that, as a result of Bradley's speech, there were public meetings of protest across the country. Two notable gatherings were in St. Anthony on the Northern Peninsula and at Lawn, a Roman Catholic community on the south coast. The St. Anthony meeting was attended by two hundred citizens—which was "practically the whole adult male population and a resolution condemning the Convention was passed unanimously." Smallwood claimed that telegrams with eleven thousand signatures had been received by February 3, of which forty-five hundred came from districts represented by members of the National Convention who had voted against the inclusion of Confederation on the ballot. Just a day later, the number of petitioners had reportedly reached twenty-four thousand. "About a third of the telegrams are from Roman Catholic communities which is a good indication that the movement embraces many denominations," Macdonald optimistically informed Ottawa.[81]

Ottawa first watched with interest as events unfolded in Newfoundland and London and then reacted to them. When asked by Whitehall what the Canadian government might do given the rejection of its proposal for union, St. Laurent insisted that Canada "was taking no part whatsoever in presenting [the] terms to the people of Newfoundland, nor would it venture to do or say anything which might be regarded as trying to influence the decision of the free people of Newfoundland." He did add, however, that the National Convention was "only an advisory body, and the matter still had to be dealt with by those who have the constitutional responsibility for a decision."[82] Even before the petitions that Smallwood and Bradley had encouraged

CHAPTER 6

reached the governor, the British government, which had long favoured the union of Newfoundland with Canada, had decided that three options would be included in the referendum: Commission of Government for a period of five years; Confederation with Canada; and responsible government as it existed in 1933. In a dispatch to Governor Gordon Macdonald, P.J. Noel-Baker, secretary of state for Commonwealth relations, explained the decision to add Confederation with Canada to the referendum ballot: "The terms offered by the Canadian government represent . . . the result of long discussion with a body of Newfoundlanders who were elected to the Convention, and the issues involved appear to have been sufficiently clarified to enable the people of Newfoundland to express an opinion as to whether Confederation with Canada would commend itself to them." Given that and the large contingent in the Convention advocating the inclusion of Confederation on the ballot paper, he said, "It would not be right that the people of Newfoundland should be deprived of an opportunity of considering the issue at the referendum."[83] Great Britain had set the rules of the final contest, Canada had agreed with them, and Newfoundlanders would now have to make a decision.

CHAPTER 7

REFERENDUM, SOCIAL CITIZENSHIP, AND CANADA: NEWFOUNDLAND BECOMES A PROVINCE, 1948–1949

IN 1948, THE PEOPLE OF NEWFOUNDLAND WENT TO THE polls twice to vote on their political future. The options on the ballot for the first referendum, held on June 3, were three: return to responsible government as it existed in 1933; continuation of government by commission; and Confederation, that is, union with Canada. On the ballot for the second referendum, held on July 22, there were only two options: responsible government as it existed in 1933 or Confederation with Canada, because the option with the fewest votes on the first referendum had been eliminated as the British wanted a clear majority in the referendum. Confederation won on the second referendum, with just over 52 percent of the almost 150,000 votes cast. The people of Newfoundland had decided, by referendum, that the Dominion of Newfoundland was to become the tenth province of the Dominion of Canada.

Essentially, two opposing organizations campaigned for Newfoundlanders' votes in 1948. The campaign for a return to responsible government was led by Peter Cashin, a veteran of the Great War

Joseph R. Smallwood campaigning in the battle over Newfoundland's constitutional future. He was the de facto leader of the Confederate Association.

and former minister of finance and customs; however, he never fully controlled the Responsible Government League, which often shared resources and people with the far smaller Economic Union Party (EUP), led by Chesley Crosbie, a wealthy St. John's merchant. The EUP wanted an economic union with the United States, although that was not an option on either of the two ballots. The challenges facing the EUP were enormous. To achieve the party's goal, there needed to be a return to responsible government—hence the EUP's cooperation

CHAPTER 7

with Cashin and his league—for only if voters opted for responsible government and independence could the EUP then try to establish an economic union between Newfoundland and the United States.[1] The EUP claimed that Newfoundland could not survive on its own in the postwar world, as did Smallwood and the Confederates. Both Crosbie and Donald Jamieson, the EUP's campaign manager, said repeatedly during the referendum campaigns that Newfoundland needed "some form of insurance, an anchor to add stability to the Newfoundland economy under self-rule." Crosbie claimed that he had never objected to joining Confederation on ideological grounds but that he "saw distinct advantages in acquiring the leverage a potential deal with the United States would provide in talks with Ottawa. As he saw it," Jamieson later wrote, "the choice of Responsible Government closed no doors."[2] Such views could only cloud the issue for voters because by suggesting that the time was not right for union with Canada or that Newfoundland might get a better deal if it first elected a government, the anti-Confederates were not denying that in the long term Confederation might be desirable. There was no organized group campaigning for the retention of Commission of Government, which had been administering the Dominion of Newfoundland since 1934 (see Chapter 4). Those for union with Canada, which would mean provincial autonomy and self-government, were organized within the Confederate Association, led by Joseph R. Smallwood, who would become the first premier of the new Province of Newfoundland, on April 1, 1949.

GAUGING PUBLIC OPINION DURING THE REFERENDUM CAMPAIGNS

No systematic polling was available to gauge the opinions of Newfoundlanders before they cast their votes in 1948. The Commission of Government did, however, observe some trends in public opinion when it asked its officials, particularly magistrates and members of the Newfoundland Ranger Force, to report back on political attitudes they were noticing in their jurisdictions. Some Rangers initially found that support for Commission of Government was strong; however, the Broadcasting Corporation of Newfoundland's live broadcast of the

National Convention debates generated considerable interest, and several Rangers throughout the country observed that support for Confederation appeared to be gathering momentum. From Burin, Ranger G.C. Jenkins reported, on December 2, 1947, "The attitude of the people has undergone a sudden change." This was not even a month after the "Proposed Arrangements for the Entry of Newfoundland into Confederation" had been presented to the National Convention. Jenkins found a perceptible decline in support for Commission of Government and a pronounced increase in support for union: "Confederation with Canada is at present the most popular form of government," he reported, adding that "Responsible Government, too, has gained considerable popularity."[3] Other such reports made mention, especially, of people's interest—attributable to the radio broadcasts—in the Dominion of Canada's social programs. Writing from St. Anthony in northern Newfoundland, on December 8, Ranger S.M. Christian noted that, in his district, there was "very little interest" in the speeches of the Responsible Government League.[4] Moreover, the Ranger at nearby Port Saunders reported that "a wide and large number have swung their opinions to favour union with Canada, owing to Mr. Smallwood's interesting and informative debates on the laws governing that country and terms laid down to govern us should we unite."[5] The public had been engaged, and the campaign to determine a winner was fierce and hard fought.

RESPONSIBLE GOVERNMENT LEAGUE

The Responsible Government League, as noted above, was launched officially in St. John's on February 11, 1947, eleven months before the dissolution of the National Convention. The league was established as a response to the growing momentum for Confederation in the National Convention, and it was dedicated to securing the return of "Responsible Government for Newfoundland and to encourag[ing] the people of Newfoundland to accept their full, personal and collective responsibilities for the good government of our country."[6] Its founding members came from leading St. John's merchants and professionals, and many who joined later were outport merchants with close ties to Water Street. It declared itself to be non-sectarian and open to all, but from its inception the Responsible

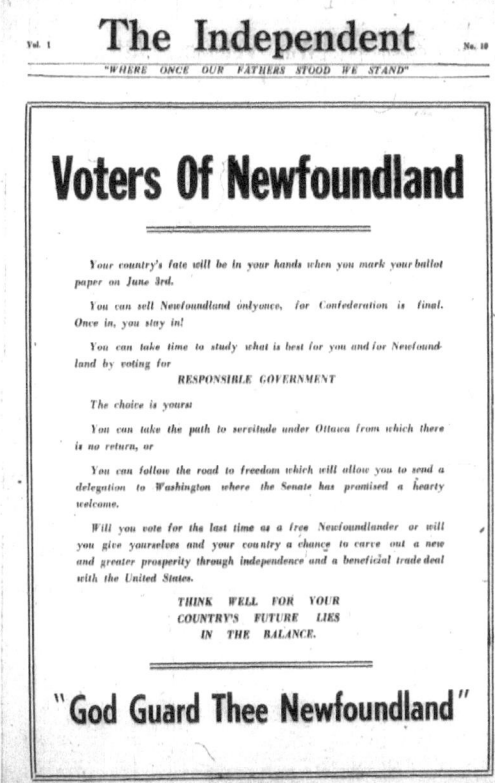

The *Independent*, the official newspaper of the Responsible Government League, played upon the patriotism of Newfoundlanders in its campaign for a return to responsible government and independence, as illustrated by the front page of the publication released a few months before the first referendum vote on June 3, 1948.

Government League was perceived by most people to be an organ of Newfoundland's business and professional elite.[7]

Many of those associated with the league were staunch nationalists and conservatives. They campaigned, as Charles Fox Bennett had successfully done in 1869 (see Chapter 1), to convince Newfoundland voters that they must remain faithful to the earlier generations of their people who had struggled and had built their own vibrant nation against terrible odds. "Responsible Government is what our forefathers fought for and won nearly one hundred years ago," proclaimed the league's declaration of July 21, 1947, and "we feel that the present generation of Newfoundlanders has a duty and a trust to restore this temporarily-lost heritage."[8] Citizens were asked not to hand over to Canada the country that their ancestors had created but to heed the words and sentiments of Governor Sir Cavendish Boyle, as expressed in his 1902 poem that became Newfoundland's national (and later, provincial) anthem. The masthead of the league's news organ, *The Independent*, read "Where once our Fathers stood we stand," playing on the words of the "Ode to Newfoundland":

As loved our fathers, so we love
Where once they stood we stand...

Yet the Responsible Government League never fully understood or appreciated the people who lived outside its own urban environs, even if they constituted nearly 70 percent of the population of Newfoundland. Members of the league were, by and large, people who had benefitted from the old regime and were comfortable in and around the old colonial capital of St. John's. They were, for the most part, out of touch with the lives of the people in the outports and throughout rural Newfoundland—the very people who in 1948 would overwhelmingly decide the constitutional future of the country. They ignored or even downplayed the obvious economic, social, and cultural divisions between the capital and the rest of their country, perhaps best exemplified politically by the rise of William Coaker and the Fishermen's Protective Union, founded in 1908 (see Chapter 3). Corner Brook and Grand Falls, of course, by that point were also significant urban areas, but with very different mentalities from both St. John's and the fishing communities.

The Responsible Government League never embraced any of the notions of social citizenship that were gaining traction throughout much of the postwar Western world (see Chapter 5). Worse, not only did the league not embrace such notions, but its supporters also, and vociferously, rejected such policies outright—as pandering to the uneducated, the lazy, and the illiterate.[9] At the time, John S. Currie was the owner of the *Daily News*, one of the leading St. John's newspapers, and stalwartly for Newfoundland's independence. In a radio speech given on February 14, 1948, Currie made his argument clear, saying, "People should accept the responsibility of self-government with the restraints and discipline that it should impose on the individual."[10] In essence, he told voters to "be content with your station in life," oblivious to the fact that Newfoundland's hard-working fishermen and loggers were growing increasingly aware of the better conditions and greater opportunities that existed throughout the rest of North America, and particularly in Canada. Newfoundlanders wanted a similar standard of living. Currie and supporters of the Responsible Government League could not seem to understand that basic reality. They tried to shame and intimidate voters through a patriotic appeal of posing to them the following question: "Are we going to admit to the rest of the world we're not fit to govern ourselves?" But such tactics held little appeal for people who were being offered social and economic security—by the side for union with Canada.[11] The Responsible Government League failed to appreciate that, since at least the late 1930s, the tide had been running towards social rights, social justice, and, importantly, social welfare and social security. Public opinion in Newfoundland, too, was running in that direction by that time.

People advocating for a return to responsible government tended to see such changes to the concept of citizenship, indeed changes towards social citizenship, in a different light altogether. They expressed considerable worry and great concern with what they regarded as the "materialism" they feared had become the new dynamism in their society. Some of their speakers throughout the referendum campaigns claimed that even if it did not have the material wealth that other nations and some of the Canadian provinces enjoyed, Newfoundland might still be better off because the material age bred selfishness and greed and embittered the lives of great sections of the population. The material age also gave rise, they claimed, to avaricious politicians, corrupting the political system and falling over each other making promises as they competed for favour with voters.[12] The Responsible Government League maintained that Newfoundlanders were content with the level of services that could be supported within their current tax system (and, of course, most league members had no desire for an increase in the levels of taxation).[13] Moreover, the league adopted a conservative, even reactionary, approach to human security, asserting that a good job was the best means for a worker to provide for one's family. A return to responsible government, it insisted, would result in the expansion of the industries, such as the fisheries, that had supported Newfoundlanders for more than two centuries and would spur the development of new ones. This would generate higher incomes and, according to the Responsible Government League, render the social welfare system being developed elsewhere unnecessary in Newfoundland.[14] Confederates were accused of bribing voters with the promise of the "baby bonus" (the family allowance), old age pensions, unemployment insurance, and other manifestations of social citizenship that Canadians

The Responsible Government League attempted to scare the electorate during the referendum campaigns by emphasizing how Confederation with Canada would result in the imposition of a wide range of taxes.

and others were by then receiving regularly and enjoying from their governments. League members also warned voters not to be fooled by short-term gains in the form of state-sponsored individual transfers if it meant permanently losing control of their political destiny and control over the Newfoundland nation. This argument was seized upon in the March 29 issue of the Responsible Government League's *Independent*, which admonished Newfoundlanders "Don't Sell Your Soul to Feed Your Body."[15] Throughout the campaign, supporters of a return to responsible government continued to voice fear that voters might be swayed by the hope of being better off materially "as a deck hand on a different ship."[16]

CHAPTER 7

Returning to responsible government was defeated, as a future option for Newfoundland, twice by the people of the Island in 1948. As the referenda results made clear, many Newfoundlanders were not willing to accept their erstwhile station with its recurrent hardships. Newfoundlanders rejected the notion propagated by the Responsible Government League that continued economic and social insecurity, and a lower level of state support through various income supplements, was the price they should be happy to pay for a return to their political independence.[17] Clearly, during the Second World War, the expansion of social rights had come to influence Newfoundlanders' understanding of citizenship.[18] In 1943, just months after the publication in London of the Beveridge Report, which provided a set of principles Lord Beveridge thought necessary to banish poverty and want from Britain, there were frequent media comments on the need for social security in Newfoundland. The *Daily News* noted on March 2, 1943, that Canada had also appointed a special parliamentary committee to study and report on a scheme of social insurance, adding that "in the relatively primitive state of the local economy, social security as envisaged by the Beveridge plan can be little more than a dream." It wondered if primary producers in Newfoundland might develop contributory plans to deal with unemployment to avoid a return to the "dole [which] must never again be allowed to rear its shameful head in our midst."[19] Later, the *Daily News* raised the matter again, asking "Can Newfoundland have its own Beveridge Plan?" The newspaper was not optimistic that it could afford such progressive legislation. It had editorialized on a number of occasions that the country first needed a more highly developed industrial economy, adding that a national scheme of social security "can only be financially possible if total employment is the normal condition and large-scale unemployment an abnormal event." It thought that a national plan to provide health and unemployment insurance and retirement pensions was clearly out of the question until Newfoundland figured out how to sustain full-time, year-round employment for all its workers.[20] It again lamented in 1944 that Newfoundland could not hope to emulate the proposals put forward in Britain for free and comprehensive health services unless it could first dramatically increase its national income, which depended on broader and better-paid employment.[21]

Clearly, the hopes for social security and a new relationship between citizen and state had come to Newfoundland.

Several years later, the Responsible Government League's view of citizenship remained firmly entrenched in the nineteenth century, however, largely unchanged from what it had been during the fight for responsible government in 1855 and in the debate over Confederation in 1869. Supporters of the league demanded democratic government, full voting rights associated with earlier notions of political citizenship, and the immediate return of responsible government. But times had changed, even if the views of the league's leadership had not. Those goals of political citizenship, although important for most voters, were not the crucial ones for an electorate still harbouring vivid memories of the devastation and destitution they had endured during the Great Depression. Moreover, by that time Newfoundlanders were informed about which government supports were being offered to citizens elsewhere, for example, to Canadians and to the British—indeed, Smallwood expended a lot of energy making sure that they were so informed. It might also be worth recalling that the report of the finance committee of the National Convention, most of whose members were strong supporters of a return of responsible government, had chastised the Commission of Government for its spending on social and public welfare during the 1930s (see Chapter 5).[22] For example, Peter Cashin, lifelong anti-Confederate and chairman of the finance committee, rejected Canada's social programs as he considered them to be immoral.[23] One of Cashin's colleagues in the fight for responsible government, Fanny Ryan Fiander, a well-known and popular journalist, who campaigned on behalf of the league, often repeated, "We'll look after our own babies." But William J. Browne, later a Conservative MP from St. John's (who, incidentally, was eventually replaced by Cashin's son, Richard, a Liberal), claimed that he had advised Peter Cashin during the campaign to embrace a program of family allowances if responsible government won. But Cashin had refused to even contemplate the idea. Some within the league did, however, consider enriched pensions for the elderly, but Browne considered the opposition to social programs, more generally, "fatal" for the anti-Confederates.[24]

Given its principles and the philosophy it embraced, the Responsible Government League faced an uphill struggle throughout the two

CHAPTER 7

The Confederates emphasized the benefits of Canada's social programs to Newfoundlanders if they voted for Confederation and reminded voters that Peter Cashin, one of the major opponents of union, called social programs such as family allowances "immoral."

referendum campaigns. Its principles and philosophy also made the league an easy target for the Confederates, who claimed that it was out of touch with the needs of ordinary workers. Moreover, the league inherited all of the negativity associated with the failure of the pre-1934 responsible government system, which was not remembered with any great enthusiasm or fondness by many Newfoundlanders and which had led to the imposition of the Commission of Government (see Chapter 4). Smallwood made certain to remind voters of those connections regularly in his adept and precocious use of the relatively new medium of radio. Indeed, responsible government had become intimately associated in Newfoundland with the economic deprivation that many citizens had experienced in the 1920s and especially in the 1930s. The Hollis Walker Report of 1924 (see Chapter 3) provided an indictment not only of a number of individuals for political corruption but also of a political system that allowed such actions within the state apparatus. A decade later, the Amulree Commission (see Chapter 4) further entrenched the notion that Newfoundland's experiment with responsible government had resulted in widespread corruption, mismanagement, and economic failure.[25] The Responsible Government League inherited all of this as its members and supporters attempted to convince voters to return to a system of responsible government as it had existed in 1933. A female voter from Trinity Bay, when asked for a donation to support the league, gave this angry retort: "What reply did we get from the old Responsible Government when we were forced to live on the Dole and had to spend days fighting for it. We were told to starve and be damned... I don't forget what we went through on 6 cents a day. I detest the word Responsible Government."[26]

Perhaps the greatest failing of the Responsible Government League was that it neglected to campaign widely and aggressively in rural Newfoundland.[27] This is particularly astonishing given that the league was politically active nearly a year before the Confederate Association was formed and had access to potential supporters with deep pockets who could have been encouraged to contribute. Moreover, the league had a palatable, even attractive, strategy had it built a narrative around national pride and capitalized on the long-standing opposition to Confederation dating from the 1860s in Newfoundland. The league's first mistake may have been the decision not to campaign while the National Convention was still doing its work, as the leadership felt it would interfere with the process already in place.[28] That the league remained distinct and separate from the supporters of responsible government in the National Convention certainly complicated matters further. In fact, league members were particularly sceptical of Peter Cashin, perhaps the most prominent

CHAPTER 7

The Confederate attempted to denigrate the notion of an independent self-governing Newfoundland "nation" and constantly associated the pre-1934 responsible government with poverty and economic deprivation.

anti-Confederate in the Convention; he was a man capable of mobilizing a mass movement in favour of responsible government, but "his drinking and notorious temper" remained a serious obstacle to their embracing him as leader.[29]

The Responsible Government League and its supporters also had limited knowledge of Canada's federal system, particularly the often-troubled relationship between Ottawa and the provincial governments—which might have been used effectively to counter Smallwood's arguments about the virtues and benefits of union. Once it had become obvious in the mid-1940s that some future arrangements would have to be decided upon, Smallwood, as we have seen (see Chapter 6), made deliberate efforts to personally learn about how Canada worked and to acquaint himself with the power brokers in Ottawa. In the autumn of 1947, for example, Edward Henley, a member of the league from Gander, had complained to Wickford Collins, the league's secretary that the league was not challenging the information Smallwood was spouting. In his reply to Henley, Collins admitted that they did not yet have the ability to do so. By the end of that year, however, the Responsible Government League was fully cognizant that its initiatives to promote the option of responsible government were failing badly. "Reports from the outport district," Collins wrote on December 29, "indicate that Confederation is high liner at the moment, with Commission of Government second in the field." He lamented that "a great deal of bitterness [had] been stirred up against responsible government by the use of class hatred against the merchant class," and he recognized that "our radio talks and pamphlets have been in the nature of academic discussion," and not the type to get voters overly excited. Yet he remained optimistic, noting, "We know our weak points and are prepared to put on a first class show in 1948."[30]

It was not to be, however. Over the next three months, the Responsible Government League expended considerable efforts on debating policy and drafting minutes, but doing little else.[31] Fred Morris, a merchant from Trinity Bay, advised the league to get "a good sprinkling of baymen [people who lived in the outport rural communities] associated with your movement [as] there's a feeling and probably justly so, that the Avalon Peninsula is Newfoundland and the remainder of the Country being 'No Man's Land.'"[32] Thereupon, the executive of the league wrote to forty-five people in rural areas hoping they would allow their names to be added to a membership list to be published in *The Independent*. The executive was not, however, interested in having those individuals contribute to the league's planning and organization or even having them campaign in the districts in which they resided. As Jeff Webb has shown, the Responsible Government League was elitist and wanted only "prominent" men as members who, the leaders believed, would give responsible government respectability. Ordinary workers, including women and outport people, had little to contribute in terms of planning and campaigning. This was very much in keeping with the league's view that the state should not embark upon a program of social security measures for ordinary citizens. Francis M. O'Leary, a St. John's merchant, wrote Morris that we "merely want the bigger places through the country to be represented on our Board of Directors, so that the Responsible Government League would not be criticized as being a bunch in St. John's." They would not have to do "any active work," nor "would [they] have to be of exceptional ability."[33] This was quite a different approach from that of the Confederates, who promised to embrace the "toiling masses." Not surprisingly, the league failed to create a country-wide campaign organization or a broadly based political movement, even though it brought several prominent St. John's labour leaders into the organization and hired Charles Bailey, who had been a member of the National Convention, to campaign for three months on the northeast coast. Bailey was dismissed two months before the first vote in June 1948, as the league campaigned hardest in the districts in which it found a receptive audience.[34] As John FitzGerald has argued, the league "with few exceptions exported its campaign from St. John's" and did not follow the lead of the Confederate Association, whose speakers and organizers often came from the communities in which they campaigned.[35]

Donald Jamieson has noted that when he and others created the Economic Union Party on March 28, 1948, "We had no confidence in those who were, at the time, the only promoters of a return to self government ... [it] was an inefficient hodge-podge of reactionary businessmen and recycled politicians. Most were sincere enough in their own blinkered way, but their stale rhetoric and threadbare arguments sounded stodgy and self-serving." Jamieson acknowledged that they might "rally the loyalists," but "they had nothing to offer the hesitant and uncommitted."[36] The Economic Union Party brought considerable enthusiasm to the campaign, and shortly thereafter the Responsible Government League changed its mind on the importance of a large organization when it attempted to establish local committees throughout rural and outport Newfoundland. "It is only in this way," the league reported in mid-April, "that we will be able to build up and consolidate an island wide organization capable of dealing with the many jobs which will be necessary in this fight against Confederation and Commission of Government."[37] League branches were established in a few of the urban centres outside St. John's, notably in Gander, Grand Falls, and Corner Brook, but they were always short of volunteers and never able to mount effective campaigns. The league gave up completely on some of the more northern regions of the country because of limited funds, and this, no doubt, had an impact on the outcome of the referendum vote.

Rural Newfoundlanders, moreover, were hesitant about an organization that called for a return to the old ways of managing the state. As we have seen earlier, there were clear divisions between St. John's and the rest of the country, and many voters in rural and outport Newfoundland had long harboured a great deal of resentment towards St. John's. They believed the country's leaders in the capital had benefitted enormously from the economic rents earned from the country's resources and their toils, especially in the fish trade. The Responsible Government League simply failed to present to Newfoundlanders an alternative to the St. John's–dominated political system that had failed fifteen years earlier, while it also failed to present to voters any virtues that the pre-1934 constitutional arrangement might have had. Members and supporters of the league could have taken a page out of Charles Fox Bennett's campaign playbook from 1869, when Bennett campaigned vigorously in coastal fishing communities and constructed a narrative to counter the arguments of the Confederates. In a sense, one might conclude that the Responsible Government League had an eye for neither the big picture nor the details, seeing neither the trees nor the forest.

CONFEDERATE ASSOCIATION

The Confederate Association was established on February 21, 1948, and it had a completely different message and campaign playbook than the Responsible Government League. It drew supporters from diverse backgrounds across Newfoundland, including business and labour. Gordon Bradley (Bonavista East, from National Convention

CHAPTER 7

days) was nominated as president, and Smallwood became campaign manager but the de facto leader of the Confederate group. The Confederate Association appointed more than a hundred vice-presidents to represent it throughout Newfoundland and to make connections with local communities, and it drew on funds supplied by donors to the Liberal Party of Canada.[38] The Confederate Association emphasized continually the social and economic benefits that would come of union with Canada, stressing how Canada's social programs and generally higher standard of living would flow to Newfoundlanders with union and, hence, improve the lives of all. At the same time, it sought to cultivate among outport Newfoundlanders, especially, a fear and distrust of an independent, self-governing nation. After all, communities come together in times of change and uncertainty to pursue measures and policies that offer a measure of protection from that uncertainty and fear.[39] The Confederate Association waged a well-organized and effective campaign, promoting its message over the radio and in a successful tabloid, *The Confederate*, first published on April 7, 1948, and widely distributed throughout the country—constantly building the case for joining Confederation. The tabloid's popular and effective political cartoons were professionally drawn by Jack Boothe, a Toronto *Globe and Mail* cartoonist, under Smallwood's direction. The paper emphasized, both graphically and in text, the social benefits of union and repeatedly exploited the resentment of outport Newfoundland against St. John's and the Avalon Peninsula. In its April 14 issue, *The Confederate* claimed that Confederation was ahead in eighteen of twenty-four constituencies. It then listed those in the eastern parts of the country near St. John's that were "weak" in their support for union, making explicit that Confederation was possible without much support in St. John's.[40] *The Confederate*'s May 31 issue asked Newfoundlanders "to give yourself a chance. Give the Children a chance. Give Newfoundland a chance. Vote for Confederation and a healthier, happier Newfoundland." To mothers, Smallwood and the Confederates promised the benefits of a modern social welfare state. Smallwood reminded parents that their children under the age of sixteen would receive "*every month* a cash allowance for every child you have or may have."[41] Family allowances in Canada were paid to the mother; therefore, if Newfoundland joined Confederation, it would be the first time most mothers would receive money in their own names. As Smallwood's biographer Richard Gwyn later recounted in 1968,

> Skilfully, he capitalized on the uninhibited enthusiasm of children, which contrasted strikingly with the deep-rooted shyness in public of most Newfoundland adults. At meeting after meeting, Smallwood cajoled children onto the stage beside him, and made a great show of asking their names and ages. Then, holding one child by the hand, he would turn to the audience and say: "Now, Peter. You are eight, and you have two brothers and one sister, all under sixteen. When Confederation comes, your mother, Mrs. X., will receive every month, $22.00 to look after you, to buy your clothes, to buy your food." He then repeated this procedure with each child on the platform.[42]

This was a familiar tactic for Smallwood and members and supporters of the Confederate Association. The May 20 issue of *The Confederate* emphasized the benefits of the new social citizenship in its bold headline, "Under Confederation *never again will there be a hungry child in Newfoundland.*"[43] These were powerful messages and directed to women as mothers and grandmothers. Women had, moreover, enjoyed employment opportunities during the war, especially on Canadian and American bases, and would have been very interested not only in Canada's social programs that were paid to women but also in the new opportunities for employment that would follow union with Canada.[44] The Responsible Government League, on the other hand, attempted to belittle and denigrate Smallwood's claims on family allowances, insisting in *The Independent* that "I don't intend to raise my family on the Canadian dole."[45] Yet Smallwood's message was powerful and effective: "If you decide, I don't want family allowances, I don't want pensions, I don't want veterans' benefits, I don't want anything from Canada," he told Newfoundlanders repeatedly, "then mark an X for Responsible Government."[46] He understood that support for children would appeal especially to mothers, and, of course, family allowance cheques were paid directly to mothers, not fathers.

CHAPTER 7

THE REFERENDUM CAMPAIGN

Smallwood travelled widely throughout the campaign, as Charles Fox Bennett had in 1869. Smallwood, however, did so mainly by aircraft. He also wrote open letters to a large number of communities that he could not visit. He expressed in a May 29, 1948, letter "To the People of Lower Island Cove" his regret that he could not visit their town and explained why he favoured joining Confederation. He appealed to what he called the "common man" or the "toiling masses." "It is the people who earn small incomes who will benefit the most by Confederation," he wrote. "They are the ones who deserve our greatest consideration because they get very little out of life." Smallwood suggested further that those who argued for a return to responsible government had not considered the interests of the worker. His attack on the privileged Water Street merchants was intense and persistent in this particular letter and elsewhere; it was a clear attempt to pit the working class against the elites and to capitalize on the dislike of the commercial elite who dominated Newfoundland economic life especially outside of St. John's. The elites, he reminded voters, cared little for those whose labour they exploited and kept in "servitude." Such rhetoric was essential to the narrative of Newfoundland's past that Smallwood had been constructing since 1946. He suggested that merchants, such as Chesley Crosbie and others who campaigned for a return to responsible government, had not "considered the interests of others. Have they ever been actuated by a desire to improve the conditions of the masses of our people?" he asked. "Don't forget the struggle is between a better living for you, or more profits for the merchants and a still lowering of your standard of living. It is a struggle," he told Newfoundlanders constantly, "in which you have only one advantage, and that is the ballot paper." Similar letters were sent to other communities that Smallwood was unable to visit. He also made the same powerful arguments in his radio broadcasts and in hundreds of speeches throughout the campaign all across Newfoundland.[47] The Confederates also made very good use of thousands of posters, photographs, letters, even airplane fly-overs, and especially community visits where Confederate rallies were chaired by prominent local citizens, including clergymen, and often held in Orange lodges (although the Responsible Government League also held meetings in some of the same lodges).[48]

Smallwood reminded Newfoundlanders that his opponents would attempt to denigrate union with Canada and attempt to frighten them with misinformation. He asked voters not to be fooled by such anti-Confederate rhetoric that they would be taxed at prohibitively high levels after union. Such rhetoric, he claimed, was a mere scare tactic to frighten them into voting against Confederation. "You do not earn enough to pay income tax," Smallwood informed his audiences. Yet Canada was a generous state, and "under Confederation you will get Family Allowances and Old Age Pensions and the cost of purchasing should average at least 25% cheaper than now." He asked voters to compare their situations with those of their relatives who had moved to Canada, many of whom were even sending remittances home as well as news of what life was like in Canada: "You know they are enjoying a better standard of living than here." "The per capita earnings of all the people of Canada are over a hundred per cent greater than in Newfoundland," he boasted, "and it is on their greater earnings they pay taxes, and they can well afford to pay them." Smallwood then claimed a "sack of flour is retailing in Canada for about half the cost here, and all other food stuffs cost considerably less." Canadian fishermen and sealers earned more for their products than did those in Newfoundland, he asserted. After reciting a litany of the benefits available to Canadians at his rallies, Smallwood would then ask voters to consider the issues carefully. The choice was theirs, he always reminded them, but he left little doubt that if they voted for Confederation they would enjoy a better standard of living.[49]

Smallwood and the Confederate Association made effective use of the radio, a medium through which many Newfoundlanders already knew and trusted him. Smallwood was a well-known media personality, having been "the Barrelman" on radio station VONF and later the Broadcasting Corporation of Newfoundland. The program, designed to cultivate pride in Newfoundland's culture and history, aired six nights a week and ran from 1937 to 1943, making Smallwood's one of the most recognized voices in the country. It was certainly an advantage during the referendum campaigns. In a radio broadcast on April 6, 1948, Smallwood outlined why he favoured the option of joining Confederation. His opening sentence, designed to cultivate trust with the listener, began, "If I did not favour Confederation with Canada I would be false to the people who reside on that bleak part of the Bay de Verde District." He pointed out that 80 percent of the people of Newfoundland resided in outports and had "much to contend with in this life. A life of strenuous toil, a life of hardship—and from the cradle to the grave one continuous struggle for existence. They do not enjoy luxurious living like some who live in St. John's and the industrial areas of Newfoundland," he said. Smallwood promised that his campaign for Confederation was to benefit all Newfoundlanders. He assured them a "brighter future" and emphasized a number of ways in which their lives would be improved: through the family allowance, veterans' benefits, cheaper products, and several other factors. He noted that the Government of Canada would take over Newfoundland's public debt, and the money-losing Newfoundland Railway System, thus providing cheaper passenger and freight rates, even though doing so would create a deficit of about $3 million a year for the Canadian government.[50] From Montreal, where he was a schoolteacher and composer of the famed "The Squid Jiggin' Ground," Art Scammell of Change Islands wrote the *Fishermen's Advocate* in May 1948 that many Newfoundlanders already lived in Canada for economic security reasons, and he suggested that the "social security benefits resulting from Confederation will be a godsend to countless families." Scammell also noted that it was easy for "those with full bellies and an assured income" in Newfoundland to "laugh and scoff at children's allowances, increased old age pensions, etc.," but those programs would help create a new and better world for most Newfoundland families.[51]

Throughout the campaigns, the Responsible Government League strutted its patriotism and, unlike the Confederate Association, saw little social responsibility for its fellow citizens. It certainly demonstrated little regard for the social-economic well-being of members of the Newfoundland political community, during a period of history when political leaders and their parties in neighbouring countries were almost bending over backward to portray their progressive and inclusive agendas. Even the old Conservative Party of John A. Macdonald changed its name in 1942 to the Progressive Conservative Party of Canada to reflect its embrace of social welfare and other progressive measures associated with social citizenship. The Responsible Government League, on the other hand, seemed to say to Newfoundlanders during the two referenda on their constitutional future: why should we pay a little more in taxes to support social welfare programs and provide better health care, better educational opportunities, and better public services when we can claim national independence and self-government for Newfoundland and fly our own flag? That message combined swaggering patriotism and supercilious nationalism with a lack of social responsibility for fellow citizens, and was a stark contrast to the Confederate Association's promise of social citizenship. By the late 1940s in many countries, such a promise had become the very basis of modern citizenship, which vowed to bestow on all members of the political community a number of protections and benefits as social rights. As such, the Confederates attacked the historical acceptance of the hierarchy of privilege that had long been entrenched in Newfoundland society and promised to expand the domain of equality and fairness for all voters and their dependants.[52]

RESULTS OF THE REFERENDA

The results of the first referendum, held June 3, 1948, failed to produce a majority for either side, although responsible government won 44.5 percent of the vote compared with joining Confederation's 41.1 percent. More than 88 percent (155,797) of eligible voters cast a ballot. Commission of Government, with 14.3 percent of the vote, was then dropped from the ballot. In the second referendum, held July 22, 1948, Confederation won a narrow victory with 52.3 percent (78,323 votes) to 47.7 percent (71,334 votes) for responsible government, although the turnout of voters dropped slightly to 84 percent (149,657).[53] The responsible government option won in seven districts, all on the Avalon Peninsula, and the Confederates carried the vote elsewhere on the Island and in Labrador, although the vote for Confederation was greater in all constituencies in the second referendum than in the first. On the Avalon Peninsula, 66 percent of voters supported responsible government, compared with 34 percent for Confederation; the rest of the Island voted 70 percent for union with Canada. Because much of the support for responsible government came from districts with Catholic majorities—and because the Catholic Church through its monthly publication, *The Monitor*, had

CHAPTER 7

promoted Newfoundland's independence and warned of the evils of Confederation, which in turn brought the Orange Order into the fray to criticize the Catholic hierarchy for bringing sectarianism into the campaign—it might appear that religion was the deciding factor in the referendum;[54] however, it was not. Region and new notions of citizenship were the decisive factors that carried Newfoundland's vote for Confederation. As historian Jeff Webb suggests, Newfoundlanders held different conceptions of national identity and different political and economic expectations depending on their place of residence.[55]

The debate on Confederation was merely the latest issue to expose the divisions within the country. People on the Avalon Peninsula had more familiarity with and a greater attachment to Newfoundland as a state, and they were more committed to an independent Newfoundland. This was the part of Newfoundland, too, that had led the fight decades earlier for responsible government, had forged the apparatus of the Newfoundland state in the nineteenth century, and had volunteered in greater numbers in the First World War. People outside of the Avalon Peninsula had had fewer interactions with that state than those living in or near St. John's, and in the 1940s, they "envisioned a different future for themselves."[56] Even those Newfoundlanders who supported responsible government realized before the votes had been counted that the antagonisms between the rural and outport regions and St. John's would be a factor in the outcomes of the referenda, as they had been in many other electoral fights in Newfoundland for decades before 1948. Writing in the *Daily News* the day after the second referendum, but before the final results were released, A.B. Perlin noted that the "fanatical zeal for union with Canada" is an expression of antagonism towards the capital which is totally irrational although it is nothing new."[57] The Most Reverend J.M. O'Neill, Bishop of Harbour Grace, accused the Confederate leaders of using communist tactics to obtain a small majority, "pitting the poor against the rich, the outports against the Catholics."[58] The two constituencies on the Avalon Peninsula among those farthest from St. John's (Trinity South and Carbonear–Bay de Verde) voted for Confederation, as did two predominantly Catholic districts off the Avalon Peninsula (Placentia West and St. George's–Port au Port). Catholic votes farthest from St. John's may have carried Confederation to victory, and many Protestants in St. John's were decidedly

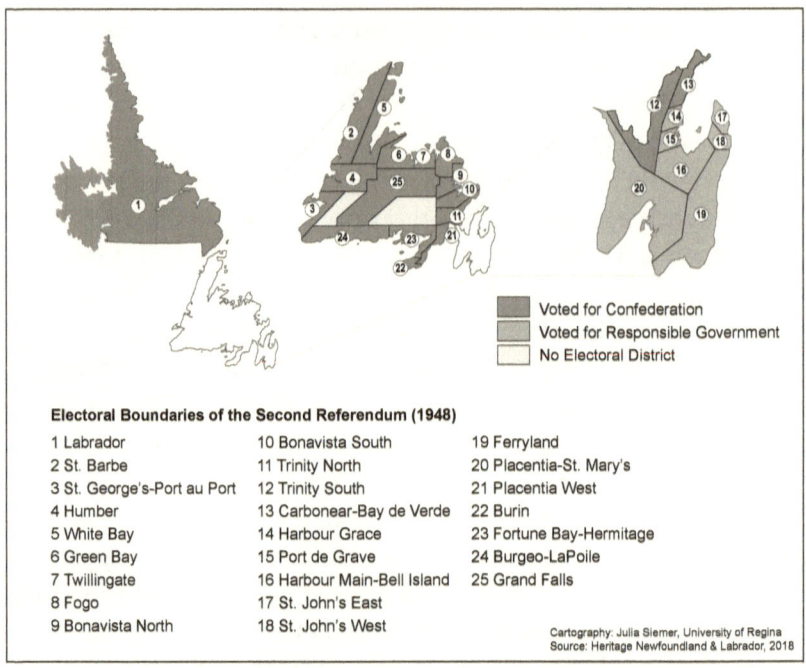

Electoral Boundaries of the Second Referendum (1948)

1 Labrador
2 St. Barbe
3 St. George's-Port au Port
4 Humber
5 White Bay
6 Green Bay
7 Twillingate
8 Fogo
9 Bonavista North
10 Bonavista South
11 Trinity North
12 Trinity South
13 Carbonear-Bay de Verde
14 Harbour Grace
15 Port de Grave
16 Harbour Main-Bell Island
17 St. John's East
18 St. John's West
19 Ferryland
20 Placentia-St. Mary's
21 Placentia West
22 Burin
23 Fortune Bay-Hermitage
24 Burgeo-LaPoile
25 Grand Falls

Cartography: Julia Siemer, University of Regina
Source: Heritage Newfoundland & Labrador, 2018

opposed to Confederation. Still, Catholic and Protestant organizations exchanged a number of barbs during the campaign leading to the second referendum, including Bradley's "Orange Letter" to the Protestant Loyal Orange Lodge encouraging members to vote against the domination of Roman Catholics of Newfoundland politics by voting for union with Canada. The letter was written in response to editorials in the Catholic *Monitor* encouraging a vote against Confederation. Also influential in the outcome of the referendum was the decision of several well-known members of the economic elite—notably Leonard Outerbridge and several other Water Street merchants, including Eric Bowring and Arthur Monroe, as well as several of the Newfoundland members of the Commission of Government, including Herman Quinton and Herbert Pottle—announcing their embrace of Confederation. The deciding factor, though, was the Confederates' promise of a new form of citizenship and engagement with the state. Confederation was a vote for social citizenship and the welfare state as embodied in the Canadian Confederation. Yet the diehards such as Peter Cashin continued to fight union, claiming that the vote was rigged and that the small majority

CHAPTER 7

District	Responsible Government (%)	Confederation (%)	Roman Catholic (%)	Protestant (%)
Labrador (1)	22.22	77.78	10.8	68.0
St. Barbe (2)	21.20	78.80	14.3	85.6
St. George's–Port au Port (3)	43.27	56.73	77.4	21.8
Humber (4)	31.27	68.73	30.0	68.8
White Bay (5)	24.19	75.81	20.1	78.2
Green Bay (6)	28.64	71.36	5.8	93.7
Twillingate (7)	24.75	75.25	2.4	97.5
Fogo (8)	38.07	61.93	11.3	87.4
Bonavista North (9)	25.51	74.49	10.1	89.4
Bonavista South (10)	48.10	51.90	15.4	83.9
Trinity North (11)	34.91	65.09	4.8	94.3
Trinity South (12)	39.73	60.27	7.7	91.8
Carbonear–Bay de Verde (13)	47.29	52.71	24.5	75.4
Harbour Grace (14)	62.32	37.68	22.4	76.8
Port de Grave (15)	50.96	49.04	19.8	79.3
Harbour Main–Bell Island (16)	82.58	17.42	56.5	42.8
St. John's West (17)	66.89	33.11	46.3	51.0
St. John's East (18)	68.78	31.22	51.1	46.1
Ferryland (19)	84.56	15.44	97.5	2.3
Placentia–St. Mary's (20)	81.60	18.40	92.1	7.8
Placentia West (21)	45.19	54.81	56.0	43.8
Burin (22)	15.04	84.96	29.9	70.0
Fortune Bay–Hermitage (23)	18.60	81.40	26.0	73.8
Burgeo–LaPoile (24)	11.09	88.91	1.00	98.5
Grand Falls (25)	43.45	56.46	25.1	80.4

FACING PAGE AND ABOVE: Electoral boundaries and results of the second referendum, July 22, 1948.

had been "obtained by unscrupulous appeals to passion and prejudice, by shameless exploitation of religious and sectional differences."[59] But their continued opposition mattered little after the Confederate victory in the second referendum.

NEWFOUNDLAND AND CANADA PREPARE FOR THEIR UNION
Newfoundland Delegation Prepares for Ottawa, August 1948

On July 27, 1948, Ottawa announced it would accept Newfoundland as Canada's tenth province despite the narrow victory for union in the referendum. Preparations began immediately in St. John's and Ottawa for final negotiations, although a few members of the Responsible Government League vowed to fight the decision in court and in the United Kingdom Parliament.[60] The 1948 Newfoundland delegation to Ottawa was chaired by Holyrood native and Dalhousie-trained lawyer Albert J. Walsh, a vice-chairman of the Commission of Government. It also included Confederate Association leaders Smallwood and Bradley; prominent businessman and leader of the Economic Union Party, Chesley Crosbie; John B. McEvoy, a St. John's lawyer and former chairman of the National Convention; Pouch Cove native Philip Gruchy, general manager of the Anglo-Newfoundland Development Company's pulp and paper mill at Grand Falls; and Gordon Winter, vice-president of T. & M. Winter and Company and former president of the Newfoundland Board of Trade. Two senior civil servants, Walter Marshall, secretary for finance, and Harold Puddester, secretary for justice, provided expert advice to the delegation, and James G. Channing, junior assistant secretary in Newfoundland's Department of Natural Resources, was appointed secretary to the delegation. Other Newfoundland civil servants were called upon as needed. The delegation was also advised by J.C. Thompson, a senior partner with the accounting firm Peat Marwick, and Professor Vincent MacDonald, a constitutional expert from Dalhousie University.[61]

The Newfoundlanders who were part of the 1948 delegation, like those who went to Ottawa in 1947, almost to a person believed in the exceptionalism of their country. They also believed it deserving of special consideration because of its unique historical and constitutional

CHAPTER 7

The Commission of Government appointed a seven-person delegation to Ottawa to negotiate the final terms of union in August 1948. From left to right: Chesley Crosbie, Philip Gruchy, Albert J. Walsh, Gordon Bradley, Joseph R. Smallwood, and Gordon Winter. John B. McEvoy is missing from the photograph.

development, even if those notions were not readily accepted in Ottawa.[62] This was particularly true of Smallwood. Newfoundland had no experience with a federal arrangement, and Smallwood, in particular, failed to appreciate that the Canadian system had developed a set of normative and general practices that had to be adhered to most of the time.[63] What Smallwood saw in union with Canada was a way to improve Newfoundlanders' standard of living and to provide better public services than existed there at the time. For him, the Canadian style of federalism held considerable promise for a bright and better future for Newfoundland while restoring democracy and self-government. The hope that Joseph Smallwood held for Newfoundland within Canada cannot be underestimated.

Members of the Newfoundland delegation held their first meeting on August 25, 1948, in St. John's. They agreed to study the various documents submitted by the Government of Canada outlining the terms of Confederation and try to identify any problems with regard to the effects of union upon Newfoundland.[64] The delegation advertised for interested parties to make submissions explaining how union might impact them.[65] The minutes of the meetings show that the delegation and Smallwood, especially, believed that Canada would do what was necessary for the social and economic well-being of Newfoundland after Confederation. They also understood that the delegation would have to demonstrate the exceptional needs of Newfoundland as a province if they hoped to make revisions to the proposed terms previously agreed to by the delegation from the National Convention. Consequently, the members of the second delegation to Ottawa did not see their task as merely to address the specific terms of union included in the "Proposed Arrangement for the Entry of Newfoundland into Confederation" (see Chapter 6) but to forge a relationship with Canada that would improve the social and economic conditions in Newfoundland. Not surprisingly, much of their attention was focused on the financial prospects of Newfoundland, especially after Marshall and Thompson had prepared a budget for Newfoundland's first six years as a province. Even though Canada had insisted that the subsidy offered to Newfoundland in 1947 was proportionately higher than that paid to any of the Maritime provinces and that it could offer no more, the delegation worried that Newfoundland's fiscal capacity would be insufficient to meet normal expenditures.[66] Smallwood reminded his colleagues on numerous occasions, however, that the Canadian government was worried about the political and fiscal repercussions, especially in the Maritime provinces, of providing greater financial assistance to Newfoundland than to the other provinces. "There was absolutely no possibility, in his estimation," Smallwood said, "of having the amount of the subsidy increased" if they simply demanded more. If, however, they were able to make a case for the special consideration of Newfoundland aside from fiscal needs, Ottawa might provide assistance of a transitory or short-term nature without having to worry about political backlash from any of the other provinces, especially those in the Maritimes.[67] The federal government, Smallwood pointed out, had consistently refused any requests from the provinces for additional monies for the

CHAPTER 7

express purpose of meeting their fiscal needs and would undoubtedly adopt a similar attitude towards Newfoundland. He suggested that if the Newfoundland delegation was to succeed in securing additional payments or additional benefits of any kind, "it must devise some formula or present some argument in support of its request which is apparently applicable to Newfoundland only, although, in fact, it need not necessarily be."[68]

After its month-long preparations in St. John's, where it met daily from ten in the morning to five in the afternoon and heard from a wide variety of interested parties and individuals, the Newfoundland delegation prepared a memorandum to be submitted to the Canadian Cabinet Committee on Newfoundland. The memorandum outlined a variety of issues for negotiations in Ottawa.[69] It pointed out that public services in Newfoundland were at a level below that of any province of Canada and that, even without providing for new services, Newfoundland would face a deficit of approximately $10 million per annum within four years of union (when it was expected that its surplus of approximately $40 million would be exhausted). The financial outlook was not encouraging: "It is apparent that there will be a wide gap between prospective revenue and expenditure, having regard to the amount reasonably required to maintain Provincial public services even at their present level, which is far below that of all other Provinces." The delegation did not see how the deficit could be overcome and warned that "the existence of this [financial] gap presents a problem which is more than a financial one. It is one the solution of which is a prerequisite to workable union. It should therefore be placed in the forefront of the discussions." The delegation also accepted Smallwood's argument about seeking better financial terms:

> The cost of maintaining services for a small population scattered over a long coastline will impose a heavy burden on the new government. Revenue to maintain these services will have to be sought from people who are, in the main, fishermen and seasonal workers accustomed to a system of indirect taxation and traditionally opposed to any system of direct taxation. It therefore follows that the most important question for consideration [during the negotiations] is the ability of the new

Province to provide public services which will remain her sole responsibility. While the standard of these services has been considerably improved within the past decade, the present standard is below that of any Province of Canada.[70]

Second Delegation to Ottawa, October 6 to December 11, 1948

Following the decisions of the Canadian Cabinet on August 3 and 11, 1948, to accept union with Newfoundland, the Interdepartmental Committee on Canada-Newfoundland Relations that had been appointed to prepare for the 1947 delegation was enlarged to include all government departments and agencies impacted by Newfoundland's entry into Canada. Coordination of the interdepartmental committee was given to a steering subcommittee under the chairmanship of Dr. Robert A. MacKay, then head of the British Commonwealth Division of the Department of External Affairs, and included representatives from the departments of External Affairs, Finance, Trade and Commerce, the Privy Council Office, and the Bank of Canada. The following five other subcommittees were established: Legal and Procedure, Fisheries, Transportation, Finance and Economic Policy, and Organization of Administrative Services.[71] The Interdepartmental Committee was particularly concerned with the procedures for bringing Newfoundland into Confederation. It had all government departments prepare for the administrative takeover of departments and agencies in Newfoundland that would pass to Canada after union and to consider any problem that might arise in that transition.

The second Newfoundland delegation to Ottawa first met the Canadian delegation on October 6, 1948, in a public session in the Canadian Senate, but all of the other nineteen meetings were held in camera. The Newfoundland delegation convened daily to discuss the matters raised with the Canadians and to receive reports from Newfoundland officials who were also in Ottawa holding discussions with their Canadian counterparts.[72] The meetings were not a series of negotiations between the two delegations, however. The federal government was limited by two factors in negotiating the terms of union with Newfoundland. First, as already noted, it was worried about the political implications of offering to Newfoundland any terms or conditions that the other provinces, particularly those in the Maritime region, might consider more advantageous than they enjoyed at the time. Second, even if the federal government had wished to negotiate a constitutional arrangement that might have been more advantageous than the Maritime provinces then enjoyed, section 146 of the *British North America Act* (since 1982, the *Constitution Act, 1867*) stated that any new provinces admitted to the federation were bound by the same constitutional conditions as every other province. Yet in practice, the federal government had frequently negotiated special arrangements with provinces that entered the union after the creation of Canada in 1867 as well as with those that were particularly unhappy with the 72 Resolutions agreed to in Quebec. One of the best known examples was "better terms" for Nova Scotia in 1869 that increased its debt allowance to $9,188,756, effectively increasing the annual subsidy by nearly $60,000 and further increasing the annual subsidy by $82,698 for the first ten years of Confederation.[73] Mitchell Sharp of the Department of Finance, who was a member of the important steering subcommittee of the Interdepartmental Committee on Newfoundland in 1948, recalled some years later that the negotiations of the financial terms of union were not of the conventional nature. Canada did not bargain directly with the Newfoundland delegation, "trying to ascertain what price had to be paid to induce them to join."[74] The negotiations were not about determining the best arrangements for Newfoundland to thrive as a province but about figuring out what could be done without creating political problems for the Liberal government of Louis St. Laurent, who had replaced Mackenzie King as prime minister on November 15, 1948—at the precise time the Newfoundland delegation was in Ottawa negotiating the final terms of union.[75] James Channing, the secretary of the Newfoundland delegation in 1948, was critical of such an approach to the negotiations in Ottawa. Canada's failure to recognize that Newfoundland had particular problems that called for special treatment only perpetuated Newfoundland's position as a backward region, he later wrote. Moreover, it was "short-sightedness and a lack of knowledge and understanding of Newfoundland's problems."[76]

Not surprisingly then, Canada's usual response to the financial issues raised by the Newfoundland delegation—at least initially—was "We're sorry but we have to treat all provinces alike." Yet Ottawa adopted a conciliatory approach early on in the negotiations with the Newfoundland delegation, which might be seen as a sign that it was willing, at times at least, to meet the special needs of Newfoundland when and where it could do so without upsetting the balance that had been achieved in the Canadian federation since 1867. For example, the Canadians agreed, in Term 46 of the draft terms of union, to allow the production of oleomargarine (which was largely prohibited by law in Canada) because Newfoundland's transportation system and dairy industry were not sufficiently developed to facilitate the efficient movement of perishable products such as butter. The Canadians also agreed to the enrichment of flour to compensate for dietary deficiencies throughout Newfoundland. Term 38 extended the benefits of Canadian veterans to Newfoundland veterans, and Term 17 provided constitutional guarantees for denominational schools in Newfoundland. Louis St. Laurent, the secretary of state for external affairs and chairman of the Canadian Cabinet Committee on Newfoundland before he became prime minister, later remarked that union was much more complex in 1949 than it had been in 1867, and the differences between Newfoundland and Canada had to be harmonized with the fundamental basis of the Canadian constitution.[77]

On November 22, 1948, the two sides began drafting an agreement that would become the Terms of Union. It would not be until December 11, thirteen drafts later and more than two months after the Newfoundland delegation arrived in Ottawa, that the negotiations would be finalized. The Terms of Union contained fifty articles. On the fiscal side, Newfoundland won a clear victory when Canada increased the twelve-year sliding transitional subsidy included in the 1947 proposals from $26.2 million to $42.7 million in the 1948 negotiations. Canada also promised a review in Term 29 of Newfoundland's finances after eight years of union in the most "sympathetic approach," according to Channing, but Newfoundland did not at the time insist on playing a role in that later investigation.[78] Chesley Crosbie broke with other members of the Newfoundland delegation and refused to sign the Terms of Union on December 11, asserting that the arrangement did not secure Newfoundland's financial future. Crosbie claimed that the arrangement left the financial future of Newfoundland far from secure. He was worried too about the fate of secondary industries in

CHAPTER 7

Newfoundland following union and particularly disappointed that greater assistance was not being offered to them during a transitional period.[79] Smallwood, too, realized that there were some uncertainties with Newfoundland's financial position going into Confederation, but he believed that Canada and Newfoundland would address any lingering problems over fiscal matters through Term 29.[80] In his 1973 autobiography, *I Chose Canada*, Smallwood points out that he had attempted to convince Crosbie to sign the terms:

> I argued with him that the terms could not properly cover all eventualities, and I was able to quote for him Sir Wilfrid Laurier's dictum, "There is no finality to the Terms of Confederation." I told him that the terms of admission of Nova Scotia, New Brunswick, Prince Edward Island, and the Prairie Provinces, had been amended again and again, always upward for the provinces. The same would happen to our terms.[81]

Later events would support Smallwood's claim that he believed the Terms of Union could be altered. After 1949, Smallwood sought special arrangements for Newfoundland's fisheries, for local manufacturers facing severe competition from new Canadian imports, and for federal tax exemptions for the province's pulp and paper mills. In each case, Ottawa usually refused to provide any assistance that was not included in the Terms of Union—but his lack of success with federal ministers never stopped Smallwood from raising other matters when he believed he could make a special case for Newfoundland.[82]

The rights of Newfoundland's Indigenous Peoples received little to no attention during the negotiations leading to union. David MacKenzie suggests the "neglect was based on ignorance."[83] There were no Indigenous representatives in the National Convention and no meaningful debate about Indigenous issues there, although there was one revealing exchange during the debate on the proposed terms in 1947. In Ottawa, the question had come up about Indigenous Peoples' voting and education rights, and members of the Newfoundland delegation believed at the time that Indigenous Peoples in Newfoundland had the same citizenship status as all Newfoundlanders and that bringing them under Canadian legislation such as the *Indian Act* would deprive them of some of the social benefits to which all citizens were entitled (including family allowance and old age pensions). Yet when Smallwood brought up the matter in the National Convention of an Indian Affairs Division that would be responsible for Indigenous Peoples, laughter was recorded from someone in the Assembly. Smallwood accused Malcolm Hollett of making light of the situation and said, "Mr. Bay Boy may not feel like laughing when I say that the Government of Newfoundland has no such division or department for the welfare of the Indians or Eskimos, of whom there are many hundreds in Labrador." Hollett denied it was he, and Smallwood apologized but not to "the member who laughed." He then said that Newfoundland had "never even allowed [Indigenous Peoples] to be citizens. Until this National Convention we never even gave them a vote. All we gave them was a bit of dole."[84]

Later, before the second delegation arrived in October 1948, Dr. P.E. Moore, director of Indian Health Services of the Department of National Health and Welfare, travelled to Newfoundland to investigate what services Newfoundland provided to Indigenous people. He estimated that there were about twelve hundred Indigenous people in Newfoundland, but no special services were provided to them by the Newfoundland state, except perhaps some financial assistance to the Grenfell and Moravian missions for the purpose of providing schools. Still, Moore found that Indigenous people were regarded as citizens and would be eligible for Canadian social programs at Confederation on the same basis as all other Newfoundlanders. Given his comments in the National Convention, it was not surprising then that Smallwood initially believed that "the administration of Indians in Newfoundland would be taken over by the Federal Government," but he eventually came around to the Canadian position that "it would be most undesirable that any group of residents in Newfoundland or Labrador should lose any rights or benefits as a result of confederation."[85] There is no indication that any attempt was ever made to consult with the people impacted, nor was there any mention in the Terms of Union of Indigenous Peoples or their relationship with the state after union. The matter of administration of Indigenous affairs would be settled after Confederation when the *Indian Act* was proclaimed in Newfoundland; however, it took years for this to happen. Only in 1984

CHAPTER 7

was the Miawpukek First Nation (at Conne River) recognized under the *Indian Act*, and in 2013 the Government of Canada officially recognized the Qalipu Mi'kmaq Band as a landless band for the Mi'kmaq of Newfoundland. In 2007, the Innu of Labrador won recognition for its members as Status Indians under Canada's *Indian Act*, but land claims remain an issue of contention to this day.[86]

Upon his return to St. John's, Albert J. Walsh, who chaired the second delegation to Ottawa, prepared a memorandum for the Commission of Government on the negotiations and the Terms of Union. His memorandum might be seen as his interpretation of what had transpired and what had been agreed upon by the two sides. He complimented the members of the delegation and its staff on their efforts and offered his view on the various terms. On Term 17 dealing with education, Walsh noted that the provincial legislature had exclusive jurisdiction to make laws over education but that it "did not have authority to make laws prejudicially affecting any right or privilege with respect to denominational schools, common (amalgamated) schools, or denominational colleges" that existed at the time of union. He also noted that "the Education clause has been agreed to by the Executive Officers of the [Newfoundland] Department of Education." He noted the gains that he believed had been made in fisheries. After "very difficult negotiation," the Canadian government allowed for a five-year continuation of the Newfoundland legislation relating to the marketing of salt fish, although the cost of administration was transferred to Canada. Walsh said the Newfoundland delegation had insisted on this arrangement, even though the Canadians maintained that the regulation of trade and commerce was a federal prerogative under the *British North America Act*. Similarly, Ottawa wished to bring the Newfoundland Fisheries Board, created in 1936 to regulate most aspects of the fishery from production to distribution, under the administrative control of the federal minister of fisheries, but the Newfoundland delegation wanted the Fisheries Board to continue. Despite the lobbying from Maritime interests that wanted the Board discontinued, Ottawa relented to the demands of the Newfoundland delegation. Walsh also believed that Term 29—the appointment of a royal commission to review Newfoundland's financial position after eight years of union—was a major gain, as it included the phrase "at the levels and standards reached subsequent to the date of union" rather than continuance of those services "at then prevailing levels." The delegation believed that it would be beneficial for Newfoundland to have an examination of the period after union, rather than the period immediately preceding the appointment of the royal commission, because it would show, Walsh believed, how the gains made in the early years of union had to be maintained without imposing burdensome taxation rates on the province. On Public Services, Works, and Property, Walsh noted, "Term 31 follows the clause in the original proposal but makes it clear that Canada will be liable for the costs of operation of the services named 'as from the date of Union.'" The Newfoundland Railway, including steamship and other marine services, were included in Term 31. These and several of the other terms, including those dealing with veterans, policing, and those losing employment after the date of union, represented considerable savings for the new provincial government. Term 47 exempted Newfoundlanders from income tax for a period of three months.[87] Walsh considered all of this very beneficial.

The Terms of Union outlined how Newfoundland was to be integrated into Canada as a province.[88] This agreement set out the roles and procedures for the union of Newfoundland with Canada. The federal government was acutely aware of the social and economic conditions in Newfoundland at the time of union, and it moved relatively quickly to make sure that Canada's social programs were immediately available to the new province. This was true of the family allowance, unemployment insurance benefits, and old age pensions. Arrangements were made immediately after the signing of the Terms of Union to register children in Newfoundland so that family allowance benefits could be paid in the first month of union.[89] Similarly, the federal government introduced measures to have Newfoundlanders avail themselves of the unemployment insurance benefits immediately after Newfoundland became a province. It also created a temporary program to enable workers in Newfoundland to qualify for such benefits even if they had not yet contributed to the national unemployment insurance program and had not qualified for benefits under the normal rules.[90] Old age pensions had to await the establishment of a provincial government in Newfoundland, but the federal government moved quickly to facilitate the program and have payments made as soon as possible after April 1, 1949.

CHAPTER 7

Accompanied by members of the Newfoundland and Canadian delegations, Prime Minister Louis St. Laurent and Hon. Albert J. Walsh shake hands following the signing of the agreement admitting Newfoundland to Confederation, December 11, 1948.

Although the federal government was committed to fulfilling its obligation regarding social benefits and individual transfers to Newfoundlanders, it did not offer a similar commitment to fostering the economic development of Newfoundland, as Chesley Crosbie had feared. In fact, it might be argued that the 1948 Newfoundland delegation to Ottawa that negotiated the Terms of Union was not intent on protecting the manufacturing sector that existed in Newfoundland at the time of union with Canada. Historian Peter Neary argues that the Canadian federal system of jurisdiction left economic development to the provinces.[91] When the Association of Newfoundland Industries Limited, representing the Island's manufacturing sector, approached the 1948 Newfoundland delegations during their preparations for negotiations in Ottawa, it asked that the delegations negotiate tax concessions for Newfoundland manufacturers and other forms of assistance to help local manufacturers transition to the new economic arrangements after union. Newfoundland manufacturers had long enjoyed protection from outside competitors through a protective tariff, but those protective tariffs were to disappear with Confederation.

However, the Newfoundland delegations did not lobby for protection for local manufacturers. In fact, the delegations were more interested in lowering the prices of consumer goods than in securing any form of protection for Newfoundland's manufacturing sector. In the months following Confederation, the Government of Canada, through its influential minister of trade and commerce, C.D. Howe, refused to offer any special consideration to Newfoundland's manufacturers, who struggled in the new economic environment. Howe insisted that the government could not treat manufacturers in one Canadian province differently from those in other provinces.[92]

The dropping of trade barriers with Canada and new competition with local producers led to a reduction in prices for many consumer goods. Smallwood's promise of improved circumstances for ordinary citizens was immediately realized, which would have pleased many of the supporters of union. Shortly after the Confederate victory, a west coast merchant sent Francis M. O'Leary, a manufacturers' agent in St. John's who did business throughout the Island, a cheque for $91.76 to settle his account. He attached a brief note that revealed his hostility to the St. John's mercantile elite, saying, "You can close the account for ever, now that we have Confederation we can buy goods from our good Canadian friends. I will be in St. John's next August to cut grass off Water Street for my horse next winter."[93] Yet despite the reduction, prices of consumer goods in Newfoundland never dropped to the levels found in most Canadian cities.

UNION—AT LAST

By the end of February 1949, the Canadian Parliament passed the appropriate legislation to enable union, which allowed the British Parliament to pass the *Newfoundland Act*, providing for the constitutional basis upon which Newfoundland would become a province of Canada.[94] Although the Progressives Conservatives voted against the bill to approve union, they joined all other members who stood and sang "O Canada" and "God Save the King." The terms came into force "immediately before the expiration" of the thirty-first day of March 1949. At long last, some eighty-five years after Newfoundland premier and attorney

CHAPTER 7

At the ceremony on Parliament Hill in Ottawa to welcome Newfoundland into Canada on April 1, 1949, Prime Minister St. Laurent initiates the work of carving Newfoundland's coat of arms at the base of the Peace Tower.

general Hugh W. Hoyles first talked with Nova Scotia premier Charles Tupper in Halifax about joining in the discussion to create a new country, Newfoundland finally became a province of Canada. Gordon Bradley, who joined St. Laurent's Cabinet as the secretary of state, referred to the day as "a day of fulfilment—fulfilment of a vision of great men who planned the nation of Canada.... We [can] see them now, bending over this scene in silent and profound approval." He acknowledged that union would transform Newfoundland but that the federal system of government "assures them of a continuance of their identity of which they have always been so proud." He warned that the new system of government would lead to "stresses and strains," but he was hopeful that the process of integration would be smooth as Canada had given already "speedy recognition" to Newfoundland's unique circumstances. Both Bradley and St. Laurent promised Canada's newest citizens full partnership and prosperity in their new country.[95] As Toronto's *Globe and*

Mail favourably noted, Newfoundland was "yielding its ancient independence, but not its identity."[96] *Fishermen's Advocate* editor Charles Granger observed a few days later, on April 8, 1949, "Now that we are a Province of Canada it will not cure all the ills and ailments of our Island. Our future will depend on what type of Provincial Government we get."[97] Whatever the future was to hold, union with Canada brought Newfoundlanders a new and improved form of citizenship, and as the province's first premier, Joseph R. Smallwood could take much of the credit for that.

CONCLUSION

"When I launched the fight for Confederation two years ago," Joseph R. Smallwood wrote in *The Star Weekly* on March 26, 1949, just a few days before union became official, "I did so with the belief that union with Canada was Newfoundland's only hope of escaping poverty and oppression." After leading the Confederates to final victory in 1948 and reversing a powerful tide of anti-Confederate sentiment dating back to the 1860s, Smallwood, who was to become the province's first premier, was undoubtedly happy and optimistic. "I am convinced," he gushed, "we have broken with an unhappy past [and] arrived at the dawn of a glorious new era." He was also insistent, as he had been throughout the campaign for union, that as citizens of a "small, isolated nation, striving to get along by our own unaided efforts, [Newfoundlanders] were doomed to eternal want and an endless but futile struggle to keep our chins above water." Newfoundlanders were wonderful, hard-working, industrious people, he insisted, but his work with fishermen and loggers in the desperate 1930s, when he witnessed "the finest fishermen in the world reduced to death's door by malnutrition, hobbling about with beri-beri... children stricken with rickets... [and] women age 10 years in a single year," made him "hate the very thought of Newfoundland reverting to responsible government as an independent nation." Hard times might indeed come again, but "if they do," he wrote, "Newfoundland will be better prepared" as a province of Canada; it would not have "to struggle along with meagre resources to keep our people alive." Confederation should have come eighty years ago, he suggested, but "at last we have learned. Now we are about to abandon our ancient isolation and join the great Canadian family." Confederation would not end all poverty, nor would it solve all issues confronting Newfoundland, he admitted, but he contended that "our families will live better" and new solutions to old problems were possible. Like the Canadian prairies with their wheat economies, he noted, Newfoundlanders could not depend solely on the fisheries. They had to stabilize their economy with the development of a diversified and vibrant industrial sector and through the development of their natural resources. Smallwood claimed that it was a "great new era," one that would "make Newfoundland great and Canada greater."[1]

The optimism was evident again a few days later when Canadians gathered on Parliament Hill in Ottawa and Canada's newest citizens assembled in St. John's to officially welcome Newfoundland as a province. Although Newfoundlanders might have had little understanding at the time of Canada's constitutional model—with its divided jurisdictions as adopted in 1867—they were reassured by Prime Minister Louis St. Laurent on April 1, 1949, that the federal system of government guaranteed the "continuance of their identity of which they have always been so proud." Those who had led the fight for Confederation understood that Canadian federalism had built a national political community that made space for and accepted the legitimacy of the various communities that comprised the nation in 1867 or were added later. St. Laurent also promised Newfoundlanders that they entered Confederation as full and equal partners and would share with all Canadians the wealth the country had to offer its citizens. Gordon Bradley, the Confederate leader who became secretary of state in St. Laurent's Cabinet, shared those sentiments; his comment, "We are all Canadians now," held considerable promise for a bright future.[2]

How has it all turned out for Newfoundlanders and Labradorians? There is a simple answer to that perplexing question, as well as a long and complicated one that is beyond the scope of this book. The simple answer is that Newfoundlanders benefitted immensely from union, especially if one accepts that the decisive factor in the 1948 campaign

CONCLUSION

was social citizenship. Yet the fiscal situation in Newfoundland and Labrador has rarely been robust since 1949, and it has deteriorated in the past decade after a brief period when the province was among the leaders in economic growth across the country. Moreover, as a province of Canada, Newfoundland and Labrador has few constitutional guarantees for addressing the economic disparities it faces within the federation. As the Newfoundland and Labrador Royal Commission on Renewing and Strengthening Our Place in Canada noted in 2003, it has relied "on the good faith, vision and courage of successive federal governments in addressing obstacles to its full participation in Confederation." The Commission also found that Newfoundlanders and Labradorians "feel ignored, misunderstood and unappreciated by their federal government and, to a lesser extent, by other Canadians. There is a deep concern," the Commission lamented, "that a future of prosperity and self-reliance is not achievable within the Canada of today."[3] Yet much of the anti-Confederate feeling in Newfoundland dissipated immediately after union in 1949, and many of those who fought against Smallwood over Confederation joined with him or gravitated to the Progressive Conservative Party of Canada. Perhaps Donald Jamieson is among the most notable examples, but he was only one of thousands who chose to quickly accept the results of the 1948 referenda. Jamieson offered assistance to Canadian business interests trying to establish themselves in Newfoundland and eventually became a Liberal politician and later a federal Cabinet minister. He recalled that in 1948 after the Confederate victory, he felt that "with Confederation a reality, it made sense to do everything possible to make it work. This meant, under the circumstances, allying myself with Smallwood provincially, and with the Liberal Party on the national scene."[4] Even though St. John's and Ottawa have fought frequently over a number of policy issues, notably the control over marine resources, the transmission of hydroelectricity, and federal transfers to the province, the quarrels have been over how to make Confederation work better for Newfoundland and Labrador, not over Confederation itself. This is extraordinary given that nearly half of Newfoundlanders voted in 1948 not to become a province of Canada.

A 2018 survey found that half of Newfoundlanders and Labradorians polled believe that their province will be bankrupt within a few years. The current level of anxiety is quite elevated across the province, and there is apparently little of the optimism that Smallwood and Bradley held in 1949. A quarter of citizens now anticipate things getting worse over the coming decade. When asked to explain the root of such pessimism, respondents pointed to some of the same factors that, in 1949, many hoped union with Canada might help to avoid—a crippling provincial debt, high unemployment and limited opportunities for young people, poor health care and outcomes, and government mismanagement. More than 70 percent of respondents in 2018 believed things were so bad in the province that they must consider new ways of doing things. There was, however, no sense among those surveyed that union with Canada was responsible for the current state of affairs in Newfoundland and Labrador.[5] Nor was Confederation blamed when, in 2017, researchers at the Harris Centre at Memorial University similarly projected serious demographic challenges for the province, partly because of the federal closure in the early 1990s of the cod fishery that led to the out-migration of many young people and their families to seek employment, particularly in western Canada. Greater labour mobility after 1949 within Canada was one of the many benefits of being citizens of the Canadian federation. Newfoundland's population is now expected to be much older and much smaller in the next two decades. If the birth rate remains low and out-migration of young people from rural areas in search of work continues, combined with a rapidly aging population—Newfoundland and Labrador is aging faster than any other province in the country—the province's population will decline by 8 percent within two decades. There are a few bright spots, especially in the urban regions adjacent to St. John's, where population growth is anticipated. However, if the current trends continue unchecked, it will be a vastly different province in 2049, at the centennial of Confederation, than it is today and certainly what it was in 1949.[6]

Yet after seventy years of union, it is difficult to attribute much of anything in Newfoundland and Labrador to Confederation anymore, except perhaps the continued benefits to individuals that all Canadians receive and federal transfers to the provincial government for a variety of programs that, again, all provinces of Canada receive. Even with the latter transfers, there is something perverse in Canada's much-vaunted equalization program that attempts to address the fiscal disparities

CONCLUSION

among provinces. Equalization payments were designed to enable less prosperous provincial governments to provide their residents with public services that are reasonably comparable to those in other provinces, at reasonably comparable levels of taxation. So committed was Canada to these notions of fairness that equalization is entrenched in the Canadian constitution. Yet through the complex and complicated formula that has been adopted to determine equalization payments, it excludes all or a portion of natural resource revenues. Newfoundland and Labrador was not eligible for such transfers between 2009 and 2018, even though its fiscal capacity was severely handicapped by the rapid decline in the price of oil since 2012.[7]

During this period, and in fact since 1949, Newfoundland and Labrador has struggled with high rates of unemployment, a huge provincial deficit, one of the highest costs of living in Canada, low education outcomes, and high rates of illiteracy. When Newfoundland joined Canada in 1949, it placed lowest on these and, indeed, most indices that measure social and economic well-being. Now, after seven decades as a province of Canada, it continues to hold that unfavourable and dubious distinction. The promise of economic security and social well-being is relative, of course, but Confederation—as Smallwood, St. Laurent, and Bradley had promised in 1949—has delivered on its promise of social citizenship. When Newfoundlanders consider their situation relative to the Canadian average, many might still wonder, nonetheless, if the fairness, justice, and fiscal and economic stability they had hoped for have been achieved. Even if they live in a province that continues to lag behind much of the rest of the country, they can be reasonably secure in the belief that as part of a prosperous nation like Canada, it is unlikely that they will ever again have to deal single-handedly with a major economic collapse as they did before Confederation. Canadian citizenship provides the basis upon which they can now make claims on the larger political community concerning not only juridical and political rights and duties but also protection against the vicissitudes of social and economic ills with which they have to deal. In the nineteenth and twentieth centuries, Newfoundlanders had not imagined themselves as citizens with the right to demand certain protections within the framework of political debate or to be guaranteed certain benefits from the state, and they had laboured under the most undesirable conditions. But through union with Canada, Newfoundlanders achieved a new social citizenship that promised them a measure of security to which they had rarely been accustomed. In Canada, Newfoundland and Labrador has become a modern society with the benefits of a social security system and a comparatively high standard of living that is among the best in the world, and, at the same time, it has maintained its unique identity and sense of place that makes it among the most culturally distinctive provinces in Canada.

The journey to Canada took eighty-two years, more if we begin with Frederic Bowker Terrington Carter and Ambrose Shea's attendance at the 1864 constitutional conference in Quebec City that laid the basis for Confederation in 1867. In the years since Canadian Confederation, union with Canada was a ballot question put to Newfoundlanders only three times, in 1869 and 1948, but Confederation was nonetheless a constant political issue throughout much of that time, even if on occasion it was only a distraction used by political leaders and their parties to smear their opponents and to score favour with the electorate. But Newfoundlanders were never fools in the process. They made informed, though certainly personal and self-interested, decisions on their relationship with Canada and on Confederation. Newfoundland voters were not ill-informed, not easily swayed by prejudice and hysteria, nor by the emotional appeals of demagogues, not in 1869 and not in 1948. On both occasions when Confederation was the ballot question—and at other times when it was tangential or peripheral—Newfoundlanders made informed and rational choices for rejecting Confederation in 1869 and for choosing Canada in 1948. By 1948, a new relationship had emerged in Newfoundland (as was the case elsewhere) between state and citizen—a social citizenship whereby the state would provide all people a basic level of social and economic stability and well-being to which many were unaccustomed but naturally aspired. The shift in the notion of citizenship based primarily on political and constitutional imperatives to social and economic ones was a decisive factor in the narrow vote for union with Canada in 1948 because it promised voters full participation in Canada's economic, social, and political life, something that an independent Newfoundland could not provide in the foreseeable future. The victory for Confederation in 1948 was not about Newfoundlanders being bribed or selling their souls and birthrights for a mess of pottage. If other citizens throughout North America and Europe, but especially in Canada, were increasingly getting more from their state, why shouldn't Newfoundlanders? The large number of outport people who voted for union with Canada believed it might provide them with a better life and more of what they believed the Water Street merchants enjoyed; they were not crass, greedy, selfish materialists, but at that point in their history they demanded full participation in the state's economic, social, and political life. In 1869, on the other hand, political (not social) citizenship and the fear of an expanding state had been the important factors in the decision to reject union with Canada and pursue a separate path in North America. By 1948, the appeal to nationalism and patriotism that had worked well in the past for those who wished to chart an independent course for Newfoundland within the world failed to resonate with voters. By then, a new model of citizenship—social citizenship, based on economic and social as well as political rights—lay at the heart of the movement for union with Canada. The rest from formal politics that had begun in 1934 also allowed for a break with the past, one that allowed for the severing of the dominant influence that the St. John's economic and political elite had over the economy and society. Newfoundland's most vulnerable families and workers, especially those in outport communities, including a large number of women, especially mothers, were determined to put their well-being and that of their families first. The respite from politics in Newfoundland also allowed Prime Minister Clement Attlee and his government in faraway Whitehall to change the ground rules for active political life in Newfoundland from 1945 to 1948, something Smallwood was quick to seize upon and outport people supported. Through Smallwood and the Confederates, they claimed their place—and voice—in the democratic process and voted for the social citizenship that was at the heart of the Confederate campaign. It was those voters who made the decision that Newfoundland would become a province of Canada.

ENDNOTES

INTRODUCTION

1   Governor Middleton to J.H. Thomas, 15 Mar. 1932 (The Rooms, Provincial Archives of Newfoundland and Labrador [RPA], GN1.1.7, box 34, file 1932).
2   *Irish Examiner*, 15 Dec. 1948. The *Irish Independent* added, "Union with Canada would seem to be the most practicable way to a solution of the administrative difficulties that have troubled Newfoundland for a considerable time" (3 Apr. 1947). Many commentators in Ireland wondered if Westminster might attempt to include Newfoundland in the United Kingdom in an arrangement similar to that in Northern Ireland (Ulster). See *Belfast Newsletter*, 4 June 1947.
3   Phillip McCann, "British Policy and Confederation," *Newfoundland Studies* 14, no. 2 (1998): 155–68; John E. FitzGerald, "The Confederation of Newfoundland with Canada, 1946–49" (MA thesis, Memorial University, 1992); Bren Walsh, *More than a Poor Majority: The Story of Newfoundland's Confederation with Canada* (St. John's: Breakwater, 1985); and *Secret Nation*, written by Edward Riche and directed by Mike Jones (1992). For a discussion of Newfoundland nationalism, see Jerry Bannister, "Whigs and Nationalists: The Legacy of Judge Prowse's *History of Newfoundland*," *Acadiensis* 32, no. 1 (Autumn 2002): 84–109; and " 'The Sport of Historic Misfortune': Judge Prowse and the Story of Newfoundland," in *Discourse and Discovery: Sir Richard Whitbourne Quatercentennial Symposium 1615–2015 and Beyond*, ed. Melvin Baker, Christopher P. Curran, and J. Derek Green (St. John's: SS *Daisy* Legal History Committee, Law Society of Newfoundland and Labrador, 2017), 263–314; and Ed Hollett, "Two Solitudes: Newfoundland's Victim Narrative," *Dorchester Review* 6, no. 1 (Spring/Summer 2016): 14–17.
4   Greg Malone, *Don't Tell the Newfoundlanders: The True Story of Newfoundland's Confederation with Canada* (Toronto: Knopf Canada, 2012).
5   Malone, *Don't Tell the Newfoundlanders*, 150–51.
6   Hill to Granville, 20 Nov. 1869 (Colonial Office Records Series 194 [CO 194], CO 194/178, 13617, Newfoundland, Centre for Newfoundland Studies, Queen Elizabeth II Libraries, Memorial University).

7   Quoted in Jeff Webb, "The Responsible Government League and the Confederation Campaigns of 1948," *Newfoundland Studies* 5, no. 2 (1989): 214.
8   Quoted in Webb, "The Responsible Government League," 214.
9   *The Monitor*, Feb. 1949.
10 On the history of Confederation in 1949, see Melvin Baker, "Falling into the Canadian Lap: The Confederation of Newfoundland and Canada, 1945–1949," in *Royal Commission on Renewing and Strengthening Our Place in Canada*, vol. 1, *Research* (St. John's: Office of the Queen's Printer, 2003): 29–88; Raymond B. Blake, *Canadians at Last: Canada Integrates Newfoundland as a Province* (Toronto: University of Toronto Press, 2004); Paul Bridle, ed., *Documents on Relations Between Canada and Newfoundland*, vol. 2, *Confederation, Parts 1 and 2* (Ottawa: Minister of Supply and Services Canada, 1984); John E. FitzGerald, " 'The True Father of Confederation'? Archbishop E.P. Roche, Term 17, and Newfoundland's Confederation with Canada," *Newfoundland Studies* 14, no. 2 (1998): 188–219; James K. Hiller, "Confederation Defeated: The Newfoundland Election of 1869," in *Newfoundland in the Nineteenth and Twentieth Centuries: Essays in Interpretation*, eds. James K. Hiller and Peter Neary (Toronto: University of Toronto Press, 1980), 67–94; James K. Hiller and Michael F. Harrington, eds., *The Newfoundland National Convention, 1946–1948*, vol. 1, *Debates* (Montreal and Kingston: McGill-Queen's University Press, 1995); David MacKenzie, *Inside the Atlantic Triangle: Canada and the Entrance of Newfoundland into Confederation, 1939–1949* (Toronto: University of Toronto Press, 1986); Peter Neary, *Newfoundland in the North Atlantic World, 1929–1949* (Montreal and Kingston: McGill-Queen's University Press, 1988); and "Newfoundland's Union with Canada: Conspiracy or Choice?" *Acadiensis* 12, no. 2 (Spring 1983): 110–19; S.J.R. Noel, *Politics in Newfoundland* (Toronto: University of Toronto Press, 1971); Corey Slumkoski, *Inventing Atlantic Canada: Regionalism and the Maritime Reaction to Newfoundland's Entry into Canadian Confederation* (Toronto: University of Toronto Press, 2011); Jeff A. Webb, "Newfoundland's National Convention, 1946–48" (MA thesis, Memorial University, 1987); "The Responsible Government League"; and "Confederation, Conspiracy and Choice: A Discussion," *Newfoundland Studies* 14, no. 2 (1998): 169–87.
11 See, for example, D.W. Prowse, *A History of Newfoundland: From the English, Colonial, and Foreign Records* (London: Eyre and Spottiswoode, 1896), 494–95; A.M. Fraser, "Relations with Canada," in *Newfoundland: Economic, Diplomatic, and Strategic Studies*, ed. R.A. MacKay (Toronto: University of Toronto Press, 1946), 411–43; William L. Morton, *The Critical Years: The Union of British North America, 1857–1873* (Toronto: McClelland and Stewart, 1964), 43–44; St. John Chadwick, *Newfoundland: Island into Province* (New York: Cambridge University Press, 1967); Hiller, "Confederation Defeated," 67–94; Peter Waite, *The Confederation Debates in the Province of Canada, 1865*, 2nd ed., introduction by Ged Martin (Montreal and Kingston: McGill-Queen's University Press, 2006); Phillip Buckner, "The 1860s: An End and a Beginning," in *The Atlantic Region to Confederation: A History*, ed. Phillip

Buckner and John G. Reid (Toronto: University of Toronto Press, 1994), 382–83; H.B. Mayo, "Newfoundland and Confederation in the Eighteen-Sixties," *Canadian Historical Review* 29, no. 2 (June 1948): 125–42; and Frederick Jones, "The Antis Gain the Day," in *The Causes of Canadian Confederation*, ed. Ged Martin (Fredericton: *Acadiensis* Press, 1990), 142–48.

12 Andrew Smith, "Toryism, Classical Liberalism, and Capitalism: The Politics of Taxation and the Struggle for Canadian Confederation," *Canadian Historical Review* 89, no. 1 (Mar. 2008): 2–25; Peter J. Smith, "The Ideological Origins of Canadian Confederation," *Canadian Journal of Political Science/Revue canadienne de science politique* 20, no. 1 (Mar. 1987): 3–29; Janet Ajzenstat, *The Canadian Founding: John Locke and Parliament* (Montreal and Kingston: McGill-Queen's University Press, 2007); and Kurt Korneski, *Conflicted Colony: Critical Episodes in Nineteenth-Century Newfoundland and Labrador* (Montreal and Kingston: McGill-Queen's University Press, 2016).

13 Smith, "Toryism, Classical Liberalism, and Capitalism."

14 See S.J.R. Noel, *Politics in Newfoundland* (Toronto: University of Toronto Press, 1971), 17–26. Noel notes that elections in nineteenth-century Newfoundland were often hotly contested and marred by "violence, intimidation and irregularities of every sort." In 1861, for instance, the local magistrate refused to open the polls in the Harbour Grace constituency. Patrick O'Flaherty, in *Lost Country: The Rise and Fall of Newfoundland, 1843–1933* (St. John's: Long Beach Press, 2005), shows that voters often became very excited about elections. See 46, 86, and 89.

15 James K. Hiller, "Research Note: James Murray and the 1882 Newfoundland General Election," *Newfoundland and Labrador Studies* 33, no. 1 (2018): 237–58. Murray's commentary on the 1882 election, Professor Hiller claims, provides "a unique account of electoral campaigning in a remote district before the introduction of the secret ballot in 1887" and an "unusual insight into how elections in that period were conducted." We wish to acknowledge our appreciation to Professor Hiller for the timely publication of this important research note and for directing our attention to the thirty articles that Mr. Murray published in the *Evening Telegram* between 21 Nov. 1882 and 1 Mar. 1883.

16 *Evening Telegram*, 28 Nov. and 8 Dec. 1882; and Hiller, "James Murray and the 1882 Newfoundland General Election," 241–42.

17 *Evening Telegram*, 23 Nov. 1882.

18 Some of those ideas are developed in studies of electoral politics. See, for example, Frank O'Gorman, "Campaign Rituals and Ceremonies: The Social Meaning of Elections in England, 1780–1860," *Past and Present* no. 135 (1992): 79–115; John Lonsdale, "Moral and Political Argument in Kenya," in *Ethnicity and Democracy in Africa*, ed. Bruce Berman, Dickson Eyoh, and Will Kymlicka (Oxford: James Currey, 2004), 76; and Thomas Bierschenk and Jean-Pierre Olivier de Sardan, "Studying the Dynamics of African Bureaucracies: An Introduction to States at Work," in *States at Work: Dynamics of African*

19 Richard Banégas, "Commodification of the Vote and Political Subjectivity in Africa: Reflections Based on the Case of Benin," in *Cultures of Voting: The Hidden History of the Secret Ballot*, ed. Romain Bertrand, Jean-Louis Briquet, and Peter Pels (London: Hurst, 2007), 186; and Timothy Mitchell, "The Limits of the State: Beyond Statist Approaches and Their Critics," *American Political Science Review* 85, no. 1 (Mar. 1991): 77–96.

20 James K. Hiller, "The Confederation Election of 1869," Newfoundland and Labrador Heritage Website, 1997, http://www.heritage.nf.ca/articles/politics/election-confederation-1869.php.

21 Some of these ideas are raised in Walter R. Fisher, "Rhetorical Fiction and the Presidency," *Quarterly Journal of Speech* 66, no. 2 (Apr. 1980): 119–26; "Narration as a Human Communication Paradigm: The Case of Public Moral Argument," *Communication Monographs* 51, no. 1 (Mar. 1984): 1–22; and "Romantic Democracy, Ronald Reagan, and Presidential Heroes," *Western Journal of Speech Communication* 46, no. 3 (Summer 1982): 299–310. For a recent look at Fisher's ideas, see Nicolas Bencherki and Joelle Basque, "Why So Many Americans Continue to Believe in Donald Trump," *The Conversation* (Canada), 6 Aug. 2018, https://theconversation.com/why-so-many-americans-continue-to-believe-in-donald-trump-100498.

22 *Monitor*, Feb. 1949.

23 See, for example, George Perlin, "The Constitutional Referendum of 1948 and the Revival of Sectarianism in Newfoundland Politics," *Queen's Quarterly* 75, no. 1 (1968): 155–60.

24 On the idea of social citizenship, see T.H. Marshall, *Citizenship and Social Class, and Other Essays* (Cambridge: Cambridge University Press, 1999); and for its application to Canada, see Raymond B. Blake, *From Rights to Needs: A History of Family Allowances in Canada, 1929–92* (Vancouver: UBC Press, 2009); Keith Banting, "Social Citizenship and the Multicultural Welfare State," in *Citizenship, Diversity, and Pluralism*, ed. Alan C. Cairns, John C. Courtney, Peter MacKinnon, Hans J. Michelmann, and David E. Smith (Montreal and Kingston: McGill-Queen's University Press, 1999), 108–36; and Janine Brodie, "Citizenship and Solidarity: Reflections on the Canadian Way," *Citizenship Studies* 6, no. 4 (2002): 377–94.

25 T.H. Marshall, *Class, Citizenship, and Social Development* (New York: Doubleday, 1964), 72.

26 Webb, "Confederation, Conspiracy and Choice." See also Peter Neary, "Newfoundland's Union with Canada," and his "Address to Convocation," Memorial University of Newfoundland, 5 May 1999, published in the *Gazette*, 8 June 1999, and available at https://www.mun.ca/president/report/1999-2000/honor/honorary_neary.html.

ENDNOTES

27 Speech by Smallwood during 1959 election campaign, n.d., 3, Coll-075, file 4.03.007 (Archives and Special Collections [ASC], Centre for Newfoundland Studies, Memorial University, St. John's, Newfoundland and Labrador).
28 Some of these ideas are discussed in James Overton, "Nationalism, Democracy, and Self-Determination: Newfoundland in the 1930s and 1940s," *Canadian Review of Studies in Nationalism* 32, nos. 1–2 (2005): 31–52.
29 Hiller and Harrington, eds., *Debates*, 21 Nov. 1947, 807.
30 Persons in Newfoundland and Labrador who identified as Indigenous at the time represented a small proportion of the population. However, when the Government of Canada and the Mi'kmaq First Nations Assembly of Newfoundland agreed to create the Qalipu First Nation in 2008, more than 100,000 people from Newfoundland and Labrador applied for membership and status under the *Indian Act*. Newfoundland and Labrador had a population of slightly more than 520,000 in 2008.
31 For a discussion of referenda and other forms of deliberative democracy, see Lawrence LeDuc, "Referendums and Deliberative Democracy," *Electoral Studies* 38 (June 2015): 139–48; Andreas R.T. Schuck and Claes H. de Vreese, "Public Support for Referendums in Europe: A Cross-National Comparison in 21 Countries," *Electoral Studies* 38 (June 2015): 149–58; Jon Henley, "Why Referendums Are Problematic—Yet More Popular than Ever," *The Guardian*, 6 Oct. 2016, https://www.theguardian.com/politics/political-science/2016/oct/06/why-referendums-are-problematic-yet-more-popular-than-ever; Dean Lacy and Emerson M.S. Niou, "A Problem with Referendums," *Journal of Theoretical Politics* 12, no. 1 (2000): 5–31; Steven J. Brams and Peter C. Fishburn, "Yes-No Voting," *Social Choice and Welfare* 10, no. 1 (1993): 35–50; and Elisabeth Gerber, "Legislative Response to the Threat of Popular Initiatives," *American Journal of Political Science* 40, no. 1 (Feb. 1996): 99–128.
32 See, for example, Lionel Marquis and Manfred Max Bergman, "Development and Consequences of Referendum Campaigns in Switzerland, 1981–1999," *Swiss Political Science Review* 15, no. 1 (Spring 2009): 63–97.

CHAPTER 1

1 Danette Dooley, "Revisiting the War of 1812," *The Telegram*, 30 Sept. 2011; and E.B. Biggar, ed., *Canada: A Memorial Volume: A Statistical and Descriptive Handbook of the Dominion* (London: Edward Stanford, 1889), 33.
2 See "Proposed Union of British North American Provinces," Cartier, Ross, and Galt to Secretary of State for the Colonies, 22 Oct. 1858 (RPA, GN1.3.A, box 2, file 2/1859).
3 *Journal of the House of Assembly* (JHA), 1865, Appendix, 845.
4 JHA, 1865, Appendix, 845; and Kent M. Haworth, "Musgrave, Sir Anthony," in *Dictionary of Canadian Biography* 11, University of Toronto/Université Laval, 1982, http://www.biographi.ca/en/bio/musgrave_anthony_11E.html.

5   See Phillip Buckner, "Beware the Canadian Wolf: The Maritimes and Confederation," *Acadiensis* 46, no. 2 (Summer/Autumn 2017): 177–95.
6   JHA, 1865, Appendix, 846–47.
7   JHA, 1865, Appendix, 848.
8   JHA, 1865, Appendix, 846–48, and R. Carter, acting colonial secretary, to F.B.T. Carter and A. Shea, 19 Sept. 1864 [JHA, 1865, Appendix, 850]. See also James K. Hiller, "The Confederation Issue in Newfoundland, 1864–1869: Selected Documents" (St. John's: Memorial University of Newfoundland, Oct. 1974), 4–5.
9   Phillip Buckner, "Tupper, Sir Charles," in *Dictionary of Canadian Biography* 14, University of Toronto/Université Laval, 1998, http://www.biographi.ca/en/bio/tupper_charles_14E.html.
10 James K. Hiller, "Shea, Sir Ambrose," in *Dictionary of Canadian Biography* 13, University of Toronto/Université Laval, 1994, http://www.biographi.ca/en/bio/shea_ambrose_13E.html. See also John E. FitzGerald, "Conflict and Culture in Irish-Newfoundland Roman Catholicism, 1829–1850" (PhD thesis, University of Ottawa, 1997).
11 James K. Hiller, "Carter, Sir Frederic Bowker Terrington," *Dictionary of Canadian Biography* 12, University of Toronto/Université Laval, 1990, http://www.biographi.ca/en/bio/carter_frederic_bowker_terrington_12E.html; and Sean T. Cadigan, *Newfoundland and Labrador: A History* (Toronto: University of Toronto Press, 2009), 130–33.
12 O'Brien to Cardwell, 20 Sept. 1864 (CO194, vol. 173); and JHA, 1865, Appendix, 848.
13 JHA, 1865, Appendix, Tupper to Hoyles, 28 Sept. 1864, 852; and Edward C. Moulton, "The Political History of Newfoundland, 1861–1869" (MA thesis, Memorial University, 1960), 161.
14 Quoted in Hiller, "Carter."
15 Quoted in Hiller, "Carter."
16 "Sir Frederic Bowker Terrington Carter," Library and Archives Canada (LAC), Canadian Confederation, https://www.collectionscanada.gc.ca/confederation/023001-4000.11-e.html.
17 Hiller, "Shea."
18 Extract from *Montreal Herald*, reprinted in the *Public Ledger*, 18 Nov. 1864.
19 JHA, 1865, Appendix, 845; and Hiller, "The Confederation Issue in Newfoundland."
20 JHA, 1865, Appendix, Report of the Resolutions Adopted at Quebec Conference, 865–66; and Moulton, "The Political History of Newfoundland," 167. See also Martha Elizabeth Walls, "Confederation and Maritime First Nations," *Acadiensis* 46, 2 (Summer/Autumn 2017): 155–76.
21 JHA, 1865, Appendix, Report of the Resolutions Adopted at Quebec Conference, 854–73.
22 R.A. MacKay, ed., *Newfoundland: Economic, Diplomatic, and Strategic Studies* (Toronto: Oxford University Press, 1946), 424.

23   JHA, 1865, Appendix, Report of the Resolutions Adopted at Quebec Conference, 865–66.
24   Hiller, "Carter."
25   Moulton, "The Political History of Newfoundland," 165.
26   JHA, Appendix, Report of the Delegates, 21 Jan. 1865, 872.
27   G.M. Story, "Prowse, Daniel Woodley," in *Dictionary of Canadian Biography* 14, University of Toronto/Université Laval, 1998, http://www.biographi.ca/en/bio/prowse_daniel_woodley_14E.html.
28   Prowse, *A History of Newfoundland*, 494–95.
29   Fraser, "Relations with Canada," 437–38.
30   Morton, *The Critical Years*, 43–44.
31   Chadwick, *Newfoundland: Island into Province*, 20.
32   Hiller, "Confederation Defeated," 83 and 79.
33   The literature is vast on voter competence, and, of course, the election in 2016 of American president Donald J. Trump has generated new interest in the topic. See Paul Goren, *On Voter Competence* (New York: Oxford University Press, 2012); Arthur Lupia, "How Elitism Undermines the Study of Voter Competence," *Critical Review: A Journal of Politics and Society* 18, nos. 1–3 (2006): 217–32; and Mark Chou, "Combatting Voter Ignorance: A Vertical Model of Epistocratic Voting," *Policy Studies* 38, no. 6 (2017): 589–603.
34   Phillip Buckner, formerly a historian at the University of New Brunswick, similarly challenged in 1990 many of the assumptions about the opposition to Confederation in the Maritime colonies to show how the stereotype of Maritime conservatism distorted the historical literature on the Maritimes and Confederation. See Phillip Buckner, "CHR Dialogue: The Maritimes and Confederation: A Reassessment," *Canadian Historical Review* 71, no. 1 (Mar. 1990): 1–45; and "Beware the Canadian Wolf."
35   Jones, "The Antis Gain the Day." Patrick O'Flaherty in *Lost Country* describes the campaign of 1869 as an "intellectual battle" (see 106–11).
36   Smith, "Toryism, Classical Liberalism, and Capitalism." Two recent works on tax history, Shirley Tillotson, *Give and Take: The Citizen-Taxpayer and the Rise of Canadian Democracy* (Vancouver: UBC Press, 2017), and Elsbeth Heaman, *Tax, Order, and Good Government: A New Political History of Canada, 1867–1917* (Montreal and Kingston: McGill-Queen's University Press, 2017), demonstrate the importance of taxation in Canadian political history. Heaman suggests that changes in tax policy were essential to moving Canada from a government based on property values to a democracy based on citizenship values.
37   Newfoundland switched to dollars from sterling in 1865 at a rate of 1 dollar = 4 shillings, 2 pence sterling. This was slightly higher than the Canadian dollar at the time (worth 4 shillings, 1.3 pence). For a discussion of Newfoundland currency, see *Encyclopedia of Newfoundland and Labrador*, vol. 1 (St. John's: Newfoundland Book, 1981).

38 James K. Hiller, "Newfoundland Confronts Canada, 1867–1949," in *The Atlantic Provinces in Confederation*, ed. Ernest Forbes and D.A. Muse (Toronto: University of Toronto Press, 1993), 351–52.
39 On the education system, see Phillip McCann, *Island in an Empire: Education, Religion, and Social Life in Newfoundland, 1800–1855* (Portugal Cove–St. Philip's: Boulder Publications, 2016).
40 Cadigan, *Newfoundland and Labrador*, especially chapters 5 and 6; and Noel, *Politics in Newfoundland*, 23–25.
41 David Alexander, "Literacy and Economic Development in Nineteenth-Century Newfoundland," in *Atlantic Canada and Confederation: Essays in Canadian Political Economy*, compiled by Eric Sager, Lewis R. Fischer, and Stuart O. Pierson (Toronto: University of Toronto Press, 1983), 113; and Michael Mann, "The Emergence of Modern European Nationalism," in *Transition to Modernity*, ed. John A. Hall and I.C. Jarvie (Cambridge: Cambridge University Press, 1992), 142.
42 Alan G. Macpherson, "The People of Newfoundland: A Longue Durée in Historical Geography," in *A Social Geography of Canada*, ed. Guy M. Robinson (Edinburgh: North British Publishing, 1988), 289.
43 Alexander, "Literacy and Economic Development," 113 and 137. These points are also made in Noel, *Politics in Newfoundland*, 18–25.
44 A 1900 obituary of an outport resident noted that the late fisherman "always took an active part in the political life of his country, [in] particular the political campaign of 1869, when Confederation was the issue before the country. He was one of those who believed in the motto, 'Newfoundland for Newfoundlanders.'" See "Well-Known Planter Dead," *Evening Herald* (St. John's), 30 July 1900.
45 Sean T. Cadigan and Jeff Hutchings, "The Ecology of Expansion: The Case of the Labrador Fishery" paper presented to the Canadian Historical Association Annual Meeting, St. John's, 1997, 7–8. They suggest that using subsidies to encourage the forestry sector and shipbuilding provided inshore fishermen with new vessels to exploit new fishing grounds, particularly in Labrador, and that these subsidies did not, in fact, represent a withdrawal from the fishery in favour of new employment opportunities.
46 Bannerman to Newcastle, 18 May 1863 (CO194/170, 5521 Newfoundland, no. 26). On the credit system, see James K. Hiller, "The Newfoundland Credit System: An Interpretation," in *Merchant Credit and Labour Strategies in Historical Perspective*, ed. Rosemary E. Ommer (Fredericton: *Acadiensis* Press, 1990), 86–101.
47 Hiller, "Newfoundland Confronts Canada," 352–55. On the role of the mercantile influence on the legislature, see Kenneth J. Kerr, "A Social Analysis of the Members of the Newfoundland House of Assembly, Executive Council, and Legislative Council for the Period 1855–1914" (MA thesis, Memorial University, 1973), 352–439.

48 See Gertrude E. Gunn, *The Political History of Newfoundland, 1832–1864* (Toronto: University of Toronto Press, 1966), 113–40; and Frederick Jones, "John Bull's Other Ireland—Nineteenth-Century Newfoundland," *Dalhousie Review* 55, no. 2 (Summer 1975): 227–35.
49 Cadigan and Hutchings, "The Ecology of Expansion," 12–13.
50 *Newfoundlander*, 2 Feb. 1865, and *Courier*, 5 Aug. 1865.
51 Quoted in Noel, *Politics in Newfoundland*, 13–14.
52 The impact of the geological surveys is discussed in Scott Eaton, "A 'Rugged, and, for the Most Part, a Barren Country': Nineteenth-Century Surveyors and the Characterization of Newfoundland's Interior," paper presented to the Canadian Historical Association Annual Meeting, Regina, May 2018, 12–13. We acknowledge with thanks his sharing of his new research with us.
53 Korneski, *Conflicted Colony*, 75. See also David Alexander, "Newfoundland's Traditional Economy and Development to 1934," *Acadiensis* 5, no. 2 (Spring 1976): 56–78.
54 Hiller, "James Murray and the 1882 Newfoundland General Election." See also Henry Winton, "A Chapter in the History of Newfoundland for the Year 1861" (St. John's: Provincial Archives of Newfoundland and Labrador, 1972), for an account of election campaign practices around that time.
55 See Hiller, "James Murray and the 1882 Newfoundland General Election."
56 Keith Mercer, "The Murder of Lieutenant Lawry: A Case Study of British Naval Impressment in Newfoundland, 1794," *Newfoundland and Labrador Studies* 21, no. 2 (2006): 254–89.
57 JHA, 6 Feb. 1865, 13–14; and Hoyles quoted in Moulton, "The Political History of Newfoundland," 179.
58 Bannerman to Newcastle, Confidential, 17 Dec. 1859 (CO 194/156, 312, Newfoundland).
59 Buckner, "The 1860s: An End and a Beginning," 382–83.
60 Cardwell to Musgrave, no. 31, 24 June 1865, printed in *Royal Gazette*, 18 July 1865.
61 Hiller, "Carter."
62 Ambrose Shea to John A. Macdonald, 14 May 1867, in Joseph Pope, ed., *Correspondence of Sir John Macdonald* (Toronto: Doubleday, Page, 1921), 44–45.
63 Mayo, "Newfoundland and Confederation in the Eighteen-Sixties," 128.
64 For a discussion of Canada's debt in 1867, see Livio Di Matteo, *A Federal Fiscal History: Canada, 1867–2017* (Toronto: Fraser Institute, 2017), https://www.fraserinstitute.org/sites/default/files/federal-fiscal-history-canada-1867-2017.pdf.
65 Hiller, "Confederation Defeated," 75.
66 Macdonald to Musgrave, 27 Dec. 1867, in Pope, ed., *Correspondence of Sir John Macdonald*, 61–62.
67 Quoted in Cadigan and Hutchings, "The Ecology of Expansion," 14.
68 Melvin Baker, "The Rejection of Confederation with Canada, 1865–1874," 1994, http://www.ucs.mun.ca/~melbaker/1860S.htm.

69   Quoted in Mayo, "Newfoundland and Confederation in the Eighteen-Sixties," 125–42.
70   Mayo, "Newfoundland and Confederation in the Eighteen-Sixties," 142.
71   JHA, 23 Feb. 1869; and Mayo, "Newfoundland and Confederation in the Eighteen-Sixties," 134.
72   Young to Granville, 2 July 1869 (LAC, RG7, Office of the Governor General of Canada Fonds, Numbered Files, 1818–1941, Governor General's Files, no. 184). See also G.F.G. Stanley, "Sir Stephen Hill's Observations on the Election of 1869 in Newfoundland," *Canadian Historical Review* 29, no. 3 (Sept. 1948): 280.
73   Granville to Hill, 25 Aug. 1869 (LAC, RG7, Office of the Governor General of Canada Fonds, Numbered Files, 1818-1941, Governor General's Files, no. 184).
74   *Encyclopedia of Newfoundland and Labrador,* vol. 1, 688.
75   Cadigan, *Newfoundland and Labrador: A History,* 132. Mullock's death was noted in several Irish newspapers, with the *Irish Examiner* noting on 29 Apr. 1869 that "As bishop his influence over people of Newfoundland was almost unbounded." The nationalist *Nation* noted a few days later, on 15 May 1869, that Bishop Mullock "took an active interest in the political affairs of the colony, and was largely instrumental in acquiring for his people the blessings of self-government, a principle he warmly cherished." It noted, too, that he acknowledged the dangers of reliance upon the fishery as the only industry in Newfoundland and that "he always advised his people to practice agriculture, or some useful art as a supplement to or, if need be, substitute for their precarious avocation."
76   Frederick Jones, "Mullock, John Thomas," in *Dictionary of Canadian Biography* 9, University of Toronto/Université Laval, 1976, http://www.biographi.ca/en/bio/mullock_john_thomas_9E.html.
77   "Charles Bennett Objections, 1864–1865" (C.F. Bennett to *The Newfoundlander,* 5 Dec. 1864), http://www.heritage.nf.ca/articles/politics/charles-bennett-objections.php.
78   *Morning Chronicle,* 13 Sept. 1869. See also *Ireland's Eye in Newfoundland and Labrador: Thomas Talbot's Letter to a Friend in Ireland (1882),* eds. Melvin Baker, Christopher P. Curran, John Joy, and Robin McGrath (St. John's: The Law Society of Newfoundland and Labrador, 2009, reprint of 1882 edition), 74–77.
79   James K. Hiller, "Bennett, Charles James Fox," in *Dictionary of Canadian Biography* 11, University of Toronto/Université Laval, 1982, http://www.biographi.ca/en/bio/bennett_charles_james_fox_11E.html.
80   Hiller, "Bennett."
81   "Charles Bennett Objections, 1864–1865."
82   *Newfoundlander,* 29 Dec. 1864.
83   Musgrave to Cardwell, 19 July 1865 (CO 194), quoted in P.B. Waite, ed., *Canadian Historical Document Series,* vol. 2, *Pre-Confederation* (Scarborough, ON: Prentice-Hall, 1965), 207–08.

ENDNOTES

84 Smith, "Toryism, Classical Liberalism, and Capitalism," 7–8; and Hiller, "Bennett."
85 On the opposition to Confederation in the Maritime provinces, see Buckner, "CHR Dialogue: The Maritimes and Confederation: A Reassessment" and "Beware the Canadian Wolf."
86 *Morning Chronicle*, 23 and 30 Aug. and 9 Sept. 1869; and Moulton, "The Political History of Newfoundland," 286. The *Newfoundlander* referred to the committee as the Committee of Public Safety, and it had been formed when two opponents of Confederation in Nova Scotia visited St. John's on 26 June 1866 hoping to form an alliance with Newfoundland against the Quebec Resolutions. See Francis J. Smith, "Newfoundland and Confederation, 1864–1870" (MA thesis, University of Ottawa, 1970), 103.
87 *Newfoundlander*, 12 Jan. 1865. On this point, also see Smith, "Toryism, Classical Liberalism, and Capitalism," 7–13.
88 P.T. McGrath, "Will Newfoundland Join Canada?," *Queen's Quarterly* 29 (1929): 254–55.
89 On this point, see Cadigan and Hutchings, "The Ecology of Expansion," 16.
90 Mayo, "Newfoundland and Confederation in the Eighteen-Sixties," 136.
91 *Newfoundlander*, 2 and 5 Dec. 1864.
92 Gerald S. Doyle, *Old-Time Songs and Poetry of Newfoundland* (St. John's: Gerald S. Doyle, 1940), 69.
93 *Newfoundlander*, 8 Jan. 1869.
94 Proceedings of House of Assembly, 4 Feb. 1869, quoted in *Newfoundlander*, 10 Feb. 1869; and Moulton, "The Political History of Newfoundland," 222–24.
95 *Newfoundlander*, 9 Nov. 1869.
96 JHA, 2 Mar. 1865; and quoted in Smith, "Toryism, Classical Liberalism, and Capitalism," 9.
97 Quoted in Hiller, "Shea."
98 Hiller, "Confederation Defeated," 79, and Hiller, "Shea."
99 Hill to Rogers, 5 Nov. 1869, with enclosure of Bennett's appeal to the voters of the District of Placentia–St. Mary's, 366 (CO 194/178, 13060, Newfoundland); and *Newfoundlander*, 1 Oct. 1869.
100 Richard Howley, *Letters on the Present State of Newfoundland and on Confederation* (St. John's, 1869).
101 Mayo, "Newfoundland and Confederation in the Eighteen-Sixties," 137.
102 *Newfoundlander*, 15 Oct. 1869.
103 Hill to Granville, 22 Oct. 1869 (CO 194/178, 12744, Newfoundland); Hill to Rogers, 5 Nov. 1869 (CO 194/178, 13060, Newfoundland); and Stanley, "Sir Stephen Hill's Observations on the Election of 1869 in Newfoundland," 280–82.
104 Jones, "The Antis Gain the Day," 147; and Buckner, "The 1860s: An End and a Beginning," 383.
105 Quoted in Jones, "The Antis Gain the Day," 143.
106 *Morning Chronicle*, 8 July 1870.

107　*Evening Telegram*, 6 Dec. 1882.
108　Hill to Granville, 20 Nov. 1869 (CO 194/178, 13617, Newfoundland).
109　Quoted in Pope, ed., *Memoirs of The Right Honourable Sir John Alexander Macdonald*, 144.
110　JHA, 3 Feb. 1870.
111　JHA, 17 Feb. 1870.

CHAPTER 2

1　Quoted in C.P. Stacey, "The Withdrawal of the Imperial Garrison from Newfoundland, 1870," *Canadian Historical Review* 17, no. 2 (June 1936): 147–58.
2　See Melvin Baker, *Aspects of Nineteenth Century St. John's Municipal History* (St. John's: Harry Cuff Publications, 1982), 5–16.
3　Lord Lisgar to Macdonald, 13 Dec. 1871, in Pope, ed., *Correspondence of Sir John Macdonald*, 152–53.
4　*Courier*, 23 Sept. 1873, as quoted in Elinor Senior, "The Origin and Political Activities of the Orange Order in Newfoundland, 1863–1890" (MA thesis, Memorial University, 1959), 1; and W. David MacWhirter, "A Political History of Newfoundland, 1865–1874" (MA thesis, Memorial University, 1963), 149–52.
5　Senior, "The Origin and Political Activities," 96, 107, and 111.
6　*Morning Chronicle*, 27 Sept. 1873.
7　Power to Governor Hill, 10 Jan. 1874 (RPA, GN1.3.A, box 7, file "Bishop Power of St. John's, re Appointment of Roman Catholic Magistrate"); and *Royal Gazette*, 30 Jan. 1974.
8　Hill to Kimberley, Secretary of State for the Colonies, 13 Dec. 1873 (CO 194/186, 13754, Newfoundland).
9　*Evening Telegram*, 2 and 7 Dec. 1882.
10　Quoted in Newfoundland Royal Commission 1933, *Report* (Cmd. 4480, 1933), 241–43.
11　Macdonald to Sir Stafford Northcote, 1 May 1878, in Pope, ed., *Correspondence of Sir John Macdonald*, 240–42.
12　Eaton, "A 'Rugged, and, for the Most Part, a Barren Country' "; Patrick O'Flaherty, "Introduction," in *Reminiscences of James P. Howley: Selected Years*, ed. William J. Kirwin, G.M. Story, and Patrick A. O'Flaherty (Toronto: Champlain Society, 1997), xx–xxxiii; and James K. Hiller, "A History of Newfoundland, 1874–1901" (PhD thesis, Cambridge University, 1971), 39–41.
13　Alexander, "Newfoundland's Traditional Economy and Development to 1934," 65.
14　A.R. Penney, *A History of the Newfoundland Railway*, vol. 1, *1881–1923* (St. John's: Harry Cuff, 1988), 6–8; *Morning Chronicle*, 22, 27, 29 July and 4, 7, 12 Aug. 1880; and *Evening Telegram*, 11 Aug. 1880.
15　On this point, see Korneski, *Conflicted Colony*, 81–84.
16　*Public Ledger*, 17 Feb. 1865. See also Cadigan, *Newfoundland and Labrador: A History*, especially 125–53; and Korneski, *Conflicted Colony*, especially 71–100.

ENDNOTES

For the Irish in Newfoundland during this period, see Patrick Mannion, *A Land of Dreams: Ethnicity, Nationalism, and the Irish in Newfoundland, Nova Scotia, and Maine, 1880–1923* (Montreal and Kingston: McGill-Queen's University Press, 2018).

17 Cadigan, *Newfoundland and Labrador: A History*, contends that the nationalist sentiment masked the realities of the economic difficulties facing Newfoundland and the divisions caused by class, gender, ethnicity, and region.
18 Korneski, *Conflicted Colony*, 76–77.
19 Hiller, "A History of Newfoundland, 1874–1901," 81–83, 100.
20 *Evening Telegram*, 8 and 14 Dec. 1882.
21 *Public Ledger*, 22 Mar. 1881.
22 Senior, "The Origin and Political Activities," 139–42.
23 Senior, "The Origin and Political Activities," 191–98.
24 Quoted in Hiller, "A History of Newfoundland, 1874–1901," 155.
25 Robert Cuff, "Alfred Bishop Morine," in *Encyclopedia of Newfoundland and Labrador*, vol. 3 (St. John's: Harry Cuff Publications, 1991), 619–21.
26 For the Greenspond Letter, see Archives and Special Collections (ASC), Memorial University Libraries, Coll-237, 2.06.005.
27 Harvey Mitchell, "Canada's Negotiations with Newfoundland, 1887–1895," *Canadian Historical Review* 40, no. 4 (Dec. 1959): 278.
28 Melvin Baker and Peter Neary, "Sir Robert Bond (1857–1927): A Biographical Sketch," *Newfoundland Studies* 15, no. 1 (Spring 1999): 1–54.
29 Tupper informed Prime Minister Macdonald on 31 Oct. 1888 that Whiteway's main interest was in succeeding Carter as Chief Justice. See G.F.G. Stanley, "Further Documents Relating to the Union of Newfoundland and Canada, 1886–1895," *Canadian Historical Review* 29, no. 4 (Dec. 1948): 375.
30 Hiller, "A History of Newfoundland, 1874–1901," 156; Mitchell, "Canada's Negotiations," 277–93; and Stanley, "Further Documents," 370–86.
31 Morine to Bond, 20 Mar. 1888 (ASC, Coll-237, file 8.03.005).
32 Bond to Whiteway, 25 Jan. 1888 (ASC, Coll-237, file 3.17.002).
33 Winter to Bond, 12 Mar. 1888 (ASC, Coll-237, file 8.03.004); and 1892 Correspondence respecting the Admission of Newfoundland into the Dominion of Canada (copy available in the Centre for Newfoundland Studies, Memorial University), Lord Lansdowne to Governor of Newfoundland, 6 Mar. 1888.
34 1892 Correspondence respecting the Admission of Newfoundland into the Dominion of Canada, Governor of Newfoundland to Lord Lansdowne, 4 Apr. 1888.
35 Whiteway to Bond, 11 May 1888 (ASC, Coll-237, file 8.03.006).
36 Quoted in O'Flaherty, *Lost Country*, 163.
37 Whiteway Party Minute Book, 1 Sept. 1888 (ASC, Coll-237, file 3.07.004); Bond to Thorburn, 5 Sept. 1888 (ASC, Coll-237, file 8.03.007); and Baker and Neary, "Sir Robert Bond," 6.
38 Sir Charles Tupper to Macdonald, 18 Sept. 1888, in Pope, ed., *Correspondence of Sir John Macdonald*, 422.

39 James K. Hiller, "Whiteway, Sir William Vallance," in *Dictionary of Canadian Biography* 13, University of Toronto/Université Laval, 1994, http://www.biographi.ca/en/bio/whiteway_william_vallance_13E.html.
40 Mitchell, "Canada's Negotiations," 280.
41 *Montreal Gazette*, 20 Sept. 1888; *Evening Telegram*, 21 and 26 Mar. 1888; and *St. John's Daily Colonist*, 21 and 26 Mar. 1888. (The *Daily Colonist* was a liberal, Roman Catholic, anti-Confederate newspaper.)
42 *Evening Telegram*, 20 Mar. 1888.
43 *Statutes of Newfoundland*, 1887, "Fiftieth Victoria, Cap. 10"; and Hiller, "A History of Newfoundland, 1874–1901," 21–22.
44 *Evening Telegram*, 15 Oct. and 26 Nov. 1889.
45 *Evening Telegram*, 19 Oct. 1889.
46 The French Shore had initially covered the shoreline from Cape Bonavista to Point Riche but was altered in 1783 as British settlers (planters) pushed into the areas west of Cape Bonavista.
47 James K. Hiller, "The Railway and Local Politics in Newfoundland, 1870–1901," in Hiller and Neary, *Newfoundland in the Nineteenth and Twentieth Centuries*, 134–35.
48 Kurt Korneski, "Colonialism, Place, and Power in Nineteenth Century Newfoundland and Labrador," paper presented to the Canadian Historical Association Annual Meeting, Regina, 2018. The paper has been accepted for publication in a forthcoming issue of *Journal of World History*.
49 On this point, see Korneski, *Conflicted Colony*, 124–25; and Peter Neary, "The French and American Shore Questions as Factors in Newfoundland History," in Hiller and Neary, *Newfoundland in the Nineteenth and Twentieth Centuries*, 95–122.
50 Quoted in Korneski, *Conflicted Colony*, 139–40.
51 Frederic F. Thompson, *The French Shore Problem in Newfoundland: An Imperial Study* (Toronto: University of Toronto Press, 1961), 104.
52 *Evening Telegram*, 20 Oct. 1881.
53 Melvin Baker, "Baird, James," in *Dictionary of Canadian Biography* 14, University of Toronto/Université Laval, 1998, http://www.biographi.ca/en/bio/baird_james_14E.html.
54 James K. Hiller, "The 1904 Anglo-French Newfoundland Fisheries Convention: Another Look," *Acadiensis* 25, no. 1 (Autumn 1995): 82–98.
55 Speech by Bond in the House of Assembly, 6 Mar. 1891 (ASC, Coll-237, file 7.04.001).
56 C.D. Howell, "W.S. Fielding and the Repeal Elections of 1886 and 1887 in Nova Scotia," *Acadiensis* 8, no. 2 (1978–79): 28–46.
57 Baker and Neary, "Sir Robert Bond (1857–1927)," 9–11; David J. Davis, "The Bond-Blaine Negotiations, 1890–1891" (MA thesis, Memorial University, 1970); and Peter Neary and S.J.R. Noel, "Newfoundland's Quest for Reciprocity, 1890–1910," in *Regionalism in the Canadian Community, 1867–1967*, ed. Mason Wade (Toronto: University of Toronto Press, 1969), 210–26. After Prince Edward

ENDNOTES

Island decided not to join Confederation in 1867, there was some interest in the American Congress to establish a reciprocity treaty with the island colony. In 1868, Congressman General Benjamin Butler went to Charlottetown in hopes of negotiating reciprocity, but there was little chance of success of either the American Congress agreeing to a treaty or the Imperial government accepting reciprocity that ignored the interests of the Dominion of Canada. On this point, see Ronald D. Tallman, "Annexation in the Maritimes? The Butler Mission to Charlottetown," *Dalhousie Review* 53, no. 1 (1973): 97–112.

58 A.M. Fraser, "Fishery Negotiations with the United States," in Mackay, *Newfoundland: Economic, Diplomatic, and Strategic Studies*, 372.
59 Macdonald to Seymour, 13 June 1890, in Pope, ed., *Correspondence of Sir John Macdonald*, 469–70.
60 Bond to Whiteway, 25 June 1891 (ASC, Coll-237, file 8.03.011); and Baker and Neary, "Sir Robert Bond (1857–1927)," 10–11.
61 Howlan to Macdonald, 3 May 1891, and Howlan to Abbott, 16 June 1891 (RPA, MG214, Sir Mackenzie Bowell Papers).
62 Melvin Baker, "Harvey, Augustus William," in *Dictionary of Canadian Biography* 13, University of Toronto/Université Laval, 1994, http://www.biographi.ca/en/bio/harvey_augustus_william_13E.html.
63 Mitchell, "Canada's Negotiations," 283.
64 Mitchell, "Canada's Negotiations," 281–84; and Hiller, "A History of Newfoundland, 1874–1901," 232.
65 Melvin Baker, "The Government of St. John's, Newfoundland, 1800–1921" (PhD thesis, University of Western Ontario, 1981), 270–86.
66 Mitchell, "Canada's Negotiations," 285; and Fraser, "Fishery Negotiations," 382.
67 For a history of the international trade in bait, see Brian Payne, *Fishing a Borderless Sea: Environmental Territorialism in the North Atlantic, 1818–1910* (Lansing: Michigan State University Press, 2010). Payne examines the multinational nature of the North Atlantic fishery, and he focuses primarily on the trade in bait. He argues bait was the "foundation of the cod fisheries, and by the nineteenth century, fishermen were paying top dollar for good, fresh bait." Moreover, bait was supplied by local fishermen, and in the North Atlantic bait trade there emerged "informal codes of conduct" that "did not necessarily correspond to official law and in fact often directly contradicted that law." "Outsiders" were excluded from catching bait, and when fishermen from outside a local area attempted to do so, local fishermen "often responded with crowd action, intimidation, and violence." Regardless of formal law or treaty rights that may have permitted "outsiders" to participate in the bait fishery, local fishermen "often continued operating their business under the guiding principals [sic] of the accepted informal codes of conduct, which allowed for such trade so long as those foreigners did not attempt to catch their own." Local fishermen retained territorial control over the bait fishery resource. See xi–xv.

68 Mitchell, "Canada's Negotiations," 285–86.
69 Morine to Thompson, 3 Nov. 1892 (RPA, MG220, Thompson Papers).
70 Quoted in Mitchell, "Canada's Negotiations," 286.
71 Hiller, "The Railway and Local Politics," 137.
72 James Thistle, "The Bank Crash of 1894" (unpublished History 6201 paper, Department of History, Memorial University, copy courtesy of Robert Hong); and James Murray, *The Commercial Crisis in Newfoundland: Cause, Consequences, and Cure* (St. John's: J.W. Withers, 1895).
73 Hiller, "The Railway and Local Politics," 137–39; and "The Trinity Bay Election Trial, 1894: Electioneering and Local Government," *Newfoundland and Labrador Studies* 26, no. 2 (2011): 215–29.
74 Hiller, "A History of Newfoundland, 1874–1901," 288–98.
75 O'Brien to Ripon, 26 Jan. 1895 (CO 194/230, Newfoundland no. 2449). See Murray, *The Commercial Crisis*; and O'Flaherty, *Lost Country*, 189–90.
76 O'Brien to Ripon, 10 Dec. 1894 (CO 194/228, Newfoundland nos. 22104 and 22105), and O'Brien to the Colonial Office, telegram dated 4 Jan. 1895 (CO 194/230, Newfoundland no. 174).
77 Greene passed legislation guaranteeing Union Bank notes at 80 cents on the dollar and those of the Commercial Bank at 20 cents.
78 Newfoundland Royal Commission 1933, *Report*, 27–29; and O'Brien to Ripon, 12 Jan. 1895 (CO 194/230, Newfoundland no. 1519), and certified copy of a minute of the Executive Council, 12 Mar. 1895 (Newfoundland no. 5300).
79 Mitchell, "Canada's Negotiations," 287.
80 O'Brien to Ripon, 4 Jan. 1895 (CO 194/230, Newfoundland no. 854), and O'Brien to Ripon, 1 Feb. 1895 (Newfoundland no. 3398).
81 *Evening Herald*, 31 Dec. 1894, 5 and 11 Jan. 1895. Many residents signed petitions calling for a "Royal Commission to investigate our Public Affairs thoroughly, and afford us such aid as our necessities demand." See O'Brien to Ripon, 26 Jan. 1895 (CO 194/230, Newfoundland no. 2130).
82 James K. Hiller, "The 1895 Newfoundland-Canada Confederation Negotiations: A Re-consideration," *Acadiensis* 40, no. 2 (Summer/Autumn 2011): 98–99.
83 *Evening Herald*, 5 Jan. 1895.
84 Whiteway to Bowell, 14 Jan. 1895, and Bowell to Whiteway, 14 Jan. 1895, reprinted in Stanley, "Further Documents," 376–78.
85 Quoted in Hiller, "The 1895 Newfoundland-Canada Confederation Negotiations," 101.
86 *Evening Herald*, 27 Mar. 1895; *Evening Telegram*, 27 Mar. 1895; and O'Brien to Ripon, 3 Apr. 1895 (CO 194/230, Newfoundland no. 8468).
87 *Evening Herald*, 17 Apr. 1895, and *Evening Telegram*, 23 Apr. 1895; also quoted in Hiller, "The 1895 Newfoundland-Canada Confederation Negotiations," 103.
88 Fraser, "Relations with Canada," 451–53.

89 For correspondence and documentation concerning the conference, see JHA 1895–1896, Appendix, 369–434.
90 Quoted in Hiller, "The 1895 Newfoundland-Canada Confederation Negotiations," 106.
91 Mitchell, "Canada's Negotiations," 277–93; and Stanley, "Further Documents," 376–86.
92 Whiteway to Bowell, 1 May 1895, in Stanley, "Further Documents," 365–66.
93 Bowell to Whiteway, 11 May 1895, in JHA 1895–1896, Appendix, 422, and *Daily News*, 17 May 1895.
94 *Evening Herald*, 19, 20, and 22 Apr. 1895; Mitchell, "Canada's Negotiations," 287–88; and Baker and Neary, "Sir Robert Bond (1857–1927)," 13.
95 See *Daily News*, 16, 20, and 22 Apr. and 11 May 1895; *Evening Telegram*, 13 Feb., 20, 22, 27, and 30 Mar., and 4 Apr. 1895. See also Maudie Whelan, "The Newspaper Press in Nineteenth-Century Newfoundland: Politics, Religion, and Personal Journalism" (PhD thesis, Memorial University, 2002), 224–25.
96 O'Brien informed Ripon on 9 Apr. 1895 that not a "single Confederate would be returned by the electorate in case the question is brought to the polls" (CO 194/230, Newfoundland no. 7007).
97 *Evening Telegram*, 27 May 1895.
98 Canada, *Senate Debates*, 7th Parliament, 5th session, vol. 1, 20 June 1895, 351; and *Proceedings of the House of Assembly*, 350–52.
99 Bond to Newfoundland Savings Bank Directors, 1 June 1895 (ASC, Coll-237, file 9.01.020); O'Brien to Ripon, 13 May 1895 (CO 194/232, Newfoundland no. 8934); and Baker and Neary, "Sir Robert Bond (1857–1927)," 12.
100 *Evening Herald*, 7 June 1895.
101 Bannister, "Whigs and Nationalists," 211–25.
102 G.M. Grant, "Newfoundland and Canada," *The Canadian Magazine* 11 (1898): 466.
103 Peter E. Pope, *The Many Landfalls of John Cabot* (Toronto: University of Toronto Press, 1997).
104 *Evening Herald*, 17, 19, 22, and 27 Nov. 1900. See also the letter from Harbour Grace native Will Tapp (who served in E Battery, Royal Field Artillery) in *Evening Herald*, 12 Sept. 1900; *Evening Herald*, 25 Sept., 9 Nov., and 1 Dec. 1900, for information about St. John's volunteer Charlie Foran; and Jack Randell, *I'm Alone* (Indianapolis: Bobbs-Merrill Company, 1930), 42–94. Randell (from Port Rexton) enlisted at Sydney in 1899. When the steamer *Carthaginian* arrived in the port of St. John's on 10 Nov. 1900 with twenty-four injured Canadian Boer War veterans aboard, the citizens of the town gave them a warm welcome. Newfoundlander Roland Penny arrived with them and was also feted for his service with the Canadians. See *Evening Herald*, 12, 13, and 14 Nov. 1900; *Evening Telegram*, 17 and 20 Nov. 1900; and *Daily News*, 12, 13, and 20 Nov. 1900. From St. John's, the Reid Newfoundland Company provided for their transportation by train and steamer to Halifax.

105 B.J. Pippy, "Sir Patrick McGrath: A Biographical Essay" (BA honours thesis, Memorial University, 1992), 9–11 and 44–45.
106 Hiller, "A History of Newfoundland, 1874–1901," 317–33 and 338.
107 Newfoundland Royal Commission 1933, *Report*, 31–34.
108 Baker and Neary, "Sir Robert Bond (1857–1927)," 13–15.
109 Hiller, "A History of Newfoundland, 1874–1901," 341–53; and *Evening Herald*, 11, 14, and 15 Aug. 1900.
110 *Evening Herald*, 11, 14, and 15 Aug. 1900.
111 *Evening Telegram*, 1 Oct. 1900; and *Evening Herald*, 3 Nov. 1900.
112 *Evening Herald*, 3, 4, 5, 6, and 9 Oct. 1900; *Daily News*, 5, 6, 8, and 11 Oct., 2 and 6 Nov. 1900; and *Evening Telegram*, 11 Sept., 6 Oct., and 6 Nov. 1900.
113 *Evening Herald*, 3 and 10 Sept. 1900.
114 James K. Hiller, *The Newfoundland Railway, 1881–1949* (St. John's: Newfoundland Historical Society, 1981), 17–18; and A.R. Penney, *A History of the Newfoundland Railway, vol. 1, 1881–1923*, 70–71.
115 Malcolm MacLeod, "Subsidized Steamers to a Foreign Country: Canada and Newfoundland, 1892–1949," *Acadiensis* 14, no. 2 (Spring 1985): 67.
116 MacLeod, "Subsidized Steamers," 66.
117 *Evening Herald*, 30 Nov. 1900. P.T. McGrath was the Newfoundland correspondent. See *Daily News*, 29 and 30 Nov. 1900.
118 *Evening Herald*, 22 Aug. 1900.

CHAPTER 3

1 Ralph Williams, *How I Became a Governor* (London: John Murray, 1913), 421.
2 P.T. McGrath, *Newfoundland in 1911* (London: Whitehead Morris, 1911), 64–69, 83–91, 105–09; and Baker and Neary, "Sir Robert Bond (1857–1927)," 15.
3 Bill Gillespie, *A Class Act: An Illustrated History of the Labour Movement in Newfoundland and Labrador* (Portugal Cove–St. Philip's: Boulder Publications, 2016), 22–38.
4 Frank Graham, *We Love Thee, Newfoundland: Biography of Sir Cavendish Boyle, Governor of Newfoundland, 1901–1904* (St. John's: Valhalla Press, 1979), 165–79; and James K. Hiller, "Robert Bond and the Pink, White, and Green: Newfoundland Nationalism in Perspective," *Acadiensis*, 36, no. 2 (Spring 2007): 113–33.
5 Fielding to Bond, 15 Sept. 1902, and Bond to Fielding, 17 Oct. 1902 (ASC, Coll-237, file 8.03.022); and Fielding to Bond, 15 Sept. 1902 (RPA, MG223, Reel 36, Borden Papers). This reel consists of Newfoundland-related materials microfilmed by Memorial University in the late 1950s as part of its efforts to organize a public archive for the province. See Memorial University, President's Office Records, Box PO-27, file "Carnegie Corporation (1958–65)," Report of the Newfoundland Archives for 1957–58.
6 A copy of Bond's 1904 election manifesto is in ASC, Coll-237, file 3.23.013.

7 *Free Press*, 4 Oct. 1904.
8 *Free Press*, 11 Oct. 1904.
9 On Newfoundland-US trade relations, see W.G. Reeves, "Alexander's Conundrum Reconsidered: The American Dimension in Newfoundland Resource Development, 1898–1910," *Newfoundland Studies* 5, no. 1 (Spring 1989): 2–37.
10 Bond to Lodge, 11 Sept. 1902 (ASC, Coll-237, file 7.08.006).
11 James K. Hiller, "The Political Career of Robert Bond," in *Twentieth-Century Newfoundland: Explorations*, ed. Hiller and Neary (St. John's: Breakwater, 1994), 39.
12 "An Act Respecting Foreign Fishing Vessels" in *Statutes of Newfoundland*, 1905, 16–18, and in *Statutes of Newfoundland*, 1906, 5–9. 5–9.
13 Baker and Neary, "Sir Robert Bond (1857–1927)," 19–20; Neary and Noel, "Newfoundland's Quest for Reciprocity, 1890–1910," 221–26; and Noel, *Politics in Newfoundland*, 45–50.
14 Baker and Neary, "Sir Robert Bond (1857–1927)," 19–20; Neary and Noel, "Newfoundland's Quest for Reciprocity, 1890–1910," 221–26; and Noel, *Politics in Newfoundland*, 45–50. See also *The North Atlantic Coast Fisheries Case* (Great Britain, United States) (1910), vol. 11, *Reports of International Arbitral Awards/Recueil des sentences arbitrales*, 167–226; and Fraser, "The Hague Arbitration," in MacKay, *Newfoundland: Economic, Diplomatic, and Strategic Studies*, 400–10. The full text is available at https://arbitrationlaw.com/library/north-atlantic-coast-fisheries-case-great-britain-v-united-states-award-september-7-1910.
15 R.B. Joyce, *Sir William MacGregor* (Melbourne: Oxford University Press, 1971), 317–26.
16 Joyce, *MacGregor*, 306–07, 339. For the 1905 visit, see his *Report of an Official Visit to the Coast of Labrador* (St. John's: J.W. Withers, 1906). In 1908, he also visited the Mi'kmaq community of Conne River in Bay d'Espoir on the Island's south coast. His report is in CO 194/273, despatch 25922, 8 July 1908.
17 *Evening Herald*, 6 and 18 June 1906.
18 *Evening Herald*, 28 June 1906.
19 Morison to William Coaker, 29 Sept. 1906, 45–50 (ASC, Coll-009, file 10.03.054).
20 Hiller, "The Political Career of Robert Bond," 27–28.
21 *Evening Herald*, 25 May 1906; and RPA, MG271.1, folder "Life in the Colony," 10.
22 As quoted in *Evening Herald*, 28 June 1906.
23 Grey to Laurier, 8/8/06, LAC, Grey Papers, vol. 13, 3616, quoted in James K. Hiller, "The Constitutional Crisis of 1908–09: A Subplot" (lecture to the Newfoundland Historical Society, 1974), 3.
24 *Evening Telegram*, 24 July and 2 Aug. 1906; *Evening Herald*, 30 July 1906; and Noel, *Politics in Newfoundland*, 41. Bond told the *Telegram* that the government would not be associated in any official way with the visit. Details of Grey's visit are in RPA, GN1.3.A, box 58, despatch 117/1906, 2 July 1906.
25 Joyce, *MacGregor*, 315–31.

26 Grey to Elgin, 16 Aug. 1906 and 29 June 1907, as quoted in Noel, *Politics in Newfoundland*, 41–42, 46.
27 Hiller, *The Newfoundland Railway, 1881–1949*, 18–19.
28 Bond to Morris, 24 July 1907 (ASC, Coll-237, file 3.26.002).
29 *Evening Chronicle*, 5 Mar. 1908; and Noel, *Politics in Newfoundland*, 51–76.
30 P.T. McGrath, "Should Newfoundland Confederate with Canada?," *Westminster Magazine* 9 (1906): 366–72.
31 *Manifesto of the Right Hon. Sir Robert Bond, P.C., K.C.M.G., Premier, 1908* (St. John's, 1908), 1.
32 *Evening Chronicle*, 10 Mar., 10 Aug., 26, 28 Sept., and 2 Oct. 1908; and *Daily News*, 18 and 24 Sept. 1908. For Morris's manifesto, see *Evening Chronicle*, 5 Oct. 1908, and see *Free Press*, 13 Apr. 1908, for the platform of the People's Party; for Bond's, see *Manifesto of the Right Hon. Sir Robert Bond, P.C., K.C.M.G., Premier, 1908*, 16.
33 The funeral reference is to the anti-Confederates in 1869 dragging a funeral casket through the streets of St. John's and dumping it in the harbour. See P.T. McGrath, "Will Newfoundland Join Canada?," *Queen's Quarterly* 29 (1929), 253–66.
34 *Evening Chronicle*, 5 Oct. 1908.
35 See Don MacGillivray, "Henry Melville Whitney comes to Cape Breton: The Saga of a Gilded Age Entrepreneur," *Acadiensis* 9, no. 1 (Autumn 1979): 44–70.
36 Melvin Baker, "Crowe, Harry Judson," in *Dictionary of Canadian Biography* 15, University of Toronto/Université Laval, 2003, http://www.biographi.ca/en/bio/crowe_harry_judson_15E.html.
37 Hiller, "The Constitutional Crisis of 1908–09," 5. See also Fraser Bond, "The Confederation Scheme that Failed," in *The Book of Newfoundland*, vol. 5, ed. Joseph R. Smallwood (St. John's: Newfoundland Book Publishers, 1967), 163–68.
38 The Crowe-Downey correspondence was published during the election campaign. See *Daily News*, 27 Apr. 1909, and *Free Press*, 3 May 1909.
39 Hiller, "The Constitutional Crisis of 1908–09," 5–8.
40 See Barbara A. Crosbie, "Howley, Michael Francis," in *Dictionary of Canadian Biography* 14, University of Toronto/Université Laval, 1998, http://www.biographi.ca/en/bio/howley_michael_francis_14E.html.
41 Hiller, "The Constitutional Crisis of 1908–09," 5–8; and "The Political Career of Robert Bond," 36.
42 Crowe to Bond, 12 Feb. 1909 (ASC, Coll-237, file 8.03.025).
43 Hiller, "The Constitutional Crisis of 1908–09," 5–8; and "The Political Career of Robert Bond," 36.
44 Morris to MacGregor, 3 Mar. 1909 (CO 194/275); Morris to MacGregor, 31 Mar. 1909, MacGregor to the Earl of Crewe, 5 Apr. 1909, and Bond to MacGregor, 6 Apr. 1909 (CO 194/276); *Evening Telegram*, 25 Feb. 1909; and *Royal Gazette*, 9 and 24 Feb. 1909 and 3 Mar. 1909. See also S.J.R. Noel, "Politics

and the Crown: The Case of the 1908 Tie Election in Newfoundland," *The Canadian Journal of Economics and Political Science* 33, no. 2 (May 1967): 285.
45   Hiller, "The Constitutional Crisis of 1908–09," 5–8.
46   As quoted in the *Evening Herald*, 30 Mar. 1914.
47   Baker, "Crowe"; *Daily News*, 30 Dec. 1918; and Crowe to Prime Minister King, 11 Dec. 1924, Crowe to Governor Allardyce, 17 Dec. 1924, and Allardyce to Amery, Secretary of State for the Colonies, 19 Dec. 1924 (ASC, CO 532/275).
48   *Evening Telegram*, 19, 22, 29, and 30 Apr., 4, 5, and 7 May 1909.
49   For his election manifesto, see *Daily News*, 12 Apr. 1909.
50   *Daily News*, 29 Apr. 1909.
51   *Daily News*, 21 Apr. 1909.
52   Melvin Baker, "Crosbie, Sir John Chalker," in *Dictionary of Canadian Biography* 16, University of Toronto/Université Laval, 2016, http://www.biographi.ca/en/bio/crosbie_john_chalker_16E.html.
53   *Evening Telegram*, 5 and 9 June 1909; *Daily News*, 1–6 May 1909. See also O'Flaherty, *Lost Country*, 243–44.
54   Williams, *How I Became a Governor*, 424.
55   See James G. Snell, "The Newfoundland Old Age Pension Programme, 1911–1949," *Acadiensis* 23, no. 1 (Autumn 1993): 86–109. Morine had first advocated such pensions as part of the 1897 general election campaign. See *Evening Telegram*, 10 Oct. 1900.
56   On this point, see Sean T. Cadigan, *Death on Two Fronts: National Tragedies and the Fate of Democracy in Newfoundland, 1914–34* (Toronto: Allen Lane, 2013), xvi–xviii.
57   Melvin Baker, "Challenging the 'Merchants' Domain': William Coaker and the Price of Fish, 1908–1919," *Newfoundland and Labrador Studies* 29, no. 2 (Fall 2014): 189–226; ASC, Coll-009, file 1.02.006, item "Mr. Coaker Replies"; and Robert Hong, " 'An Agency for the Common Weal': The Newfoundland Board of Trade, 1909–1915" (MA thesis, Memorial University, 1998), 22.
58   The FPU anthem was sung to the tune of the American Civil War song "We Are Coming, Father Abraham, Three Hundred Thousand More," written in 1862 by James Sloan Gibbons. Like the American song, the FPU anthem was a call for action. See https://en.wikipedia.org/wiki/Fishermen%27s_Protective_Union.
59   *Fishermen's Advocate*, 29 Oct., 19 and 26 Nov. 1910; and Melvin Baker, "The Rise of the Fishermen's Protective Union, the First World War and the National Government, 1908–1919," 1994, http://www.ucs.mun.ca/~melbaker/fpuhis.html.
60   Smallwood to George H. Tucker, 5 Apr. 1925 (ASC, Coll-213, George H. Tucker Papers, file 1.06); and Melvin Baker, "J.R. Smallwood—Labour and Socialist Leader," *Newfoundland Quarterly* 93, no. 1 (Fall 1999): 23–28.
61   G. Panting, " 'The People' in Politics," *Newfoundland Quarterly* 65, no. 4 (June 1967): 15–17; and W.F. Coaker, ed., *Twenty Years of the Fishermen's Protective Union of Newfoundland* (St. John's: Creative Publishers, 1984, reprint of 1930

edition), 50. The balance of power strategy is examined in Ian McDonald, "W.F. Coaker and the Balance of Power Strategy: The Fishermen's Protective Union in Newfoundland Politics," in Hiller and Neary, *Newfoundland in the Nineteenth and Twentieth Centuries*, 148–60.

62 Crowe to Coaker, 27 Nov. 1912 (RPA, MG223).
63 Crowe to Borden, 2 May 1913 (RPA, MG223).
64 *Evening Herald*, 4 July 1912.
65 *Fishermen's Advocate*, 6 July 1912; *Evening Herald*, 6 Aug. 1912; and *Fishermen's Advocate*, 3 Aug. 1912.
66 *Fishermen's Advocate*, 10 Aug. 1912.
67 Tait to Morine, 14 Oct. 1912, and Morine cable to Tait, 19 Oct. 1912 (ASC, Coll-237, file 3.33.005).
68 *Evening Herald*, 22 Nov. 1912.
69 *Fishermen's Advocate*, 30 Nov. 1912.
70 *Fishermen's Advocate*, 11 Jan. 1913. On Coaker's need for a solicitor, see Melvin Baker, "Plaindealing and the Fishermen's Protective Union, 1908–1910," *Newfoundland Quarterly* 105, no. 4 (Spring 2013): 43–51; and "The Struggle for Influence and Power: William Coaker, Abram Kean, and the Newfoundland Sealing Industry, 1908–1915," *Newfoundland and Labrador Studies* 28, no. 1 (Spring 2013): 63–96.
71 Bond to Coaker, 15 and 26 Aug. 1913 (ASC, Coll-237, file 3.32.004).
72 *Evening Herald*, 7 Oct. 1913.
73 See Noel, *Politics in Newfoundland*, 103–05.
74 *Evening Telegram*, 4 Oct. 1913.
75 *Fishermen's Advocate*, 22 Aug. 1913.
76 Bond to Stephen Loveridge, 3 Jan. 1914, in *Evening Telegram*, 13 Jan. 1914.
77 Bond to James A. Clift, 2 Jan. 1914, in *Evening Telegram*, 10 Jan. 1914.
78 *Daily Mail* and *Advocate*, 17 Jan. 1914.
79 G.W.L. Nicholson, *The Fighting Newfoundlander: A History of the Royal Newfoundland Regiment* (Montreal and Kingston: McGill-Queen's University Press, 2006, reprint of 1964 edition), 89–154; and Patricia O'Brien, "The Newfoundland Patriotic Association: The Administration of the War Effort, 1914–1918" (MA thesis, Memorial University, 1982).
80 As regulation khaki serge material was then unavailable in St. John's, army recruits were first dressed in makeshift fatigues with blue serge puttees and white duck kitbags made locally. The five hundred recruits who answered the first call became known as the "Blue Puttees."
81 David R. Facey-Crowther, ed., *Lieutenant Owen William Steele of the Newfoundland Regiment* (Montreal and Kingston: McGill-Queen's University Press, 2002), 16–17, 19, and 30.
82 Christopher Sharpe, "The 'Race of Honour': An Analysis of Enlistments and Casualties in the Armed Forces of Newfoundland: 1914–1918," *Newfoundland Studies* 4, no. 1 (1988): 27–28; and O'Brien, "The Newfoundland Patriotic Association," 35.

ENDNOTES

83 Melvin Baker and Janet Miller Pitt, "Jack Turner," *Newfoundland Quarterly* 90, no. 2 (Spring 1996): 24. Jack Turner enlisted in Nov. 1914 in Vancouver, rising to the rank of captain. He received the Military Cross for his service at Vimy Ridge and in 1918 published a book of poetry entitled *Buddy's Blithe and Other Verses from the Trenches*. Frost's memoir was published in 2014 as *A Blue Puttee at War: The Memoir of Captain Sydney Frost, MC*. For Newfoundlanders in the American Forces, see Melvin Baker, "Repatriated Newfoundlanders from the American Expeditionary Forces," *The Newfoundland Ancestor* 30, no. 3 (Fall 2014): 98–101.
84 Terry Bishop-Stirling, " 'Such Sights One Will Never Forget': Newfoundland Women and Overseas Nursing in the First World War," in *A Sisterhood of Suffering and Service: Women and Girls of Canada and Newfoundland during the First World War*, ed. Sarah Glassford and Amy Shaw (Vancouver: UBC Press, 2012), 126–47.
85 Quoted in Noel, *Politics in Newfoundland*, 130.
86 O'Brien, "The Newfoundland Patriotic Association," 31–51.
87 O'Brien, "The Newfoundland Patriotic Association"; and Cadigan, *Newfoundland and Labrador*, 188–89.
88 Frost, *Blue Puttee*, 127, 143, 147–53; P. Whitney Lackenbauer, "War, Memory, and the Newfoundland Regiment at Gallipoli," *Newfoundland and Labrador Studies* 15, no. 2 (1999): 176–214; and Robert Harding, "Glorious Tragedy: Newfoundland's Cultural Memory of the Attack at Beaumont Hamel, 1916–1925," *Newfoundland and Labrador Studies* 21, no. 1 (2006): 3–40.
89 Christopher J.A. Morry, *When the Great Red Dawn Is Shining: Howard L. Morry's Memoirs of Life in the Newfoundland Regiment* (St. John's: Breakwater, 2014), 137; Frost, *Blue Puttee*, 143, 147–53; Harding, "Glorious Tragedy," 3–40; Mike O'Brien, "Producers versus Profiteers: The Politics of Class in Newfoundland during the First World War," *Acadiensis* 40, no. 1 (Winter 2011): 45–69; and Melvin Baker and Peter Neary, "P.T. McGrath's 1918 Account of 'Newfoundland's Part in the Great War,' " *Newfoundland and Labrador Studies* 29, no. 2 (2014): 279.
90 Baker and Neary, "P.T. McGrath's 1918 Account," 283.
91 Davidson to Secretary of State, 11 July 1917 (RPA, GN1.3.A, box 97, despatch 36); and *Evening Advocate* 17 and 18 July 1917.
92 *Evening Advocate*, 19 July 1917.
93 Minutes of Executive Council, 31 Dec. 1917 and 5 Jan. 1918 (RPA, GN9.25).
94 O'Brien, "The Newfoundland Patriotic Association," 289–303. The income tax was "practically the same as the Canadian Act" on the same subject. See *Proceedings of the House of Assembly and Legislative Council*, 1918, 198.
95 Minutes of Executive Council, 19 July 1917 (RPA, GN9.25); *Evening Advocate*, 19 July 1917; and Coaker, ed., *Twenty Years*, 119.
96 Sharpe, "The 'Race of Honour' "; O'Brien, "The Newfoundland Patriotic Association," 312; and Chris Martin, "The Right Course, the Best Course,

the Only Course: Voluntary Recruitment in the Newfoundland Regiment, 1914–1918," *Newfoundland and Labrador Studies* 24, no. 1 (2009): 55–90.

97 On the conscription issue, see O'Brien, "The Newfoundland Patriotic Association," 319–29; Ian McDonald, *"To Each His Own": William Coaker and the Fishermen's Protective Union in Newfoundland Politics, 1908–1925*, ed James K. Hiller (St. John's: ISER Books, 1987), 54–72; and Martin, "The Right Course, the Best Course, the Only Course," 71–89.

98 Hiller, "A History," 265–66.

99 Morton, *The Critical Years*, 212–13.

100 William C. Gilmore, *Newfoundland and Dominion Status: The External Affairs Competence and International Law Status of Newfoundland, 1855–1934* (Toronto: Carswell, 1988), 25–26.

101 See, for example, *Proceedings of the House of Assembly and Legislative Council*, 1918, 3 and 5.

102 *Proceedings of the House of Assembly and Legislative Council*, 1919, 5–8, 17–18; and Harris to Halfyard, 29 July 1918, with attached memorandum (RPA, GN2.6, Correspondence with the Governor).

103 Gilmore, *Newfoundland and Dominion Status*, 25–26; and Margaret Macmillan, *Paris 1919: Six Months That Changed the World* (New York: Random House, 2001), 43.

104 Gilmore, *Newfoundland and Dominion Status*, 53–63.

105 Harris to Harding, 5 Apr. 1921 (RPA, GN1.3.A, box 106, despatch 1108).

106 Harding to Bowring, 14 Mar. 1921 (RPA, GN13.1.B, box 142, file 5).

107 Foreign Office to Sir L. Carnegie, 4 Feb. 1921, telegrams 7 and 11 (CO 194/302, Newfoundland Dominions 3966).

108 Quoted in Gilmore, *Newfoundland and Dominion Status*, 108. See 109–10 for a full discussion of the 1926 Imperial Conference.

109 Quoted in Gilmore, *Newfoundland and Dominion Status*, 109.

110 A good overview of the Confederation issue is McDonald, *"To Each His Own,"* 54–72.

111 Morine to Borden, 16 Jan. 1914 (RPA, MG223).

112 Morine to Borden, 16 Jan. and 5 Feb. 1914 (RPA, MG223).

113 Crowe to Borden, 2 May 1913 (RPA, MG223).

114 Morine to Borden, 23 Oct. 1914 (RPA, MG223).

115 Morris to Borden, 22 Oct. 1914 (RPA, MG223).

116 Borden to Morris, 20 Nov. 1914 (RPA, MG223).

117 Morine to Borden, 25 Feb. 1915 (RPA, MG223). On the lecture, see *Mail and Advocate*, 11 and 12 Feb. 1915, and *Daily News*, 11 Feb. 1915.

118 W.D. Reid to Lord Shaughnessy, 29 Nov. 1917 (Roman Catholic Archdiocesan Archives of St. John's [RCAASt-J], Reid Papers).

119 McDonald, *"To Each His Own,"* 54–55.

120 White to Borden, 10 June 1916 (RPA, MG223).

121 *Mail and Advocate*, 26 Feb. 1916.

ENDNOTES

122   *Mail and Advocate*, 28 Feb. 1916.
123   W.D. Reid to Lord Shaughnessy, 17 Dec. 1917 (RCAASt-J, Reid Papers).
124   McDonald, *"To Each His Own,"* 56.
125   Davidson to Bonar Law, 28 Mar. and 17 May 1916 (RPA, GN1.3.A, box 95, despatch 120).
126   Morris to Davidson, 6 May 1916, Davidson to the Duke of Connaught, 10 May 1916, and Davidson to Laurier, 22 May 1916 (RPA, GN1.3.A, box 96, despatch 34).
127   Davidson to Long, 7 Apr. 1917 (RPA, GN1.3.A, box 95, despatch 120).
128   A summary of the Reid family problems is provided by Governor Davidson in CO 194/293, Davidson to Walter Long, 24 Oct. 1917. See also *Evening Telegram*, 9 Jan. 1918; *Evening Advocate*, 16 Feb., 5 Apr., and 11 May 1918; W.D. Reid to Lord Shaughnessy, 29 Nov. and 17 Dec. 1917, and W.D. Reid to M.F. Cashin, R.A. Squires, J.R. Bennett, M.P. Gibbs, and J.C. Crosbie, 17 Dec. 1917 (RCAASt-J, Reid Papers); McDonald, *"To Each His Own,"* 65–68; *Daily News*, 18 Feb. 1918; W.D. Reid to Lord Shaughnessy, 29 Nov. and 1 Dec. 1917 (RPA, GN2.5.3419[2], Colonial Secretary Office Correspondence); and ASC, Richard Anderson Squires Papers, Coll-250, file 3.17.026, for the legal documents associated with Coaker's lawsuit. Coaker gave a spirited self-defence in the House of Assembly on 11 May 1918. See *Proceedings of the House of Assembly and Legislative Council, 1918*, 167–76.
129   McDonald, *"To Each His Own,"* 74–79; Proceedings of the House of Assembly and Legislative Council 1918, 6 May 1918, 107; and *St. John's Daily Star*, 11 Oct. 1919.
130   *St. John's Daily Star*, 9, 22, and 24 Sept. 1919.
131   *Evening Herald*, 27 Sept. 1919.
132   *St. John's Daily Star*, 11, 15, and 22 Oct. 1919.
133   *Evening Herald*, 30 Sept. 1919.
134   *Evening Herald*, 14, 15, and 17 Oct. 1919.
135   On the fishery regulations in 1919 and 1920, see Baker, "Challenging the 'Merchants' Domain,'" 214–15. See also McDonald, *"To Each His Own,"* 100–105; Edward Roberts, "Nothing Venture, Nothing Have: Mr. Coaker's Regulations" (MA thesis, Memorial University, 2006), 59–69; O'Flaherty, *Lost Country*, 299–303, 466; Cadigan, *Newfoundland and Labrador*, 194–95; and Cadigan, *Death on Two Fronts*, 210–29.
136   On the bank's role with Coaker and the Fishermen's Trading Company, for example, see Roberts, "Nothing Venture, Nothing Have," 46–50. O'Flaherty in *Lost Country* notes that in adopting the Canadian currency in 1894, "in effect the government relinquished control of money as a tool to regulate the economy" (187).
137   *Free Press*, 22 May and 6 June 1922; and *Daily News*, 20 May 1922.
138   *Daily News*, 31 Dec. 1921.
139   *Evening Advocate*, 13 Dec. 1921.

140 Hiller, *The Newfoundland Railway, 1881–1949*, and "The Politics of Newsprint: The Newfoundland Pulp and Paper Industry, 1915–1939," *Acadiensis* 19, no. 2 (Spring 1990): 3–25; and McDonald, *"To Each His Own,"* 106–18.

141 Melvin Baker, ed., "Dear Friends: Coaker's Circular Letters to Councils, 1909–1927" (unpublished manuscript, 2014), Circular Letter #3 for 9 Feb. 1923.

142 Allardyce to the Duke of Devonshire, 5 Apr. 1923 (RPA, GN1.3.A, box 127, despatch 215/23); and *Daily News*, 5 Apr. 1923.

143 *Daily News*, 5 Apr. 1923.

144 E.R. Forbes, "Newfoundland Politics in 1921: A Canadian View," *Acadiensis* 9, no. 1 (Fall 1979): 102. Morine told William Smith, deputy archivist at the Public Archives of Canada, that "he was opposed to Confederation until Newfoundland had put her house in order, so that the Island would not come into the negotiation, in pauperis forma" (103).

145 *Evening Advocate*, 21 Apr. 1923.

146 *Daily News*, 11 Apr. 1923.

147 In transmitting the report to the Colonial Office, Governor Allardyce provided a list of examples where Squires and others had mismanaged public expenditures. See Allardyce to J.H. Thomas, 17 Mar. 1924 (CO 532/275).

148 An account of the "chaos and confusion" of the politics in this period is in Governor Allardyce to J.H. Thomas, 10 May 1924, and "Report for Quarter Ending 30th June 1924" (CO 532/275); *Evening Advocate*, 25 and 26 Apr. 1924; *Daily Mail*, 7 May 1924; R.M. Elliott, "Newfoundland Politics in the 1920s: The Genesis and Significance of the Hollis Walker Enquiry," in Hiller and Neary, *Newfoundland in the Nineteenth and Twentieth Centuries*, 181–204; and O'Flaherty, *Lost Country*, 321–23. Transcripts of the enquiry are in ASC, Coll-250, files 8.01.001–19, and "The Report of T. Hollis Walker, K.C. on Corruption in the Newfoundland Government" in 8.02.001.

149 *The Royalist*, May 1924, a copy of which is in CO 532/275, 186.

150 *Evening Telegram*, 25 Mar. 1924.

151 Melvin Baker and James Overton, "Document: J.R. Smallwood on Liberalism in 1926," *Newfoundland Studies* 11, no. 1 (1995): 75–126.

152 MacLeod, "Subsidized Steamers," 78–80.

153 Quoted in MacLeod, "Subsidized Steamers," 74.

154 Quoted in MacLeod, "Subsidized Steamers," 74.

155 MacLeod, "Subsidized Steamers," 83.

156 Colonial Secretary to T.A. Low, 5 Aug. 1924, 14 Feb. 1925, and 30 Jan. 1926 (RPA, GN8.111).

157 Colonial Secretary to James Malcolm, 25 Aug. 1927, and Malcolm to Bennett, 31 Jan. 1928 (RPA, GN8.111).

158 See *In the Privy Council, in the Matter of the Boundary between the Dominion of Canada and the Colony of Newfoundland in the Labrador Peninsula* [Labrador Boundary Dispute Documents], vol. 2 of Joint Appendix, 341; and Augustus G.

Lilly and Christopher P. Curran, "Introduction," in *The Journals of George Simms, J.P., and the Records of the Labrador Court 1826–1833*, vol. 1, ed. Lilly and Curran (St. John's: ss *Daisy* Legal History Committee, Law Society of Newfoundland and Labrador, 2017); and Chadwick, *Newfoundland: Island into Province*, 134.

159 J. Johnston to Burgess, 12 July 1889 (RPA, GN1.11.1); Labrador Boundary Dispute Documents, vol. 2 of Joint Appendix, 341, Pinsent to Blake, 22 May 1888; and A.M. Fraser, "The Labrador Boundary Dispute," in MacKay, *Newfoundland: Economic, Diplomatic, and Strategic Studies*, 460–64.

160 For a discussion of the Royal Proclamation, see Indigenous and Northern Affairs Canada, https://www.aadnc-aandc.gc.ca/eng/1370355181092/1370355203645.

161 Tache to Dickie, 6 Dec. 1902, and Dickie to Tache, 9 Dec. 1902 (RPA, GN1.11.2). On Dickie, see L. Anders Sandberg, "Dickie, Alfred," in *Dictionary of Canadian Biography* 15, University of Toronto/Université Laval, 2005, http://www.biographi.ca/en/bio/dickie_alfred_15E.html.

162 Richard Budgel and Michael Staveley, *The Labrador Boundary* (Happy Valley–Goose Bay: Labrador Institute of Northern Studies, 1987), 7. The legislation was the Quebec Boundary Extension Act, S.C. 1898, Vic. C.3, to be found in the Labrador Boundary Dispute Documents, vol. 1, 246–47.

163 Wilfrid Laurier to Robert Bond, 16 Sept. and 2 Oct. 1907 (ASC, Coll-237, file 8.04.005); and Fraser, "The Labrador Boundary Dispute," 467.

164 *Proceedings of the House of Assembly and the Legislative Council of Newfoundland*, 1914, 691; Minutes of Executive Council, 25 Apr. 1914 (RPA, GN9.23).

165 Minute by Sir Walter Davidson on the Labrador Boundary, 12 Oct. 1917 (RPA, MG9.20); and Joseph R. Smallwood, "The Labrador Boundary Case," in *The Book of Newfoundland*, vol. 4, ed. Joseph R. Smallwood (St. John's: Newfoundland Book Publishers, 1967), 11.

166 Gouvin to Harris, 10 Dec. 1918 (RPA, GN1.11.4); Labrador Boundary Dispute Documents, vol. 1 of Joint Appendix, 125; and Smallwood, "The Labrador Boundary Case," 11.

167 Warren to P.T. [McGrath], 12 Nov. 1922 (RPA, MG8.3).

168 Quoted in O'Flaherty, *Lost Country*, 314.

169 McGrath to Warren, 4 Jan. 1924 (RPA, MG8.3).

170 See Governor Allardyce to Lord Amery, secretary of state for the colonies, 21 and 25 Nov. and 3 Dec 1924 (RPA, GN1.3.A, box 131, despatch 868/24).

171 *Evening Telegram* newspaper clippings, 5 and 8 Dec. 1924 (RPA, MG8.109).

172 RPA, MG8.7, Taschereau telegram to Monroe, 10 Dec. 1924; *Daily News*, 2 Mar. 1925, for copies of the Monroe-Taschereau correspondence leading to the conference in Montreal; and Smallwood, "The Labrador Boundary Case," 8. Besides Monroe, the delegates were Minister of Justice W.J. Higgins, Colonial Secretary John R. Bennett, and McGrath. Governor Allardyce speculated that Harry Crowe might have been influential in urging Newfoundland to attend this conference. See CO 532/275, Allardyce to Amery, secretary of state for the

colonies, 19 Dec. 1924, Crowe to Allardyce, 17 Dec. 1924, and to King, 11 Dec. 1924.
173 Monroe to Taschereau, 13 Jan. 1925, and Monroe to Taschereau, 10 Feb. 1925 (RPA, MG8.7).
174 Monroe to Taschereau, 4 Mar. 1925, Lapointe to Monroe, 6 Mar. 1925, Monroe telegram to Taschereau, 24 Mar. 1925, and Taschereau's reply, 27 Mar. 1925 (RPA, MG8.7); *Daily News*, 13 Apr. 1925; and Lord Amery to Monroe, 7 July 1925 (RPA, GN1.3.A, box 131, despatch 868/24).
175 Text of the *Report of the Privy Council on the Labrador Boundary Dispute. Great Britain*. Privy Council. Judicial Committee. (St. John's: Robinson, 1927).
176 *Daily News*, 2 Mar. 1927.
177 *The Newfoundland Weekly*, 5 Mar. 1927.
178 See Peter Neary, "Newfoundland and Quebec: Provincial Neighbours across an Uneasy Frontier," *Bulletin of Canadian Studies* 2, no. 2 (Dec. 1978): 35–51.

CHAPTER 4

1 Newfoundland Royal Commission 1933, *Report*, 251; *Evening Telegram*, 17 May 1929; and Noel, *Politics in Newfoundland*, 184–89.
2 *Evening Telegram*, 4 Mar. 1927.
3 *Evening Telegram*, 25 Mar. 1927; and Coaker, *Twenty Years*, 236. On the commission idea, see Gene Long, *Suspended State: Newfoundland before Canada* (St. John's: Breakwater, 1999), and O'Flaherty, *Lost Country*, 330.
4 On 4 Feb. 1932, two city clubs debated whether Newfoundland should join Canada, for instance, at a time of severe economic crisis in the country. See *Daily News*, 6 Feb. 1932.
5 Newfoundland Royal Commission 1933, *Report*, 47.
6 See Malcolm MacLeod, *Connections: Newfoundland's Pre-Confederation Links with Canada and the World* (St. John's: Creative Publishers, 2003), 55–98.
7 Noel, *Politics in Newfoundland*, 184.
8 Quoted in Michael Harris, *Rare Ambition: The Crosbies of Newfoundland* (Toronto: Viking, 1992), 98–99.
9 O'Flaherty, *Lost Country*, 340; and JHA, 1928, Appendix, 233–53, for Crosbie's 1928 Budget Speech.
10 Cashin quoted in Noel, *Politics in Newfoundland*, 182; and O'Flaherty, *Lost Country*, 330. On Peter Cashin, see his *My Life and Times, 1890–1919*, ed. R.E. Buehler (Portugal Cove: Breakwater, 1976) and *Peter Cashin: My Fight for Newfoundland*, ed. Edward Roberts (St. John's: Flanker Press, 2012).
11 Joseph R. Smallwood, *The New Newfoundland* (New York: Macmillan, 1931); and O'Flaherty, *Lost Country*, 343.
12 Noel, *Politics in Newfoundland*, 185. Smallwood claimed some of the credit in 1926 and 1927 for working to bring about a political reconciliation between Coaker and Squires. See Smallwood, *I Chose Canada* (Toronto: Macmillan,

ENDNOTES

1973), 166; and Memoir, "I got those two men together" (ASC, Coll-285, file 2.06.001).

13 Allardyce to Secretary of State, 9 Feb. 1928 (RPA, GN1.3.A, box 139, despatch 115/28). See Sir William Horwood to L.S. Amery, 16 Aug. 1928 (GN1.3.A, box 139, despatch 689/28).

14 Doug Letto, *Newfoundland's Last Prime Minister: Frederick Alderdice and the Death of a Nation* (Portugal Cove–St. Philip's: Boulder Publications, 2014), 42.

15 *Daily News*, 29 Sept. 1928; Horwood telegram to Secretary of State, 28 Sept. 1928 (RPA, GN1.3.A, box 139, despatch 689/28).

16 *Daily News* and *Evening Telegram*, 28 Sept. 1928. On the campaign for women's suffrage, see Margot I. Duley, *Where Once Our Mothers Stood We Stand: Women's Suffrage in Newfoundland, 1890–1925* (Charlottetown: Gynergy Books, 1993), 88–96; Anne Hart, "Knowling, Fannie (McNeil)," in *Dictionary of Canadian Biography* 15, University of Toronto/Université Laval, 2005, http://www.biographi.ca/en/bio/knowling_fannie_15E.html; and Heidi MacDonald, "Woman's Suffrage and Confederation," *Acadiensis* 46, no. 1 (Winter/Spring 2017): 163–76.

17 O'Flaherty, *Lost Country*, 346; and *Evening Telegram*, 10 and 11 Apr. 1930.

18 *Twillingate Sun*, 27 Oct. 1928.

19 Newfoundland Royal Commission 1933, *Report*, 10.

20 Budget Speech as published in the *Evening Telegram*, 14, 15, and 16 May 1929.

21 *Evening Telegram*, *Daily News*, 14 May 1929, and *Fishermen's Advocate*, 3 May 1929.

22 Newfoundland Royal Commission 1933, *Report*, 251; and *Evening Telegram*, 17 May 1929.

23 Cadigan, *Death on Two Fronts*, 275.

24 *Fishermen's Advocate*, 27 Dec. 1929.

25 See also *Evening Telegram*, 27 Aug. and 7 Sept. 1931; *Daily News*, 2, 7, 13, and 14 Jan., 6 Feb., 17 and 26 Aug. 1931; and *Fishermen's Advocate*, 30 Jan., 14 and 21 Aug., 4 Dec. 1931.

26 *Evening Telegram*, 13 and 14 Nov. 1931; and *Fishermen's Advocate*, 30 Oct., 10 Nov. 1931.

27 Telegram from Governor Middleton to Secretary of State, 12 Dec. 1930 (RPA, GN1.3.A, box 146, despatch 1361A/31).

28 Cyril Fox, Speaker of the House of Assembly, to Administrator Sir William Horwood, 2 May 1928 (RPA, GN1.3.A, box 139, despatch 418/28).

29 *Evening Telegram*, 3, 15, 22, 23, 30, and 31 Mar., 7 Apr. 1928; *Daily News*, 12, 30, and 31 Mar. 1928

30 *Evening Telegram*, 15 Mar. 1928.

31 I.C. Morris letter in the *Evening Telegram*, 28 Apr. 1928.

32 *Evening Telegram*, 6 Mar. 1928.

33 *Evening Telegram*, 28 and 29 Aug. 1929.

34 Middleton to Lord Passfield, 18 Oct. 1929 (RPA, GN1.3.A, box 141, despatch 20/29). See also *Evening Telegram*, 29 Aug. 1929, for an exchange of letters between Alderice and Lapointe dated 3 Oct. and 10 Nov. 1928.
35 Middleton to Lord Passfield, 18 Oct. 1929 (RPA, GN1.3.A, box 141, despatch 20/29); and *Daily News*, 26, 27, 28, and 29 Aug. 1929.
36 Barnes, Cashin, Coaker, and Mosdell to Bennett, 7 Oct. 1931, and Bennett's reply, 14 Oct. 1931 (RPA, GN2.563); and Peter Neary, " 'That Thin Red Cord of Sentiment and of Blood': Newfoundland in the Great Depression, 1929–34" (unpublished manuscript, 1988, available at the Centre for Newfoundland Studies, Memorial University Libraries), 16–22. The correspondence dealing with these negotiations was tabled on 16 Feb. 1932 in the House of Assembly. See *Daily News*, 19 Feb. 1932.
37 O'Flaherty, *Lost Country*, 404.
38 On Newfoundland's political problems in the early 1930s, see Newfoundland Royal Commission 1933, *Report*, 43–72; Noel, *Politics in Newfoundland*, 186–214; Neary, "'That Thin Red Cord'"; O'Flaherty, *Lost Country*, 347–409; and Valerie Summers, *Regime Change in a Resource Economy: The Politics of Underdevelopment in Newfoundland since 1825* (St. John's: Breakwater, 1994), 90–120.
39 Squires to J.H. Thomas, secretary of state for Dominion Affairs, 11 July 1931, and Thompson to Squires, 14 Aug. 1931 (RPA, GN1.3.A, box 146, despatch 840/31); Noel, *Politics in Newfoundland*, 187–200; and Neary, "'That Thin Red Cord,'" 12.
40 Thomas to Middleton, 21 Sept. 1931 (RPA, GN1.3.A, box 146, despatch 840/31). J.H. Penson, acting principal in the Treasury, was also seconded to assist Thompson.
41 Thompson memorandum, 10 Nov. 1931, Thompson to Middleton, 26 Nov. 1931, and Thompson to Sir Herbert Hambling, 4 Dec. 1931 (RPA, GN1.3.A, box 148, despatch 609/31); and *Evening Telegram*, 8 Feb. and 27 May 1932. His first interim report was published in the *Evening Telegram*, 9 Feb. 1932, and *Daily News*, 6 Feb. 1932.
42 Middleton to Thomas, 12 Nov. 1931, and Middleton telegram to Thomas 15 Nov. 1931 (RPA, GN1.3.A, box 148, despatch 609/31). The four Canadian banks were the Bank of Montreal, the Bank of Nova Scotia, the Royal Bank of Canada, and the Canadian Bank of Commerce.
43 Thompson to Hambling, 4 Dec. 1931 (RPA, GN1.3.A, box 148, despatch 609/31).
44 Quoted in Noel, *Politics in Newfoundland*, 191.
45 Thomas telegram to Middleton, 28 Nov. 1931 (RPA, GN1.3.A, box 148, despatch 609/31).
46 *Evening Telegram*, 2 Jan. 1932; *Daily News*, 2 and 4 Jan. 1932; and Middleton to Thomas, 7 Jan. 1932, with enclosure containing the banks' conditions for the loan (RPA, GN1.3.A, box 146, despatch 840/31), and despatch 609/31, containing foreign press coverage of Newfoundland's financial problems.

47 Noel, *Politics in Newfoundland*, 196–97.
48 O'Flaherty, *Lost Country*, 404.
49 David Hale, "The Newfoundland Lesson," *International Economy* (Summer 2003): 52–61, http://www.international-economy.com/TIE_Su03_Hale.pdf.
50 K.C. Wheare, *The Statute of Westminster and Dominion Status*, 4th edn (London: Oxford University Press, 1949), 237–38; *Statutes of Newfoundland, 1931*, Cap. 1, 22 Geo. V.; William C. Gilmore, "Law, Constitutional Convention, and the Union of Newfoundland and Canada," *Acadiensis* 18, no. 2 (Spring 1989): 111–26; and *Proceedings of the House of Assembly and the Legislative Council*, 1931, 489–90, 500.
51 *Statutes of Newfoundland*, 1931, Cap. 19, "National Flag Act," and Cap. 14, "External Affairs Act."
52 *Evening Telegram*, 4 Feb. 1932.
53 Notes by Middleton, 6, 8, 9, 13, 15, 19, and 21 Apr., 5 May 1932 (RPA, GN1.3.A, box 151, despatch 349/32); and *Evening Telegram*, 1, 2, 5, 6, and 18 Feb., 8 Apr. 1932.
54 P.J. O'Neill to Charles Hutchings, 15 Feb. 1932 (RPA, GN13.1.B, box 371, file 23).
55 Middleton to Thomas, 26 Mar. 1932 (RPA, GN1.3.A, box 150, despatch 181/32); and Neary, "'That Thin Red Cord,'" 32–36.
56 Collingwood to Dick, 22 Apr. 1932 (RPA, MG4, box 2C, file Collingwood 1932).
57 On Smallwood's role in the escape, see his *I Chose Canada*, 182–85.
58 Quoted in Cadigan, *Death on Two Fronts*, 293; and W.F. Coaker, *Past, Present and Future: Being a Series of Articles Contributed to the* Fishermen's Advocate, 1932 (Port Union: *Fishermen's Advocate*, 1932), Article 10, 21 Sept. 1932.
59 RPA, GN1.3.A, box 151, despatch 541/32; *Fishermen's Advocate*, 14 July 1933; *Daily News*, 21 May 1932; and *Evening Telegram*, 25 May 1932.
60 James K. Hiller, "Corruption and Collapse, or Did Squires Do It?," in *Amulree's Legacy: Truth, Lies, and Consequences. Symposium March 2000* (papers and presentations), ed. Garfield Fizzard (St. John's: Newfoundland Historical Society, 2001), 90. In her visits to England, Lady Squires was keenly interested in the spiritualism movement, then popular among political and literary leaders of society. In a letter to a fellow spiritualism believer, Sir William Coaker, on 10 Oct. 1930, she wondered whether British Prime Minister Ramsay MacDonald, whom she was to meet a few days later at Chequers (the prime minister's country residence), had "any particular interest in spiritualism." See Lady Squires to Coaker, 10 Oct. 1930 (ASC, Coll-486, file 1.02.026); and Smallwood, *I Chose Canada*, 166, where Smallwood recalls attending spiritualist meetings with her in early 1927 when he was in London. On the spiritualism movement in Britain and Canada at this time, see Christopher Dummitt, *Unbuttoned: A History of Mackenzie King's Secret Life* (Montreal and Kingston: McGill-Queen's University Press, 2017), 34–36, and 56–70.

61 Peter Neary, "'With Great Regret and after the Most Anxious Consideration': Newfoundland's 1932 Plan to Reschedule Interest Payments," *Newfoundland Studies* 10, no. 22 (Fall 1994): 250–59; and Neary, "'That Thin Red Cord,'" 22–57. Alderdice wrote the General Manager of the Bank of Montreal in Montreal that despite the government's retrenchment efforts, it "looks almost like a confession of failure on my part to bring this country back to a stabilized condition." See Alderdice to Jackson Dodds, 27 Sept. 1932 (RPA, GN2.5.582.1).

62 Collingwood to Newman, 23 Dec. 1932 (RPA, MG4, box 2C, file Collingwood 1932).

63 Letto, *Newfoundland's Last Prime Minister*, 115–34.

64 MacLeod, "Subsidized Steamers," 88–89; and Alderdice to Stevens, 8 Oct. 1932 (RPA, GN8.243). With the end of the subsidy in 1924, Newfoundland claimed that by 1932 Canada owed a total of $297,500 in arrears.

65 Peter Neary, "Canadian Immigration Policy and the Newfoundlanders, 1912–1939," *Acadiensis* 11, no. 2 (Spring 1982): 69–75; and Minister of Immigration and Colonization to Prime Minister Squires, 7 May 1921 (RPA, GN8.140).

66 Peter Neary, "Canada and the Newfoundland Labour Market, 1939–49," *Canadian Historical Review* 62, no. 4 (Dec. 1981): 470–95.

67 *Evening Telegram*, 27 and 28 July 1932; and "Statement by the Leader of the Newfoundland Delegation" (RPA, GN8.244, folder 14).

68 Newfoundland Royal Commission 1933, *Report*, 1.

69 Quoted in Neary, *Newfoundland in the North Atlantic World*, 20.

70 Newfoundland Royal Commission 1933, *Report*, 1–3. Biographical details and the work schedule of the commissioners are in RPA, GN2.5.582, box 97. See also Newfoundland Affairs, *Correspondence and Papers, 1931–1933* (Dominions Office no. 151), 45–163.

71 Peter Fenwick, "Witnesses to the Lord: An Analysis of the Testimony Presented to the Newfoundland Royal Commission, 1933, Lord Amulree, Chairman" (Paper submitted for Political Science 6610, Memorial University, 1994), 24–25.

72 Alderdice to Amulree, 22 June 1933 (RPA, GN2.5.582, box 88).

73 Alderdice to Amulree, 22 June 1933 (RPA, GN2.5.582, box 88); and Newfoundland Affairs, *Correspondence and Papers, 1931–1933* (Dominions Office no. 151, D.O. 114/58), 4.

74 Note by Clutterbuck, 20 Mar. 1933, on the evidence of Frederick Alderdice given that day (RPA, GB 16, Reel 13, Newfoundland Royal Commission 1933).

75 Evidence of Dr. H.M. Mosdell, 31 May 1933, 1–2 (LAC, MG 30, E82, vol. 17, file 82).

76 *Evening Telegram*, 27 Nov. 1933.

77 Board of Trade Minute Books, Minute 24, Nov. 1933 (RPA, MG73, box 75); and GB 16, Newfoundland Royal Commission 1933, Reel 13, "Newspaper Clippings, Nov. 1933."

78 *Evening Telegram*, 27 Nov. 1933; and *Daily News*, 25 Nov. 1933.

79 *Fishermen's Advocate*, 24 Nov., 1 Dec. 1933, and 11 Aug. 1939; and telegram from Squires to Secretary of State for Dominion Affairs, 30 Nov. 1933 (RPA, GN2.5.582.6, box 99).
80 *Fishermen's Advocate*, 23 Feb. and 9 Mar. 1934.
81 John B. McEvoy, "Our New Constitution," in *The Book of Newfoundland*, vol. 1, ed. Joseph R. Smallwood (St. John's: Newfoundland Book Publishers, 1937), 43.
82 Quoted in Neary, "'With Great Regret and after the Most Anxious Consideration,'" 253.
83 See RPA, GN1.3.A, box 155, despatch 1011/34, for a copy of the resolutions.
84 See RPA, GN1.3.A, box 156, file 6/34, for a copy of the commission to the commissioners.
85 On the 1980s disputes between Ottawa and Newfoundland, see Raymond B. Blake, *Lions or Jellyfish: Newfoundland-Ottawa Relations since 1957* (Toronto: University of Toronto Press, 2015), 152–220.
86 Lodge wrote a memoir of his time in Newfoundland entitled *Dictatorship in Newfoundland* (London: Cassell, 1939); On Hope Simpson, see Neary, *White Tie and Decorations: Sir John and Lady Hope Simpson in Newfoundland, 1934–1936* (Toronto: University of Toronto Press, 1996), 3–10.
87 Quoted in the *Daily News*, 10 Feb. 1934.
88 Hope Simpson quoted in the *Daily News*, 19 Mar. 1934.
89 Thomas Lodge, "Memorandum on General Policy," 25 Jan. 1935 (ASC, Dominions Office Newfoundland Correspondence, DO35/504, N1051/7).
90 *Daily News*, 20 Nov. 1934; and Gordon Handcock, "The Commission of Government's Land Settlement Scheme in Newfoundland," in *Twentieth-Century Newfoundland: Explorations*, ed. Hiller and Neary (St. John's: Breakwater, 1994), 123–51.
91 There is a substantial history on the Commission of Government. Noel, in his *Politics in Newfoundland*, sees little good in its work, claiming it was saved only with the economic activity created in Newfoundland by the Second World War. Patrick O'Flaherty takes a similar stance in *Leaving the Past Behind: Newfoundland History from 1934* (St. John's: Long Beach Press, 2011). Peter Neary offers a more nuanced and sympathetic view of the Commission in his *Newfoundland in the North Atlantic World*.
92 *Observer's Weekly*, 20 Jan. and 3 Feb. 1934.
93 "Personal Diary and Views of Commission of Government," Chapter 1 (ASC, Coll-285, file 2.06.002).
94 Smallwood to Anderson, 6 Feb. 1934 (RPA, GN38, box S1-2-7, file 19); and Smallwood to the *Observer's Weekly*, 31 Mar. 1934, original emphasis.
95 Smallwood to the *Observer's Weekly*, 24 Nov. 1934.
96 An overview of social unrest in 1930s Newfoundland is discussed in James Overton, "Riots, Raids, and Relief, Police, Prisons, and Parsimony: The Political Economy of Public Order in Newfoundland in the 1930s," in *Violence and Public Anxiety*, ed. Elliott Leyton, William O'Grady, and James Overton (St. John's:

ISER Books, 1992), 195–334; and Overton, "Nationalism, Democracy, and Self-Determination."

97 "Unemployment in Newfoundland," Anderson to Thomas, 9 May 1935 (RPA, GN1.3.A, box 168, file 353.34); Newfoundland, *Report by the Commission of Government on the Unemployment Situation May 1935*, Cmd. 4910 (London: His Majesty's Stationery Office, 1935); and *Daily News*, 10, 11, 26, 29, and 30 May 1935.

98 Simpson to Harding, 24 Sept. 1935 (DO35/500, N1029/10).

99 Commissioner John Hope Simpson quoted in Peter Neary, "Ebb and Flow of Citizenship in Newfoundland, 1929–1949," in *Belonging: The Meaning and Future of Canadian Citizenship*, ed. William Kaplan (Montreal and Kingston: McGill-Queen's University Press, 1993), 87.

100 *Fishermen's Advocate*, 6 July, 3 Aug. 1934.

101 *Fishermen's Advocate*, 9 Nov. 1934.

102 *Evening Telegram*, 13 June 1932, and *Daily News*, 7 Dec. 1934. Cashin was the managing director of the Newfoundland Insurance Agencies, Ltd, which in June 1932 represented the Merchants Casualty Insurance Co. of Waterloo, Ontario. A summary of Cashin's business activities is in Walwyn to Thomas, 2 Nov. 1935 (RPA, GN1.3.A, box 189, despatch 208/36).

103 Captain R. Schwerdt, private secretary, to P.J. Cashin, 6 Mar. 1936, with attached document "Prospectus for Proposed Sweepstake to Be Operated at St. John's, Newfoundland" (RPA, GN1.3.A, box 188, despatch 179/36).

104 John Walsh, Michael Keough, M.P. Mahoney, and A. Matthews to P.J. O'Neill, chief of police, 30 Oct. 1934 (RPA, GN1.3.A, box 189, despatch 208/36).

105 Walwyn to Thomas, 2 Nov. 1935 (RPA, GN1.3.A, box 189, despatch 208/36), and Newfoundland Crusaders to Governor Anderson, 10 Jan. 1936 (GN1.3.A, box 189, despatch 208/36). Similar charges were made by journalist John T. Meaney in his short-lived 1934 newspaper, the *Newfoundlander*, "dedicated to the restoration of parliamentary institutions." A newspaper scrapbook of Meaney's writings for the mid-1930s is in ASC, Coll-285, file 4.02.035.

106 Cashin to Puddester, 11 June 1936, and to Walwyn, 11 June 1936 (RPA, GN1.15, box 2, despatch 366/36).

107 Notes by Clutterbuck, 19 Nov. and 29 Dec. 1936 (DO35/497, N1017/65).

108 MacDonald to Walwyn, 22 Oct. 1936 (RPA, GN1.3.A, box 191, despatch 568/36).

109 See Jeff A. Webb, *The Voice of Newfoundland: A Social History of the Broadcasting Corporation of Newfoundland, 1939–1949* (Toronto: University of Toronto Press, 2008).

110 Neary, *Newfoundland in the North Atlantic World*, 75–76; and Walwyn to Schwerdt, 26 Nov. 1936, and Walwyn to MacDonald, 15 Dec. 1936 (RPA, GN1.3.A, box 193, despatch 851/36).

111 Quoted in Walwyn to MacDonald, 19 Aug. 1937, H.T. Renouf to W.J. Carew, 3 Aug. 1937, and Clutterbuck to the Assistant Secretary, the British Empire Union, 12 Aug. 1937 (RPA, GN1.3.A, box 192, despatch 568/46).

112 Walwyn to Secretary of State for Dominion Affairs, n.d., 1937 (RPA, GN1.3.A, box 199, despatch 234/37, draft despatch).
113 Simpson to Harding, 24 Sept. 1935 (DO35/500, N1029/10). See also Neary, *White Tie and Decorations*, 15–18, 85, 168.
114 Quoted in Neary, "Ebb and Flow of Citizenship in Newfoundland," 86.
115 Draft "Memorandum Submitted by Commissioner for Natural Resources for Consideration of Commission of Government," N.R. 41–40, prepared by J.H. Gorvin, 24 Apr. 1940 (RPA, GN13.1.B, box 414, file Reorganization of Fisheries–1940).
116 Neary, *Newfoundland in the North Atlantic World*, 349.
117 Extract from House of Commons Official Report of 10 May 1938 (RPA, GN1.3.A, box 207, despatch 88/38); and *Daily News*, 11 May 1938.
118 Walwyn to Harding, 4 July 1938 (DO 35/725).
119 *Observer's Weekly*, 3 Feb. 1934; and Francis G. Hollohan, *Albert Perlin: A Biography* (St. John's: Jesperson Press, 1985), 51. Perlin's 1933 evidence before the Amulree Commission is in LAC, MG 30, E82, vol. 18, file 97.
120 Alexander, "Literacy and Economic Development in Nineteenth-Century Newfoundland," 136–37.
121 Alexander, "Literacy and Economic Development in Nineteenth-Century Newfoundland," 113.
122 Anderson to Thomas, 29 Jan. 1936, enclosing "Memorandum on General Policy" by Thomas Lodge (DO 35/504, N1051/7).
123 Neary, *Newfoundland in the North Atlantic World*, 75–81; Phillip McCann, "The Educational Policy of the Commission of Government," *Newfoundland Studies* 3, no. 2 (Fall 1987): 201–15; and for the role of women in education, see Kay Whitehead and Judith Peppard, "Women Teachers in the Turbulent Educational World of St. John's, Newfoundland, 1920–1949," *Acadiensis* 37, no. 1 (Winter/Spring 2008): 56–75.
124 Neary, *Newfoundland in the North Atlantic World*, 78–79. See also his "Document: The Commission of Government on Reconstruction, Dec. 1936," *Newfoundland and Labrador Studies* 26, no. 2 (2011): 241–88.
125 Quoted in Neary, *Newfoundland in the North Atlantic World*, 75–76.
126 Neary, *Newfoundland in the North Atlantic World*, 85.
127 Peter Neary, "P.A. Clutterbuck on Morley Richards and the Record of the Commission of Government, 1939," *Newfoundland and Labrador Studies* 27, no. 1 (2012): 79–98.
128 *Evening Telegram*, 15, 20, and 21 July, and 16 Aug. 1939; *Daily News*, 20 July 1939; and Walwyn to Anthony Eden, 5 Oct. 1939 (DO35/725, N8/19).
129 See *Evening Telegram*, 19 Oct. 1938, for a report of a talk he gave to the young men's section of the Toronto Board of Trade regarding Newfoundland's strategic importance to the defence of Canada.
130 *Daily News*, 2 and 4 Apr. 1940; and *Observer's Weekly*, 9 Apr. 1940.
131 *Evening Telegram*, 20 June 1939.
132 *Daily News*, 23 and 26 May 1939, and *Observer's Weekly*, 30 May 1939.

133 Melvin Baker and Peter Neary, " 'Pigs Is My Business': Joey Smallwood on Himself, 1945," *Newfoundland and Labrador Studies* 28, no. 1 (Spring 2013): 117–34; and Jeff Webb, "Constructing Community and Consumers: Joseph R. Smallwood's Barrelman Radio Programme," *Journal of the Canadian Historical Association* 8, no. 1 (1997): 165–86.

134 *Evening Telegram*, 9, 14, and 15 Apr. 1936. See also Philip D. Hiscock, "The Barrelman Radio Programs, 1937–1943: The Mediation and Use of Folklore in Newfoundland" (PhD thesis, Memorial University, 1994); Peter Narváez, "Joseph R. Smallwood, 'The Barrelman': The Broadcaster as Folklorist," in *Media Sense: The Folklore-Popular Culture Continuum*, ed. Peter Narváez and Martin Laba (Bowling Green, OH: Bowling Green State University Popular Press, 1986), 47–64; James R. Thoms, ed., *Call Me Joey* (St. John's: Harry Cuff Publications, 1990, reprint of 1969 edition); William Connors, ed., *The Best of the Barrelman, 1938–1940* (St. John's: Creative Publishers, 1998); and Webb, *The Voice of Newfoundland: A Social History of the Broadcasting Corporation of Newfoundland, 1939–1949*, 94–107; and ASC, Moakler Papers, box 6, file "Agreement between Joey Smallwood and F.M. O'Leary Ltd."

135 *Daily News*, 12 May 1938.

136 On Newfoundland at war, see Neary, *Newfoundland in the North Atlantic World*, 109–82, and "Canada and the Newfoundland Labour Market"; and Steven High, ed., *Occupied St. John's: A Social History of a City at War, 1939–1945* (Montreal and Kingston: McGill-Queen's University Press, 2010).

137 *Daily News*, 31 Dec. 1948. Clarence Powell, acting director of local government affairs, observed in 1948 that it was "impossible to escape the conviction that local government provides education in citizenship and a training ground for democracy."

138 Quoted in Melvin Baker and Peter Neary, "Document: Governor Sir Humphrey Walwyn's Account of His Meetings with Churchill and Roosevelt, Placentia Bay, Newfoundland, August 1941," *Newfoundland and Labrador Studies* 31, no. 1 (2016): 166.

139 See Steven High, "Working for Uncle Sam: The 'Comings' and 'Goings' of Newfoundland Base Construction Labour, 1940–1945," *Acadiensis* 32, no. 2 (Spring 2003): 84–107.

CHAPTER 5

1 Smallwood, *I Chose Canada*, 255–61; and *Daily News*, 29 Oct. 1946.
2 *Daily News*, 29 Oct. 1946.
3 *Daily News*, 30 Oct., 5 and 6 Nov. 1946.
4 Noel, *Politics in Newfoundland*, 252.
5 *Daily News*, 25 Oct. 1940.
6 *Daily News*, 27 July, 6 Aug. 1940; and *Observer's Weekly*, 30 July 1940. See the address by William White to the Association in Nov. 1940 in the *Daily News*, 22 Nov. 1940.

7   *Express*, 15 Feb., 12 Apr. 1941.
8   *Daily News*, 11 Mar. 1941.
9   RPA, MG73, box 41, folder 17; and *Daily News*, 27 June 1942.
10 *Observer's Weekly*, 9 and 16 Mar. 1943; *Fishermen's Advocate*, 2 Apr. 1943; and Report of Special Committees, 8 Mar. and 2 Apr. 1943 (RPA, MG73, box 43, folder 1). In the early 1940s, Cashin had split his time between Montreal and St. John's. See *Peter Cashin: My Fight for Newfoundland*, 97–98.
11 MacKenzie, *Inside the Atlantic Triangle*, 141–42; Peter Neary, "Great Britain and the Future of Newfoundland, 1939–45," *Newfoundland Studies* 1, no. 1 (1985): 37–38; Attlee to Walwyn, 29 Apr. 1943 (RPA, GN1.3.A, box 232, file 167/40); and *Fishermen's Advocate*, 12 Nov. 1943. Herbert recounted his Newfoundland visit in his 1950 autobiography, *Independent Member* (London: Methuen, 1950).
12 *Observer's Weekly*, 21 Dec. 1943.
13 Attlee's assessment is discussed below.
14 Neary, "Ebb and Flow of Citizenship in Newfoundland," 94; and Attlee quoted in the *Daily News*, 17 Dec. 1943.
15 Neary, *Newfoundland in the North Atlantic World*, 224–28.
16 Quoted in Neary, *Newfoundland in the North Atlantic World*, 228.
17 MacKenzie, *Inside the Atlantic Triangle*, 143–44.
18 Bridle, ed., *Documents on Relations Between Canada and Newfoundland*, vol. 2, 73–74; and Raymond B. Blake, "WLMK's Attitude towards Newfoundland's Entry into Confederation," *Newfoundland Quarterly* 82, no. 4 (Spring 1987): 26–37.
19 Blake, *Canadians at Last*, 11.
20 MacKenzie, *Inside the Atlantic Triangle*, 146–47.
21 Robertson Memo, 18 Aug. 1943 (LAC, King Papers, Series J4, vol. 308, file 3270).
22 Cabinet Minutes, 12 Apr. 1944 (LAC, Privy Council Records, RG2).
23 MacKenzie, *Inside the Atlantic Triangle*, 155–56.
24 Chadwick, *Newfoundland*, 182.
25 Attlee to Walywn, 25 Nov. 1942 (RPA, GN1.3.A, box 247, file 206/42); Neary, "Great Britain and the Future of Newfoundland, 1939–45," 33–35, and "Clement Attlee's Visit to Newfoundland, September 1942," *Acadiensis* 13, no. 2 (Spring 1984): 101–09.
26 RPA, GN1.3.A, box 247, file 306/42.
27 Attlee radio speech from Government House, St. John's, 17 Sept. 1942 (RPA, GN1.3.A, Governor's Office–Local and Miscellaneous Correspondence, 1942, box 247, file 306/42).
28 Newfoundland Government telegram no. 2 to Dominions Secretary, 7 Jan. 1943 (RPA, GN1.3.A, box 232, file 167/40).
29 A.J.P. Taylor, *English History 1914–1945* (New York: Oxford University Press, 1992), 543–44.

30 See Bridle, *Documents on Relations Between Canada and Newfoundland*, vol. 2, 80–95 and 88–93.
31 Sir William Beveridge, *Social Insurance and Allied Services* (London: King's Printer, 1942).
32 MacKenzie, *Inside the Atlantic Triangle*, 155–56.
33 Blake, *Canadians at Last*, 13–14.
34 MacKenzie, *Inside the Atlantic Triangle*, 157–59.
35 Neary, "Clement Attlee's Visit to Newfoundland, September 1942," 101–09; and Nicklaus Thomas-Symonds, *Attlee: A Life in Politics* (London: I.B. Tauris, 2010).
36 National Archives, London, Government of the United Kingdom, Cabinet Conclusions and Minutes, 1 Nov. 1945, 212–13, http://discovery.nationalarchives.gov.uk/details/r/D7662859.
37 "Reports—House of Commons, Official," excerpt from British House of Commons, 11 Dec. 1945, 210–11 (RPA, GN1.3.A, box 269, file 352/45); Great Britain, House of Commons, *Debates*, 11 Dec. 1945, 210–11; and *Daily News*, 12 Dec. 1945.
38 *Fishermen's Advocate*, 14 Dec. 1945.
39 Walwyn to Viscount Addison, 4 Jan. 1946 (RPA, GN1.3.A, box 253, file 52/43).
40 *Evening Telegram*, 3 June 1944.
41 Smallwood, *I Chose Canada*, 226–28.
42 Quoted in Melvin Baker, "J.R. Smallwood—Labour and Socialist Leader," *Newfoundland Quarterly* 93, no. 1 (Fall 1999): 26.
43 *Daily News*, 24 Jan. 1946.
44 Smallwood, ed., *The Book of Newfoundland*, vol. 3, 38–62, and *I Chose Canada*, 230–31.
45 See, for example, Blake, *From Rights to Needs*; Banting, "Social Citizenship and the Multicultural Welfare State"; Brodie, "Citizenship and Solidarity: Reflections on the Canadian Way"; and Gøsta Esping-Andersen, *Three Worlds of Welfare Capitalism* (Princeton: Princeton University Press, 1990).
46 See, for example, Karen Stanbridge, "Framing Children in the Newfoundland Confederation Debate, 1948," *Canadian Journal of Sociology* 32, no. 2 (Spring 2007): 177–201; and Linda Cullum and Marilyn Porter, eds., *Creating This Place: Women, Family, and Class in St. John's, 1900–1950* (Montreal and Kingston: McGill-Queen's University Press, 2014).
47 Cadigan, *Death on Two Fronts*, xxiv.
48 Neary, *Newfoundland in the North Atlantic World*, 195–97.
49 Macdonald to Addison, 29 June 1946 (DO35/1360), original emphasis.
50 Walwyn to Viscount Addison, 4 Jan. 1946 (RPA, GN1.3.A, box 253, file 52/43).
51 Albert Walsh to Kenneth Macdonald, 4 July 1946 (RPA, GN1.3.A, box 276, file Newfoundland Affairs).
52 On the BCN, see Jeff A. Webb, *The Voice of Newfoundland*; and http://collections.mun.ca/cdm/landingpage/collection/nconvention.
53 *Evening Telegram*, 7 Jan. 1947.

54 RPA, GN 38/S-2-5-2, Ranger Reports, file 21, Hermitage for 31 Dec. 1947, file 29, Marystown for 7 Jan. 1948, file 42, Rose Blanche for 24 Oct. 1947. On the Rangers' activities, see Marilyn Tuck, "The Newfoundland Ranger Force, 1935–1950" (MA thesis, Memorial University, 1983), 98–105.
55 Raymond B. Blake, "Newfoundland's Search for Citizenship: The Confederation Debates, 1948" (paper presented to the Atlantic Studies Conference, Mount Allison University, May 2016).
56 Burchell to King, 11 Oct. 1943 (LAC, W.L. Mackenzie King Papers, MG 26 J1, vol. 337, item 290071); and column by Wayfarer, *St. John's Daily News*, 8 Oct. 1943.
57 These points are evident from reading the debates from the National Convention. See Hiller and Harrington, eds., *Debates*.
58 For a discussion of St. Laurent's response to some of Premier Smallwood's demands after 1949, see Blake, *Lions or Jellyfish*, especially 28–32.
59 On this point, see J.W. Pickersgill, *My Years with Louis St. Laurent: A Political Memoir* (Toronto: University of Toronto Press, 1975); and Richard Gwyn, *Smallwood: The Unlikely Revolutionary* (Toronto: McClelland and Stewart, 1972), 170–80.
60 Quoted in Noel, *Politics in Newfoundland*, 253; and Gwyn, *Smallwood*, 76–77.
61 Smallwood, *I Chose Canada*, 255–61; and *Daily News*, 29 Oct. 1946.
62 Neary, *Newfoundland in the North Atlantic World*, 287.
63 James K. Hiller and Michael F. Harrington, eds., *The Newfoundland National Convention, 1946–1948*, vol. 2, *Reports and Papers* (Montreal and Kingston: McGill-Queen's University Press, 1995), *Report of the Fisheries Committee of the National Convention*, 47–48.
64 Hiller and Harrington, eds., *Reports and Papers*, *Report of the Committee on Public Health and Welfare*, 286.
65 Hiller and Harrington, eds., Reports and Papers, *Report of the Fisheries Committee of the National Convention*, 47–48.
66 Hiller and Harrington, eds., Reports and Papers, 17–19.
67 Linda White, "The Rev. Lester Burry Collection: United Church Conference Archives," *Newfoundland Quarterly* 105, no. 2 (Fall 2012): 10.
68 Hiller and Harrington, eds., *Debates*, 32–33.
69 Hiller and Harrington, eds., *Debates*, 728.
70 Hiller and Harrington, eds., *Debates*, 37.
71 Hiller and Harrington, eds., *Debates*, 34–35.
72 William J. Keough, "We Knew What We Wanted," in *The Book of Newfoundland*, vol. 3, ed. Joseph R. Smallwood, 62–63.
73 Hiller and Harrington, eds., *Debates*, 747.
74 Hiller and Harrington, eds., *Debates*, 35.
75 Hiller and Harrington, eds., *Debates*, 37.
76 Hiller and Harrington, eds., *Debates*, 40.
77 *Evening Telegram*, 1 June 1944.
78 *Evening Telegram*, 16 June 1944.

79 Hiller and Harrington, eds., *Debates*, 51.
80 Memorandum from the Newfoundland Tuberculosis Association to Ottawa Delegation, Sept. 1948 (RPA, GN154.6).
81 "Further Notes on the Impact of Confederation on the Health Services of the Newfoundland Department of Public Health and Welfare, Submitted by Leonard Miller, No Date" (RPA, GN154.6). The file also contained an Address by the Honourable Paul Martin, Minister of National Health and Welfare, entitled "New Deal for Health in Canada," which explained how the Government of Canada was heavily investing in improving the health of Canadians. In his speech (which is included in the documents attached), Martin made the following point that the proponents of Confederation had been making since their election to the National Convention: "In the wider comprehension of health as one of the fundamental rights of every human being, there can be no greater goal for national cooperative effort and the expenditure of the nation's financial resources than to build the health of its citizens." See also Eric Strikwerda, "Newfoundland and Labrador Maligned: Taking Stock of Nutritional Health in Rural Newfoundland and Labrador, 1912–1949," *Acadiensis* 47, no. 1 (Winter/Spring 2018): 118–39.
82 *Western Star*, letters to the editor, 8 Mar. 1946 (two letters).
83 Hiller and Harrington, eds., *Reports and Papers*, 444.
84 Webb, "Newfoundland's National Convention," 112.
85 Hiller and Harrington, eds., *Debates*, 594–603.
86 Webb, "Newfoundland's National Convention," 133, and Hiller and Harrington, eds., *Debates*, 1370–72.
87 Hiller and Harrington, eds., *Debates*, 1370–72.

CHAPTER 6

1 W.G. Warren to W.J. Carew, 5 Feb. 1947, enclosing a copy of the 4 Feb. resolution (RPA, GN1.3.A, box 279, file 449/46 "National Convention"); and *Evening Telegram*, 5 Feb. 1947.
2 Smallwood, *I Chose Canada*, 266–68.
3 "Report of Conference of a Committee of the National Convention with His Excellency the Governor in Commission, Held at Government House on Saturday, February 8th, 1947" (RPA, GN1.3.A, box 279, file 449/46). The response was the same again from the Commission when on 22 May 1947 the Convention passed a resolution calling for a delegation of six members to visit the United States for "general trade discussions and other relevant matters affecting the future economy of Newfoundland with the government of the United States of America." See Carew to Warren, 26 May 1947 (GN1.3.A, box 287, file 449/36 "National Convention, May–October 1947"). The second resolution was "entirely outside the terms of reference and the powers and authority of the Convention."

ENDNOTES

4 *Evening Telegram*, 10 May 1947.
5 *The Times*, 14 Jan. 1944.
6 The *Daily News* claimed that "we should not seek financial aid at all but we have every right to ask for reasonable economic assistance" (13 Dec. 1945).
7 On this point, see Webb, "Newfoundland's National Convention," 70–80.
8 Hiller and Harrington, eds., *Reports and Papers*, 451–56. See also Robert Holland, "Newfoundland and the Pattern of British Decolonization," *Newfoundland Studies* 14, no. 2 (1998): 141–53; and McCann, "British Policy and Confederation."
9 Hiller and Harrington, eds., *Reports and Papers*, 451–56.
10 *Evening Telegram*, 13 May 1947.
11 Smallwood to St. Laurent, 21 Mar. 1947, in Bridle, ed., *Documents on Relations Between Canada and Newfoundland*, vol. 2, 414–15.
12 On the London visit, see *Evening Telegram*, 12 and 14 May 1947; and Roberts, ed., *Peter Cashin: My Fight for Newfoundland*. Their hopes and disappointments have been told in two sympathetic accounts: Walsh, *More than a Poor Majority*, 136–50; and Malone, *Don't Tell the Newfoundlanders*, 109–27.
13 *Evening Telegram*, 10 May 1947.
14 Hiller and Harrington, eds., *Reports and Papers*, 500–03.
15 More research is needed on Lord Addison's role in this period. See Catalogue of the Papers of Viscount Addison, Department of Special Collections, Bodleian Library, Oxford, http://www.bodley.ox.ac.uk/dept/scwmss/wmss/online/modern/addison/addison.html.
16 Hiller and Harrington, eds., *Reports and Papers*, 500–03.
17 Webb, "Newfoundland's National Convention," 91–92. See also *Evening Telegram*, 20 May 1947; Report of the Public Relations Officer of the Convention Proceedings for 19, 20, 21, and 22 May 1947 (GN1.3.A, box 287, file 449/46 "National Convention, May–October 1947"); and Hiller and Harrington, eds., *Reports and Papers*, 527–35.
18 *Evening Herald* (Dublin), 21 May 1947.
19 Indeed, Bradley was quoted in the British press as predicting that he saw a swing in Newfoundland sentiment moving towards Confederation, especially if Ottawa's terms were favourable once a Newfoundland delegation went to the Canadian capital. See *Evening Telegram*, 8 May 1947.
20 *Evening Telegram*, 8 and 9 May 1947.
21 Hiller and Harrington, eds., *Debates*, 550–53; and *Evening Telegram*, 12, 13, 20, and 21 May 1947.
22 Neary, *Newfoundland in the North Atlantic World*, 248.
23 Excerpt from British House of Commons, 11 Dec. 1945, 210–11 (RPA, GN1.3.A, box 269, file 352/45, "Reports—House of Commons, Official").
24 Quoted in Neary, *Newfoundland in the North Atlantic World*, 244. For the number of persons and expenditures on relief, see Appendix C, Table 8, of the "Report on the Financial and Economic Position of Newfoundland,"

25 *Irish Independent*, 3 Apr. 1947.
26 J.S. Macdonald to Honourable Secretary of State for External Affairs, 30 Mar. 1946 (LAC, Brooke Claxton Papers, MG 32 B5, vol. 114, file Newfoundland: Cables between Canada and High Commissioner for Canada in Newfoundland, 1945–1947 [file 2]).
27 MacKenzie, *Inside the Atlantic Triangle*, 172.
28 Cabinet Minutes, 12 Apr. 1944 (LAC, Privy Council Records, RG2).
29 MacKenzie, *Inside the Atlantic Triangle*, 169–70.
30 Diaries, 27 Sept. 1947 (LAC, W.L. Mackenzie King Papers).
31 For Labrador's potential value to Canada, see John E. FitzGerald, ed., *Newfoundland at the Crossroads: Documents on Confederation with Canada* (St. John's: Terra Nova Publishing, 2002), 29–40, 99–104.
32 *Evening Telegram*, 25 June 1947.
33 "Outline on Points to Be Considered in Connection with the Forthcoming Discussions with Newfoundland, 11 June 1947," prepared by J.S. Macdonald, High Commissioner for Canada (LAC, R.A. MacKay Papers, MG 30 E159, vol. 3, file Interdepartmental Committee on Canada-Newfoundland Relations: General Correspondence and Memoranda, May 1947–48).
34 Hiller, "The Career of F. Gordon Bradley," *Newfoundland Studies* 4, no. 2 (1988): 165.
35 Quoted in Neary, *Newfoundland in the North Atlantic World*, 304.
36 Cabinet Conclusions, 19 June 1947 (LAC, Privy Council Records, RG2, Series A-5a, vol. 2640); and *Evening Telegram*, 26 June 1947.
37 "General Correspondence and Departmental Memoranda, Part I: March–November, 1946, Despatch no. 585 of November 27th 1946 from the High Commissioner for Canada in St. John's, Newfoundland" (LAC, R.A. MacKay Papers, MG 30 E159, vol. 2, file I.C.C.N.R.); and *Evening Telegram*, 26 Nov. 1946.
38 Bridle, ed., *Documents on Relations Between Canada and Newfoundland*, vol. 2, Part 1, Minutes of a Meeting between the Delegation to Ottawa from the National Convention of Newfoundland and Representatives of the Government of Canada, 25 June 1947, 522–29; and Minutes of Meetings 25/08/48–16/09/48 (ASC, Coll-075, box 300, file 4.01.005, Newfoundland Delegation).
39 "Some Notes on the Constitution and Government of Canada and the Canadian Federal System," 23, 41 (ASC, Coll-075, box 299, file 4.01.004, Newfoundland Delegation, 1947).
40 Ira Wild to R.A. MacKay, 18 July 1946 (LAC, R.A. MacKay Papers, MG 30 E159, vol. 2, file I.C.C.N.R. General Correspondence and Departmental Memoranda, Part I: March–November, 1946).
41 J.S. Macdonald to MacKay, 20 Aug. 1946, and Macdonald to MacKay, 9 Apr. 1946 (LAC, R.A. MacKay Papers, MG 30 E159, vol. 2, file I.C.C.N.R, General

Correspondence and Departmental Memoranda, Part I: March–November, 1946).
42 Memorandum, Baldwin to St. Laurent, 11 July 1947 (LAC, St. Laurent Papers MG26 L253, vol. 19, file 100–08).
43 Cabinet Conclusions, 18 July 1947 (LAC, Privy Council Records, RG2, Series A-5a, vol. 2640); and MacKenzie, *Inside the Atlantic Triangle*, 188.
44 Gerald H. Warring to J.S. Currie, 12 July 1947 (RPA, MG955, 1000–2000 Series, box 9, 1090 file 13, "Confederation 1947").
45 For a discussion of post-Confederation relations, see Blake, *Lions and Jellyfish*.
46 Webb, "Newfoundland's National Convention," 99.
47 For an excellent discussion of the Maritime reaction to the union of Newfoundland with Canada, see Slumkoski, *Inventing Atlantic Canada*; and for Premier Macdonald, see T. Stephen Henderson, *Angus L. Macdonald: A Provincial Liberal* (Toronto: University of Toronto Press, 2007).
48 J.W. Pickersgill, *Mackenzie King Record*, vol. 4, 1947–1948 (Toronto: University of Toronto Press, 1970), 76–80.
49 *Evening Telegram*, 19 July 1947.
50 *Evening Telegram*, 17, 18, and 19 July 1947.
51 *Evening Telegram*, 19 and 21 July 1947; and *Observer's Weekly*, 11 Feb. 1947.
52 *Evening Telegram*, 24 July 1947.
53 *Evening Telegram*, 9 Sept. 1947; and Walwyn telegram to Bradley, 17 July 1947, and Bradley to Walwyn, 17 July 1947 (RPA, GN1.3.A, box 287, file 449/46, "National Convention, May–October 1947").
54 *Evening Telegram*, 10 and 13 Sept. 1947; J.S. Macdonald to Department of External Affairs and attachments (LAC, MacKay Papers, MG 30 E159, vol. 3, file Newfoundland, Despatches and Memos, Oct. 46–Sept. 47); and Neary, *Newfoundland in the North Atlantic World*, 306.
55 "Basis for the Admission of Newfoundland as a Province of Canada," prepared on 23 Sept. 1947, 12 (LAC, R.A. MacKay Papers, MG 30 E159, vol. 5, file Draft Committee Meetings, Rough Drafts of Proposals, 1947 [2 of 2]); and *Evening Telegram*, 30 Sept. and 2 Oct. 1947.
56 Pickersgill, *Mackenzie King Record*, vol. 4, 81.
57 Minutes of Newfoundland-Canada Discussions, Meeting, 13 Sept. 1947 (LAC, R.A. MacKay Papers, MG 30 E159, vol. 5, file Committee Reports Submitted to Newfoundland National Convention, 1946–47).
58 *Evening Telegram*, 4 Oct. 1947.
59 Cabinet Conclusions, 28 Oct. 1947 (LAC, Privy Council Records, RG2, Series A-5-a, vol. 2641).
60 Bridle, ed., *Documents*, vol. 2, Part 1, Prime Minister King to Governor of Newfoundland, 29 Oct. 1947, 682. The proposed arrangements were included in the correspondence.
61 *Evening Telegram*, 11 Oct. 1947.
62 Smallwood, *I Chose Canada*, 416–17.
63 Quoted in Neary, *Newfoundland in the North Atlantic World*, 310.

64 Francis G. Hollohan and Melvin Baker, eds., *A Clear Head in Tempestuous Times: Albert B. Perlin, The Wayfarer. Observations on the National Convention and the Confederation Issue 1946–1949* (St. John's: Harry Cuff Publications, 1986), 75–76.
65 Smallwood, *I Chose Canada*, 278.
66 Blake, *Canadians at Last*, 18.
67 Bridle, ed., *Documents on Relations Between Canada and Newfoundland*, vol. 2, Part 1, 526 and 528.
68 See Webb, *The Voice of Newfoundland*; and Darrell Varga, "Radio and the Invention of Newfoundland," *Acadiensis* 38, no. 2 (Summer/Autumn 2009): 168–71.
69 Hiller and Harrington, eds., *Debates*, 1187.
70 Hiller and Harrington, eds., *Debates*, 811 and 1064–65.
71 High Commissioner in Newfoundland to Secretary of State for External Affairs, 10 Nov. 1947, in Bridle, ed., *Documents on Relations Between Canada and Newfoundland*, vol. 2, Part 2, 734–35.
72 *Evening Telegram*, 6 Jan. 1948; and Webb, "Newfoundland's National Convention," 127.
73 Smallwood, *I Chose Canada*, 278; and J.B. McEvoy to Secretary of State for Commonwealth Relations, 29 Jan. 1948, and Minutes of the National Convention, 22 Jan. 1948 (RPA, GN1.3.A, box 287, file 1/48 "National Convention").
74 *Evening Telegram*, 20 Jan. 1948.
75 Hiller and Harrington, eds., *Debates*, 1358.
76 Hiller and Harrington, eds., *Debates*, 1363–43.
77 Hiller and Harrington, eds., *Debates*, 1370.
78 Webb, "Newfoundland's National Convention," 134.
79 *Evening Telegram*, 28 Jan. 1948.
80 J.B. McEvoy, Chairman, to W.G. Warren, Secretary, 29 Jan. 1948 (RPA, GN1.3.A, box 287, file 1/48 "National Convention"); and *Evening Telegram*, 30 and 31 Jan. 1948.
81 J.S. Macdonald to Louis St. Laurent, 2 and 4 Feb. 1948 (LAC, R.A. MacKay Papers, MG 30 E159, vol. 3, file Interdepartmental Committee on Canada-Newfoundland Relations: General Correspondence and Memoranda, May 1947–48); and J.R. Smallwood to W.J. Carew, 14 Feb. 1948 (RPA, GN1.3.A, box 287, file 1/48 "National Convention").
82 Canada, *House of Commons Debates*, 30 Jan. 1948.
83 Noel-Baker to Macdonald, 2 Mar. 1948, published in the *Evening Telegram*, 11 Mar. 1948, and *Observer's Weekly*, 16 Mar. 1948.

CHAPTER 7

1 See David Sorensen, "The Economic Union with America Party and the Referenda of 1948" (MA thesis, Memorial University, 2004); and Donald C.

ENDNOTES

Jamieson, "I Saw the Fight for Confederation," in *The Book of Newfoundland*, vol. 3, ed. Joseph R. Smallwood, 70–104.

2   Quoted in Donald Jamieson, *No Place for Fools: The Political Memoirs of Don Jamieson* (St. John's: Breakwater, 1989), 87–92 and 124–25.

3   "Burin," report by G.C. Jenkins, 2 Dec. 1947 (RPA, GN 38/S-2-5-2, file 7); and Webb, "Newfoundland's National Convention," 138. On the Rangers' activities in this period, see Tuck, "The Newfoundland Ranger Force, 1935–1950," 98–105.

4   "St. Anthony," report by S.M. Christian, 8 Dec. 1947 (RPA, GN 38/S-2-5-2, file 44).

5   Webb, "Newfoundland's National Convention," 138–39.

6   Quoted in Webb, "The Responsible Government League," 205; and *Observer's Weekly*, 11 Feb. 1947.

7   Webb, "The Responsible Government League," 205.

8   *Evening Telegram*, 21 July 1947; and *Observer's Weekly*, 22 July 1947.

9   Although Karen Stanbridge does not consider the wider notions of social citizenship in Newfoundland in the late 1940s, she notes that "advocates for Responsible Government failed to utilise the prevailing discourse surrounding the child and nation-state in their framing efforts." See "Framing Children in the Newfoundland Confederation Debate, 1948," 177–201.

10 Speech by J.S. Currie, 14 Feb. 1948 (ASC, Coll-087, box 19, file 3.01.032).

11 *Independent*, 29 Apr. 1948.

12 Radio speech by F.W. Marshall, Dominion President of the Great War Veterans' Association, 5 May 1948 (ASC, Coll-087, box 19, file 3.01.033).

13 Radio speech by Frank Fogwill, 6 Mar. 1948 (ASC, Coll-087, box 19, file 3.01.033).

14 The Responsible Government League, *The Case for Responsible Government* (pamphlet published by Responsible Government League, St. John's, 1949; copy in Centre for Newfoundland Studies, Memorial University).

15 *Independent*, 29 Mar. 1948.

16 Broadcast speech by A.B. Butt, 10 Apr. 1948 (ASC, Coll-087, box 19, file 3.01.033).

17 Speech by J.S. Currie, 14 Feb. 1948 (ASC, Coll-087, box 19, file 3.01.032); broadcast speech by A.B. Butt, 10 Apr. 1948; radio speech by F.W. Marshall, Dominion President of the Great War Veterans' Association, 5 May 1948; and radio speech by Frank Fogwill, 6 Mar. 1948 (file 3.01.033).

18 On this point, see T.H. Marshall, *Citizenship and Social Class, and Other Essays*; and for the Canadian situation, see Blake, *From Rights to Needs*.

19 *Daily News*, 2 Mar. 1943.

20 *Daily News*, 13 Aug. 1943.

21 *Daily News*, 19 Feb. 1944.

22 Webb, "Newfoundland's National Convention," 112–14.

23 Webb, "Newfoundland's National Convention," 133.

24 Quoted in FitzGerald, "The Confederation of Newfoundland with Canada, 1946–49," 236; and William J. Browne, *Eighty-Four Years a Newfoundlander: Memoirs*, vol. 1, *1897–1949* (St. John's: Dicks, 1981), 300–01.

25 This was also a view sometimes expressed by Newfoundland governors to officials at the Dominions Office. In 1923, for example, in commenting on the re-election of Prime Minister Squires, Governor Allardyce wrote that "for weeks prior to a General Election it appears to be the practice in Newfoundland for the newspapers of both parties to carry on a campaign of personal invective and abuse such as I have not met with in any other part of the world. The characters of the various political candidates are, with few exceptions, subject to the most poisonous misrepresentation and actions for libel are not infrequent." (Allardyce to the Duke of Devonshire, 2 Apr. 1923, 83 [CO 532/237]).

26 Quoted in Webb, "The Responsible Government League," 208.

27 On the Newfoundland referendum and the Responsible Government League, see Webb, "The Responsible Government League," 204–20; and FitzGerald, "The Confederation of Newfoundland with Canada, 1946–49."

28 Bridle, ed., *Documents on Relations Between Canada and Newfoundland*, vol. 2, Part 1, 366–67.

29 Webb, "The Responsible Government League," 206.

30 Collins to Herbert B. Morgan, 29 Dec. 1947 (ASC, Coll-087, file 3.01.020). See also Webb, "The National Convention," 125–26.

31 Webb, "The National Convention," 142–43.

32 Quoted in Webb, "The Responsible Government League," 209.

33 Quoted in Webb, "The Responsible Government League," 209–10.

34 Webb, "The Responsible Government League," 212; and FitzGerald, "The Confederation of Newfoundland with Canada, 1946–49," 145.

35 FitzGerald, "The Confederation of Newfoundland with Canada, 1946–49," 177–78.

36 Quoted in Jamieson, *No Place for Fools*, 90.

37 Quoted in Webb, "The Responsible Government League," 212.

38 For a discussion of the Confederate campaign, see Smallwood, *I Chose Canada*, 285–324; Gwyn, *Smallwood*, 96–124; and Harold Horwood, *Joey: The Life and Political Times of Joey Smallwood* (Toronto: Stoddart, 1989), 72–144.

39 On this general idea, see Karl Polanyi, *The Great Transformation: The Political and Economic Origins of Our Times* (Boston: Beacon Press, 2001, reprint of 1944 edition).

40 *Confederate*, 14 Apr. 1948.

41 Peter Neary, *The Political Economy of Newfoundland, 1929–1972* (Toronto: Copp Clark, 1973), 140–41, original emphasis.

42 Gwyn, *Smallwood*, 98. See also Stanbridge, "Framing Children in the Newfoundland Confederation Debate, 1948," 177–201, which examines the place of children in political debate and in the Newfoundland referenda more generally.

ENDNOTES

43   *Confederate*, 20 May 1948, original emphasis.
44   On the role of women on the American bases, see High, "Working for Uncle Sam," 90–91.
45   *Independent*, 22 Mar. 1948.
46   Gwyn, *Smallwood*, 98.
47   Newfoundland Confederate Association, "To the People of Lower Island Cove from C.F. Garland (Secretary Treasurer, Confederate Association), 29 May 1948," letter from Confederate Headquarters (ASC, Coll-075, box 299, file 4.01.001); and Speech, "Why I Favour Confederation," 6 Apr. and 23 Apr. 1948 (file 4.01.004).
48   FitzGerald, "The Confederation of Newfoundland with Canada, 1946–49," 158–59.
49   Newfoundland Confederate Association, "To the People of Lower Island Cove from C.F. Garland (Secretary Treasurer, Confederate Association), 29 May 1948," letter from Confederate headquarters (ASC, Coll-075, box 299, file 4.01.001). He also wrote many letters to the press extolling the benefits of Canada's social welfare programs. See his letter in the *Fishermen's Advocate*, 9 Jan. 1948, for example, where he outlined how residents in the Bonavista area could gain by the Canadian family allowance and old age pension programs. Catalina, with two hundred children under the age of sixteen years, would receive a monthly total of $1,200. Its twenty-four senior citizens would receive a monthly total of $1,020.
50   Speech, "Why I Favour Confederation," 6 Apr. and 23 Apr. 1948 (ASC, Coll-075, file 4.01.004).
51   Scammell letter in the *Fishermen's Advocate*, 21 May 1948.
52   Some of the ideas here come from reading Mitchell Cohen, "T.H. Marshall's 'Citizenship and Social Class,'" *Dissent Magazine* 57, no. 4 (Fall 2010): 81–85. Available at https://www.dissentmagazine.org/article/t-h-marshalls-citizenship-and-social-class.
53   One account of the second referendum is FitzGerald, "The Confederation of Newfoundland with Canada, 1946–49." It contends that sectarianism was the dominant factor in the outcome.
54   O'Flaherty, *Leaving the Past Behind*, 193–98.
55   Webb, "The Responsible Government League," 204; and Neary, *Newfoundland in the North Atlantic World*, 321–25.
56   Webb, "The Responsible Government League," 204.
57   *Daily News*, 23 July 1948.
58   *The Ensign*, 11 Dec. 1948, article by Most Rev. J.M. O'Neill, "Not-So-Forgotten Land," 9 and 33. *The Ensign* was a lay Catholic weekly published in Montreal, 1948–56. A few days later, on 15 Dec. 1948, the lead editorial in *Le Droit*, a French-language newspaper in Ottawa, established and owned by the Missionary Oblates of Mary Immaculate, echoed Bishop O'Neill's sentiments: "Nous serons heureux d'accueillir Terre-Neuve comme dixième

province, lorsqu'elle en manifestera librement et dèmocratiquement le dèsir. Mais jamais nous ne saurions approuver les mèthodes hitlériennes et soviétiques auxquelles on a eu recours jusqu'á présent. Il n'y a qu'une morale internationale. Il faut en respecter les principes dans tous ses actes."

59 *Daily News*, 17 Nov. 1948.
60 *Evening Telegram*, 31 July 1948; and RPA, GN1.3.A, box 287, file 1/48, "National Convention," for a copy of King's statement dated 30 July 1948.
61 The minutes for those meetings are available at Newfoundland Delegation, Minutes of Meetings, 25/08/48–16/09/48 (ASC, Coll-075, file 4.01.005), and RPA, GN154.1.
62 See Raymond B. Blake, "Canada, Newfoundland, and Term 29: The Failure of Intergovernmentalism," *Acadiensis* 41, no. 1 (Winter/Spring, 2012): 49–74.
63 For a detailed discussion, see Blake, *Lions or Jellyfish*.
64 Minutes, 25 Aug. 1948 (RPA, GN154.1, Minutes, 25 Aug.–24 Sept. 1948).
65 Minutes, 25 Aug. 1948 (RPA, GN154.1, Minutes, 25 Aug.–24 Sept. 1948); and Blake, *Canadians at Last*, 25.
66 Minutes, 28 Aug. 1948 (RPA, GN154.1, Minutes, 25 Aug.–24 Sept. 1948).
67 Minutes, 28 Aug. 1948 (RPA, GN154.1, Minutes, 25 Aug.–24 Sept. 1948).
68 Minutes, 28 Aug. 1948 (RPA, GN154.1, Minutes, 25 Aug.–24 Sept. 1948).
69 Memorandum submitted by the Newfoundland Delegation, Oct. 1948 (RPA, GN154.38).
70 Memorandum submitted by the Newfoundland Delegation, Oct. 1948 (RPA, GN154.38).
71 "Newfoundland—Progress Report," prepared in Privy Council Office, 31 Aug. 1948; and letter from Paul Pelletier, Secretary, Interdepartmental Committee on Newfoundland, 12 Oct. 1948 (LAC, R.A. MacKay Papers, MG 30 E159, vol. 3, file I.C.C.N.R.: Minutes and Correspondence, 1948–49).
72 Confederation with Canada, Memorandum for Commission, prepared by A.J. Walsh, 24 Jan. 1949, 1–2 (RPA, GN158.103, Department of Finance Records).
73 See J. Murray Beck, *Joseph Howe*, vol. 2, *The Briton Becomes Canadian, 1848–1873* (Montreal and Kingston: McGill-Queen's University Press, 1983), 248–50.
74 Blake, *Canadians at Last*, 29–30.
75 Mitchell Sharp, *Which Reminds Me . . . A Memoir* (Toronto: University of Toronto Press, 1994), 33.
76 J.G. Channing, *The Effects of Transition to Confederation on Public Administration in Newfoundland* (Toronto: Institute of Public Administration of Canada, 1982), 42.
77 Blake, *Canadians at Last*, 29–30.
78 Channing, *The Effects of Transition to Confederation*, 42–43; and Blake, *Canadians at Last*, 28–36.

ENDNOTES

79 "National Convention—Confederation," Crosbie to Albert Walsh, 9 Dec. 1948 (RPA, GN1.3.A, box 287, file 1/48); and *Evening Telegram*, 10 Dec. 1948. In accepting his appointment to the delegation, Crosbie had made it known that he would not sign if he felt the terms were not in the best interests of Newfoundlanders. See *Daily News*, 11 Dec. 1948.
80 Blake, *Canadians at Last*, 37.
81 Smallwood, *I Chose Canada*, 320.
82 Blake, *Lions or Jellyfish*, 21.
83 David MacKenzie, "The Indian Act and the Aboriginal Peoples of Newfoundland at the Time of Confederation," *Newfoundland and Labrador Studies* 25, no. 2 (2010): 163.
84 Hiller and Harrington, eds., *Debates*, 808.
85 Quoted in MacKenzie, "The Indian Act and the Aboriginal Peoples of Newfoundland at the Time of Confederation," 172–73.
86 MacKenzie, "The Indian Act and the Aboriginal Peoples of Newfoundland at the Time of Confederation," 161–81; and Peter Neary, "The First Nations and the Entry of Newfoundland into Confederation, 1945–1954. Part 1," *Newfoundland Quarterly* 105, no. 2 (Fall 2012): 36–42.
87 Confederation with Canada, Memorandum for Commission, prepared by A.J. Walsh, 24 Jan. 1949 (RPA, GN158.103, Department of Finance Records).
88 David MacKenzie, "The Terms of Union in Historical Perspective," *Newfoundland Studies* 14, no. 2 (1998): 220–37. The only full-length treatment of this process and how Newfoundland was integrated into Canada is found in Blake, *Canadians at Last*.
89 Blake, *Canadians at Last*, 70–93.
90 Blake, *Canadians at Last*, 94–114.
91 Peter Neary, "Party Politics in Newfoundland, 1949–71: A Survey and Analysis," in Hiller and Neary, *Newfoundland in the Nineteenth and Twentieth Centuries*, 232.
92 Blake, *Canadians at Last*, 177–84.
93 Quoted in Webb, "The Responsible Government League," 218.
94 Stephen May, "The Terms of Union: An Analysis of Their Current Relevance," in *Royal Commission on Renewing and Strengthening Our Place in Canada*, vol. 1, Research, (St. John's: Office of the Queen's Printer, 2003), 161.
95 CBC Radio broadcast, 1 Apr. 1949. See https://www.bac-lac.gc.ca/eng/discover/politics-government/canadian-confederation/Pages/newfoundland-labrador-1949.aspx#i; and Bridle, ed., *Documents on Relations Between Canada and Newfoundland*, vol. 2, 1675–89.
96 *Globe and Mail*, 1 Apr. 1949.
97 *Fishermen's Advocate*, 8 Apr. 1949.

CONCLUSION

1. *The Star Weekly*, 26 Mar. 1949.
2. Bridle, ed., *Documents on Relations Between Canada and Newfoundland*, vol. 2, 1675–89.
3. Royal Commission on Renewing and Strengthening Our Place in Canada, *Main Report: Our Place in Canada* (St. John's, Office of the Queen's Printer, 2003), 2, 8, 24–26.
4. Jamieson, *No Place for Fools*, 151.
5. David Coletto and Tim Powers, "NL residents recognize dire circumstances in province; Want political leadership," *Abacus Data*, 8 Feb. 2018, abacusdata.ca/nl-residents-recognize-dire-circumstances-in-province-want-political-leadership/.
6. Sarah Smellie, "Report Predicts Plummeting Population for Rural Newfoundland and Labrador," CBC News, 8 Sept. 2017, http://www.cbc.ca/news/canada/newfoundland-labrador/population-decline-newfoundland-labrador-harris-centre-report-1.4279580.
7. See Canada, Department of Finance, *Federal Support to Provinces and Territories*, Oct. 2017, https://www.fin.gc.ca/access/fedprov-eng.asp#Major.

BIBLIOGRAPHY

PRIMARY SOURCES
Memorial University
Archives and Special Collections, Centre for Newfoundland Studies

GOVERNMENTS, ORGANIZATIONS, AND INSTITUTIONS

CO194, CO532/275, and DO35: Colonial Office and Dominions Office, Newfoundland correspondence, available on microfilm at the Centre for Newfoundland Studies [and also at the Rooms Provincial Archives].
Dominions Office No. 151, *Newfoundland Affairs, Correspondence and Papers, 1931–1933*, available at the Centre for Newfoundland Studies.
Memorial University, President's Office Records, Box PO-27, file "Carnegie Corporation (1958–65)," Report of the Newfoundland Archives for 1957–58.

PRIVATE PAPERS, ARCHIVES AND SPECIAL COLLECTIONS

Sir Robert Bond Papers, Coll-237
Sir William Coaker Papers, Coll-009
John Gilbert Higgins Papers, Coll-087
Joseph R. Smallwood Papers, Coll-075 and Coll-285
Helena Squires Papers, Coll-486
Richard Anderson Squires Papers, Coll-250
George H. Tucker Papers, Coll-213

Rooms Provincial Archives, Newfoundland and Labrador
RPA, GN9, Minutes of Executive Council
RPA, GN1.11, Governor's Files on the Labrador Boundary
RPA, GN1.1.7, Governor's Files
RPA, GN158.103, Department of Finance Records
RPA, MG220, John Sparrow David Thompson Papers
RPA, MG223, Reel 36, Robert Borden Papers

RPA, MG214, Sir Mackenzie Bowell Papers
RPA, MG271, A.B. Morine Papers
RPA, MG4, Baine Johnston & Co Records
RPA, MG8, Sir P.T. McGrath Papers
RPA, MG955, 1000–2000 Series
RPA, GB16, Newfoundland Royal Commission 1933
RPA, GN1.3.A, 1858–1949, General Correspondence of the Governor's Office
RPA, GN2.6, Colonial Office Correspondence with the Governor
RPA, GN2.5, Colonial Secretary Office Correspondence
RPA, GN13.1.B, Department of Justice
RPA, GN154, Newfoundland Delegation to Ottawa (1948)
RPA, GN38/S-2-5-2, Newfoundland Ranger Force Reports
RPA, GN8, Office of the Prime Minister
RPA, MG73, Newfoundland Board of Trade Papers
RPA, GN1.15, Local Correspondence of the Governor's Office, Newfoundland

Library and Archives Canada
Governor General's Files, RG7
W.L. Mackenzie King Papers, MG26 J1 and Series J4
Brooke Claxton Papers, MG32 B5
R.A. MacKay Papers, MG30 E159
Privy Council Records, RG2
Louis St. Laurent Papers, MG26 L253
C.A. Magrath Papers, MG30, E82

Roman Catholic Archdiocesan Archives of St. John's
Reid Newfoundland Correspondences

Newspapers

Belfast Newsletter	Globe and Mail	Royal Gazette
Courier	Irish Examiner	St. John's Daily Star
Daily Colonist	Irish Independent	The Confederate
Daily Mail and Advocate	Le Droit	The Ensign
Daily News	Mail and Advocate	The Express
Evening Advocate	Montreal Gazette	The Gazette
Evening Chronicle	Montreal Herald	The Independent
Evening Herald (Dublin)	Morning Chronicle	The Monitor
Evening Herald (St. John's)	Nation	The Star Weekly
	Newfoundland Weekly	The Times
Evening Telegram	Newfoundlander	Twillingate Sun
Fishermen's Advocate	Observer's Weekly	Western Star
Free Press	Public Ledger	

BIBLIOGRAPHY

Published Primary Sources and Websites

1892 Correspondence respecting the Admission of Newfoundland into the Dominion of Canada. Copy available in the Centre for Newfoundland Studies, Memorial University.

Bridle, Paul, ed. *Documents on Relations Between Canada and Newfoundland*, vol. 2, *Confederation, Parts 1 and 2.* Ottawa: Minister of Supply and Services Canada, 1984.

Canada. *House of Commons Debates.*

Canada. *Senate Debates.*

Catalogue of the Papers of Christopher Addison, 1st Viscount Addison (1869–1951). Compiled by Hannah Lowery. Department of Special Collections, Bodleian Library, 1999. http://www.bodley.ox.ac.uk/dept/scwmss/wmss/online/modern/addison/addison.html.

Doyle, Gerald S. *Old-Time Songs and Poetry of Newfoundland.* St. John's: Gerald S. Doyle, 1940.

Fishermen's Protective Union. Wikipedia. 12 July 2018. https://en.wikipedia.org/wiki/Fishermen%27s_Protective_Union.

Heritage Newfoundland and Labrador. 2018. http://www.heritage.nf.ca/.

Hiller, James K., ed. *The Confederation Issue in Newfoundland, 1864–1869. Selected Documents.* St. John's: Memorial University of Newfoundland, Oct. 1974.

Hiller, James K., and Michael F. Harrington, eds. *The Newfoundland National Convention, 1946–1948*, vols. 1 and 2, *Debates* and *Reports and Papers.* Montreal and Kingston: McGill-Queen's University Press, 1995.

In the Privy Council, in the Matter of the Boundary between the Dominion of Canada and the Colony of Newfoundland in the Labrador Peninsula, vols. 1 and 2 of Joint Appendix, available at http://www.heritage.nf.ca/articles/politics/privy-council-introduction.php.

Ireland's Eye in Newfoundland and Labrador: Thomas Talbot's Letter to a Friend in Ireland (1882), edited by Melvin Baker, Christopher P. Curran, John Joy, and Robin McGrath. St. John's: Law Society of Newfoundland and Labrador, 2009. Reprint of 1882 edition.

Journals and Appendices of the House of Assembly of Newfoundland.

Manifesto of the Right Hon. Sir Robert Bond, P.C., K.C.M.G., Premier, 1908. St. John's, 1908.

Newfoundland. *Report by the Commission of Government on the Unemployment Situation May 1935*, Cmd. 4910. London: His Majesty's Stationery Office, 1935.

Newfoundland Royal Commission 1933. *Report* (Cmd. 4480, 1933).

The North Atlantic Coast Fisheries Case (Great Britain, United States) (1910), vol. 11 of *Reports of International Arbitral Awards / Recueil des sentences arbitrales*, 167–226.

Pope, J., ed. *Correspondence of Sir John Macdonald.* Toronto: Doubleday, Page, 1921.

———. *Memoirs of the Right Honourable Sir John Alexander Macdonald*, vol. 2. London: Edward Arnold, 1894.

Proceedings of the House of Assembly and Legislative Council, 1909–1931.

Responsible Government League. *The Case for Responsible Government.* Pamphlet published by Responsible Government League, St. John's, 1949; copy in Centre for Newfoundland Studies.

Statutes of Newfoundland.

Text of the Report of the Privy Council on the Labrador Boundary Dispute. Great Britain. Privy Council. Judicial Committee. St. John's: Robinson, 1927.

United Kingdom. *House of Commons Debates.*

Waite, P.B., ed. *Canadian Historical Document Series*, vol. 2, *Pre-Confederation*. Scarborough, ON: Prentice-Hall, 1965.

SECONDARY SOURCES

Ajzenstat, Janet. *The Canadian Founding: John Locke and Parliament.* Montreal and Kingston: McGill-Queen's University Press, 2007.

Alexander, David. "Literacy and Economic Development in Nineteenth-Century Newfoundland." In *Atlantic Canada and Confederation: Essays in Canadian Political Economy*. Compiled by Eric Sager, Lewis R. Fischer, and Stuart O. Pierson, 110–43. Toronto: University of Toronto Press, 1983.

———. "Newfoundland's Traditional Economy and Development to 1934." *Acadiensis* 5, no. 2 (Spring 1976): 56–78.

Anders Sandberg, L. "Dickie, Alfred." In *Dictionary of Canadian Biography* 15. University of Toronto/Université Laval, 2005. http://www.biographi.ca/en/bio/dickie_alfred_15E.html.

Baker, Melvin. *Aspects of Nineteenth Century St. John's Municipal History.* St. John's: Harry Cuff Publications, 1982.

———. "Baird, James." In *Dictionary of Canadian Biography* 14. University of Toronto/Université Laval, 1998. http://www.biographi.ca/en/bio/baird_james_14E.html.

———. "Challenging the 'Merchants' Domain': William Coaker and the Price of Fish, 1908–1919." *Newfoundland and Labrador Studies* 29, no. 2 (Fall 2014): 189–226.

———. "Crosbie, Sir John Chalker." In *Dictionary of Canadian Biography* 16. University of Toronto/Université Laval, 2016. http://www.biographi.ca/en/bio/crosbie_john_chalker_16E.html.

———. "Crowe, Harry Judson." In *Dictionary of Canadian Biography* 15. University of Toronto/Université Laval, 2005. http://www.biographi.ca/en/bio/crowe_harry_judson_15E.html.

———, ed. *Dear Friends: Coaker's Circular Letters to Councils, 1909–1927.* Unpublished manuscript, 2014. Circular Letter #3 for 9 Feb. 1923.

———. "Falling into the Canadian Lap: The Confederation of Newfoundland and Canada, 1945–1949." In *Royal Commission on Renewing and Strengthening Our Place in Canada*. Research, vol. 1. St. John's: Office of the Queen's Printer, 2003: 29–88.

———. "The Government of St. John's, Newfoundland, 1800–1921." PhD thesis, University of Western Ontario, 1981.

———. "Harvey, Augustus William." In *Dictionary of Canadian Biography* 13. University of Toronto/Université Laval, 1994. http://www.biographi.ca/en/bio/harvey_augustus_william_13E.html.
———. "J.R. Smallwood—Labour and Socialist Leader." *Newfoundland Quarterly* 93, no. 1 (Fall 1999): 23–28.
———. "Plaindealing and the Fishermen's Protective Union, 1908–1910." *Newfoundland Quarterly* 105, no. 4 (Spring 2013): 43–51.
———. "The Rejection of Confederation with Canada, 1865–1874." 1994. http://www.ucs.mun.ca/~melbaker/1860S.htm.
———. "Repatriated Newfoundlanders from the American Expeditionary Forces." *The Newfoundland Ancestor* 30, no. 3 (Fall 2014): 98–101.
———. "The Rise of the Fishermen's Protective Union, the First World War and the National Government, 1908–1919." 1994. http://www.ucs.mun.ca/~melbaker/fpuhis.html.
———. "The Struggle for Influence and Power: William Coaker, Abram Kean, and the Newfoundland Sealing Industry, 1908–1915." *Newfoundland and Labrador Studies* 28, no. 1 (Spring 2013): 63–96.
Baker, Melvin, and Janet Miller Pitt. "Jack Turner." *Newfoundland Quarterly* 90, no. 2 (Spring 1996): 24.
Baker, Melvin, and Peter Neary. "Document: Governor Sir Humphrey Walwyn's Account of His Meetings with Churchill and Roosevelt, Placentia Bay, Newfoundland, August 1941." *Newfoundland and Labrador Studies* 31, no. 1 (2016): 165–80.
———. " 'Pigs Is My Business': Joey Smallwood on Himself, 1945." *Newfoundland and Labrador Studies* 28, no. 1 (Spring 2013): 117–34.
———. "P.T. McGrath's 1918 Account of 'Newfoundland's Part in the Great War.' " *Newfoundland and Labrador Studies* 29, no. 2 (2014): 272–302.
———. "Sir Robert Bond (1857–1927): A Biographical Sketch." *Newfoundland Studies* 15, no. 1 (Spring 1999): 1–54.
Baker, Melvin, and James Overton. "Document: J.R. Smallwood on Liberalism in 1926." *Newfoundland Studies* 11, no. 1 (1995): 75–126.
Banégas, Richard. "Commodification of the Vote and Political Subjectivity in Africa: Reflections Based on the Case of Benin." In *Cultures of Voting: The Hidden History of the Secret Ballot*, edited by Romain Bertrand, Jean-Louis Briquet, and Peter Pels, 180–96. London: Hurst, 2007.
Bannister, Jerry. "The Campaign for Representative Government in Newfoundland," *Journal of the Canadian Historical Association*, vol. 5 (1994), 19–40.
———. " 'The Sport of Historic Misfortune': Judge Prowse and the Story of Newfoundland." In *Discourse and Discovery: Sir Richard Whitbourne Quatercentennial Symposium 1615–2015 and Beyond*, edited by Melvin Baker, Christopher P. Curran, and J. Derek Green, 263–314. St. John's: SS *Daisy* Legal History Committee, Law Society of Newfoundland and Labrador, 2017.
———. "Whigs and Nationalists: The Legacy of Judge Prowse's *History of Newfoundland*." *Acadiensis* 32, no. 1 (Autumn 2002): 84–109.

Banting, Keith. "Social Citizenship and the Multicultural Welfare State." In *Citizenship, Diversity, and Pluralism*, edited by Alan C. Cairns, John C. Courtney, Peter MacKinnon, Hans J. Michelmann, and David E. Smith, 108–36. Montreal and Kingston: McGill-Queen's University Press, 1999.

Beck, J. Murray. *Joseph Howe*, vol. 2, *The Briton Becomes Canadian, 1848–1873*. Montreal and Kingston: McGill-Queen's University Press, 1983.

Bencherki, Nicolas, and Joelle Basque. "Why So Many Americans Continue to Believe in Donald Trump." *The Conversation* (Canada), 6 Aug. 2018. https://theconversation.com/why-so-many-americans-continue-to-believe-in-donald-trump-100498.

Beveridge, Sir William. *Social Insurance and Allied Services*. London: King's Printer, 1942.

Bierschenk, Thomas, and Jean-Pierre Oliver de Sardan. "Studying the Dynamics of African Bureaucracies: An Introduction to States at Work." In *States at Work: Dynamics of African Bureaucracies*, edited by Thomas Bierschenk and Jean-Pierre Olivier de Sardan, 3–32. Leiden, Netherlands: Brill, 2004.

Biggar, E.B., ed. *Canada: A Memorial Volume: A Statistical and Descriptive Handbook of the Dominion*. London: Edward Stanford, 1889.

Bishop-Stirling, Terry. " 'Such Sights One Will Never Forget': Newfoundland Women and Overseas Nursing in the First World War." In *A Sisterhood of Suffering and Service: Women and Girls of Canada and Newfoundland during the First World War*, edited by Sarah Glassford and Amy J. Shaw, 126–47. Vancouver: UBC Press, 2012.

Blake, Raymond B. "Canada, Newfoundland, and Term 29: The Failure of Intergovernmentalism." *Acadiensis* 41, no. 1 (Winter/Spring 2012): 49–74.

———. *Canadians at Last: Canada Integrates Newfoundland as a Province*. Toronto: University of Toronto Press, 2004.

———. *From Rights to Needs: A History of Family Allowances in Canada, 1929–92*. Vancouver: UBC Press, 2009.

———. *Lions or Jellyfish: Newfoundland-Ottawa Relations since 1957*. Toronto: University of Toronto Press, 2015.

———. "Newfoundland's Search for Citizenship: The Confederation Debates, 1948." Paper presented to the Atlantic Studies Conference, Mount Allison University, May 2016.

———. "WLMK's Attitude towards Newfoundland's Entry into Confederation." *Newfoundland Quarterly* 82, no. 4 (Spring 1987): 26–37.

Bond, Fraser. "The Confederation Scheme that Failed." In Smallwood, *The Book of Newfoundland*, vol. 5, 163–68.

Brams, Steven J., and Peter C. Fishburn. "Yes-No Voting." *Social Choice and Welfare* 10, no. 1 (1993): 35–50.

Brodie, Janine. "Citizenship and Solidarity: Reflections on the Canadian Way." *Citizenship Studies* 6, no. 4 (2002): 377–94.

Browne, William J. *Eighty-Four Years a Newfoundlander: Memoirs of William J. Browne*, vol. 1, *1897–1949*. St. John's: Dicks, 1981.

Buckner, Phillip. "Beware the Canadian Wolf: The Maritimes and Confederation." *Acadiensis* 46, no. 2 (Summer/Autumn 2017): 177–95.
———. "CHR Dialogue: The Maritimes and Confederation: A Reassessment." *Canadian Historical Review* 71, no. 1 (Mar. 1990): 1–45.
———. "The 1860s: An End and a Beginning." In *The Atlantic Region to Confederation: A History*, edited by Phillip Buckner and John G. Reid, 360–86. Toronto: University of Toronto Press, 1994.
———. "Tupper, Sir Charles." In *Dictionary of Canadian Biography* 14. University of Toronto/Université Laval, 1998. http://www.biographi.ca/en/bio/tupper_charles_14E.html.
Budgel, Richard, and Michael Staveley. *The Labrador Boundary*. Happy Valley–Goose Bay: Labrador Institute of Northern Studies, 1987.
Cadigan, Sean T. *Death on Two Fronts. National Tragedies and the Fate of Democracy in Newfoundland, 1914–34*. Toronto: Allen Lane, 2013.
———. *Newfoundland and Labrador: A History*. Toronto: University of Toronto Press, 2009.
Cadigan, Sean T., and Jeff Hutchings. "The Ecology of Expansion: The Case of the Labrador Fishery." Paper presented to the Canadian Historical Association Annual Meeting, St. John's, 1997.
Cashin, Peter. *My Life and Times, 1890–1919*, edited by R.E. Buehler. Portugal Cove: Breakwater, 1976.
———. *Peter Cashin: My Fight for Newfoundland*, edited by Edward Roberts. St. John's: Flanker Press, 2012.
Chadwick, St. John. *Newfoundland: Island into Province*. New York: Cambridge University Press, 1967.
Channing, J.G. *The Effects of Transition to Confederation on Public Administration in Newfoundland*. Toronto: Institute of Public Administration of Canada, 1982.
Chou, Mark. "Combatting Voter Ignorance: A Vertical Model of Epistocratic Voting." *Policy Studies* 38, no. 6 (2017): 589–603.
Coaker, W.F. *Past, Present and Future: Being a Series of Articles Contributed to the Fishermen's Advocate, 1932*. Port Union: Fishermen's Advocate, 1932.
———. ed., *Twenty Years of the Fishermen's Protective Union of Newfoundland*. St. John's: Creative Publishers, 1984. Reprint of 1930 edition.
Cohen, Mitchell. "T.H. Marshall's 'Citizenship and Social Class.'" *Dissent Magazine* 57, no. 4 (Fall 2010): 81–85.
Coletto, David, and Tim Powers. "NL residents recognize dire circumstances in province; Want political leadership." *Abacus Data*, 8 Feb. 2018, abacusdata.ca/nl-residents-recognize-dire-circumstances-in-province-want-political-leadership/.
Connors, William, ed. *The Best of the Barrelman, 1938–1940*. St. John's: Creative Publishers, 1998.
Crosbie, Barbara A. "Howley, Michael Francis." In *Dictionary of Canadian Biography* 14. University of Toronto/Université Laval, 1998. http://www.biographi.ca/en/bio/howley_michael_francis_14E.html.

Cuff, Robert. "Alfred Bishop Morine." In *Encyclopedia of Newfoundland and Labrador*, vol. 3, 619–21. St. John's: Harry Cuff Publications, 1991.

Cullum, Linda, and Marilyn Porter, eds. *Creating This Place: Women, Family, and Class in St. John's, 1900–1950*. Montreal and Kingston: McGill-Queen's University Press, 2014.

Davis, David J. "The Bond-Blaine Negotiations, 1890–1891." MA thesis, Memorial University, 1970.

Di Matteo, Livio. *A Federal Fiscal History: Canada, 1867–2017*. Toronto: The Fraser Institute, 2017. https://www.fraserinstitute.org/sites/default/files/federal-fiscal-history-canada-1867-2017.pdf.

Duley, Margot I. *Where Once Our Mothers Stood We Stand: Women's Suffrage in Newfoundland, 1890–1925*. Charlottetown: Gynergy Books, 1993.

Dummitt, Christopher. *Unbuttoned: A History of Mackenzie King's Secret Life*. Montreal and Kingston: McGill-Queen's University Press, 2017.

Eaton, Scott. "A 'Rugged, and, for the Most Part, a Barren Country': Nineteenth-Century Surveyors and the Characterization of Newfoundland's Interior." Paper presented to the Canadian Historical Association Annual Meeting, Regina, 2018.

Elliott, R.M. "Newfoundland Politics in the 1920s: The Genesis and Significance of the Hollis Walker Enquiry." In Hiller and Neary, *Newfoundland in the Nineteenth and Twentieth Centuries*, 181–204.

Encyclopedia of Newfoundland and Labrador, vols. 1 and 3. St. John's: Newfoundland Book, 1981 and 1991.

Esping-Andersen, Gøsta. *Three Worlds of Welfare Capitalism*. Princeton: Princeton University Press, 1990.

Facey-Crowther, David R., ed. *Lieutenant Owen William Steele of the Newfoundland Regiment*. Montreal and Kingston: McGill-Queen's University Press, 2002.

Fenwick, Peter. "Witnesses to the Lord: An Analysis of the Testimony presented to the Newfoundland Royal Commission 1933, Lord Amulree, Chairman." Paper submitted for Political Science 6610, Memorial University, 1994.

FitzGerald, John Edward. "The Confederation of Newfoundland with Canada, 1946–49." MA thesis, Memorial University, 1992.

——. "Conflict and Culture in Irish-Newfoundland Roman Catholicism, 1829–1850." PhD thesis, University of Ottawa, 1997.

——. " 'The True Father of Confederation'? Archbishop E.P. Roche, Term 17, and Newfoundland's Confederation with Canada." *Newfoundland Studies* 14, no. 2 (1998): 188–219.

——, ed. Newfoundland at the Crossroads: Documents on Confederation with Canada. St. John's: Terra Nova Publishing, 2002.

Fisher, Walter R. "Narration as a Human Communication Paradigm: The Case of Public Moral Argument." *Communication Monographs* 51, no. 1 (Mar. 1984): 1–22.

——. "Rhetorical Fiction and the Presidency." *Quarterly Journal of Speech* 6, no. 2 (Apr. 1980): 119–26.

———. "Romantic Democracy, Ronald Reagan, and Presidential Heroes." *Western Journal of Speech Communication* 46, no. 3 (Summer 1982): 299–310.
Forbes, E.R. "Newfoundland Politics in 1921: A Canadian View." *Acadiensis* 9, no. 1 (Fall 1979): 95–103.
Fraser, A.M. "Fishery Negotiations with the United States." In MacKay, *Newfoundland: Economic, Diplomatic, and Strategic Studies*, 333–410.
———. "The Hague Arbitration." In MacKay, *Newfoundland: Economic, Diplomatic, and Strategic Studies*, 400–10.
———. "The Labrador Boundary Dispute." In MacKay, *Newfoundland: Economic, Diplomatic, and Strategic Studies*, 460–84.
———. "Relations with Canada." In MacKay, *Newfoundland: Economic, Diplomatic, and Strategic Studies*, 411–43.
Frost, Sydney. *A Blue Puttee at War: The Memoir of Captain Sydney Frost, MC*, edited by Edward Roberts. St. John's: Flanker Press, 2014.
Gerber, Elisabeth. "Legislative Response to the Threat of Popular Initiatives." *American Journal of Political Science* 40, no. 1 (Feb. 1996): 99–128.
Gillespie, Bill. *A Class Act: An Illustrated History of the Labour Movement in Newfoundland & Labrador*. Portugal Cove–St. Philip's: Boulder Publications, 2016.
Gilmore, William C. "Law, Constitutional Convention, and the Union of Newfoundland and Canada." *Acadiensis* 18, no. 2 (Spring 1989): 111–26.
———. *Newfoundland and Dominion Status: The External Affairs Competence and International Law Status of Newfoundland, 1855–1934*. Toronto: Carswell, 1988.
Goren, Paul. *On Voter Competence*. New York: Oxford University Press, 2012.
Graham, Frank. *We Love Thee, Newfoundland: Biography of Sir Cavendish Boyle, Governor of Newfoundland, 1901–1904*. St. John's: Valhalla Press, 1979.
Grant, G.M. "Newfoundland and Canada." *The Canadian Magazine* 11 (1898): 466.
Gunn, Gertrude E. *The Political History of Newfoundland, 1832–1864*. Toronto: University of Toronto Press, 1966.
Gwyn, Richard. *Smallwood: The Unlikely Revolutionary*. Toronto: McClelland and Stewart, 1972.
Hale, David. "The Newfoundland Lesson." *International Economy* (Summer 2003): 52–61. http://www.international-economy.com/TIE_Su03_Hale.pdf.
Handcock, Gordon. "The Commission of Government's Land Settlement Scheme in Newfoundland." In *Twentieth-Century Newfoundland: Explorations*, edited by James K. Hiller and Peter Neary, 123–51. St. John's: Breakwater, 1994.
Harding, Robert. "Glorious Tragedy: Newfoundland's Cultural Memory of the Attack at Beaumont Hamel, 1916–1925." *Newfoundland and Labrador Studies* 21, no. 1 (2006): 3–40.
Harris, Michael. *Rare Ambition: The Crosbies of Newfoundland*. Toronto: Viking, 1992.
Hart, Anne. "Knowling, Fannie (McNeil)." In *Dictionary of Canadian Biography* 15. University of Toronto/Université Laval, 2005. http://www.biographi.ca/en/bio/knowling_fannie_15E.html.

Haworth, Kent M. "Musgrave, Sir Anthony." In *Dictionary of Canadian Biography* 11. University of Toronto/Université Laval, 1982. http://www.biographi.ca/en/bio/musgrave_anthony_11E.html.

Heaman, Elsbeth. *Tax, Order, and Good Government: A New Political History of Canada, 1867–1917*. Montreal and Kingston: McGill-Queen's University Press, 2017.

Henderson, T. Stephen. *Angus L. Macdonald: A Provincial Liberal*. Toronto: University of Toronto Press, 2007.

Henley, Jon. "Why Referendums Are Problematic—Yet More Popular than Ever." *The Guardian*, 6 Oct. 2016. https://www.theguardian.com/politics/political-science/2016/oct/06/why-referendums-are-problematic-yet-more-popular-than-ever.

Herbert, A.P. *Independent Member*. London: Methuen, 1950.

High, Steven. "Working for Uncle Sam: The 'Comings' and 'Goings' of Newfoundland Base Construction Labour, 1940–1945." *Acadiensis* 32, no. 2 (Spring 2003): 84–107.

———. ed. *Occupied St. John's: A Social History of a City at War, 1939–1945*. Montreal and Kingston: McGill-Queen's University Press, 2010.

Hiller, James K. "Bennett, Charles James Fox." In *Dictionary of Canadian Biography* 11. University of Toronto/Université Laval, 1982. http://www.biographi.ca/en/bio/bennett_charles_james_fox_11E.html.

———. "The Career of F. Gordon Bradley." *Newfoundland Studies* 4, no. 2 (1988): 163–80.

———. "Carter, Sir Frederic Bowker Terrington." In *Dictionary of Canadian Biography* 12. University of Toronto/Université Laval, 1990. http://www.biographi.ca/en/bio/carter_frederic_bowker_terrington_12E.html.

———. "Confederation Defeated: The Newfoundland Election of 1869." In Hiller and Neary, *Newfoundland in the Nineteenth and Twentieth Centuries: Essays in Interpretation*, 67–94.

———. "The Confederation Election of 1869." *Newfoundland and Labrador Heritage Website*, 1997. http://www.heritage.nf.ca/articles/politics/election-confederation-1869.php.

———. "The Constitutional Crisis of 1908–09: A Subplot." Lecture to the Newfoundland Historical Society, 1974.

———. "Corruption and Collapse, or Did Squires Do It?" In *Amulree's Legacy: Truth, Lies and Consequences. Symposium March 2000* (papers and presentations), edited by Garfield Fizzard, 83–90. St. John's: Newfoundland Historical Society, 2001.

———. "The 1895 Newfoundland-Canada Confederation Negotiations: A Reconsideration." *Acadiensis* 40, no. 2 (Summer/Autumn 2011): 94–111.

———. "A History of Newfoundland, 1874–1901." PhD thesis, Cambridge University, 1971.

———. "James Murray and the 1882 Newfoundland General Election." Research Note. *Newfoundland and Labrador Studies* 33, no. 1 (2018): 237–58.

———. "Newfoundland Confronts Canada, 1867–1949." In *The Atlantic Provinces in Confederation*, edited by Ernest Forbes and D.A. Muse, 349–81. Toronto: University of Toronto Press, 1993.

———. "The Newfoundland Credit System: An Interpretation." In *Merchant Credit and Labour Strategies in Historical Perspective*, edited by Rosemary E. Ommer, 86–101. Fredericton: Acadiensis Press, 1990.

———. *The Newfoundland Railway, 1881–1949*. St. John's: Newfoundland Historical Society, 1981.

———. "The 1904 Anglo-French Newfoundland Fisheries Convention: Another Look." *Acadiensis* 25, no. 1 (Autumn 1995): 82–98.

———. "The Political Career of Robert Bond." In *Twentieth-Century Newfoundland: Explorations*, edited by James K. Hiller and Peter Neary, 11–46. St. John's: Breakwater, 1994.

———. "The Politics of Newsprint: The Newfoundland Pulp and Paper Industry, 1915–1939." *Acadiensis* 19, no. 2 (Spring 1990): 3–39.

———. "The Railway and Local Politics in Newfoundland, 1870–1901." In Hiller and Neary, *Newfoundland in the Nineteenth and Twentieth Centuries: Essays in Interpretation*, 123–47.

———. "Robert Bond and the Pink, White and Green: Newfoundland Nationalism in Perspective." *Acadiensis* 36, no. 2 (Spring 2007): 113–33.

———. "Shea, Sir Ambrose." In *Dictionary of Canadian Biography* 13 University of Toronto/Université Laval, 1994. http://www.biographi.ca/en/bio/shea_ambrose_13E.html.

———. "The Trinity Bay Election Trial, 1894: Electioneering and Local Government." *Newfoundland and Labrador Studies* 26, no. 2 (2011): 215–29.

———. "Whiteway, Sir William Vallance." In *Dictionary of Canadian Biography* 13. University of Toronto/Université Laval, 1994. http://www.biographi.ca/en/bio/whiteway_william_vallance_13E.html.

Hiller, James K., and Peter Neary, eds. *Newfoundland in the Nineteenth and Twentieth Centuries: Essays in Interpretation*. Toronto: University of Toronto Press, 1980.

Hiscock, Philip D. "The Barrelman Radio Programs, 1937–1943: The Mediation and Use of Folklore in Newfoundland." PhD thesis, Memorial University, 1994.

Holland, Robert. "Newfoundland and the Pattern of British Decolonization." *Newfoundland Studies* 14, no. 2 (1998): 141–53.

Hollett, Edward. "Newfoundland Nationalism," *Dorchester Review* 7, no. 2 (Autumn/Winter 2017): 51–5.

———. "Two Solitudes: Newfoundland's Victim Narrative." *Dorchester Review* 6, no. 1 (Spring/Summer 2016): 14–17.

Hollohan, Francis G. *Albert Perlin: A Biography*. St. John's: Jesperson Press, 1985.

Hollohan, Francis G., and Melvin Baker, eds. *A Clear Head in Tempestuous Times: Albert B. Perlin, The Wayfarer. Observations on the National Convention and the Confederation Issue, 1946–1949*. St. John's: Harry Cuff Publications, 1986.

Hong, Robert. " 'An Agency for the Common Weal': The Newfoundland Board of Trade, 1909–1915." MA thesis, Memorial University, 1998.

Horwood, Harold. *Joey: The Life and Political Times of Joey Smallwood.* Toronto: Stoddart, 1989.

Howell, C.D. "W.S. Fielding and the Repeal Elections of 1886 and 1887 in Nova Scotia." *Acadiensis* 8, no. 2 (1978–79): 28–46.

Howley, Richard. *Letters on the Present State of Newfoundland and on Confederation.* St. John's, 1869.

Jamieson, Donald C. "I Saw the Fight for Confederation." In Smallwood, *The Book of Newfoundland*, vol. 3, 70–104.

———. *No Place for Fools: The Political Memoirs of Don Jamieson.* St. John's: Breakwater, 1989.

Jones, Frederick. " 'The Antis Gain the Day': Newfoundland and Confederation in 1869." In *The Causes of Canadian Confederation*, edited by Ged Martin, 142–48. Fredericton: Acadiensis Press, 1990.

———. "John Bull's Other Ireland—Nineteenth-Century Newfoundland." *Dalhousie Review* 55, no. 2 (Summer 1975): 227–35.

———. "Mullock, John Thomas." In *Dictionary of Canadian Biography* 9. University of Toronto/Université Laval, 1976. http://www.biographi.ca/en/bio/mullock_john_thomas_9E.html.

Jones, Michael, dir. *Secret Nation.* Black Spot, Newfoundland Independent Filmmakers Co-operative, 1992.

Joyce, R.B. *Sir William MacGregor.* Melbourne: Oxford University Press, 1971.

Keough, William J. "We Knew What We Wanted." In Smallwood, *The Book of Newfoundland*, vol 3, 62–63.

Kerr, Kenneth J. "A Social Analysis of the Members of the Newfoundland House of Assembly, Executive Council, and Legislative Council for the Period 1855–1914." MA thesis, Memorial University, 1973.

Korneski, Kurt. "Colonialism, Place, and Power in Nineteenth Century Newfoundland and Labrador." Paper presented to the Canadian Historical Association Annual Meeting, Regina, 2018.

———. *Conflicted Colony: Critical Episodes in Nineteenth-Century Newfoundland and Labrador.* Montreal and Kingston: McGill-Queen's University Press, 2016.

Lackenbauer, P. Whitney. "War, Memory and the Newfoundland Regiment at Gallipoli." *Newfoundland Studies* 15, no. 2 (1999): 176–214.

Lacy, Dean, and Emerson M.S. Niou. "A Problem with Referendums." *Journal of Theoretical Politics* 12, no. 1 (2000): 5–31.

LeDuc, Lawrence. "Referendums and Deliberative Democracy." *Electoral Studies* 38 (June 2015): 139–48.

Letto, Doug. *Newfoundland's Last Prime Minister: Frederick Alderdice and the Death of a Nation.* Portugal Cove–St. Philip's: Boulder Publications, 2014.

Lilly, Augustus G., and Christopher P. Curran. "Introduction." In *The Journals of George Simms, J.P., and the Records of the Labrador Court 1826–1833*, vol. 1, edited

by Lilly and Curran. St. John's: ss *Daisy* Legal History Committee, Law Society of Newfoundland and Labrador, 2017.
Lodge, Thomas. *Dictatorship in Newfoundland*. London: Cassell, 1939.
Long, Gene. *Suspended State: Newfoundland before Canada*. St. John's: Breakwater, 1999.
Lonsdale, John. "Moral and Political Argument in Kenya." In *Ethnicity and Democracy in Africa*, edited by Bruce Berman, Dickson Eyoh, and Will Kymlicka, 73–95. Oxford: James Currey, 2004.
Lupia, Arthur. "How Elitism Undermines the Study of Voter Competence." *Critical Review: A Journal of Politics and Society* 18, nos. 1–3 (2006): 217–32.
MacDonald, Heidi. "Woman's Suffrage and Confederation." *Acadiensis* 46, no. 1 (Winter/Spring 2017): 163–76.
MacGillivray, Don. "Henry Melville Whitney Comes to Cape Breton: The Saga of a Gilded Age Entrepreneur." *Acadiensis* 9, no. 1 (Autumn 1979): 44–70.
MacGregor, William. *Report of an Official Visit to the Coast of Labrador*. St. John's: J.W. Withers, 1906.
MacKay, R.A., ed. *Newfoundland: Economic, Diplomatic, and Strategic Studies*. Toronto: Oxford University Press, 1946.
MacKenzie, David. "The Indian Act and the Aboriginal Peoples of Newfoundland at the Time of Confederation." *Newfoundland and Labrador Studies* 25, no. 2 (2010): 161–81.
———. *Inside the Atlantic Triangle: Canada and the Entrance of Newfoundland into Confederation, 1939–1949*. Toronto: University of Toronto Press, 1986.
———. "The Terms of Union in Historical Perspective." *Newfoundland Studies* 14, no. 2 (1998): 220–37.
MacLeod, Malcolm. *Connections: Newfoundland's Pre-Confederation Links with Canada and the World*. St. John's: Creative Publishers, 2003.
———. "Subsidized Steamers to a Foreign Country: Canada and Newfoundland, 1892–1949." *Acadiensis* 14, no. 2 (Spring 1985): 66–92.
Macmillan, Margaret. *Paris 1919: Six Months That Changed the World*. New York: Random House, 2001.
Macpherson, Alan G. "The People of Newfoundland: A Longue Durée in Historical Geography." In *A Social Geography of Canada*, edited by Guy M. Robinson, 280–94. Edinburgh: North British Publishing, 1988.
MacWhirter, W. David. "A Political History of Newfoundland, 1865–1874." MA thesis, Memorial University, 1963.
Malone, Greg. *Don't Tell the Newfoundlanders: The True Story of Newfoundland's Confederation with Canada*. Toronto: Knopf Canada, 2012.
Mann, Michael. "The Emergence of Modern European Nationalism." In *Transition to Modernity*, edited by John A. Hall and I.C. Jarvie, 137–84. Cambridge: Cambridge University Press, 1992.
Mannion, Patrick. *A Land of Dreams: Ethnicity, Nationalism, and the Irish in Newfoundland, Nova Scotia, and Maine, 1880–1923*. Montreal and Kingston: McGill-Queen's University Press, 2018.

Marquis, Lionel, and Manfred Max Bergman. "Development and Consequences of Referendum Campaigns in Switzerland, 1981–1999." *Swiss Political Science Review* 15, no. 1 (Spring 2009): 63–97.

Marshall, T.H. *Citizenship and Social Class, and Other Essays*. Cambridge: Cambridge University Press, 1999.

———. *Class, Citizenship, and Social Development*. New York: Doubleday, 1964.

Martin, Chris. "The Right Course, the Best Course, the Only Course: Voluntary Recruitment in the Newfoundland Regiment, 1914–1918." *Newfoundland and Labrador Studies* 24, no. 1 (2009): 55–89.

May, Stephen. "The Terms of Union: An Analysis of Their Current Relevance." In *Royal Commission on Renewing and Strengthening Our Place in Canada*, vol. 1, *Research*, 167–206. St. John's: Office of the Queen's Printer, 2003.

Mayo, H.B. "Newfoundland and Confederation in the Eighteen-Sixties." *Canadian Historical Review* 29, no. 2 (1948): 125–42.

McCann, Phillip. "British Policy and Confederation." *Newfoundland Studies* 14, no. 2 (1998): 155–68.

———. "The Educational Policy of the Commission of Government." *Newfoundland Studies* 3, no. 2 (Fall 1987): 201–15.

———. *Island in an Empire: Education, Religion, and Social Life in Newfoundland, 1800–1855*. Portugal Cove–St. Philip's: Boulder Publications, 2016.

McDonald, Ian. *"To Each His Own": William Coaker and the Fishermen's Protective Union in Newfoundland Politics, 1908–1925*, edited by James K. Hiller. St. John's: ISER Books, 1987.

———. "W.F. Coaker and the Balance of Power Strategy: The Fishermen's Protective Union in Newfoundland Politics." In Hiller and Neary, *Newfoundland in the Nineteenth and Twentieth Centuries*, 148–60.

McEvoy, John B. "Our New Constitution." In Smallwood, *The Book of Newfoundland*, vol. 1, 43–46.

McGrath, P.T. *Newfoundland in 1911*. London: Whitehead Morris, 1911.

———. "Should Newfoundland Confederate with Canada?" *Westminster Magazine* 9 (1906): 366–72.

———. "Will Newfoundland Join Canada?" *Queen's Quarterly* 29 (1929): 253–66.

Mercer, Keith. "The Murder of Lieutenant Lawry: A Case Study of British Naval Impressment in Newfoundland, 1794." *Newfoundland and Labrador Studies* 21, no. 2 (2006): 254–89.

Mitchell, Harvey. "Canada's Negotiations with Newfoundland, 1887–1895." *Canadian Historical Review* 40, no. 4 (Dec. 1959): 277–93.

Mitchell, Timothy. "The Limits of the State: Beyond Statist Approaches and Their Critics." *American Political Science Review* 85, no. 1 (Mar. 1991): 77–96.

Morry, Christopher J.A. *When the Great Red Dawn Is Shining: Howard L. Morry's Memoirs of Life in the Newfoundland Regiment*. St. John's: Breakwater, 2014.

Morton, William L. *The Critical Years: The Union of British North America, 1857–1873*. Toronto: McClelland and Stewart, 1964.

Moulton, Edward C. "The Political History of Newfoundland, 1861–1869." MA thesis, Memorial University, 1960.

Murray, James. *The Commercial Crisis in Newfoundland: Cause, Consequences, and Cure.* St. John's: J.W. Withers, 1895.

Narváez, Peter. "Joseph R. Smallwood, 'The Barrelman': The Broadcaster as Folklorist." In *Media Sense: The Folklore–Popular Culture Continuum*, edited by Peter Narváez and Martin Laba, 47–64. Bowling Green, OH: Bowling Green State University Popular Press, 1986.

Neary, Peter. "Canada and the Newfoundland Labour Market, 1939–49." *Canadian Historical Review* 62, no. 4 (Dec. 1981): 470–95.

———. "Canadian Immigration Policy and the Newfoundlanders, 1912–1939." *Acadiensis* 11, no. 2 (Spring 1982): 69–83.

———. "Clement Attlee's Visit to Newfoundland, September 1942." *Acadiensis* 13, no. 2 (Spring 1984): 101–09.

———. "Document: The Commission of Government on Reconstruction, December 1936." *Newfoundland and Labrador Studies* 26, no. 2 (Fall 2011): 241–88.

———. "Ebb and Flow of Citizenship in Newfoundland, 1929–1949." In *Belonging: The Meaning and Future of Canadian Citizenship*, edited by William Kaplan, 79–103. Montreal and Kingston: McGill-Queen's University Press, 1993.

———. "The First Nations and the Entry of Newfoundland into Confederation, 1945–1954. Part 1." *Newfoundland Quarterly* 105, no. 2 (Fall 2012): 36–42.

———. "The French and American Shore Questions as Factors in Newfoundland History." In Hiller and Neary, *Newfoundland in the Nineteenth and Twentieth Centuries*, 95–122.

———. "Great Britain and the Future of Newfoundland, 1939–45." *Newfoundland Studies* 1, no. 1 (1985): 29–56.

———. "Newfoundland and Quebec: Provincial Neighbours across an Uneasy Frontier." *Bulletin of Canadian Studies* 2, no. 2 (Dec. 1978): 35–51.

———. *Newfoundland in the North Atlantic World, 1929–1949.* Montreal and Kingston: McGill-Queen's University Press, 1988.

———. "Newfoundland's Union with Canada: Conspiracy or Choice?" *Acadiensis* 12, no. 2 (Spring 1983): 110–19.

———. "P.A. Clutterbuck on Morley Richards and the Record of the Commission of Government, 1939." *Newfoundland and Labrador Studies* 27, no. 1 (2012): 79–98.

———. "Party Politics in Newfoundland, 1949–71: A Survey and Analysis." In Hiller and Neary, *Newfoundland in the Nineteenth and Twentieth Centuries*, 205–45.

———. *The Political Economy of Newfoundland, 1929–1972.* Toronto: Copp Clark, 1973.

———. " 'That Thin Red Cord of Sentiment and of Blood': Newfoundland in the Great Depression, 1929–34." Unpublished manuscript, 1988. Available at the Centre for Newfoundland Studies, Memorial University Libraries.

———. " 'With Great Regret and after the Most Anxious Consideration': Newfoundland's 1932 Plan to Reschedule Interest Payments." *Newfoundland Studies* 10, no. 22 (Fall 1994): 250–59.

———, ed. *White Tie and Decorations: Sir John and Lady Hope Simpson in Newfoundland, 1934–1936*. Toronto: University of Toronto Press, 1996.

Neary, Peter, and S.J.R. Noel. "Newfoundland's Quest for Reciprocity, 1890–1910." In *Regionalism in the Canadian Community, 1867–1967*, edited by Mason Wade, 210–26. Toronto: University of Toronto Press, 1969.

Nicholson, G.W.L. *The Fighting Newfoundlander: A History of the Royal Newfoundland Regiment*. Montreal and Kingston: McGill-Queen's University Press, 2006. Reprint of 1964 edition.

Noel, S.J.R. "Politics and the Crown: The Case of the 1908 Tie Election in Newfoundland." *The Canadian Journal of Economics and Political Science* 33, no. 2 (1967): 285–91.

———. *Politics in Newfoundland*. Toronto: University of Toronto Press, 1971.

O'Brien, Mike. "Producers versus Profiteers: The Politics of Class in Newfoundland during the First World War." *Acadiensis* 40, no. 1 (Winter 2011): 45–69.

O'Brien, Patricia. "The Newfoundland Patriotic Association: The Administration of the War Effort, 1914–1918." MA Thesis, Memorial University, 1982.

O'Flaherty, Patrick. "'Holding the Baby': Parliamentary Responses in Britain and Newfoundland to the Crisis of 1931," *Newfoundland Quarterly*, vol. XCI, no. 2 (Summer/Fall 1997): 23–32.

———. "Introduction." In *Reminiscences of James P. Howley: Selected Years*, edited by William J. Kirwin, G.M. Story, and Patrick O'Flaherty, xx–xxxiii. Toronto: Champlain Society, 1997.

———. *Leaving the Past Behind: Newfoundland History from 1934*. St. John's: Long Beach Press, 2011.

———. *Lost Country: The Rise and Fall of Newfoundland, 1843–1933*. St. John's: Long Beach Press, 2005.

———. *The Rock Observed: Studies in the Literature of Newfoundland*. Toronto: University of Toronto Press, 1979.

O'Gorman, Frank. "Campaign Rituals and Ceremonies: The Social Meaning of Elections in England, 1780–1860." *Past and Present* no. 135 (1992): 79–115.

Overton, James. "Nationalism, Democracy, and Self-Determination: Newfoundland in the 1930s and 1940s." *Canadian Review of Studies in Nationalism* 32, nos. 1–2 (2005): 31–52.

———. "Riots, Raids and Relief, Police, Prisons and Parsimony: The Political Economy of Public Order in Newfoundland in the 1930s." In *Violence and Public Anxiety*, edited by Elliott Leyton, William O'Grady, and James Overton, 195–334. St. John's: ISER Books, 1992.

Panting, Gerald. " 'The People' in Politics." *Newfoundland Quarterly* 65, no. 4 (June 1967): 15–17.

Payne, Brian. *Fishing a Borderless Sea: Environmental Territorialism in the North Atlantic, 1818–1910*. Lansing: Michigan State University Press, 2010.

Penney, A.R. *A History of the Newfoundland Railway*, vol. 1, *1881–1923*. St. John's: Harry Cuff, 1988.

Perlin, George. "The Constitutional Referendum of 1948 and the Revival of Sectarianism in Newfoundland Politics." *Queen's Quarterly* 75, no. 1 (1968): 155–60.
Pickersgill, J.W. *Mackenzie King Record*, vol. 4, 1947–1948. Toronto: University of Toronto Press, 1970.
———. *My Years with Louis St. Laurent. A Political Memoir.* Toronto: University of Toronto Press, 1975.
Pippy, B.J. "Sir Patrick McGrath: A Biographical Essay." BA honours thesis, Memorial University, 1992.
Polanyi, Karl. *The Great Transformation: The Political and Economic Origins of Our Times.* Boston: Beacon Press, 2001. Reprint of 1944 edition.
Pope, Peter E. *The Many Landfalls of John Cabot.* Toronto: University of Toronto Press, 1997.
Prowse, D.W. *A History of Newfoundland: From the English, Colonial, and Foreign Records.* London: Eyre and Spottiswoode, 1896.
Randell, Jack. *I'm Alone.* Indianapolis: Bobbs-Merrill Company, 1930.
Reeves, W.G. "Alexander's Conundrum Reconsidered: The American Dimension in Newfoundland Resource Development, 1898–1910." *Newfoundland Studies* 5, no. 1 (Spring 1989): 2–37.
Roberts, Edward. "Nothing Venture, Nothing Have: Mr. Coaker's Regulations." MA thesis, Memorial University, 2006.
Schuck, Andreas R.T., and Claes H. de Vreese. "Public Support for Referendums in Europe: A Cross-National Comparison in 21 Countries." *Electoral Studies* 38 (June 2015): 149–58.
Senior, Elinor. "The Origin and Political Activities of the Orange Order in Newfoundland, 1863–1890." MA thesis, Memorial University, 1959.
Sharp, Mitchell. *Which Reminds Me . . . A Memoir.* Toronto: University of Toronto Press, 1994.
Sharpe, Christopher. "The 'Race of Honour': An Analysis of Enlistments and Casualties in the Armed Forces of Newfoundland: 1914–1918." *Newfoundland Studies* 4, no. 1 (1988): 27–55.
Slumkoski, Corey. *Inventing Atlantic Canada: Regionalism and the Maritime Reaction to Newfoundland's Entry into Canadian Confederation.* Toronto: University of Toronto Press, 2011.
Smallwood, Joseph R., ed. *The Book of Newfoundland*, 4 vols. St. John's: Newfoundland Book Publishers, 1937 and 1967.
———. *I Chose Canada.* Toronto: Macmillan, 1973.
———. *The New Newfoundland.* New York: Macmillan, 1931.
Smellie, Sarah. "Report Predicts Plummeting Population for Rural Newfoundland and Labrador." CBC News, 8 Sept. 2017. http://www.cbc.ca/news/canada/newfoundland-labrador/population-decline-newfoundland-labrador-harris-centre-report-1.4279580.

Smith, Andrew. "Toryism, Classical Liberalism, and Capitalism: The Politics of Taxation and the Struggle for Canadian Confederation." *Canadian Historical Review* 89, no. 1 (Mar. 2008): 2–25.

Smith, Francis J. "Newfoundland and Confederation, 1864–1870." MA thesis, University of Ottawa, 1970.

Smith, Peter J. "The Ideological Origins of Canadian Confederation." *Canadian Journal of Political Science/Revue canadienne de science politique* 20, no. 1 (Mar. 1987): 3–29.

Snell, James G. "The Newfoundland Old Age Pension Programme, 1911–1949." *Acadiensis* 23, no. 1 (Autumn 1993): 86–109.

Sorensen, David. "The Economic Union with America Party and the Referenda of 1948." MA thesis, Memorial University, 2004.

Stacey, C.P. "The Withdrawal of the Imperial Garrison from Newfoundland, 1870." *Canadian Historical Review* 17, no. 2 (June 1936): 147–58.

Stanbridge, Karen. "Framing Children in the Newfoundland Confederation Debate, 1948." *The Canadian Journal of Sociology* 32, no. 2 (Spring 2007): 177–201.

Stanley, G.F.G. "Further Documents Relating to the Union of Newfoundland and Canada, 1886–1895." *Canadian Historical Review* 29, no. 4 (Dec. 1948): 370–86.

———. "Sir Stephen Hill's Observations on the Election of 1869 in Newfoundland." *Canadian Historical Review* 29, no. 3 (Sept. 1948): 278–85.

Story, G.M. "Prowse, Daniel Woodley." In *Dictionary of Canadian Biography* 14. University of Toronto/Université Laval, 1998. http://www.biographi.ca/en/bio/prowse_daniel_woodley_14E.html.

Strikwerda, Eric. "Newfoundland and Labrador Maligned: Taking Stock of Nutritional Health in Rural Newfoundland and Labrador, 1912–1949." *Acadiensis* 47, no. 1 (Winter/Spring 2018): 118–39.

Summers, Valerie. *Regime Change in a Resource Economy: The Politics of Underdevelopment in Newfoundland since 1825*. St. John's: Breakwater, 1994.

Tallman, Ronald D. "Annexation in the Maritimes? The Butler Mission to Charlottetown." *Dalhousie Review* 53, no. 1 (1973): 97–112.

Taylor, A.J.P. *English History 1914–1945*. New York: Oxford University Press, 1992.

Thistle, James. "The Bank Crash of 1894." Unpublished History 6201 paper, Department of History, Memorial University, n.d. Copy courtesy of Robert Hong.

Thomas-Symonds, Nicklaus. *Attlee: A Life in Politics*. London: I.B. Tauris, 2010.

Thompson, Frederic F. *The French Shore Problem in Newfoundland: An Imperial Study*. Toronto: University of Toronto Press, 1961.

Thoms, James R., ed. *Call Me Joey*. St. John's: Harry Cuff Publications, 1990. Reprint of 1969 edition.

Tillotson, Shirley. *Give and Take: The Citizen-Taxpayer and the Rise of Canadian Democracy*. Vancouver: UBC Press, 2017.

Tuck, Marilyn. "The Newfoundland Ranger Force, 1935–1950." MA thesis, Memorial University, 1983.

Varga, Darrell. "Radio and the Invention of Newfoundland." *Acadiensis* 38, no. 2 (Summer/Autumn 2009): 168–71.

Waite, Peter. *The Confederation Debates in the Province of Canada, 1865*. 2nd ed. Introduction by Ged Martin. Montreal and Kingston: McGill-Queen's University Press, 2006.

Walls, Martha Elizabeth. "Confederation and Maritime First Nations." *Acadiensis* 46, no. 2 (Summer/Autumn 2017): 155–76.

Walsh, Bren. *More than a Poor Majority: The Story of Newfoundland's Confederation with Canada*. St. John's: Breakwater, 1985.

Webb, Jeff A. "Confederation, Conspiracy and Choice: A Discussion." *Newfoundland Studies* 14, no. 2 (1998): 169–87.

———. "Constructing Community and Consumers: Joseph R. Smallwood's Barrelman Radio Programme." *Journal of the Canadian Historical Association* 8, no. 1 (1997): 165–86.

———. "Newfoundland's National Convention, 1946–48." MA thesis, Memorial University, 1987.

———. "The Responsible Government League and the Confederation Campaigns of 1948." *Newfoundland Studies* 5, no. 2 (1989): 203–20.

———. *The Voice of Newfoundland: A Social History of the Broadcasting Corporation of Newfoundland, 1939–1949*. Toronto: University of Toronto Press, 2008.

Wheare, K.C. *The Statute of Westminster and Dominion Status*. 4th ed. London: Oxford University Press, 1949.

Whelan, Maudie. "The Newspaper Press in Nineteenth-Century Newfoundland: Politics, Religion, and Personal Journalism." PhD thesis, Memorial University, 2002.

White, Linda. "The Rev. Lester Burry Collection: United Church Conference Archives." *Newfoundland Quarterly* 105, no. 2 (Fall 2012): 10.

Whitehead, Kay, and Judith Peppard. "Women Teachers in the Turbulent Educational World of St. John's, Newfoundland, 1920–1949." *Acadiensis* 37, no. 1 (Winter/Spring 2008): 56–75.

Williams, Ralph. *How I Became a Governor*. London: John Murray, 1913.

Winton, Henry. "A Chapter in the History of Newfoundland for the Year 1861." St. John's: Provincial Archives of Newfoundland and Labrador, 1972.

PHOTO CREDITS

(by page number)

8   Cartography: J. Siemer, University of Regina. Source: Atlas of Canada, 2006.
25   (Left) The Rooms Provincial Archives, VA 19-99; (Right) The Rooms Provincial Archives, B 1-145.
27   Photo by James Ashfield of Canadian artist Robert Harris's 1884 painting, "Conference at Québec in 1864, to settle the basics of a union of the British North American Provinces" (also known as "The Fathers of Confederation"). The original painting was destroyed in the 1916 Parliament Buildings fire. Library and Archives Canada, C-001855.
33   *Encyclopedia of Newfoundland and Labrador*, vol. 1, p. 176.
47   *Morning Chronicle*, St. John's, NL, September 29, 1869.
64   William Notman, McCord Museum.
69   The Rooms Provincial Archives, B4-53.
86   The Rooms Provincial Archives, B4-25.
87   Photographer unknown. Reproduced by permission of Archives and Special Collections (Department of Geography Photography Collection, Coll-137, 05.01.005), Queen Elizabeth II Library, Memorial University of Newfoundland, St. John's, NL.
93   Photographer unknown. Reproduced by permission of Archives and Special Collections (Department of Geography Photography Collection, Coll-137 01.10.006), Queen Elizabeth II Library, Memorial University of Newfoundland, St. John's, NL.
95   From D.W. Prowse, *A History of Newfoundland: From the English, Colonial, and Foreign Records*, 2nd ed. (London: Eyre and Spottiswoode, 1896), 542.
123   The Rooms Provincial Archives, A 51-98.
131   Reproduced with permission of the Johnson Family Foundation, St. John's, NL.
145   Archives and Special Collections (Department of Geography Photography Collection, Coll-137, 16.03.001), Memorial University of Newfoundland, St. John's, NL.

149	The Rooms Provincial Archives, Camilla Coaker Album, VA81-84.2.
161	Archives and Special Collections, Memorial University Libraries, Janet Miller Ayre Murray Collection, Coll-158, file 8.11 (Collection MF-137), Queen Elizabeth II Library, Memorial University of Newfoundland, St. John's, NL.
163	The Rooms Provincial Archives, VA 157-89.
173	(Top) Reproduced with permission of the Johnson Family Foundation, St. John's, NL; (Bottom) The Rooms Provincial Archives, A 19-20.
181	The Rooms Provincial Archives, E 23-29.
193	Reproduced with permission of the Johnson Family Foundation, St. John's, NL.
198	Joseph R. Smallwood Collection, Coll-075, Archives and Special Collections, Memorial University Libraries.
206	I.H. Withers. Canada Deptartment of National Defence. Library and Archives Canada, PA-177671.
217	Joseph R. Smallwood, ed. *The Book of Newfoundland*, vol. 3 (St. John's: Newfoundland Book Publishers, 1967), 26.
224	Rev. H. Maxwell Dawe Collection, United Church of Canada, Newfoundland Conference Archives, St. John's, photo WY500 available at http://collections.mun.ca/cdm/ref/collection/hmdawe/id/3267.
225, 228	Michael Harrington Collection, Coll-307, Archives and Special Collections, Memorial University Libraries.
233	Joseph R. Smallwood Collection, Coll-075, Archives and Special Collections, Memorial University Libraries.
237	Joseph R. Smallwood, ed. "The Story of Confederation." In *The Book of Newfoundland*, vol. 3 (St. John's: Newfoundland Book Publishers, 1967), 18.
245	George Hunter. National Film Board of Canada. Library and Archives Canada, PA-128073.
264	Joseph R. Smallwood Collection, Coll-285, Archives and Special Collections, Memorial University Libraries.
267	*The Independent*, vol. 1, no. 10, March 22, 1948.
270	*The Independent*, vol. 1, no. 3, April 5, 1948.
273	*The Confederate*, vol. 1, no. 10, June 16, 1948.
275	*The Confederate*, vol. 1, no. 11, June 23, 1948.
286, 287	Cartography: Julia Siemer, University of Regina. Source: Heritage Newfoundland & Labrador, 2018.
289	Archives and Special Collections, Memorial University Libraries, Gordon Winter Collection, Coll-363, file 4.01, "Newfoundland Delegation, Ottawa 1948 Photo Album," available at http://collections.mun.ca/PDFs/archives/GordonWinterPhotographAlbum.pdf
299	National Film Board of Canada. Library and Archives Canada, PA-133280.
301	National Film Board of Canada. Library and Archives Canada, C-006255.

INDEX

A

Abbott, Douglas, 243, 245
Act of Union of 1801, 50
Addison, Lord, 207, 209–10, 216, 234–39, 259
A.E. Reed and Company Limited, 117
agriculture sector, 39–40, 51, 78, 191; development in, 174, 181, 190
Ajzenstat, Janet, 6
Alderdice, Frederick, 160, 164–65, 168, 175–77, 180, 185
Alexander, David, 37, 189
Allardyce, Sir William Lamond, 144, 160
Amery, Leo, 160
Ammon, Charles, 203
Amulree, Baron (William Warrender Mackenzie), 176–79
Amulree Commission, 178, 274
Amulree Report, 215
Anderson, Sir David Murray, 180–81
Anglo–American Convention of 1818, 108, 110
Anglo-Newfoundland Development Company Limited, 105, 116, 288
Anti-Confederate (newspaper), 99
Anti-Confederate Committee, 53
Anti-Confederate League, 76, 99
anti-Confederation movement, 5, 28, 32, 34, 39–41, 44, 46, 50–51, 53–55; campaigns in, 47, 59–61, 71, 107;

leadership of, 11, 33–34, 42, 57, 75, 94, 98, 127; sentiments of, 106, 118–20, 275, 282, 303, 305. *See also* Confederation, with Canada
Archibald, Samuel George, 22
Ashbourne, Thomas G.W., 220, 224, 244–45
Association of Newfoundland Industries Limited, 299
Atlantic Charter (1941), 3, 13, 124, 195
Attlee, Clement, 203–4, 207–9, 211–12, 214, 234, 236–38, 240, 309
Ayre, Agnes, 161
Ayre, George, 213
Ayre, Janet, 161
Ayre, Ronald, 201

B

Bailey, Charles, 277
Baird, James, 81
Bait Act, 78, 83–84
bait trade, 78, 86, 97, 108
Baldwin, John R., 243
Balfour Declaration, 135
Ballam, Charles, 244–45
banking sector, 85, 90–91; crash of 1894, 93
Bank of Canada, 242, 292
Bank of Montreal, 92, 111, 114, 118, 137

bankruptcy, on verge of, 43, 72, 89,
    91, 98–100, 115, 159, 170, 305
Bannerman, Sir Alexander, 38–39, 44
Barnes, Arthur, 165
Beaverbrook, Lord (Max
    Aitken), 205, 209
Bennett, Charles Fox, 62, 64, 281;
    as Newfoundland nationalist,
    51–56, 58, 60, 267; as opposed to
    Confederation, 32–34, 43, 49,
    68, 278; as premier, 66–67, 71
Bennett, John R., 146–47, 150–51
Bennett, R.B., 165–66
Bennett, Thomas, 51
Beveridge, Sir William, 13, 271
Beveridge Report, 13, 209, 271
Bishop, Alfred, 120–21
Blackman, Albert L., 71
Blackman Company, 72
Blaine, James G., 82
Blair, Andrew George, 103
Boer War, 100, 106
Bonavista Platform of 1912, 125
Bond, Robert, 74, 92, 117–18, 121, 125–
    27, 140, 142; and fisheries, 109–10;
    manifesto of, 77; as Newfoundland
    nationalist, 78, 101, 112, 115,
    119–20; and old age pensions,
    122; as part of Newfoundland
    delegation, 94–96; as Prime
    Minister of Newfoundland,
    102, 105–6, 113, 116, 152; as saving
    Newfoundland from bankruptcy,
    100; and trade agreements, 82–86,
    103, 108, 111; and union with
    Canada, 88, 99, 107, 114, 136–38
Bond–Blaine Convention,
    82–83, 88, 96
Bond–Blaine trade agreement, 107
Bond–Hay Convention, 108
Boothe, Jack, 279
Borden, Robert, 111, 126,
    134, 136–38, 140

Bowell, Sir Mackenzie, 86,
    88, 93, 98–99, 104
Bowring, Eric, 286
Bowring, Sir Edgar, 134
Boyle, Sir Cavendish, 106, 267
Bradley, F. Gordon, 94, 159–60, 216,
    255–56, 304, 306; as negotiating
    terms for Confederation,
    288–89; as part of National
    Convention, 232–33, 240, 244–45,
    247, 251–52, 254, 278; and social
    rights, 222–23, 246, 307; as
    supporting Confederation, 202,
    212, 219, 239, 241, 249, 260, 301
Bridges, Frank, 243, 245, 250
British Colonial Office, 46, 63,
    82–83, 87, 102, 113–14, 118, 133–34,
    139; and financial assistance
    for Newfoundland, 92, 98;
    and French fishing rights, 78,
    80–81; and trade, 85–86
British North America Act, 44,
    49, 133, 247–48, 293, 297
British North America union, 1, 3,
    6–8, 21–23, 33–34, 40, 104; benefits
    of, 29, 43, 58; campaign for, 33
British Voluntary Aid Detachment, 129
Broadcasting Corporation of
    Newfoundland, 186, 198, 217,
    223, 239, 256, 265, 282
Bromley, Sir Arthur, 235
Brookes, H.R., 147
Brown, Ken, 161, 186, 216
Browne, William J., 272
Burchell, Charles J., 205, 241
Burry, Lester, 220, 222–24, 244–45
Butt, Albert B., 232

C

cable connections to Europe, 128
Cabot, John, 100
Cabot Lodge, Henry, 108
Cadigan, Sean, 50

INDEX

Campbell, Dr. Alex, 171
Canada: as Dominion, 23, 45, 49, 70, 87, 133, 135, 155, 231, 238, 244; expansionist strategy of, 104; federal system of, 247–48, 276, 305–6; as multinational state, 16; offer to Newfoundland for union, 246–49, 255, 259, 261. *See also* Terms of Union, for Confederation
Canadian banks, 92–93, 142, 185; control over Newfoundland, 176; credit to Newfoundland, 166–69
Canadian Expeditionary Force, 128
Canadian Pacific Railway, 103, 111, 118, 137
Cardwell, Edward, 44, 52
Carter, Frederic Bowker Terrington: as a Father of Confederation, 28; as premier, 39–40, 46, 50, 56–58, 60, 67–68; at Quebec Conference, 27, 31, 47, 308; as supporting Confederation, 25–26, 29, 32, 44, 49, 74, 90, 117
Carter, William, 26
Cartier, George-Étienne, 41
Cartwright, Richard, 103
Cashin, Michael, 140–41
Cashin, Peter, 4, 159, 179, 186, 192, 202, 216; as finance minister, 160, 162, 165, 171; as opposed to Confederation, 242, 251, 259, 272–74, 286; as part of delegation to London, 232, 235–38, 240; as supporter of responsible government, 185, 200, 222, 227–29, 241, 258, 263, 265
Cashin, Richard, 272
Cayley, Douglas Edward, 130
Chadwick, G.W. St. John, 34, 221
Chadwick-Jones Report, 222
Channing, James G., 288, 293–94
Chapleau, Joseph-Adolphe, 86
Charlottetown Conference, 22–23, 28–29, 34

Christian, S.M., 266
Churchill, Winston, 124, 195, 204, 207, 209
citizenship, 29, 178, 201, 271; changing notion of, 214, 217–18, 229, 269, 308; and gender and race, 215; rights and benefits of, 10, 13. *See also* political citizenship; social citizenship
Clark, William Clifford, 246
Claxton, Brooke, 242–43
Clouston, Sir Edward S., 118
Clouter, Nellie, 149
Clutterbuck, Peter Alexander, 177, 186, 209–10, 250, 255
Coady, Michael, 186
Coaker, Camilla, 149
Coaker, William Ford, 13, 127–28, 136, 147, 149, 158, 179, 192–93, 214, 268; in coalition government, 131, 160; and conscription, 133; as favouring social reforms, 125–26, 162, 184–85, 200; as fisheries minister, 135, 141–43; as opposed to Confederation, 138–40; as supporting fishermen, 122–24, 132, 163, 174, 215; as supporting sale of Labrador, 144–45, 165
Coaker Plan, 145
Coaker Regulations, 142
coal mining. *See* mining industry
Coates, Son and Company, 99
coat of arms, of Newfoundland, 301
cod fishery, 59, 65, 70, 142, 306
Codfish Standardization Act (1920), 142
Coercion Bill, 81
Collingwood, Tom, 172, 175
Collins, Wickford, 276
Colonial Building, Newfoundland: storming of, 2, 172–73, 184
Colonial Conference (London), 106, 110
Colonial Office. *See* British Colonial Office
Commercial Bank, 89–91

— 385 —

Commission of Government: as communicating with people, 187, 190, 217; as dealing with local issues, 182–84, 191–95, 215, 218, 225, 229, 272; delegation of to negotiate terms of union, 288–89, 297; discontent with, 185–86, 189, 193, 201–2, 212–14; expectations for, 163, 187; membership of, 178, 181, 286; opposition to, 183–86, 276, 278; populist approach of, 188; as referendum 1948 option, 15, 240, 258, 261, 263, 265, 284; as ruling Newfoundland, 2, 179–80, 208, 220, 232, 235–36, 238, 274; as social experiment, 182

Confederate, 275, 279–80

Confederate Association, 264–65, 274, 277–80, 282–84, 288

Confederation, with Canada: benefits of, 210, 219, 276, 304, 306; as best option for Newfoundland, 199, 203, 208–9, 213, 224; campaigns for, 249, 260, 283, 303, 309; economic benefits of, 47, 97, 112, 242, 279; and economic/political integration, 247, 301; negotiations for, 95, 99, 249–53, 255, 288–89, 291–94, 297; opposition to, 1, 3, 7, 24, 33–34, 65, 84, 121, 137, 164, 204, 259–60, 274, 278; problems and costs of, 243, 248–49; proposals for, 74, 76, 253, 255; rejection of, 33–35, 42–43, 64–65, 77; social benefits of, 273, 279, 281–83; as solution to economic problems, 46, 75, 142; support for, 16, 26, 74, 114, 140, 216, 227, 232, 239, 242, 266; terms/conditions for, 75, 96–98, 248–49, 253–54, 256, 292–93. *See also* referenda, on Confederation; Terms of Union, for Confederation

Conference at Québec in 1864 (painting), 28

conscription, 47, 132–33

Conservative Party, 56–57, 68, 70, 73, 92, 98, 107, 137, 272, 283

Constitution Act, 1867, 293

consumer goods, prices of, 112, 300

Cook, Eric, 201–2

copper, 176

Corner Brook Pulp and Paper Mill, 145

Corrupt Practices Act, 90

Cranborne, Lord, 204–5

Crosbie, Chesley, 179, 192, 216, 232, 264–65, 281, 288–89, 294–95, 299

Crosbie, George, 201

Crosbie, John C., 120–21, 159

Crowe, Harry, 116–19, 125–26, 136–37

Crowe–Bond Confederation scheme, 117

Crown lands, transfer to Canada, 48, 97, 99

Crummey, P.W., 244–45

Currie, John S., 268

customs duties, 30, 85, 97, 112, 125, 151, 162, 167–68, 172, 242, 257. *See also* import duties; tariffs

D

Daily News, 99, 142, 163, 165, 213, 218, 255, 268, 271, 285

Dalhousie University, 206, 245, 254, 288

Dalton, Hugh, 207

Davidson, Sir Walter E., 128–31, 139

debates, on joining Confederation, 40–41, 43, 50, 104, 187, 200–202, 272, 285; at National Convention, 217–18, 220, 223, 225, 256, 258, 260, 266

debt. *See* public debt

de Champlain, Joseph, 154, 164–65

democracy, 3, 6, 9, 11, 125, 148; impediments to, 37; referendum as tool of, 17; restoration of, 192, 219, 241, 289; and rights, 12

INDEX

denominational schools, 36, 48–49, 50, 94, 190, 294, 297. *See also* education
destitution. *See* poverty
Devine, J.M., 192
Dickie, Alfred, 152
disability, insurance policies for, 215
divisions: between St. John's and outpost residents, 15, 58, 78–79, 112, 130, 132–33
Doherty, Charles, 153
Dominion Coal Company, 116
Dominion Iron and Steel Company, 116
Don't Tell the Newfoundlanders, 4
Downey, Joseph, 117, 119
dry dock, St. John's, 71, 101, 103, 159, 167
Duplessis, Maurice, 250

E

Economic Union Party (EUP), 264–65, 277, 288
economy: as depressed, 36, 275; development of, 39, 41, 50, 70, 80, 84, 102, 105, 203, 299; difficulties in, 23, 27, 46, 142; diversification of, 26, 37–38, 46, 69–70, 121, 157; as insecure, 12, 18, 214, 222, 271, 298; management of during war, 130; and prosperity, 102, 106, 200, 222; reconstruction of, 190–92; and security, 13, 15, 19, 40, 66, 199, 225; and social security, 218, 241–42, 256, 269, 279, 307–8. *See also* finances, in Newfoundland
education, 13, 37; as compulsory, 189, 194; denominational control of, 190; reforms in, 191. *See also* denominational schools
election campaigns, 1, 9; of 1865, 44; of 1869, 6, 10, 35, 41, 51, 58–60, 63; of 1873, 67; of 1878, 68, 70; of 1882, 61, 72; of 1889, 77; of 1904, 107; of 1908, 118, 122; of 1909,

117, 119–21, 126; of 1913, 126–27; of 1919, 141; of 1928, 160, 162, 164, 170; of 1932, 174–75, 182
electrification, 13, 101
Elizabeth, Queen, 192–93
Emerson, George H., 94–95
Emerson, Prescott, 68
equalization payments program, 306–7
Evening Advocate, 143
Evening Chronicle, 114
Evening Herald, 93, 100, 102, 112, 114
Evening Mercury, 73
Evening Telegram, 68, 72, 76, 80, 120, 125, 140, 154, 163–64, 192, 212, 217, 224, 246, 258
The Express, 58, 201

F

family allowances, 6, 210, 214, 217, 272, 279; as accruing through Confederation, 242, 247, 257–58, 269, 282–83, 296, 298; criticism of, 16, 273, 280
farming. *See* agriculture sector
ferry service, 19, 101, 150, 245, 248; Port aux Basques–North Sydney connection, 103, 149, 151, 159, 176
Fiander, Fanny Ryan, 272
Fielding, William Stevens, 83, 106, 111, 146
finances, in Newfoundland: crisis in, 94, 101, 138, 144, 166, 170, 175, 179; difficulties of, 89, 99, 157–58, 189–90, 222, 226; as secure and stable, 19, 32, 92, 197, 257; and wartime surplus, 194, 201, 209, 226–28, 234, 240, 254. *See also* economy; prosperity; public debt
Financial and Economic Position Report, 221, 227
First World War, 285
fish, marketing/exporting of, 132, 135, 141–42, 162, 176, 181, 185

— 387 —

fisheries, 7, 42, 85–86, 108, 174, 192, 295; competition in, 65, 78; and Confederation, 23–24, 97, 244; and cooperatives, 125, 182, 191, 194, 254; development/diversification of, 37, 40, 48, 190, 269; economic difficulties in, 40, 46, 69, 89–90, 221, 304; as economic mainstay, 157; licences for, 141; Newfoundland control of, 39, 78, 113, 125, 138, 154, 297, 305; reforms of, 143, 181, 188, 195; regulations for, 38, 109–10, 141, 143, 297. *See also* cod fishery; frozen fish industry; herring fishery; lobster industry; salmon fishing; salt cod fishery; seal fishery

Fisheries Committee Report, 221

fishermen, 42–43, 61, 91, 108, 111, 139, 154, 257, 268, 291; attitude towards Confederation, 99, 219; and bait licences/supplies, 83, 85–86; betterment of, 174, 185, 191, 282; as British men, 124; credit system for, 37–38, 89; economic and social security of, 122–25, 215; influence of, 5, 11, 34–35, 50, 54, 58–60, 64–65; injury insurance for, 215; rights and privileges of, 164–65; and social citizenship, 215, 221; standard of living of, 38, 46, 84, 181, 187, 303; and taxation, 99. *See also* French fishermen

Fishermen's Advocate, 124, 126, 179, 184, 211, 283, 302

Fishermen's Protective Union (FPU), 122–23, 126–27, 131–32, 139–41, 162, 214, 268; and Commission of Government, 158, 186; legacy of, 163; as opposed to Confederation, 142–44; and social citizenship, 13, 174, 185, 215; and social reforms, 106, 124–25, 133

FitzGerald, John, 277

Foreign Fishing Vessels Act (1893), 109–10
foreign goods and trade, 115, 239, 242
forestry, 70, 92
Fox, Cyril J., 233
Franklin, Benjamin, 21
Fraser, Allan MacPherson, 33–34
Free Press, 107, 142
free trade, 40, 62, 65, 108; with rest of Canada, 31; with United States, 76. *See also* trade and commerce; United States
French fishermen, 79–80, 89
French Shore problem, 27, 39–40, 45, 66, 78–81, 96
Frost, Sydney, 128
frozen fish industry, 195
Fudge, H. Pierce, 232, 239, 258

G

Galt, Alexander Tilloch, 22–23
Geological Survey of Newfoundland, 40
George VI, King, 192–93
Gibbs, Michael, 192
Gilmore, William, 134
Glen, Thomas, 61
Globe and Mail, 279, 301
Godden, Edwin John, 179
Goodridge, A.F., 90, 92, 107
Gorvin, John H., 187–88, 191
Granger, Charles, 211, 302
Grant, George, 100
grant, transitional: after Confederation, 254–55
Granville, Earl, 49, 58, 61–63
Great Britain: control over Newfoundland, 197, 206, 234, 238, 259, 261; and future of Newfoundland, 235; support for union with Canada, 237–38, 241
Great Depression, 13, 241; impact of, 163, 169–71, 173, 187, 189, 247, 272

INDEX

Great Fire (St. John's), 86–87, 94
Great War, 106, 128, 133–34, 142, 153, 158, 163, 166, 263
Great War Veterans' Association, 179
Greene, Daniel J., 92
Greenspond Letter, 73
Grey, Earl, 111, 113–15, 118
Grieve, Walter, 53
Gruchy, Philip, 288–89
Gunston, Sir Derrick, 203
Gushue, Raymond, 179
Gwyn, Richard, 280

H

Haig, Sir Douglas, 131
Halifax Chronicle, 119
Halifax Conference, 86–88, 152
Hall, Glenvil, 234–35
Hall, Henry, 91
Hanson Brothers (Montreal), 99–100
Harbour Grace Standard, 58
Harding, Sir Edward J., 134, 187–88
harmonization: of differences between Newfoundland and Canada, 294
Harrington, Julian, 246
Harris, Robert, 28
Harris, Sir Charles Alexander, 134, 140
Harvey, Augustus, 85–86
Harvey, Moses, 76
Hawco, Matthew, 147
Hawes, George, 141
Hay, John, 108
health care, 13, 190–91, 222, 247, 284; as comprehensive, 271; hospital facilities, 190, 195; national programs for, 214
health insurance, national (Britain), 236
Henley, Edward, 276
Herbert, Alan, 203, 207
Herder, William J., 140
herring fishery, 108
Hickman, Albert, 140, 147, 164

Higgins, Gordon, 17, 146, 244–45, 258
Higgins, John G., 5
Higgins, William J., 145, 147
Hill, Sir Stephen, 5, 49, 58–59, 61–64, 66, 68
Hiller, James K., 34, 44, 76, 119, 133
Hillier, Daniel, 224
A History of Newfoundland, 100
HMCS *Niobe*, 128
HMS *Boston*, 43
HMS *Prince of Wales*, 195
HMS *Raleigh*, 235
Hollett, Malcolm, 232, 251, 296
Hollis Walker, Thomas, 147, 171
Hollis Walker Report, 158, 161, 274
Home Rule, 26
Hope Simpson, Lady, 187–88
Hope Simpson, Sir John, 180–81, 184, 187
Horwood, William H., 94–95
Howe, C.D., 243, 300
Howlan, George William, 84
Howley, Michael F., 114, 117
Howley, William R., 180
Hoyles, Hugh William, 22–25, 27, 39–40, 43–44, 301
Humber proposal, 144
Hutchings, Mary Ellen, 224
hydroelectrical resources, 244, 305

I

I Chose Canada, 295
illiteracy. *See* literacy rates
Ilsley, J.L., 243, 245
immigration, to Newfoundland, 36
Imperial Conference, 133–35
Imperial Economic Conference, 175–76
Imperial Oil Company, 175
Imperial War Conference, 132
import duties, 247. *See also* customs duties; tariffs

income tax, on residents, 133, 159, 162, 171, 248, 282, 298
The Independent, 267, 270, 276, 280
Indian Act, 295–97
Indigenous Peoples, 14, 17, 30, 32, 111; and social benefits, 296; voting and education rights, 295–96. *See also* land claims
industrialization, 78, 160, 170, 191, 271; and development, 77, 143, 157, 161–62, 174; as diverse and vibrant, 304
Innu of Labrador, as status Indians, 297
Intercolonial Railway, 45, 57
Interdepartmental Committee on Canada–Newfoundland Relations (ICCNR), 243, 248, 292–93
International Grenfell Association, 222
International Power and Paper Company, 145
Irish Examiner, 4
iron ore, 175–76
isolation, of Newfoundlanders, 31, 43, 48, 100, 182, 191, 199, 221, 304

J

Jackman, Edward, 137
Jamieson, Donald J., 265, 277, 305
Job, Robert, 227, 231–32
Johnston, James William, 22
Jones, E., 221
Jones, Frederick, 35
Jones, Mike, 4
Judicial Committee of the Privy Council (JCPC), 152–53, 155, 164, 250

K

Kent, John, 44, 48
Keough, William, 223, 225, 227–29, 232, 239–40, 251
Keynes, John Maynard, 204
King, William Lyon Mackenzie, 149, 219, 237, 249, 293; attitude towards Newfoundland, 205, 207, 210, 213, 241; and National Conference delegation, 243, 245; and terms of union, 252–53, 255
Korneski, Kurt, 6, 40, 72, 78

L

Labouchere, Henry, 40
labour mobility: as outcome of Confederation, 306
Labour Party, 237
Labrador: possible sale of, 144–46, 154, 157, 164–66; Quebec boundary dispute, 113, 146, 150–55, 157, 250, 252
Lanctôt, Charles, 153–54
land claims, with Indigenous Peoples, 297
Lapointe, Ernest, 164
Laurier, Sir Wilfrid, 106, 110, 113, 118–19, 138–39, 149, 295
Lawry, Richard, 43
Law Society of Newfoundland, 5
Leased Bases Agreement, 205, 234
Lewis, Philip J., 201
Liberal–Conservative Party, 159
liberalism, 35, 53, 148
Liberal-Labour-Progressive party, 141, 146
Liberal Party, 49, 77, 84, 90, 117, 125, 127, 131, 138, 237; and alliance with Catholics, 26, 50, 57, 140; as anti-Confederation, 107; as friend of labour, 148, 213
Liberal Party of Canada, 138, 205, 279, 305
Liberal Reform Party, 140–41, 147
Lisgar, Lord (John Young), 49
literacy rates, 7–8, 13, 36–37, 41, 58, 182, 188–90, 194, 307
Livernois, Jules I., 28
Lloyd, William Frederick, 125, 131–33
lobster industry, 79–81
Lodge, Thomas, 180–82, 185–87, 189

Logan, William, 40
loggers, 5, 257, 268, 303. *See also* timber trade
London Bank, 90
London School of Economics, 209
London *Times*, 104, 119
Long, Walter, 139
Longshoremen's Protective Union, 186
Low, Thomas Andrew, 150
lumbering. *See* timber trade

M

Macdonald, Angus L., 250
Macdonald, Gordon, 4, 216, 251, 253, 261
Macdonald, John A., 23, 29, 45–46, 49, 63, 70, 73, 75–76, 83–85, 283
Macdonald, J. Scott, 210, 219, 241–42, 244, 248–49, 260
MacDonald, Malcolm, 186, 188, 206–7, 210
MacDonald, Vincent, 288
MacGregor, William, 111, 113–14, 118–19
MacKay, Robert A., 206–7, 210, 243, 248, 254, 292
MacKenzie, David, 205, 295
Mackenzie King. *See* King, William Lyon Mackenzie
MacLeod, Malcolm, 104
Macpherson, Alan, 37
Magor, Robert J., 167
Magrath, Charles A., 176
Mail and Advocate, 138
Mail and Empire, 111
Malcolm, James, 151
Malone, Greg, 4–5
manufacturing sector, 45, 51, 66, 85, 191; protections as not negotiated, 299–300
Maritime colonies/provinces, 22, 45, 53, 57–58, 205, 254, 290, 293
Marshall, T.H., 13
Marshall, Walter, 288, 290

Massey, Vincent, 135
McCann, J.J., 245
McEvoy, John B., 202, 242, 254, 288–89
McGee, Thomas D'Arcy, 41
McGrath, P.T., 100, 102, 114–15, 153–55
McNair, John B., 251
McNeil, Fannie, 161
Mercer, Keith, 42
Methodist College Literary Institute (MCLI), 147, 158
Miawpukek First Nation, 297
Middleton, G.H., 88
Middleton, John, 167–68, 170–71
military bases, British, 194, 205
military service, by Newfoundlanders, 7–8, 10, 42–43
Militia Act, 48
Miller, Leonard, 226
mining industry, 40, 92, 157, 162, 175–76; exploration in, 51, 182; resources of, 112, 244; rights to, 48, 52, 180
Monck, Charles Stanley, 23
The Monitor, 6, 11, 284, 286
Monroe, Arthur, 286
Monroe, Moses, 85
Monroe, Walter Stanley, 154, 159, 161, 164, 192
Montreal Gazette, 76, 212
Montreal Star, 112, 164
Moore, P.E., 296
Moores, Silas, 201
Morgan, R.C., 144
Morine, Alfred B., 90, 120–22, 126–28, 140, 147–48, 192; as minister of finance, 101–2; as pro-Confederation, 73–74, 76, 84–85, 88, 92–93, 99, 107, 112–13, 136–37
Morison, Donald, 85, 99
Morning Chronicle, 50, 53, 67
Morris, Edward Patrick, 102, 117–18, 125, 132, 136–37, 139; attitude towards Confederation, 114–15, 119–21; and Newfoundland delegation, 94–95, 116; and old age pensions,

122; as PM of Newfoundland, 119, 121, 127–29, 131, 149, 152, 163
Morris, Fred, 276–77
mortality rates, 225–26; of infants, 190, 226
Morton, Rose and Company, 99
Morton, W.L., 34
Mosdell, Harris M., 165, 178
Mullock, John James, 39
Mullock, John Thomas, 50, 60
Murray, Alexander, 40
Murray, James, 8–9, 42, 61, 68, 99
Musgrave, Sir Anthony, 23, 44–46, 49, 52

N

National Convention: debates of, 217–18, 221; dissolution of, 266; election to, in 1946, 211, 216, 219; and Indigenous Peoples, 295–96; as negotiating union with Canada, 231, 234, 236, 241, 243–47, 251–55, 259, 290; and referenda options, 236–39, 245; and social citizenship, 214, 220, 222, 225, 229; support for responsible government, 226, 228, 272
nationalism, 2–3, 18, 55, 71, 81–82, 99–100, 102, 106, 140, 284, 309
National Policy, 70
Natives' Society of Newfoundland, 26–27
natural resources, 105, 141, 143, 157, 194, 256; development of, 77, 304, 307
Neary, Peter, 240, 299
Newell, Isaac, 222–23
Newfoundland: as British colony, 36, 53, 92, 108, 116, 135, 138; debt of, 36, 45, 48, 76, 96, 127, 153, 234, 249–50, 254, 306; as Dominion, 2, 134–35, 142, 162, 164, 166, 170, 178, 180, 201, 205, 265; as equal in status to Canada, 133–34; financial assistance to, 48, 97, 212, 240, 290, 296; future, as pessimist, 306; as independent, 12, 68, 77, 208–9, 244, 265, 268, 285, 308; and nation-building, 66, 70–72, 78, 120, 128, 133, 197; political culture of, 10, 16, 19, 29, 37, 41, 125, 189; suspension of democratic government in, 178; territorial rights of, 81. *See also* bankruptcy; public debt; public expenditures; public services; self-government
Newfoundland Act, 300
Newfoundland and Labrador Royal Commission on Renewing and Strengthening Our Place in Canada, 305
Newfoundland Board of Trade, 113, 123, 142, 179, 187, 202, 288
Newfoundland delegation, to Ottawa: in 1947, 288, 290, 292; in 1948, 288–94, 296–97, 299–300
Newfoundland: Economic, Diplomatic, and Strategic Studies, 206
Newfoundlander, 26, 54, 56, 58
Newfoundland Fisheries Board, 297
Newfoundland Forestry Corps, 128
Newfoundland National Association, 201
Newfoundland Patriotic Association (NPA), 129, 132
Newfoundland Policy, 210, 243
Newfoundland Power and Paper Company, 145
Newfoundland Railway Commission, 150
Newfoundland Railway System, 111, 137, 149–51, 166, 249, 254, 283, 298
Newfoundland Ranger Force, 217, 265–66
Newfoundland Regiment, 128–30, 132
Newfoundland Royal Commission, 176, 180
Newfoundland Savings Bank, 89–91, 100, 168

Newfoundland Timber Estates
    Company Limited, 116
New Party, 72
Noel, S.J.R., 200
Noel-Baker, P.J., 261
North Atlantic Treaty Organization, 3
Northcote, Sir Stafford, 70
Noseworthy, Joe W., 205

O

O'Brien, Terence Nicholls, 90
Observer's Weekly, 182–83
"Ode to Newfoundland,"
    106, 185, 239, 267
O'Flaherty, Patrick, 35
O'Keefe, Edward, 60
old age pensions. *See* pension plans
O'Leary, Francis M., 193,
    201, 251, 277, 300
O'Neill, J.M., 285
Orange Order, 60, 67, 73, 99,
    160, 219, 281, 285–86
O'Reilly, Thomas, 56
Outerbridge, Leonard, 286
Outerbridge, P.E., 5
out-migration, 46, 107, 158, 176, 185, 306

P

Paris Peace Conference, 134
Patriot, 46, 54
Patriotic Association, 80–81
patriotism, 4, 11, 50, 52, 96,
    256, 267, 283–84, 309
patronage, 36, 44, 62
Pauncefote, Julian, 82
Pearson, Benjamin Franklin, 116
Peat Marwick, 288
Penney, Albert, 259
pension plans: in old age, 6, 115, 122,
    215, 217, 242, 247, 269, 272, 282–83,
    296, 298; for veterans, 139, 172,
    214, 247, 257, 283; for widows, 130

People's Party, 115–17, 120,
    122, 127, 140–41
Perlin, Albert, 182, 189, 218, 255, 285
Pickersgill, Jack, 219
Pinsent, Robert, 151–52
Pitts, James, 85
Plunkett, Edmund W., 70
"Policy of Progress" platform, 72, 101
political citizenship, 9–10,
    12, 14, 272, 309
Political Reform and Labour
    Association, 99
poor relief. *See* relief assistance
Poor Relief Association, 56
Pottle, Herbert, 286
poverty, 34, 39, 41, 57, 189, 199,
    214, 225, 272, 275; banishing of,
    209, 271; and Confederation,
    303–4; of fishermen, 38, 124,
    187; as widespread, 56
Progressive Conservative Party
    of Canada, 283, 300, 305
Progressive Era, 13
prosperity, 221, 242, 256, 305; after
    Second World War, 201. *See also*
    finances, in Newfoundland
Prowse, Daniel W., 32–34, 71, 100, 202
Prowse, Hall and Morris, 91
public debt, 30, 97–98, 169, 227;
    as crisis, 2, 19, 33, 96, 169; as
    mounting, 144, 146, 158–59;
    responsibility for, 247, 283
public expenditures, 66, 147, 158–59,
    167, 172, 185; retrenchment of,
    101, 158, 160, 162, 167
Public Health and Welfare Report, 220
Public Ledger, 58
public opinion: as different in
    urban and outposts, 268,
    276, 283, 285; regarding 1948
    referenda, 265; towards social
    rights, social welfare, 269
public services, 16, 284, 292;
    deficiencies in, 159, 188, 220,

228, 291; improvements in, 167, 169, 191, 194, 215; as part of social citizenship, 13; standards for, 199, 246, 289, 307
Puddester, Harold, 288
Puddester, John C., 180, 184
pulp and paper industry, 105, 117, 121, 143, 157, 162, 194, 221, 288, 295

Q

Qalipu Mi'kmaq Band, 297
Quebec Board of Trade, 28
Quebec Conference, 24, 27–28, 30–31, 48–50, 57, 205, 308; Newfoundland delegation, 25; terms of, 73
Quinton, Herman, 286

R

radio broadcasting, 186–87, 191
Railway Act (1898), 102
railways, 36, 84, 92, 98, 104, 137, 150, 167, 246; branch line policy, 121, 127; construction of, 19, 39, 55, 71–72, 77, 80, 88–89, 96–97, 101, 162; deficits of, 97, 144, 146; expansion of, 55, 88–89, 127, 159; street system, 105; as trans-island, 26, 66, 89, 97, 103
Rand School of Social Science, 148
reconstruction, postwar, 203–4, 207, 215, 218, 234, 240
referenda, on Confederation, 1, 4, 203, 219; in 1869, 7–8, 11, 32, 308; in 1948, 5, 7, 11–12, 14, 18, 278, 284, 308; campaigns in 1948, 265, 269–70, 273, 277, 281–82, 284–86, 304; options for, 236, 238–41, 244, 252, 258–61, 263, 267, 271; outcomes in 1948, 284–88, 304–5, 308
Reform Party, 72, 74
Reid, Harry, 101–2, 112, 116, 118, 120, 137, 140, 143–44, 149–50
Reid, Robert Gillespie, 102–3, 112, 114, 116, 118, 120, 150; as pro-Confederation, 104, 107, 140; and railways, 19, 88–89, 91–92, 99, 101, 105, 137; and steamship service, 144, 149
Reid, William, 101–2, 112, 116, 118, 120, 137–41, 143–44, 149–50
Reid Newfoundland Company, 103, 105, 114–15, 136–37, 139, 144–45
Reid Railway Company, 149
relief assistance, 27, 42, 56, 169, 171, 184, 191, 241
responsible government, 3, 9, 19, 38, 179, 255, 264, 281; as democracy/independence, 199–200, 202, 226, 244, 265, 303; failure of, 273–74; opposition to, 27, 51, 53, 58, 87, 178, 209, 213, 259; support for, 26, 42, 232, 235, 245, 251–52, 258, 261, 275; surrender/suspension of, 1–2, 12, 92, 189, 204, 215, 219
responsible government, return to: and National Convention, 225, 236; opposition to, 228, 239; as patriotic, political reform, 184–85, 192, 201, 267; as referendum 1948 option, 13, 240–42, 263, 271, 276, 284–85; and social citizenship, 258, 269; support for, 15, 216, 218, 227, 229, 270
Responsible Government League, 16, 251, 264, 266–67, 270, 276–77, 281, 288; failings of, 274–75, 278; as against social assistance, 280; support for, 274; view of citizenship, 268–69, 271–72, 283
retrenchment. *See* public expenditures
Rhodes, Edgar Nelson, 177
Riche, Edward, 4
road construction, 191, 247–48
Robertson, Norman, 206–7, 210, 243
Robertson, Wishart M., 243
Roche, Edward, 140
Roddick, Dr. Thomas, 111
Rogerson, James J., 72

Roman Catholic Church, 6, 11, 38, 50, 67, 76, 140, 190, 216, 260, 284, 286
Roosevelt, Franklin D., 124, 171, 195
Roosevelt, Theodore, 110
Rosalind (liner), 142
Royal Commission of Enquiry, 202
Royal Proclamation of 1763, 152
Russell, Herbert J., 151

S

salmon fishing, 111, 113, 126
salt cod fishery, 109, 123, 130, 297
Scammell, Art, 283
schools, separate. *See* denominational schools
seal fishery, 35–36, 130, 282
secessionist movement, in Nova Scotia, 58, 83
Second World War, 188, 199, 207, 232; employment/prosperity during, 176, 191, 201, 227–28; interest in union during, 19, 205–6, 243; and social citizenship, 13, 214–15, 218, 271
Secret Nation (film), 4
sectarianism, 28, 34, 36, 41–42, 44, 50, 60, 67, 72–73, 285
self-government, 3–4, 26, 52, 148, 265, 268, 284; and equality in British world, 2, 66, 205; return to, 188–90, 195, 208, 232, 289. *See also* Commission of Government
separate schools. *See* denominational schools
separation allowances, for married troops, 130
72 Resolutions, 29, 31, 43, 52, 293
Seymour, Alfred H., 83
Sharp, Mitchell, 293
Shaughnessy, Sir Thomas George, 103, 118, 137, 139
Shea, Ambrose, 60, 72–73, 75, 90, 117; as a Father of Confederation, 28; at Quebec Conference, 25, 27, 29, 31, 57, 308; as supporting Confederation, 26, 32, 44–45, 49, 57, 76
Shea, E.D., 44
Shea, Hugh, 76
Smallwood, Joseph R., 17, 149, 185, 197, 212, 223, 242, 276, 280, 305–6; and 1948 referenda, 259, 272, 274, 281–83; and Commission of Government, 182–83, 235; and debates in National Convention, 219, 222, 256, 260, 266; as first premier of Newfoundland, 18, 172, 265; and Indigenous Peoples, 296; as journalist, 124, 160, 193, 202; as part of Newfoundland delegation to Ottawa, 244–46, 249–50, 288–91, 295; and social citizenship, 214, 302, 307, 309; as supporting Confederation, 6, 16, 198–201, 213, 216, 231, 241, 252, 254–55, 257–58, 264, 279, 300, 303; as supporting Liberal Party, 148
Smith, Andrew, 6–7, 35
Smith, Baxter A., 226
Smith, Peter J., 6
Smith, William, 146
social citizenship, 18, 208, 214, 218, 284; to be improved with Confederation, 19, 126, 246, 269, 286, 305, 307–9; benefits of, 12, 122, 280; criticism of, 258, 268; promotion of, 15, 211; as replacing political citizenship, 14; and social rights, 13, 215, 283
Social Insurance and Allied Services, 13
Socialist Party of America, 148
social justice, 220, 222, 269
social rights, 122, 215, 269; expansion of, 214, 219, 222, 271. *See also* social citizenship
social welfare, in Newfoundland, 13, 15, 37, 122, 125, 194, 247, 254, 257, 286; reforms in, 148, 211, 213, 225,

258; and social programs, 203, 217, 229, 236, 246, 258, 266, 272–73, 279, 296, 298; and social responsibility, 283–84; social security system, 209–10, 219, 277, 283, 308; and stability, 220, 269, 271–72

Squires, Lady Helena, 163, 175

Squires, Sir Richard, 159, 161, 164–67, 174–75, 183, 186; alliance with W. Coaker, 140, 145, 147, 179, 193; as Confederation supporter, 192; and corruption allegations, 171–72; government of, 144, 146, 170; as Prime Minister of Newfoundland, 14, 141, 153, 162–63, 168–69; scandal concerning, 147, 158, 160

SS *Caribou*, 151, 159

SS *Great Eastern*, 72

Stabb, Nicholas, 47–48

Stacey, Charles, 66

standard of living, 12, 124, 181, 184, 195, 223, 225, 228, 281, 283; as costing more in Newfoundland, 307; as improved with Confederation, 15, 242, 256, 268, 279, 282, 289, 304, 308–9

starvation. *See* poverty

The Star Weekly, 303

Statute of Westminster (1931), 2, 170

steamship services, 48, 66, 97, 101, 103, 144, 149–50, 176, 246, 298

Steele, Owen, 128

steel industry, 112, 143

St. John's *Globe*, 148

St. Laurent, Louis, 219, 235, 242, 294, 301, 304, 307; and Confederation negotiations, 243, 245, 249, 251–52, 260, 293, 299

Stone, John, 140

subsidies, 191, 254, 290, 293–94; from Canada, 30, 48, 97–98; to French fishermen, 78; for railway service, 104, 149; for steamship services, 101, 103–4, 149–51

T

Talbot, Thomas, 50

tariffs, 70, 101, 126, 151, 159, 242; on Canadian flour, 83; on cod liver oil, 176; imposed by Canada, 45; on manufacturing sector, 299; on salmon, 176; with United Kingdom, 234; and United States, 232

Taschereau, Louis-Alexandre, 153–54, 165

taxation, 42, 62, 153, 202, 269, 298, 307; on business profits (1917), 133; as direct, 30, 52, 112, 291; increase in, 47, 52–54, 57, 99, 113, 139, 167; as indirect, 291; to make up deficit, 30; opposition to, 35; politics of, 7, 10; reduction in, 144; as result of Confederation, 32; on staple goods, 46

Telegraph, 58

telegraph operators' union, 123

telegraph system, 71–72, 101, 103, 167

Terms of Union, for Confederation, 289–90, 294–98

Tessier, Peter G., 48

Thomas, James Henry, 167

Thompson, J.C., 288, 290

Thompson, Sir John Sparrow David, 76, 85–86, 88

Thompson, Sir Percy, 169

Thorburn, Robert, 71–72, 74–80, 85

Tilley, Samuel Leonard, 25

timber trade, 39, 112, 116, 164–65, 185

T. & M. Winter and Company, 288

Tory Party, 101, 112, 115, 163

tourism, 182

trade and commerce, 51, 62, 82, 111, 175, 192; and dropping of barriers, 300; as focused eastward, 43, 45; between Newfoundland and U.K., 234. *See also* free trade; United States

trade unions, 106

trans-island railway. *See* railways
Treaty of Utrecht, 78, 81
Trentham, E.N.R., 180
tuberculosis, 195, 222, 225–26, 259
Tupper, Dr. Charles, 23–25, 27–28, 49, 74–76, 84, 98, 103, 301

U

unemployment, 57, 182, 214, 241–42, 271, 306–7; insurance benefits, 16, 214, 257, 269, 271, 298
Union Bank, 89, 91
United Opposition Party, 107
United States: economic union with, 264; fishermen from, 110; and fishing rights, 108–9; and free trade agreement, 33; trade relations with, 19, 26, 65, 76, 85, 103; trade treaty with, 73–74, 82, 84, 107, 111, 113, 227, 231–32; and union with Newfoundland, 83

V

Victoria, Queen, 71
VONF (Voice of Newfoundland) station, 186, 193, 282
voter behaviour, 18, 35, 42, 56, 62, 64, 175, 217; in 1948 referenda, 238, 284; ability to choose options, 41, 61, 178, 265, 282, 308; and election turnout, 37, 162, 216, 284; as having final say, 49, 309; of women, 14–15, 162
voting rights, 10, 214, 229, 272, 295–96

W

Walker, Sir Baldwin, 81
Walsh, Albert J., 232, 238, 288–89, 297–99
Walwyn, Sir Humphrey, 185–86, 188, 212, 216
war effort, by Newfoundlanders, 128–31

War Measures Act, 129, 141
War of 1812, 7, 22, 43
Warren, Gordon, 252
Warren, William Robertson, 143, 147, 153
War Reparations Commission, 172
Water Street merchants, 38, 41, 70, 92, 129, 140, 174–75, 266, 281, 286, 309
Watkins, John, 224
Watton, Alfred, 225
Webb, Jeff, 15, 227, 276, 285
Webb, Sidney, 209
welfare state. *See* social welfare, in Newfoundland
Western Star, 226
Westminster (magazine), 115
White, Thomas, 137
Whiteway, Jesse, 192
Whiteway, William Vallance: as Confederation supporter, 39, 67, 70, 74–75, 88, 93–94, 98; and economic growth, 77–78; as premier, 68–69, 72–73, 79–81, 83–86, 90–92, 99, 101
Whitney, Henry Melville, 116
Whitworth, Armstrong, 144
Wild, Ira, 202, 248
Williams, Ralph C., 121
Winter, Gordon, 288–89
Winter, James Spearman, 73–74, 85, 90, 101–2
women, 71, 109, 129, 142, 277, 303; and citizenship, 215; as elected to National Convention, 216; employment opportunities for, 194, 280; franchise to, 14, 160–61; voting behaviour of, 14–15, 162; well-being of, 215, 309
Women's Franchise League, 161
Wood, Joseph, 103
working people, rights of, 77, 215, 258. *See also* fishermen; loggers
Wrong, Hume, 210

ABOUT THE AUTHORS

Born and raised in Newfoundland, RAYMOND B. BLAKE is the author and editor of over twenty books, publishing widely on Canadian political history, in particular on areas of federalism, citizenship, social welfare, and national identity. Professor of History at the University of Regina, Blake was elected to the prestigious Royal Society of Canada in 2018. He lives in Regina, Saskatchewan.

MELVIN BAKER received a PhD in history and has published extensively in nineteenth- and twentieth-century Newfoundland history. He was formerly archivist-historian for Memorial University. He lives in St. John's, Newfoundland.

www.ingramcontent.com/pod-product-compliance
Lightning Source LLC
Chambersburg PA
CBHW022112290426
44112CB00008B/648